Conservatism and Racism, and Why in America They Are the Same

SUNY series in African American Studies

John R. Howard and Robert C. Smith, *editors*

Conservatism and Racism, and Why in America They Are the Same

Robert C. Smith

Published by State University of New York Press, Albany

© 2010 State University of New York

All rights reserved

Printed in the United States of America

No part of this book may be used or reproduced in any manner whatsoever without written permission. No part of this book may be stored in a retrieval system or transmitted in any form or by any means including electronic, electrostatic, magnetic tape, mechanical, photocopying, recording, or otherwise without the prior permission in writing of the publisher.

For information, contact State University of New York Press, Albany, NY
www.sunypress.edu

Production by Eileen Meehan
Marketing by Michael Campochiaro

Library of Congress Cataloging-in-Publication Data

Smith, Robert Charles, 1947–
   Conservatism and racism, and why in America they are the same / Robert C. Smith.
      p. cm. — (SUNY series in african american studies)
   Includes bibliographical references and index.
   ISBN 978-1-4384-3233-5 (hardcover : alk. paper)
   ISBN 978-1-4384-3232-8 (pbk: alk. paper)
   1. United States—Race relations. 2. Racism—United States. 3. Conservatism—United States. I. Title.

E185.615.S5814 2010
305.800973—dc22
                                                  2009054443

10 9 8 7 6 5 4 3 2 1

*To my granddaughter, Karysa Rae Smith Ortega.
May she live in liberal times.*

Contents

List of Tables — ix

Acknowledgments — xi

Introduction — 1

Chapter 1
Defining the Terms of Discourse — 7

Chapter 2
Lockean "Liberalism" as the Conservative Ideology in America — 15

Chapter 3
The Special Place of the South in American Conservatism — 33

Chapter 4
The Rise of the Liberal Remnant — 41

Chapter 5
African American Thought and the Conservative Remnant — 63

Chapter 6
Racism and the Conservative Intellectual Movement, 1945–1970 — 77

Chapter 7
Racism and Neoconservatism, 1968–1980 91

Chapter 8
The Ascendancy of Ronald Reagan and the Parts Played by
Ideology and Race 107

Chapter 9
The Reagan Presidency and Race 143

Chapter 10
Conclusion 185

Notes 195

About the Author 261

Index 263

List of Tables

Table 5.1   Racial Differences in Attitudes toward Government
            Spending on Selected Programs, Even if Tax Increase
            Is Required (percent in favor)   65

Table 5.2   Racial Differences in Attitudes toward the
            Social Welfare Responsibilities of Government   65

Table 5.3   Racial Differences in Attitudes toward Government
            Ownership of Selected Enterprises (percent in favor)   65

Acknowledgments

I usually at the end acknowledge the assistance of my beautiful bird in the preparation of manuscripts. This time, however, I do so at the outset. For over thirty years beginning with my dissertation and through ten books and dozens of papers and articles my wife, Scottie, as critic, editor, typist, and word processor has been the indispensable person. She has provided this assistance discerningly and unselfishly, while at the same time being a grand wife, mother, and grandmother and a tireless advocate for disadvantaged children. I could never find words to adequately express my love, appreciation, and happiness.

David Covin, Mack Jones, Martin Carceri, Ronald Walters, William Strickland, Hanes Walton Jr., Georgia Persons, and James Martell read the manuscript in whole or part and made suggestions that led to improvements. I am especially grateful to Professors Walters and Jones for detailed essay-by-essay commentaries. Their critical insights helped to clarify my thinking and the writing. Their own writings in their unvarnished commitment to the liberation of black people have been an inspiration for me throughout my career.

Professors Walton and Strickland called my attention to several important sources that I had overlooked and along with Professor Covin suggested ways to make clearer the philosophical-ideological linkages. Professors Strickland and Martel also urged me to pay closer attention to the limits of liberalism as a reform ideology and think more rigorously about the idea of the bastardization of Locke. I also appreciate the comments of the anonymous reviewers selected by the State University of New York Press.

This book is published as a title in SUNY's African American Studies series, which I have coedited since 1981. This is my fifth title in the series, and as always my series coeditor, John Howard, gave me a clear and candid critique.

Patrick McCarthy, a graduate student at San Francisco State, provided able research assistance. I am especially grateful for his help in locating obscure but relevant *National Review* articles. Kelly Barton, Shelly Williams, and the other archivists at the Reagan Presidential Library efficiently facilitated access to the archival material. But my research at the library would not have been possible without the help of my sister, Cleo Barnes. The use of her sofa and car were the indispensable source of financial support needed to defray the costs of my numerous visits to Simi Valley. In addition, the College of Behavioral and Social Sciences and the Department of Political Science at San Francisco State provided support for the preparation of the manuscript.

I had the opportunity to present some of the ideas in this book at Behavioral and Social Science College colloquia at San Francisco State, at a 2004 symposium on blacks and conservatism sponsored by the Stanford University Black Law Students Association and at the 2009 Alan B. Larkin Conference on the Presidency at Florida Atlantic University.

Introduction

I decided to write this book shortly after Ronald Reagan's funeral. In the long lines of mourners who gathered to pay their respects to the president at the Capitol in Washington and the presidential library in Simi Valley, California, there were very few African Americans. In the course of the nearly week-long commemoration of Reagan's life and legacy—where he was lauded as one of the nation's greatest presidents—I did a number of interviews where I was asked to explain the absence of black mourners in Washington and Simi Valley. My explanations dealt less with Reagan as an individual or as president than with conservatism as a philosophy and ideology. Ronald Reagan was not mourned by many African Americans because he was a conservative, the most successful conservative president of the post–civil rights era and one of the most successful conservative presidents in the twentieth century. Conservatism as a philosophy and ideology, I explained, is and always has been hostile to the aspirations of Africans in America, incompatible with their struggle for freedom and equality. Thus, very few blacks could mourn the passing of a man who was an icon in the cause of twentieth-century American conservatism.

In the nature of modern media it was difficult to convey this rather complex idea in a brief interview. However, I found that even in extended hour-long interviews it was difficult to fully explore this complex relationship between conservatism and black aspirations. Repeatedly, I was asked, "Are you saying that conservatism is racism, that all conservatives are racist?" "Aren't there black conservatives? Are they racist?" "Are the millions of Americans who supported President Reagan racist?" "Are President George W. Bush and the conservatives who control the Congress and the courts hostile to African American interests?"

My answer to most of these questions was a qualified yes. But the many qualifications and caveats left me, the interviewers, and the audience without the kind of clarity one would hope for when professors are called upon to explain complex issues to the public. In going through the literature on the subject of conservatism and race in the United States, I was not surprised to find that there was no systematic treatment of the relationship between the two phenomena. Since the 1980s in the wake of the election of Reagan to the presidency, there have been a few books on blacks and conservatism and a couple of dozen articles. These works, however, are largely descriptive and deal mainly with the rise of black conservatives during the Reagan presidency. Thus, I wrote this book.[1]

In my interviews I contended that conservatism *in America* (I emphasize *in America* because my argument about conservatism and racism is specific historically and situationally to the United States) as a set of philosophical principles and as a governing ideology was hostile to black Americans. I also contended that as a separate matter the conservative movement that came to power with Reagan did so partly on the basis of racism. That is, I contended that a major part of the support of the conservative movement that elected Reagan was based on appeals to white supremacists and racists. In this regard, I noted that Reagan's first campaign appearance after he received the Republican nomination was in Philadelphia, Mississippi. As other commentators noted during Reagan's funeral, Philadelphia was the site of the murder of three civil rights workers by the Ku Klux Klan. In his Philadelphia speech Reagan invoked *states rights*, code words in the South for the right of whites to oppress blacks. In his first campaign for governor, Reagan made similar subtle appeals to racist whites in California. Thus, conservatism as a set of ideas is hostile to African Americans; Reagan as a candidate and as a president expressed this hostility; and the means by which he ascended to national power was rooted in a movement that was hostile to African Americans.

Unlike the relationship between conservative ideas and race where there are hardly any studies, there is an extensive literature on the relationships among race, racism, and the ascendancy of the conservative movement in American politics beginning in the 1960s. Kevin Phillips, who in his 1968 book, *The Emerging Republican Majority*, did as much as any single individual to lay out the "southern strategy" that facilitated the conservative ascendancy, estimates that 35 percent of the Republican ascendancy can be attributed to racism.[2] In this book I will need only to present a synthesis of this extensive historical and social science literature. This literature has never been brought together in a single volume. But, when this is done in conjunction with analysis of the historically and contextually racist nature of conservative ideas then one can more readily see the racism inherent in conservatism in America.

But the book begins with conservative ideas. This is a tricky problem as scholars of both liberalism and conservatism have long acknowledged. This is because in the United States, as Louis Hartz demonstrated in his classic work *The Liberal Tradition in America*, classical liberalism has dominated the country since its founding, leaving little room for classical, Burkean conservatism. As Gunnar Myrdal put it, "America is conservative.... But the principles conserved are liberal."³ Or, to relate this problem to the purposes of this book, in the 1930s Kelly Miller, the Dean of the College of Liberal Arts at Howard University, visited the Soviet Union. In the course of discussions with Soviet intellectuals, he remarked that there were black conservatives in America. Shocked, his Russian interlocutors responded, "[W]hy, what do they have to conserve?"⁴ A similar remark might be made historically about conservatives in America, What do they have to conserve? What they have to conserve is liberalism, the philosophical foundations of the nation's culture, economy, and government derived principally from the ideas of John Locke.

Thus, we will have to distinguish between the classical liberal ideas of Locke and the ideas of classical conservatism derived from Edmund Burke. Locke's classical liberalism is American conservatism, a conservatism whose core ideas went virtually unchallenged until the New Deal. Burke's ideas—universally regarded as the major intellectual source of Western conservatism—had relatively few adherents in the American political tradition. That is, what we call "conservatism" and "liberalism" in the United States are generally variations on or different emphases on the broad liberal tradition bequeathed by Locke. "We are Lockeans, and Locke was both a liberal and a conservative," writes Jay Sigler in *The Conservative Tradition in American Thought*.⁵

However, when examined up close we will see that the ideas in both the dominant Lockean tradition in the United States and the remnants of the Burkean tradition have been almost equally hostile to the African American quest for freedom and equality. Indeed, I will argue that it is only when the nation has been forced—and it has always been forced—to break with these traditions have blacks received a taste of the honey of freedom and equality.

Another problem that makes conservatism as a set of ideas problematic for the question of race in the United States is that the Burkean remnant in particular but conservatism generally has found its most hospitable place in the southern part of the country. The South—the site of the most systematic and brutal oppression of blacks—has always been the most conservative region of the country. John Calhoun of South Carolina is widely regarded as one of the leading conservative statesmen in early American history. His ideas expose in quite intellectually interesting ways the relationship between conservatism and racism. In *The Conservative Intellectual Movement in America* George Nash writes that the South was the "least American," the "least liberal" section of the nation.⁶ In *The Southern Tradition: The Achievements and Limitations of American Conservatism*, Eugene Genovese writes, "The principal tradition of the South—the mainstream of its cultural development—has been quintessentially conservative." And "from its origins [the South] constituted America's most impressive native-born critique of our national development, of liberalism, of the modern world."⁷

One of the more frequent refrains one encounters in studying the conservative movement in America, from the ultraconservatism of William F. Buckley Jr. and *National Review* to the neoconservatism of Irving Kristol and *The Public Interest*, is that "Ideas Have Consequences." This quote is borrowed from a book of that title by Richard Weaver, who in one of his other books offered a forthright defense of slavery and the overthrow of Reconstruction.[8] Ideas do have consequences, and I will show how the marshaling and marketing of ideas were consequential in the ascendancy of the conservative movement and the election of President Reagan.

The thesis or argument of this study is that in United States conservatism and racism are the same. The first thing necessary to do to advance the argument is to define the terms of the discourse, *racism* and *conservatism*. This is the purpose of chapter 1. Although scholars of racism have not agreed on a common definition, and racism is often confused with such related phenomena as prejudice, bigotry, and the belief in white supremacy, compared to conservatism the conceptual parameters of racism as it is manifested in the United States are reasonably well established. But if racism is difficult to define with precision, conservatism in general and conservatism in the United States present particularly nettlesome problems. Indeed, the most difficult problem in writing this book was the need to clear away a lot of philosophical, conceptual, and ideological contradictions in the historical and social science literatures on conservatism and its relationship to liberalism in the United States.

The second chapter studies the philosophy of John Locke and its impact on American society. I argue that Locke was a conservative, and his conservative philosophy permeates virtually all aspects of American life, the economy, culture, and polity. In order to advance the argument about Lockean conservatism I contrast his ideas with those of Rousseau, as a representative of left-liberal ideological traditions in Western thought. It will be necessary to plow over some elementary philosophical turf in order to flesh out this analysis, but this is necessary because of the frequent association of Locke with liberalism and democracy. I argue that ideologically he was neither a liberal nor a democrat, and this argument will become the epistemic framework for the subsequent chapters. In this chapter I also examine the influence of Locke's thought on the development of capitalism and slavery in the United States. Locke is a major source of the ideas that all men are created equal and have a divine right to the fruits of their labor. These Lockean ideas about free labor were bastardized in the United States from the beginning, in that Africans were deprived of these "inalienable" rights.

A defense of this bastardized Locke has been at the center of American conservatism since the 1870s, and it is one of the major reasons conservatism and racism in America have always been the same. This chapter ends with a discussion of Locke's influence on the Constitution—the most conservative and undemocratic set of governing arrangements of any Western democracy. An important explanation for the adoption and endurance of this conservative Constitution is the important role it has played as a bulwark of racism. Thus, for much of American history, defending the Constitution was the same as defending racism. Indeed, even today conservative yearnings for the "Constitution in Exile" are partly a defense of modern, debastardized Lockean racism.

Chapter 3 is on the special place of the South in conservatism in America, its special place intellectually and politically.

A principal argument of this book is that America is a profoundly and pervasively conservative country. However, for reasons discussed in chapters 1 and 2 this is often misunderstood, and the United States is often viewed as the quintessentially liberal nation. In my view just the opposite is the case; Roussean liberalism, not Lockean conservatism, has been the "thankless persuasion," the ideological remnant in the United States. Chapter 4 examines the emergence of this liberal remnant first cautiously during the Civil War–Reconstruction era and then more boldly during the New Deal. The relationship of this liberal remnant to the fight against racism is an important part of this chapter, demonstrating that while liberalism is not racist in America, it only has the *potential* to be antiracist. And this antiracist potential is always fragile, timid, tentative, cautious, and ambivalent in a country that is pervasively conservative.

Chapter 5 is a kind of digression, but a necessary one. It examines African American thought. In no country, none, anywhere, ever can a people be ideologically conservative if they are dissatisfied with the status quo. Africans in America have always been dissatisfied with America. They have, therefore, always been the most left, liberal, radical component of the nation's population. Among a group so profoundly and pervasively liberal, conservatism is the remnant, the thankless persuasion. The conservative remnant—Lockean and Burkean—has always been present in black thought, sometimes existing in uneasy tension in the thought of single individuals such as Douglass or DuBois. However, most persons usually thought of as black conservatives—Booker Washington or George Schuyler—were really accommodationists, cowards, or opportunists. Genuine, autonomous conservatism has always been a remnant in black thought because as Miller's Soviet interlocutors pointed out, What has there been to conserve?

Chapters 6 and 7 examine the rise of the conservative intellectual movement in the 1950s and 1960s and the neoconservatives of the 1960s and 1970s. Although both of these movements have multiple origins, and their ascendancy to power and respectability may be accounted for in multiple ways, racism and the struggles of blacks to overcome it are crucial parts of the explanation.

Chapter 8 analyzes the ascendancy of Ronald Reagan—the conservative movement's prophet—to the presidency and the part played by racism. This is done through analysis of presidential elections from 1948 to 1980. For much of American history the more racially liberal party worked to "mobilize bias" in order to keep race off the partisan and policy agendas. This is because when race is on the partisan agenda the more racially liberal party loses. Between 1948 and 1980, however, through the combination of a unique set of circumstances, race was forced on to the national agenda, eventually facilitating the election of the most ideologically conservative president of the twentieth century.

The presidency of Ronald Reagan was a triumph of the conservative movement and to some extent of conservative ideas. However, on a broad range of issues, the Reagan presidency was a disappointment to conservatives because of its failure to translate conservative ideas into practice. One area of disappointment to conservatives was how the administration dealt with race-related issues. Chapter 9, based on extensive research in the archives of the Reagan library, is a detailed analysis of how the administration dealt with six race-related issues: affirmative action, renewal of the 1965 Voting Rights Act, welfare reform, the Civil Rights Restoration Act, the Martin Luther King Jr. holiday, and sanctions against the apartheid South African regime. On each of these issues conservative ideas and principles were abandoned or to the extent they were pursued were defeated in Congress. In other words, on each of the major race-related issues of the Reagan presidency the civil rights movement and its ideas prevailed over conservatism. How and why this came about are explored in this chapter.

Substantively, on race the Reagan presidency was an ideological failure. Symbolically, however, it was a triumph. Reagan the rhetorical "reconstructive" president helped to change the ideological, political, partisan, and policy contexts for the discussion of racism in America, thereby foreclosing the possibilities of making further progress in undoing the legacies of the long bastardization of Locke in America.

Perhaps Reagan's most important legacy with respect to race has been on the Democratic Party. By discrediting liberalism in general and racial liberalism in particular Reagan forced the Democratic Party to move from racial liberalism to conservatism. The concluding chapter examines this legacy by studying the work of the Democratic Leadership Council and the election and presidency of Bill Clinton. Clinton's Reaganizing of the Democratic Party on race has worrisome consequences for the lives and well-being of poor black Americans, which I discuss in the last part of chapter 10.

CHAPTER ONE

Defining the Terms of Discourse

In the first part of this chapter I develop an understanding and definition of conservatism. This is followed by a much briefer discussion of racism and its correlative ideology of white supremacy.

Conservatism in America

Most of the literature on the American political tradition asserts that the United States is a liberal society, without a significant conservative tradition. I contend that the American political tradition is pervasively conservative with, contrary to much of the literature, liberalism rather than conservatism being the "remnant," the "illusion," or the "thankless persuasion."[1]

There are three related problems in the study of conservatism in America. The first has been the tendency of historians and social scientists to ignore conservatism in their teaching and research. (In my years of study in political science I was assigned only two books on conservatism, Edmund Burke's *Reflections on the Revolution in France* and Clinton Rossiter's *Conservatism in America*.) As the editors of *American Conservatism: An Encyclopedia* write: "The historiography of American conservatism . . . remains immature. For decades, the academic historical establishment largely ignored American Conservatism or dealt with it as some sort of fringe group. Only after the surprising and enduring appeal of Ronald Reagan did most historians begin to take serious scholarly notice of self-proclaimed conservatism. . . . But for now the story of conservatism in America, as told by academics, is fractured and inconclusive."[2]

Alan Brinkley, the historian of liberalism, writes, "[T]wentieth century American conservatism has been something of an orphan in historical scholarship." Brinkley attributes this inattention to conservatism to the tendency of scholars to view it as "a kind of pathology," a "paranoid style," but he writes, "A better explanation for the inattention of historians may be that much American conservatism in the twentieth century has rested on a philosophical foundation not readily distinguishable from the liberal tradition, to which it is, in theory opposed."[3]

This tendency to ignore "self-proclaimed" conservatism or treat it as a kind of pathology is related to the larger tendency of American scholarship to understand the American tradition as profoundly and pervasively liberal, rooted in the philosophy of John Locke. This view was stated most persuasively in Louis Hartz's seminal 1955 work, *The Liberal Tradition in America*. Although few scholars today fully embrace Hartz's thesis, the work exerted and exerts a powerful influence on teaching and research on ideology in the American political tradition.[4]

The third problem is the tendency to locate conservative thought in the writings of Burke, and finding little self-conscious Burke in the American tradition, it is concluded that there is little conservatism in the tradition or that it is an illusion, a remnant, or a "kind of pathology."[5]

Understanding Conservatism

Conservatism as a self-conscious ideology is usually understood in terms of a set of enduring principles, usually derived from Burke but in some cases traced to Plato and the Ancients.[6] But Huntington is largely correct when he contends that, unlike most ideologies, conservatism lacks what he calls a "substantive ideal" or "vision."[7] Building on Mannheim's classic essay "Conservative Thought," Huntington argues that conservatism as an ideology is best understood "situationally."[8] Or as Mannheim wrote, "conservatism ... is always dependent on a concrete set of circumstances in a [particular] period and country."[9] In other words, conservatism is always a reaction to a challenge to an existing order becoming "conscious and reflective when other ways of life and thought appear on the scene, against which it is compelled to take up arms in an ideological struggle."[10] Situationally conservatism is defined as

> the ideology arising out of a distinct but recurring type of historical situation in which a fundamental challenge is directed at established institutions and in which the supporters of those institutions employ the conservative ideology in their defense. Thus, conservatism is that system of ideas employed to justify any established social order, no matter where or when it exists, against any fundamental challenge to its nature or being, no matter from what quarter.... Conservatism in this sense is possible in the United States today only if there is a basic challenge to existing American institutions which impels their defenders to articulate conservative values.[11]

Writing in 1954 Huntington did not anticipate that the civil rights and black power movements in a few years would mount a sustained challenge to the existing order; therefore, he declared there was no conservative intellectual tradition or movement in the United States, and the effort to create one was "futile or irrelevant."[12]

Huntington also downplayed the challenge of the New Deal to the Lockean order, arguing that the only threat that could spark a conservative movement in the United States was the threat of international Communism. However, in addition to Communism, the New Deal was, as we shall see, formative in the emergence of a self-conscious conservative tradition and movement in the United States.

Conservatism as an ideology is thus a reaction to a system under challenge, a defense of the status-quo in a period of intense ideological and social conflict.[13]

In addition to understanding conservatism situationally, Huntington writes that the ideology may be understood in two other ways. First is the classic "aristocratic theory" associated mainly with Burke, which is the reaction of a specific class (the feudal aristocracy) to a specific historical circumstance (the French Revolution). Second is the "autonomous theory" in which any individual from any class can embrace a set of universal ideas—liberty, justice, moderation, balance, order—thought to constitute the essence of a conservative outlook. Although Huntington contends that conservatism is best understood situationally, he believes that in whatever situation the ideology emerges it will represent the "manifestations in history of Burke's ideas."[14] Thus, unlike Mannheim, Huntington continues to tie conservatism to a specific set of ideas rather than viewing it having no substantive ideal or vision. This appears to contradict his situational argument that conservatism is the defense of any existing order against any organized challenge, whether the established order is liberal, conservative, or Marxist. However, he suggests any system under stress will employ Burkean ideas in its defense because Burke was inclined to "defend all existing institutions wherever located and however challenged."[15] For Huntington Burke therefore becomes "the conservative archetype." Burke, however, would not likely defend a radical Marxist regime or perhaps even a militant liberal one. Huntington seems to acknowledge this when he writes,

> No necessary dichotomy exists, therefore, between conservatism and liberalism. The assumption that such an opposition does exist derives, of course, from the aristocratic theory of conservatism and reflects an over concern with a single phase of western history.... The effort to erect this ephemeral relationship into a continuing phenomenon of history only serves to obscure the fact that in the proper historical circumstances conservatism may well

be necessary for the defense of liberal institutions. The true enemy of the conservative is not the liberal but the extreme radical no matter what the ideational theory he may espouse.[16]

But the postwar conservative tradition and movement that emerged in the United States after 1945 did reject New Deal liberalism, and it did so more in the tradition of Locke, then Burke. In other words conservatism in the United States is a manifestation in history of Locke's ideas. Again, at other places Huntington appears to acknowledge this as in his critique of Russell Kirk's *Conservative Mind*. Huntington describes this seminal work in American conservative thought as "out of time and out of step in America because in Burkean fashion "it is dreaming of a world of less democracy, less equality, less industrialism, an age in which the elite ruled and the mass know their place."[17] In other words, Kirk wished to manifest Burkean ideas in modern American history. Huntington's analysis as useful as it is is nevertheless yet another manifestation of the confusion surrounding the discussion of conservatism in the historical and social science literature.

This confusion not withstanding, however conservatism as an ideology is understood, it could never be appealing to African Americans because collectively they have never been satisfied with the status-quo or the established order, and "manifestly, the ideology has little appeal to any one discontented with the status-quo."[18]

As I will demonstrate in a subsequent chapter, African American thought has always been mainly a system-challenging, dissident thought. However, until the 1950s and 1960s this thought had not been linked to a powerful mass movement. And "the mere articulation of a dissident ideology does not produce conservatism until that ideology is embraced by significant social groups."[19] Once it appeared that the black movement presented "a clear and present danger" to the existing order, a self-conscious conservative movement would necessarily emerge, and it would also necessarily be for the most part a racist movement. Although as I will show in chapters 6 and 7 conservatism in the post World War II period was a product of multiple challenges to the Lockean order—the New Deal, international Communism, and countercultural challenges to traditional values and institutions—the defense of racism was probably indispensable to the movement's acceleration in the 1960s and 1970s and its ascendancy to presidential power in 1980.

Understanding Racism

Race was taken into consideration—was a predicate for policies and decisions—in the creation of the American republic in order to subordinate

Africans and maintain control over them. Four Clauses of the Constitution reflect explicit decisions at Philadelphia to subordinate and oppress Africans.[20] Of the most infamous of these clauses Donald Robinson writes, "It bears repeating... that Madison's formula did not make blacks three fifths of a human being. It was much worse then that. It gave slave owners a bonus in representation for their human property, while doing nothing for blacks as non-persons under the law."[21]

Race was taken into consideration for the same purposes in the design of the economy, including the use of African women and children as well as men as enslaved labor in the South and subordinate labor in the North. Meanwhile, race was used to exclude nonenslaved Africans from capital and credit markets. In the South race was used to deny Africans not only the fruits of their labor but the fruits of their love as well, as the children of the enslaved were traded like ordinary articles of commerce.[22]

In the North so-called free Negros because of their race were routinely denied access to inns, schools, hospitals, churches, and cemeteries. Frequently, they were also victims of extraordinary violence because of their race. In 1741, for example, in New York City amidst rumors of a slave rebellion, thirteen black men were burned at the stake, seventeen were hanged, and more than one hundred black women and men were thrown into a dungeon beneath city hall.[23]

The making of these kinds of race-based decisions to subordinate Africans in America is the meaning of racism as used in this study. It is based on the definition advanced by Stokely Carmichael and Charles Hamilton in their 1967 book, *Black Power: Politics of Liberation in America*, where they define racism as "the predication of decisions and policies on considerations of race for the purpose of subordinating a racial group and maintaining control over it."[24] The Carmichael and Hamilton definition breaks with the way racism is traditionally defined by social scientists and historians because it focuses on behavior, rather than attitudes or ideology or the relationship between ideas and behavior. For example, many scholars of racism define it using some variations of the definition developed by Pierre Van den Berghe as "any set of beliefs that organic, genetically transmitted differences (whether real or imagined) between human groups are intrinsically associated with the presence or absence of certain socially relevant abilities or characteristics, hence that such differences are a legitimate basis of invidious distinctions between groups socially defined as races."[25] For purposes of the scientific study of racist behavior—historically and structurally—the Carmichael and Hamilton definition is preferred because the Van den Berghe type definitions tend to conflate a theory or explanation of the phenomenon with its empirical observation by stating that racism exists only if a belief in racial group inferiority is used to rationalize racial group mistreatment or subordination.

But, theoretically, it is possible that racism could be based not on perceived racial group inferiority but for simple economic or political reasons. (It is also possible that a group could be subordinated on the basis of the belief that it is superior). Antiblack racism in the United States, for example, has its origins not in the perceived differences between blacks and whites but in economic necessity and power. Frederickson writes, "The evidence strongly suggests that Africans and other non-Europeans were initially enslaved not so much because of their color and physical type as because of their legal and cultural vulnerability." And "it is clear from authoritative discussions of the legal, moral and religious foundations of slavery taking place in seventeenth-century England and the Netherlands that there was little or no overt sense that biological race or skin color played a determinative role in making some human beings absolute masters over others."[26]

The Van den Berghe type definitions of racism also complicates the process of research because it requires first identification of the beliefs in group inferiority and then a showing that these beliefs are in fact the basis for the racism, rather than mere rationalizations.[27]

However, as a historical matter racism by Europeans toward all the other peoples of the world but especially African peoples was rationalized on the basis of an ideology of white or European supremacy or, more precisely, an ideology of the inferiority of nonwhites. In the Anglo-American case the ideology that posited the inferiority of African peoples is deeply rooted in Western philosophy. Hegel wrote of Africans that they have not yet "attained to the realization of any substantial objective existence . . . in which the interest of man's volition is involved and in which he realized his own being . . . and the Negro . . . exhibits the natural man in his completely wild and untamed state" and that "among Negroes moral sentiments are quite weak, or more strictly speaking, non-existent." And Kant also concluded that blacks were inferior to whites in moral and rational capabilities and have by nature "no feelings that rise above the trifling."[28]

The ideology of white supremacy is also rooted in the Judeo-Christian faiths,[29] cultural chauvinism,[30] and scientific pretensions.[31] Thus, although racism in the United States is fundamentally about economics and relationships of power it has also been buttressed by a powerful ideology.

Racism in the United States, as Joe Feagin so ably demonstrates, is not merely individual acts of racism or bigotry, prejudice or racial stereotyping, or even racially discriminatory institutional practices. Rather it is systemic—a complex, interdependent, interactive series of behavioral and ideational components.[32] This "systemic racism" is reflected historically in the unjustly gained economic resources and political power of whites; empirically in a complex array of anti-black practices; and in the ideology of white supremacy and the attitudes of whites that developed in order to rationalize the system.

This complex systemic phenomenon is what African American thought challenges and African American movements have sought to overthrow. Conservatives, however, have sought to maintain it or, at best, to change it gradually, always prioritizing stability over justice. This, then, historically and situationally, is what in the first instance makes conservatism and racism in America the same.

It is more than this, however. For in the second instance the "substantive ideals" or "vision" of America and their economic, cultural, and political manifestations were also conservative, which are the subjects of the next chapter.

CHAPTER TWO

Lockean "Liberalism" as the Conservative Ideology in America

The philosophy of John Locke, by any contemporary understanding, postulates an ideology of conservatism. Yet as C. B. Macpherson writes, "Locke has suffered as much as anyone and more than most, from having had modern liberal-democratic assumptions read into his political thought."[1] Locke's ideology is fundamentally concerned with defending laissez-faire capitalism, limiting the power of the state, and thereby protecting the power and privileges of the wealthy against the claims of the poor. Much of the literature in American thought, however, describes Locke as the quintessential liberal, in some cases even as the philosophical father of liberalism.[2] Macpherson avers that Locke's work invites this confusion because Locke's writings are confusing and contradictory, blending—perhaps deliberately—in an ambiguous way important liberal principles such as government by consent, majority rule, minority rights, and the moral supremacy of the individual along with conservative ideas about property rights, voting rights, and the limited purposes and powers of government.

In order to extract ourselves from this confusion it seems useful to view liberalism in two ways, as a philosophy and as an ideology. Some scholars make this distinction by describing the philosophy as classical liberalism and the ideology as modern liberalism. I think, however, that this distinction only contributes to the confusion by using the label *liberalism* to describe distinct phenomena, philosophy, and ideology. Of course this to some extent is a mere quibble over words. Hartz, for example, uses the classical-modern distinction in order to make the case for Locke as a liberal and America as the quintessential liberal state. However, he also writes that "there has never been a 'liberal movement' or a real 'liberal party' " in America. . . . Ironically, 'liberalism' is a stranger in the land of its greatest realization and fulfillment."[3] Douglas Brinkley uses a similar distinction while writing that 'liberalism' is a "versatile and controversial term."[4] And in his aptly titled article "The Protean Character of American Liberalism" Gary Gerstle writes of the "malleability" of the liberal tradition in America, which he traces in part to "its use as a surrogate for socialism in America."⁵ Clifford Girvetz traces the "evolution" of liberalism from the classical to modern, and in his recent work Paul Starr draws a distinction between "constitutional liberalism" (classical) and "modern democratic liberalism" (ideology).⁶ Although I recognize it risks further confusion, I think for purposes of this study it is more useful to draw the philosophy-ideology distinction than the classical-modern and refer to the American tradition as philosophically liberal (as is the tradition of most of the Western world) and ideologically as conservative, which is not the case for most of the Western democracies.

Philosophy is understood as abstract reasoning, rational, systematic thought about the nature of reality or parts of it, and in the case of philosophical liberalism about those parts of reality dealing with the nature of man and the origins and purposes of government or, more precisely, the state.⁷ Ideology, like liberalism and conservatism, is a contested concept;⁸ however, generally we may understand it in a broad sense as a set of interrelated ideas and values used to justify a political program and plan of action. A narrower understanding would limit ideology to a set of ideas about the role, purposes, powers and appropriate size of government, particular in its relationship to private property. The narrower sense is the way I understand Locke's ideology.

Liberalism as a Philosophy

Locke is frequently referred to as the "philosophical father of liberalism," but it is Hobbes who is probably more deserving of this honor because he was the first major Western philosopher to introduce the idea that governments have their origins in a contract (he used the word *covenant*) entered into by free men.⁹ Subsequently, Locke and Rousseau developed similar understandings, and together these three social contract theorists are considered the architects of the liberal philosophy of the state. Methodologically, Hobbes, Locke, and Rousseau reach their conclusions on the basis of the same rational, deductive procedure and claim a universal validity and applicability of those conclusions. Sometimes referred to as "natural rights theorists," each begins with an assumption about the nature of men: how men think and behave innately or naturally. From this assumption it is logically deduced how life was in the "state of nature," that is, when there was no government and men were free to act in accordance with their nature. Finally, the conditions in this state of nature form the logical basis for understanding why men entered into the social contract to create the government. Critical to the philosophy of liberalism is the idea of the social contract because on it rests two of liberalism's core values: the natural rights of individuals and the idea that governments are created and derive their powers from those autonomous individuals acting collectively.

In this philosophical sense, Hartz is correct the American tradition is quintessential liberal. Although a few American thinkers have rejected philosophical liberalism, in general there has been broad consensus across the ideological divide on the liberal philosophical principles. This consensus is partly the result, as Hartz shows, of the absence in America of feudal hierarchies, traditions, and customs. Thus, Americans could embrace philosophical liberalism as natural "[b]ecause the fundamental feudal oppressions of Europe had not taken root, the fundamental social norm of Locke ceased in part to look like a norm and began, of all things, to look like a sober description of fact.... Thus, in the beginning, Locke once wrote 'all the world was America.' "[10]

Government by consent, majority rule, minority rights, the rule of law, the sanctity of private property, and the primacy of the individual are integral to the American tradition and are embraced even today by both ideological liberals and conservatives. Of these values Hartz writes that individualism—atomistic individual freedom—is the "master assumption" from which all of American attitudes flow.[11]

Needless to repeat, this master assumption was not applied to all individuals. As Rogers Smith has masterfully argued, alongside the liberal tradition in America, there also exists "liberal strategies of exclusion" of blacks, other ethnic minorities, and women.[12] But what Smith refers to as "multiple traditions" is to me really a single liberal tradition, bastardized by racism for sure but nevertheless hegemonic, so hegemonic that it is embraced in the thought of excluded groups.[13]

Although Hobbes, Locke, and Rousseau share similar epistemologies and reach similar understandings about the role of men in creating the state, each has relatively distinct theories on man's nature and conditions in the state of nature. These different theories give rise to ideologies, that is, different ideas about the origins and purposes of government as well as the appropriate way to structure government so it might most efficiently serve its purposes. Central to understanding the different ideologies embedded in the writings of Hobbes, Locke, and Rousseau is how they treat the emergence of private property and consequently the appropriate role of the state in relationship to it. Examining these differences, Locke's ideology is clearly the most conservative, conservative because, unlike Hobbes and Rousseau, Locke contends, "The great and chief end, therefore, of men uniting into commonwealths, and putting themselves under government is the preservation of their property."[14] From this master assumption flow all of the major tenets of Lockean conservatism, a conservatism that in America was hegemonic ideologically until the arrival of the New Deal in the 1930s.

Mannheim contends that philosophical conservatism of the Burkean variant *must* reject philosophical liberalism with respect to both its method of reasoning and its conclusions. Its method of reasoning is rejected because it is abstract and rational, and its conclusions are rejected because the government is understood as an evolved institution rather than a rationally planned or created one. The idea of natural rights is also rejected because philosophical conservatives believe that individual rights derive from and are dependent on society and that men are not equal but are entitled only to those rights established by custom and tradition.[15] Philosophical conservatism is thus more comfortable with the understanding of the origins and purposes of the state developed by the "ancients," with their concern about justice and virtue rather than the vindication of individual natural rights.

John C. Calhoun, for example, categorically rejected the idea of natural rights and the social contract, but since his writings are largely apologia for slavery, one has to be skeptical about their intellectual integrity. I discuss Calhoun in the next chapter. Aside from Calhoun, Willmore Kendall is probably the best known American conservative critic of philosophical liberalism, arguing that it was a "libel" on the framers to say they were Lockeans and believed in a social contract among equals emerging from a state of nature. Rather, Kendall concluded that the framers drew their inspiration from classical political philosophy.[16] Among other things, Kendall insists that the American political tradition is not committed to individual rights and equality, emphasizing that the word equality never appears in the Constitution and that most of the framers were opposed to the Bill of Rights.

Kendall was an idiosyncratic individual and thinker whose work has largely been ignored by mainstream historians and political scientists. Kendall did, however, exercise some influence on the conservative movement in the 1950s and 1960s as one of the founding editors of *National Review*. At Yale he taught William F. Buckley Jr. and may have influenced Buckley's thinking, at least on the issues of natural rights and equality.[17]

Conservatism as an Ideology in the Philosophy of Locke

In understanding Locke's conservative ideology it is useful to compare his thought with that of Rousseau, particularly their thinking on private property and its relationship to the state. As I indicated in the introduction, it will be necessary here to go over some rather elementary material.

Rousseau's Ideological Liberalism

Of the three philosophers of the liberal tradition, Rousseau is notoriously the most difficult to understand and interpret. Or to put it another way, his philosophy is open to varying interpretations, in part because parts of his writings are paradoxical—probably deliberately so—and also because he uses rhetorical flourishes to make his points sometimes it seems as if to simply surprise or shock the reader. Also, Rousseau presents two distinct social contracts in his writings. In the *Discourse on Inequality* he writes as a kind of philosophical anthropologist trying to account as best he can for the actual origins of the social contract that established the state. Here his writings very much resemble the Marxist view, as expressed by Engels in *The Origin of the Family, Private Property and the State*.[18] And then in *The Social Contract* he presents his ideal social contract or his vision of the kind of state men ought to establish. Here he resembles more his philosophical partners Hobbes and Locke. These two social contracts—the anthropological and philosophical—create ambiguity in interpreting his philosophy.

In presenting Rousseau's ideas, I divide the discussion in two parts. The first focuses on the philosophical anthropology of the *Discourse* and the second on the philosophy of the state in *The Social Contract*.

For Rousseau, man in his original nature was good. This was primitive man, with no capacity to reason, no ego, no will to exercise power or dominate others. Guided by a natural inclination to self-preservation individuals sought food, shelter, and sex but not at the expense of others because they are guided by concern, compassion, and pity for others. In Rousseau's words people had a "natural repugnance to seeing any sentient being, especially [their] fellow man suffer."[19] Thus, in acquiring the necessities of life, women and men were guided by the principle of the golden rule: "Do what is good for you with as little harm as possible to others."[20]

In this primitive state of nature men and women initially lived alone, but gradually as reason and language emerged people begin to develop lasting relationships, forming families and villages. Private property in a rudimentary form emerges, but it does not create any problems because no person possesses more than he or she needs, and there is enough for everyone. This state of nature, Rousseau believes, must have been the happiest in human history. As he puts it, people lived as "free, healthy, good and happy as they could in accordance with their nature, and they continued to enjoy among themselves the sweet reward of independent intercourse."[21]

What happened to end this free, good, and happy state? In answering this question Rousseau's philosophical anthropology closely resembles Engels historical materialism. Both Rousseau and Engels conclude that the invention of metallurgy and agriculture, the division of labor, and the subsequent development of private property in land and herds were the decisive transformative phenomena. Private property's development was the most important of these developments. In the state of nature a simple form of property had existed, but it was crude and communal. This new form is genuinely private and therefore in Rousseau's views far more destructive of society. Here is how he put it in a famous passage: "The true founder of civil society was the first man who having enclosed a piece of land, thought of saying 'This is mine' and came across people simple enough to believe him. How many crimes, wars, murders and how much misery and horror the human race might have been spared if someone had pulled up the stakes or filled in the ditch, and cried out to his fellows: Beware of listening to this charlatan. You are lost if you forget that the fruits of the earth belong to all and that the earth itself belongs to no one."[22]

Why is this development so destructive? It is destructive because it fundamentally transforms man's caring and compassionate nature and thereby the free and happy conditions of life in the state of nature. This is because genuine private property necessarily fosters inequality. And inequality alters man's nature, causing him to become selfish, competitive, and greedy.[23]

In other words, Rousseau's naturally compassionate man, living by the golden rule, is transformed into Hobbes' egoistical, ego-driven, power-seeking every man for himself. And the state of nature, it logically follows, is transformed into Hobbes' state of war: everyman against everyman where life is short, nasty and brutish.

This situation gave rise to the state. How did this come about? It came about through fraud. According to Rousseau a few rich men, knowing they had no legitimate right to their property and wealth and knowing they could not defend themselves against constant attacks of the masses of poor people decided to establish a state. Rousseau describes this development as the "shrewdest scheme to enter the human mind" because the "uncultivated and gullible masses" were persuaded to transfer their natural freedoms to a state that would have the power to oppress them. Rousseau observes that the terms of the contract must have been stated in terms of equality, fairness, and justice for all, which led the poor to believe that the state would secure their safety and liberty. But it was all a lie. Instead, he writes, this state "put new shackles on the weak and gave new powers to the rich, which destroyed natural freedom irretrievable, laid down for all time the law of property and inequality, made clever usurpation into an irrevocable right, and henceforth subjected, for the benefit of a few ambitious men, the human race to labor, servitude and misery."[24]

Rousseau's last paragraph in the *Discourse* is a call for revolution, for a new state based on an honest and just social contract, "for it is manifestly contrary to the law of nature, however it is defined, that a child should guide a wise man, and that a handful of men should gorge themselves with superfluities while the starving multitude goes in want of necessities."[25]

Given that the historical social contract was based on inequality and fraud and intimidation of the gullible and unsophisticated, Rousseau in *The Social Contract* attempts to develop a legitimate state based on the will of the people and equality. In doing so, he imagines that man will be returned to his original caring and compassionate nature.

The Social Contract outlines Rousseau's vision of a communitarian state in which individual rights and freedoms are subordinated to the good of society. An enigmatic and utopian book, its ideas have been used to justify totalitarianism on the one hand and participatory democracy on the other.

The origins of Rousseau's ideal state is, he says, based on the following "premise: men have reached a point where the obstacles hindering their preservation in the state of nature are so obstructive as to defy the resources each individual, while in that state, can devote to his preservation. This being the case that primitive condition cannot continue: humankind would perish if it did not change its way of life."[26] Thus, man enters into a compact or contract to create the state. The decision to enter into the agreement is made by free and equal individuals and requires unanimity. In this unanimous decision men agree to surrender all of their rights to the state. Like Hobbes, but unlike Locke, Rousseau's social contract requires men to surrender all of their rights to the state. In a famous passage Rousseau refers to these terms of the contract as the submission of each individual to "the general will" or "a collective moral body." And in words that forever link his philosophy to dictatorships or totalitarian government Rousseau went on to write that "whoever refuses to obey the general will shall be constrained to do so by the entire body politics, which is only another way of saying that his fellows shall force him to be free."[27] "What is the origin and nature of property in this new state? First, the land in question must not yet be inhabited by anybody. Secondly, one must occupy only that amount that one needs for one's subsistence. Thirdly, one must take possession of the amount not going through some idle ritual, but by working and cultivating it—this being the only evidence of ownership that, in the absence of positive title, ought to be respected by others."[28]

However, an individual's property is "always subservient to the community's right over all the holdings" because without such subservience "the exercise of sovereignty would lack genuine power."[29]

Several chapters in *The Social Contract* are devoted to analysis of various types of constitutions and governments (monarchy, aristocracy, democracy), but Rousseau does not appear to be passionately interested in these questions, mainly because it appears that he did not think constitutions and specific forms of government matter very much. For example, although he appears to lean toward monarchy (because it possesses "greater vigor"), like Locke he worries that it is "never healthy for the maker of laws to execute them."[30] In the end, however, he is pessimistic that any form of government that requires the selection of one man (monarch) or assembly of men (parliament) can achieve the ends of democracy. He writes "no real democracy—taking this term in its most rigorous sense—ever existed, none ever will exist. For the many to govern and the few to be governed is to go against natural order."[31]

Rousseau thought there could never be real democracy except in small states because once it was necessary to have legislators to pass laws and bureaucrats to implement them inevitably they would win "supreme power" and constitute themselves an aristocracy. In other words "the moment a people gives itself representatives it ceases to be free; it ceases, indeed, to exist."[32] In another passage probably written to shock, he writes, "The English people thinks itself free, but it is badly mistaken. It is free only during elections: once the members of parliament have been elected, it lapses back into slavery, and becomes nothing."[33]

Of the three major philosophers of liberalism, Rousseau is the only one who was committed to the ideology of liberalism and equality and social security, at least equality among men.[34] The framers of the Constitution viewed Rousseau's ideas as dangerous radicalism, the dreaded "French disease."[35] More congenial to their thinking and their interests was Locke's ideology of laissez-faire capitalism and a weak state.

Locke's Ideological Conservatism

Locke believed the nature of man was neither good nor evil but that by and large he was, as Thomas Reardon puts it, "a pretty decent fellow, far removed from the quarrelsome, selfish creature found in Hobbes."[36] But neither was he, I might add, the naturally kind and compassionate man Rousseau described. For Locke, the distinguishing feature of man's nature is his capacity to reason, and this capacity—which all men are endowed with by God—allows them to discern and live by the law of nature. It is this law of nature that makes him a pretty good fellow. Simply put, for Locke the law of nature requires all men to try to preserve their fellow men and that no man should seek to take away another's life, liberty, or property.[37]

Given this law of nature and man's capacity to discern it, life in the state of nature is pretty good. Indeed, rather than being the Hobbesian situation of a war of all against all, it is a rather peaceful place where men, guided by natural law, establish families, form communities, acquire property, and live in relative harmony. As Locke wrote, the state of nature was a "state of peace, goodwill, mutual assistance and preservation."[38] It is important to understand that for Locke property exists in the state of nature. In his famous chapter 5, "On Property," Locke begins by observing that God has given "the earth and all inferior creatures" to all men in common. But he also writes that God commands men to use the land and its creatures to the "best advantage of life and convenience." Hence, whoever mixes his labor with the land creates private property; something he alone has the right to possess and control.[39]

This, then, is the origin of private property; in the divine command that men labor "[s]o, that God, by commanding to subdue gave authority so far to appropriate; and the condition of human life which requires labor and material to work on necessarily introduces private possessions."[40] These initial private possessions were limited to "a very moderate proportion" because men were allowed to possess only the property they could use or consume. However, with the invention of money this limitation of property to a moderate proportion was destroyed, and the possibilities for gross inequalities of wealth were introduced. The creation of money defined by Locke as "some lasting thing that men might keep without spoiling and that by mutual consent men would take in exchange for the truly useful perishable supports of life" automatically creates the conditions for capitalism.[41] Money made possible the emergence of bourgeois men and capitalism and the "disproportionate and unequal possession of the earth" because it provides "a way how a man may fairly possess more land than he himself can use the product of, by receiving in exchange for the over plus gold and silver which may be hoarded up without injury to any one, these metals not spoiling or decaying in the hands of the possessor."[42] It was this unequal possession of property that made necessary the creation of the state. But why would men hoard up more than they can use, in a word, capital. Macpherson writes, "Indeed its function as a medium of exchange was seen as subordinate to its function as capital, for in his view the purpose of agriculture, industry and commerce was the accumulation of capital. And the purpose of capital was not to provide a consumable income for its owners, but to beget further capital by profitable investment."[43]

When Locke uses "property," he is not referring to property only in the sense of land or money but also to natural rights or what we would refer to today as "civil liberties" or "human rights." That is, men have property in their persons as well as their possessions. However, as McPherson writes, "In his crucial argument on the limitation of governments, he is clearly using property in the more usual sense of lands and goods."[44]

Given that the state has its origins in the wish of men to preserve their property, it has, according to Locke, three basic functions that are found "wanting in the state of nature": (1) to provide for "established, settled, known law," (2) to establish "a known and indifferent judge with authority to determine all differences according to the established law," and (3) to establish a police "power to back up and support when right, and to give it due execution."[45] In other words, it is the responsibility of the government to protect life and property or maintain law and order and provide for defense against foreign enemies. Unlike Rousseau, government's purpose for Locke is not to promote equality or provide social security.

In these ways the basic purposes of Locke's state resemble Hobbes': to maintain law and order and provide for the national defense. It differs, however, in several important respects. First, the government's power is not unlimited, and it may not be exercised in an authoritarian way. Second, the people retain sovereignty, which gives them the right to dissolve the government if they wish. Third, the state may not deprive people of their property without their consent. And fourth, the powers of the government cannot be placed in the hands of one man or one assembly of men.

For Locke the legislative power—an assembly of men—is the "supreme power of the commonwealth." But the legislature elected by the people—or at least property-holding males—may not exercise its power in an absolute or arbitrary manner.[46] The legislative power must be especially limited in terms of its authority to violate or subordinate property rights because preservation of property was the reason government was created in the first place. Thus, Locke said it would be absurd if the government itself could take away a man's property or wealth.

In order to secure the property and liberty of the people against arbitrary or tyrannical government, Locke insists on the absolute indispensability of the separation of power. Although he does not develop the separation-of-powers argument in great detail, implicit is the idea that a government in one person or body would constitute a greater threat to property than one of divided powers.

Locke's natural, God-given right of men to possess as much land as one's individual initiatives would allow over time in any given territory also naturally exhausts all the land, leaving many men landless and without money. The only recourse for these men, Locke argued, would be to sell their labor. And since every man has a property in his person, he is free to enter into a contract with other men in order to earn money. The men with money, however, are free to contract to purchase that labor at the lowest price possible, at a bare subsistence level. But McPherson writes: "[T]he laborer's share [of national income], being seldom more than a bare subsistence, never allows that body of men, time, or opportunity to raise their thoughts above that of, or struggle with the richer for theirs (as one common interest) unless when some common and great distress, uniting them in one universal ferment, makes them forget respect, and emboldens them to carve to their wants with armed force: and then sometimes they break in upon the rich, and sweep all like a deluge. But this rarely happens but in the mal-administration of neglected, or mismanaged government."[47] This "deluge" gives rise to the need of the "policeman" state; a view not unlike that expressed by Rousseau regarding the origins of the state in the *Discourse*.[48] In words that would soothe the minds of nineteenth- and early-twentieth-century laissez-faire capitalists and *Lochner*-era Supreme Court justices Locke suggested: "Masters of workhouses ('houses of correction') were to be encouraged to make them into sweated-labor manufacturing establishments; justices of the peace were to be encouraged to make them into forced labor establishments. The children of the unemployed 'above the age of three' were unnecessarily a burden on the nation; they should be set to work, and could be made to earn more than their keep. All this was justified on the explicit ground that unemployment was due not to economic causes but to moral depravity."[49]

Locke also argued that the poor should be denied the suffrage ostensibly because they lacked the mental faculties to participate in government but also as a further means to secure the protection of private property. In concluding that Locke was a "majority rule democrat," Macpherson writes that theorists have overlooked "all the evidence that Locke was not a democrat all."[50] Rather, his philosophical postulate about rule by the consent of the majority ideologically meant rule by the "consent of the majority of property owners."[51]

Locke also had little sympathy for poor relief, welfare, or any kind of redistributionist policy by the state. As Huyler puts it, he did not "evidence the keen sensibilities toward the hard-pressed that, say, Rousseau would a century later."[52] Instead, Locke emphasized the responsibility of the poor for their own condition, and in Reagan-like, neoconservative language he attributed the spread of "pauperism" to the "relaxation of discipline and the corruption of manners."[53] He also expressed more sympathy for "the burden that lies upon the industrious for maintaining the poor" than for those "begging drones, who live unnecessarily upon other people's labor."[54]

As a Christian Locke believed that "individuals may part with as much of their own goods as their charitable instincts may incline them," but he insisted the government had "no power to seize the goods of others for purposes they may deem worthy."[55]

Slavery in the Philosophy of Liberalism

The philosophy of liberalism is at war with the idea of slavery; and here again it represents a fundamental break with the ancients where slavery was common in thought and practice. From the time of the Greeks, slave trading and slavery had been integral components of Western societies. Of the two to three hundred thousand persons in Plato's Athens, it is estimated that approximately 30 to 40 percent were enslaved.[56] For Plato, slavery in his Republic was so commonplace, so unremarkable, that it did not require extensive elaboration, discussion or justification. Rather, it was in the natural order of things, as night follows day, that some persons would be enslaved because in their nature, Plato said, some men lacked "logos" and therefore needed wise, benevolent masters to guide them; otherwise they would become "vicious" and "disorderly."[57] Aristotle used similar arguments to justify slavery, writing that slaves should be "naturally inferior" to their masters; thus Greeks should not be enslaved because they were not an inferior people. Like many others throughout history Aristotle also justified slavery on the basis of war. That is, persons conquered and captured in a just war could be enslaved, but the war is just in his view only when it is waged against an inferior people who are intended by nature to be slaves but refused to submit. In an argument that anticipates justifications for slavery in the United States, Aristotle in his *Politics* wrote, "Therefore, whenever there is this same wide discrepancy between human beings as between soul and body or between man and beast, then those whose conditions is such that their function is the use of their bodies and nothing better can be expected of them, those, I say are slaves by nature."[58]

Philosophical liberalism with its focus on the natural rights of individuals breaks with this ancient tradition. It asserts that every man has a "property in his person" and an inalienable right to the fruits of his labor. Rousseau is unequivocal in his rejection of slavery, writing in *The Social Contract* that "no man, as we have seen, has any natural authority over his fellow man, and might, as we have seen also, makes no rights. Any way you look at it, then, the right to enslave is nonexistent; it is not merely illegitimate, but absurd and meaningless as well."[59] Hobbes and Locke, however, embrace the idea that slavery might be justifiable on the basis of war.[60] Although there was no basis for it, in colonial America some apologists for slavery cited Locke's just-war theory in making their case for the enslavement of Africans.[61]

Although Locke's philosophy in general rejects slavery, he was personally involved in profiting from slave trade as a stockholder in the Royal African Company and was one of the principal authors of the Charter of the Carolina Colonies in which it was mandated that "every freeman of Carolina shall have absolute power and authority over his Negro slave."[62] Yet in his voluminous writings on a wide range of subjects he never addressed the question of African slavery. On this question Farr writes that "silence seems to have been his principal bequest to posterity."[63] This bequest allowed slavery's apologists to use Locke by suggesting he thought Africans were not fully human. Although Locke was almost certainly a white supremacist, none of his writings disparage African humanity in the ways Kant or Hegel did in their works. And even if he had done so it would not have undermined his core principle that men, even "savages," are born free and equal with the natural right to individual liberty.[64] Locke also rejected the Hobbesian notion of slavery by contract or covenant, writing that a man cannot by "compact or his own consent enslave himself to anyone."[65] As Jefferson, paraphrasing Locke, put it, an individual's liberty was inalienable.

Thus, the only Lockean basis for slavery is when aggressors in an unjust war against "innocents" are conquered. Such aggressors, Locke contends, deserve death, but the victor "may (when he has him in his power) delay to take it, and make use of him to his own service and he does him no injury."⁶⁶ Slavery is justified in this instance because the enslaved persons themselves have violated the natural rights of other persons. This so-called just-war theory was obviously irrelevant to the enslavement of Africans in the Americas, since if anything they were the innocents, and if they had it within their power they could have justly enslaved Locke and all the others who engaged in the wars of aggression that resulted in the capture and enslavement of innocent African men, women, and children.

But even if this was not the case—that is, if some African men had been enslaved as a result of unjust wars—this still would not have provided a Lockean basis for the peculiar institution in the United States. This is because only those who actually engaged in the war may justly be enslaved, excluding noncombatants, women, and children. And certainly the children of the justly enslaved could not be held in bondage since they are the truly innocent. As Farr concludes, "whatever else might be said of Locke's just-war theory of slavery this much is clear: *It neither explains or justifies the practice of seventeenth century slavery.* The African slave trade and the institution of chattel slavery in the Americas flagrantly violated the theoretical constraints he so painstakingly set."⁶⁷

In other words, while the founders of America were chaste Lockeans in giving birth to laissez-faire capitalism and limited government, they were bastards when it came to his ideas about the natural rights of all men to liberty. And they (and Locke) knew it, because during the colonial era popular pamphleteers frequently used the word *slavery* to refer to their situation under British rule.⁶⁸ But as one wrote, the slavery we complain of "is lighter than a feather compared to their [African] heavy doom, and may be called liberty and happiness when contrasted with the most object slavery and intolerable wretchedness to which they are subjected."⁶⁹

The bastardization of Locke nevertheless became an integral component of what was to be conserved in America, and to challenge it was as radical, as un-American, and as unconstitutional as challenging the prohibition on taking of private property without just compensation or the liberty of capital to employ labor on its own terms. Locke's investments in and support of African slavery and the silence in his writings on the hypocrisy of it all makes him complicit in the bastardization of his own theory of the liberty of the individual.⁷⁰ In the context of the times Locke's just-war theory of slavery is morally bankrupt.⁷¹

Bastardization and moral obtuseness notwithstanding, racism has been integral to conservatism in America since the founding.⁷² Racism in the form of the exploitation of labor is of course not incidental to conservatism's principles of political economy. The historian William Freehling writes, "If the Founding Fathers unquestionably dreamed of universal freedom, their ideological posture was weighed down equally with conceptions of priorities, profits and prejudices that would long make the dream utopian."[73] The first priority of the framers of the Constitution was the preservation of the union of the states, which required the bastardization of Locke and the sanctioning of racism by the Constitution. The priority of the union of the states was thought by them to be indispensable to the priority of profit, that is, the economic and commercial success of the new nation. And as Freehling observes, their concern with profits grew out of their preoccupation with property, and slaves as property were crucial to the economy; thus "it made the slaves' right to freedom no more 'natural' than the master's right to property."[74]

It is this crucial nexus among profits, property, and slavery that from the beginning made conservatism and racism the same in America.

Lockean Conservative Institutional Arrangements: The Constitution

Each of the philosophers of liberalism influenced the development of liberal democratic states throughout Western Europe and many other parts of the world. However, in the United States it is Locke's philosophy that had the most profound and pervasive influence.[75] Thomas Jefferson wrote, "Locke's little book on government is perfect as far as it goes." Richard Lee, another of the founders, went so far as to accuse Jefferson of plagiarizing Locke in writing the Declaration of Independence. Jefferson replied that he consulted "neither book nor pamphlet while writing it." But, as Carl Becker writes, "most Americans had absorbed Locke's words as a kind of gospel; and the Declaration in its form and its philosophy follows closely certain sentences in Locke's second treatise on government. Jefferson having read Locke's treatise on government, was so taken with it that he read it again and still again, so that its very phrases reappear in his own writings."[76]

The philosophy of Locke also shaped the drafting of the Constitution. The ideas of natural rights (codified in the Bill of Rights); of government by the consent of or contract with the people (expressed in the Preamble); of limited government (expressed in article I's limits on congressional power only to those powers" herein granted"); of legislative supremacy (seen in the detailed grant of powers to Congress in article I, section 8), the centrality of private property (as found in the Fifth Amendment's prohibition against the "taking of private property without just compensation," and the contract clause) all may be traced to Locke's "little book." And of course the separation of powers—the most distinctive feature of the American government—is straight out of Locke.

In designing the Constitution the framers were guided by two overarching and interrelated principles. First, the primary object of government was the protection of private property, and second, the power of government had to be limited to avoid tyranny. These two principles are interrelated because a government of unlimited powers could itself become a threat to private property. These two principles gave rise to what are the most important contributions of the framers to the art and practice of government: the idea of the separation of powers and federalism.

In *The Federalist Papers* number 10, James Madison wrote, "The diversities in faculties of men from which the rights of property originates is no less an insuperable obstacle to uniformity of interests. The protection of these faculties is the first object of government."[77] How does government carry out this first object in a democratic society? The problem confronting Madison and his colleagues was simply this: in a democratic, capitalist state where only a minority has property but a majority may have the right to vote, it is likely that there might be a democratic "deluge" in which the propertyless majority uses its suffrage to threaten the property of the minority. To avoid this possible deluge while preserving what Madison called the "spirit and form" of democracy was a principal object of the framers in designing the Constitution.

How is this objective attained? The principal means is through the separation of powers. It was not, however, the mere separation of the government into four distinct parts (including the two parts of the Congress) but also the fact that the people were allowed to directly elect only one of the four parts—the House of Representatives—arguably the least powerful of the four. The second means that accomplishes this objective is federalism. The major powers of the federal government were limited to regulating commerce and the currency, conducting diplomacy, and waging war. Everything else done by the government was to be done by the states or not at all.[78]

Most mainstream scholars of the Constitution reject the neo-Marxist thesis advanced by Charles Beard in his famous 1913 book, *An Economic Interpretation of the Constitution*. In this work Beard argued that the Constitution was an undemocratic document written by wealthy men to protect their property (including their property in persons).[79] But in 2002 Robert Dahl, then perhaps the nation's most eminent political scientist and its leading student of democracy, published *How Democratic Is the American Constitution?* in which he demonstrated in his usual elegant way that the Constitution was substantially undemocratic. Dahl identified seven "undemocratic elements" in the Constitution, including slavery; its failure to establish universal suffrage and instead leaving voter qualifications up to each state,[80] election of the president by the electoral college rather than the people; the election of senators by state legislatures; the violation of the principle of one person, one role in the election of senators; the judicial veto over acts of Congress and the limited grant of power to Congress to legislate.[81] Although not a formal part of the Constitution, Dahl also concludes that the two-party system is undemocratic when compared to multiparty systems.[82]

Although Dahl does not include federalism as an undemocratic element, in its operation, it has allowed minorities in some parts of the country to act contrary to the will of national majorities.

Finally, Dahl does not mention the Constitution's Three-fifths Clause, which severely undermined democratic principles, giving, for example, a white man in Virginia who owned a hundred slaves the equivalent of sixty votes compared to a Rhode Island white man who owned no slaves one vote.[83] This clause until it was repealed after the Civil War allowed a minority of southern slaveholders to dominate the national government until Lincoln's election.[84]

These conservative Lockean institutions are also Burkean, reflecting Burke's concern with the sanctity of private property, the inevitability of inequality, skepticism about democracy, restraints on the power of government, and institutional arrangements that allow for gradual change within stable, traditional boundaries. American conservatives have long recognized and celebrated the conservatism of the American Revolution and the Constitution.[85] Russell Kirk, for example, writes that the Constitution "has been the most successful conservative device in the history of the world,"[86] and that "federalism had a great share in keeping the United States the most conservative power in the world."[87] Rossiter writes, "The Constitution was a triumph of conservatism," and that the two-party system is "the most conservative political arrangement in the Western World" and the Supreme Court and judicial review is "the last and most essential stone in the wall of conservative constitutionalism."[88] And Peter Viereck writes, "[T]he American Constitution performs an aristocratic and conservative function."[89]

Many of the Constitution's conservative and undemocratic elements are directly related to racism, the wish to secure to slaveholders property in African persons from anticipated attacks from the northern, nonslaveholding majority. These include the Electoral College, separation of powers, federalism, and the two-party system. Frederick Douglass recognized the impediments of the Madisonian system to democracy and to the freedom of the emancipated slaves and called for the removal of all of the Constitution's "countermajoritarian features," including the independent executive, the presidential veto, and the judicial review.[90]

For the framers the separation of powers was a safeguard against tyranny. As Madison wrote, "[T]he accumulation of all powers, legislative, executive and judiciary in the same hands . . . may be justly pronounced the very definition of tyranny."[91] Although the principle may be a safeguard against tyranny, it is not, however, as Madison contends, indispensable as the parliamentary democracies of most of the world demonstrate. And as Donald Robinson shows in *Slavery in the Structure of American Politics*, concerns about slavery also influenced the decision to adopt the principle. This is because a divided government with little unitary or centralized power would be less capable of acting against slavery.

Throughout American history the separation of powers has most often worked to impede the struggle against racism. Prior to the Civil War, the separation of powers allowed the Senate to block actions to halt the spread of slavery, and when this failed, the Supreme Court in the *Dred Scott* case interpreted the Constitution in a way that allowed the spread of slavery throughout the country. During Reconstruction President Andrew Johnson used the powers of the presidency (including the veto) to block or frustrate the efforts of Congress to pass laws guaranteeing freedom and equality. When Johnson's efforts failed and civil rights laws and amendments to the Constitution were enacted, the Supreme Court once again used its powers to block their implementation. And for more than half of the twentieth century southern senators used the filibuster to block antilynching and other civil rights legislation. Until the protests of the 1960s the Senate blocked or compromised most civil rights legislation, although there was support for such legislation in public opinion and the other parts of the national government.[92]

Without federalism it is unlikely there could have been a union of all thirteen states, but some of the framers, including Madison with his Virginia plan, favored a unitary government with unlimited congressional powers and the right to veto legislation enacted by the states. The Virginia plan was rejected for a number of reasons, among which was the need to protect property in persons in the southern states. In his classic work *Federalism: Origins and Operations* William Riker flatly concludes that "if in the United States one disapproves of racism one should disapprove of federalism" because "[t]he main beneficiaries throughout American history have been southern whites, who have been given the freedom to oppress Negroes, first as slaves and later as a depressed caste."[93]

Similarly there were several reasons the framers choose not to allow for the direct election of the president, but Robinson concludes that racism or the wish to further secure slavery was "absolutely decisive" in the determination to adopt the electoral college.[94]

Finally in *Uneasy Alliances: Race and Party Completion* Paul Frymer argues that the two-party system was established at least partly for racist reasons, that is, to keep the issue of slavery off the national partisan agenda.[95]

Generally of the Constitution Robinson writes that "tensions about slavery were prominent among the forces that maintained the resolve to develop the country without strong direction from Washington."[96] In limiting the power of the national government the Constitution itself made racism and conservatism the same in America, the same from the founding.

Ideology: Burke and Locke in America

When writing about conservatism in America scholars usually posit a sharp divide between Locke and Burke, labeling the former the "patron of liberalism" and the latter the "patron of conservatism." Kramnick, for example, is typical writing that Burke's work is the bible of conservatism, and he is its prophet in "much the same way that *The Second Treatise of Government* and *The Communist Manifesto* and John Locke and Karl Marx are the bibles and prophets of liberalism and communism respectively."[97] Yet as should be apparent by now, there are many congruencies in the thought of Locke and Burke.

Both men believed in limiting the powers of government and in stability and incremental change. Both prioritized private property and asserted that there is natural inequality between individuals (who nevertheless are morally equal), and the government should be restrained from trying to create an equalitarian society. Burke and Locke also believe in the importance of religion, especially for the maintenance of stable relationships between citizens and the state.[98] They also believed in government by an aristocracy of property and wealth, although Burke also favored rule by Britain's hereditary aristocracy as well.

Thus, while conservatives in America may attempt—awkwardly as in the case of Russell Kirk—to use the ideology of Burke to defend Lockean America from liberalism, Huntington to the contrary, they need not do so. They can and have—and have more intellectually honestly—used Locke himself.

CHAPTER THREE

The Special Place of the South in American Conservatism

The South is and always has been the most conservative part of America, conservative in an almost militant espousal of Lockean principles and institutions, as well as the only part of the country that claimed some sort of Burkean aristocratic or organic conservatism. The South also has always been the most racist part of the country. Here in a very simple and direct sense is the connection between racism and conservatism in America; for in spite of all the denials of southern intellectuals and politicians, past and present, the South's militant conservatism was rooted fundamentally in its hyperracism. But it is more complex than this since, as observers from a wide range of vantage points have noted, southern conservatism is a fraud, schizophrenic, or what Hartz called the "madhouse of southern thought." He called it a madhouse because it embraced Locke for whites, while, like virtually all white Americans, denying Locke to blacks. But almost at the same time many of the South's leading thinkers rejected Locke because slavery could not be squared with his idea of inalienable natural rights. It is one thing to deny Africans civil rights as northern whites did, but to deny them liberty and their property in their labor was more difficult, leading to a full-throated embrace of a bastardized Burke.

Although the South did have "something that resembled an aristocracy,"[1] it rested on slavery, and no amount of "intellectual gymnastics" could make slavery justifiable on either Lockean or Burkean principles. Auerbach notes the irony: "Slavery had made southern conservatism possible; now conservatism was being used to justify slavery."[2] Thus, Southern conservatism was morally bankrupt, intellectually dishonest, and superficial.

But there is more. A self-conscious conservatism did not emerge in the South until the rise of industrialism in the North, the emergence of the abolitionist movement, and the periodic slave rebellions and rumors of revolt. These developments posed a serious threat to the slaveocracy.[3] Huntington draws the connection this way: "The combination of these forces which these events [Nat Turner's revolt and the founding of William Lloyd Garrison's *The Liberator in 1831*] symbolized forced the South on the defensive and led it to abandon its Jeffersonian heritage and develop a considerable apologia in the language of Burke."[4]

Similarly, George Fitzhugh, after Calhoun perhaps the leading intellectual expositor of a distinctive southern conservatism, wrote "until the advent of abolitionism . . . the abstractions of the Declaration did little harm."[5]

Localism and federalism are often considered abiding principles of southern conservatism. However, as Fehrenbacher and others have shown, it was not until southerners began losing or perceiving a loss in their predominant power in the federal government that they began to embrace states rights. "Thus, at a critical juncture, the Jeffersonian strategy of majoritarian politics had failed to provide adequate protection for the sectional institution of slavery, and many southerners accordingly began to place more reliance on the Jeffersonian theory of states-rights constitutionalism."[6] In other words, states rights, like many principles of southern conservatism, is not principled but reactionary, reaction in large part to the stirrings of oppressed Africans.

In his sagacious *Mind of the South* W. J. Cash analyzed several enduring elements of southern tradition, of the southern mind. These include an intense individualism, a glorification of the agrarian, hostility to modernism, anti-intellectualism, localism, a tendency to violence, and a militant, evangelical Protestantism.[7] However, Cash writes that the "ancient fixation on the Negro was always perhaps the single most primary thing. . . . The maintenance of the superiority to that black man is the thing in southern life."[8] This "hypnotic Negro-fixation," this "fear and hatred" and the "terrorization of the Negro" and not the "shell of aristocracy" is the essential element in the distinctiveness of southern thought.[9] As we briefly excavate the special place of the South in American conservatism, whatever its intellectual pretensions, not far below the surface is the "Negro bogey-man."[10]

Slavery and the Burkean Variant of Southern Aristocratic Conservatism

Slavery was not feudalism and the owners of the large plantations were not an aristocracy and there was little basis for an organic, society of harmony in the South that would sustain the European style conservatism validated by Burke. Instead, as Barrington Moore Jr. shows, rather than feudalism the southern plantation economy was a bastardized form of capitalism that generated an ideology of aristocratic pretensions based on an organic solidarity of whites in defense of racism.[11] Therefore, the non-Lockean ideas expressed by southern writers such as Fitzhugh and Calhoun were largely rationalizations for keeping the philosophy of Locke for whites while denying it to blacks. Students of southern thought have not found it difficult to identify this fraud. In chapter 4 of *The Liberal Tradition in America,* "The Feudal Dream of the South," Hartz is contemptuous: "When we penetrate beneath the surface of southern thought, we do not find feudalism: we find slavery. The distinction is not unimportant. For it leads us to see at a glance that this massive revival of Burke ... below the Mason-Dixon Line was in large measure a simple fraud, and that instead of symbolizing something new in American life, it symbolized the impending disappearance of something very old. Fraud, alas, was the inevitable fate of southern thought."[12]

This fraud is easily observed in the thought of the two leading antebellum era conservative intellectuals, Fitzhugh and Calhoun. As I indicated earlier, Fitzhugh and Calhoun developed their ideas mainly in reaction to the abolitionist movement. Thus, they are to some extent situational or specific to that particular historical context. But as will be shown in chapter 6 on the modern conservative movement, variations on their ideas were employed by Russell Kirk, William F. Buckley Jr., and James J. Kilpatrick in response to the civil rights movement. Thus, while situational they are also integral to conservatism's racism in America.

Fitzhugh, who some credit with being a founder of American sociology on the basis of his 1854 *Treatise on Sociology: Theoretical and Practical,* wrote explicitly to defend slavery as preferable to Lockean free labor and African slavery on the basis of the inferiority of African peoples. Calhoun was animated by the same purpose but less honest.

In Burkean fashion, Fitzhugh attacked Locke and the contract theory, arguing that men were not born free and equal with natural rights to liberty. Rather, he famously argued, "slavery is the natural, normal condition of the laboring man, white or black."[13] Slavery, Fitzhugh contended, was superior to the free labor in Lockean laissez-faire capitalism because there was an inevitable tendency "toward the enslavement of labor by capital."[14] Enslaved Africans in the South, he wrote, were treated better than the "degraded" white workers in the northern cities who were often reduced to "beggary, suicide and starvation."[15] Fitzhugh, of course, could have left it at that and called for the deporting of Africans and their replacement as slave labor by southern working-class whites. This would not do, however, because he identified white workers as possessing a superior humanity. As Calhoun, in a different context, put it "with us the two great divisions of society are not the rich and the poor, but white and black; and all the former, the poor as the rich, belong to the upper class, and are respected as equals."[16]

In addition, Africans were peculiarly fit for slavery because of their "inherent intellectual imbecility." In language echoing James J. Kilpatrick in the 1950s and 1960s, Fitzhugh wrote, "In no age or condition has the real negro shown a capacity to throw off the chains of barbarism and brutality that has long bound down the nations of that race; or to rise above the common cloud of darkness that still broods over them.... While every other nation from China to Peru had advanced along the road of civilization, the Negro had not, possessing inherent imbecility."[17]

In other words, like Locke said, some men do have inalienable rights, but they are not Africans. Fitzhugh's southern aristocracy is one of caste and color, not Burke's aristocracy of wealth, learning, and nobility.

Fitzhugh as a seminal contributor to southern conservatism is an embarrassment today largely ignored because as Wish writes, "there is little doubt that this 'system' belongs within the ideological orbit of contemporary Fascism. From Fitzhugh to Mussolini the step is startling brief."[18]

By contrast Calhoun remains a highly revered figure in the conservative tradition in America—"the Moses of states rights conservatism"—highly regarded for his arguments about the limited powers of the federal government, states rights, and the doctrine of concurrent majorities. As the editor of one collection of his writings puts it "leaving aside the issue of slavery, Calhoun's thought... will forever assure him a high place in the history of American thought."[19] But Henry Jaffa, a leading conservative intellectual in a definitive analysis of Calhoun's thought, dismisses it as "perverse," "absurd and archaic," "ingenious sophism," "utterly devoid of reason," and "breathtaking[ly] inconsistent."[20]

Virtually all of Calhoun's work politically (he was a major antebellum era statesman; secretaries of state and war, congressman, senator, and vice president) and intellectually was in various disguises defenses of slavery. For example, his embrace of states rights, as indicated earlier, came about mainly because of his concern that the South was losing power in the federal government, and his theory of the concurrent majorities was a way to defend slavery when the South eventually lost its dominance in the Congress.

Calhoun, like Burke, but for unBurkean reasons, rejects the idea of natural rights and the social contract.[21] Calhoun argued that government inheres in man's nature, and the rights that men have are not natural or inalienable but derive from the society. Therefore southern society, if it wished, could deprive some men of all of their rights. On this reasoning Calhoun could justify the enslavement of Africans, without engaging, like Fitzhugh, in vulgar racism or berating laissez-faire capitalism. Africans in America, like all men, had only those rights granted by those in power in the society in which they lived.[22] In other words, it was the power of groups rather than the rights of individuals that mattered. And since Africans in America had little power, they had no rights. Thus, he wrote, "It is not the individual that counts but only the rights of those groups, whether counted as majorities or minorities that have the power to control their destinies."[23]

However, Calhoun also wished to preserve for some men the Lockean idea that men have a property in their persons and in the fruits of their labor, which government should not violate. That is, he wishes to make a case for Lockean individualism and inequality generally. So, he writes that "now, as individuals differ greatly from each other in intelligence, sagacity, energy, perseverance, skill, habits of industry and economy, physical power, position and opportunity—the necessary effect of leaving all free to exert themselves ... must be a corresponding inequality.... The only means by which this can be prevented is to impose such restrictions on the exertions of those ... or to deprive them of the fruits of their exertions."[24]

Leaving aside slavery, this strand of Calhoun's conservatism is consistent with the ideology's fixation on limiting the power of government to the narrow confines of the Constitution. This then is southern conservatism at its origins: racism and a militant Lockean conservatism about limited government, laissez faire capitalism, and its resulting inequality, and a commitment to states rights including the right of the states to deny rights to any persons within their power.[25]

Some crucial aspects of this tradition of southern conservatism were upended by the Civil War, but they reasserted themselves with even greater militancy in the post-Reconstruction era. This conservative reaction to Reconstruction set at the core of American politics until the New Deal and became an important part of the movement that elected President Reagan.

One final element of hypocrisy in southern conservatism is Calhoun's doctrine of the concurrent majority, which he developed as the ultimate defense of slavery against northern attack. Calhoun argued that any major minority interest or section of the country should be accorded the rights to veto any legislation passed by a congressional majority if a majority of the affected minority viewed the legislation as adverse to its interest. That is, for such legislation to pass it would require concurrent majorities of the majority and the minority. This scheme would have operated to preserve slavery forever, no matter how large an antislavery majority in the north might have become.[26]

The preservation of slavery was clearly the purpose of Calhoun's proposal; however, as a principle of governance to protect minority rights, it is a commendable contribution to political theory. The hypocrisy or fraud of Calhoun is that he could urge this principle to protect minority interests while ignoring African Americans—the largest distinctive minority interest—in the South and the nation. Indeed, he could present his theory without the slightest appreciation of its irony or trace of embarrassment because it never troubled his mind that the principle of concurrent majorities would apply with greater moral urgency to the enslaved than to the enslavers.[27] What better way to illustrate the madhouse of southern conservative thought? As Jaffa writes, "The same principle that condemned any other manifestation of majority tyranny condemned slavery. Calhoun could not see this."[28]

Southern Agrarianism

The Civil War destroyed what little there was of a southern aristocracy, with the emancipation of the slaves and Reconstruction. The spread of industrial capitalism also threatened to erode what was left of the old order. In this situation a second important strand of thought emerged in southern conservatism. In many ways it was as much an illusion as the thought of Calhoun or Fitzhugh, given the inevitability of industrialization and the hunger for it throughout most of the region. And the southern agrarians, like their forebears, could not break free from the racism that is integral to the southern mind.[29]

Southern agrarianism emerged as a distinctive element of southern conservatism among southern intellectuals in the early twentieth century. It sought first to restore what it viewed as the harmony and organic unity of white southern society prior to the disruptions caused by the Civil War and Reconstruction. It also sought to resist industrialism, science, and modernity in favor of the maintenance of an agrarian way of life, holding that a civilized way of life requires rootedness in the soil. For the agrarians, then, conservatism rested on the soil, religion, and tradition.

The tradition received its most famous expression in the collection of essays *I'll Take My Stand,* edited by John Crowe Ransom, published in 1931 and republished in 1951.[30] The work was widely read in southern intellectual circles and is viewed by some as agrarianism's manifesto. Another critical contribution was made by Richard Weaver in his *Ideas Have Consequences* and *The Southern Tradition at Bay: A History of Antebellum Thought.*[31] *Ideas Have Consequences* is an important work in the post–World War II conservative intellectual movement, and Weaver was a frequent contributor to *National Review* during the 1950s and 1960s.

Although the southern agrarians tried to downplay or obscure their racism, this strain of conservatism was rooted in the racism as well as the soil of the South.[32] Weaver's *Ideas Have Consequences* romanticized the traditions of the antebellum South, and his *Southern Tradition at Bay* was an outright defense of slavery and the overthrow of Reconstruction on the basis of the ideology of white supremacy.[33] The writers in *I'll Take My Stand* mostly avoided discussion of race, writing almost as if blacks were invisible.[34]

The gathering forces of the civil rights movement brought the racism at the roots of southern agrarianism to the forefront because "they [could] tiptoe no longer, and it is revealing that Donald Davidson, the ranking agrarian still left in the South, has come to see a greater threat to his section in *Brown v. Board of Education* than he ever saw in the Coca-Cola company."[35]

Conclusion

Southern conservatism is an integral part of American conservatism. And if one looks at southern conservatism it has racism at its core; the bastardized Locke that is an important component of American conservatism in general. Its militant laissez-faire capitalism, its emphasis on the soil, limited government, states rights, concurrent majorities, tradition, and all the rest are little more than reactions to modernity and to antiracist movements. V. O. Key got it right many years ago when he wrote, "In the last analysis the major peculiarities of southern politics go back to the Negro. Whatever phase of the southern political process one seeks to understand, sooner or later the trail of inquiry leads to the Negro."[36]

In 1953 Rossiter wrote that the "urge to link up formally with the conservatism of the South" would be a powerful one for the Republican Party, but he advised against it because he thought it would be morally reprehensible but also because he thought it risked "political annihilation" for the party in the north.[37] However, as we shall see in chapter 6 conservative Republican intellectuals and politicians did embrace their "natural allies" in the South, and instead of political annihilation they became politically ascendant.

CHAPTER FOUR

The Rise of the Liberal Remnant

Liberalism in the United States is understood as the rejection of the Lockean idea of the "negative" policeman state in favor of the Roussean "positive" welfare state, in which the government intervenes in the economy, society, and the states in order to secure the rights of individuals and provide them with some degree of social security in the form of education, housing, health, and retirement income.[1] In a word, it replaces the Lockean laissez-faire state with a Roussean regulatory-welfare state.

Liberalism understood in this sense has been the remnant, a kind of rejected, almost un-American strain in American politics. Hartz, whose seminal work does so much to confuse thinking about ideology and liberalism in America, correctly wrote, "There has never been a 'liberal movement' or a real 'liberal party' in America: we have only had the American way of life, a nationalist articulation of Locke which usually does not know Locke is involved."[2]

Hartz was correct when he wrote in 1955, and his observation is by and large correct today. There has certainly never been a liberal *movement* in the United States. And the Democratic Party since it embraced liberalism during the New Deal has always been a fractured, vacillating, ambivalent, hesitant, schizophrenic instrument of liberalism. Liberalism therefore has always been the remnant ascendant only during periods of crisis, and when the crisis subsides liberalism is routed, relegated to its remnant status.

Three Periods in the Emergence of the Liberal Remnant

Historically, the liberal ideology or the positive state becomes prominent in three periods in American history: the Civil War/Reconstruction, the New Deal and the civil rights–Great Society period of the 1960s. Four things are remarkable about these three periods of liberal ascendancy. First, each was marked by a system crisis, more or less severe. Second, each was marked by war.[3] Third, two of the three—Civil War/Reconstruction and civil rights–Great

Society—involved struggles against racism, indicative of the enduring impact the presence of Africans has had on the development of American politics.[4] Fourth, each of these periods of liberal ascendancy was relatively short lived, in the case of the New Deal and Great Society compromised and stalled within a couple of years and in the case of the Civil War/Reconstruction reversed in less than a decade by conservative reaction.

Lincoln and the Liberal Remnant

Both African Americans and conservatives are ambivalent about Lincoln. African Americans are ambivalent because they know Lincoln was both a racist and a white supremacist who only reluctantly emancipated the slaves because he concluded it was necessary to win the war and save the union.[5] He wrote in his famous letter to Horace Greeley, "[W]hat I do about slavery and the colored race I do because it helps save the union."[6] Describing abolitionism as "dangerous radicalism," Lincoln, although strongly opposed to slavery on Lockean natural rights grounds, was nevertheless prepared to see it continue in the United States forever.[7] However, he, like most so-called Radical Republicans was committed to preventing its spread beyond the boundaries of the South.[8]

In addition, Lincoln did not favor full equality and incorporation. Instead, he was for either colonialization or a subordinate status for blacks, telling a delegation of blacks at the White House in 1863 that "insurmountable white prejudice made equality impossible in the United States."[9] And "on this broad continent, not a single man of your race is made the equal of a single man of ours. Go where you are treated the best and the ban is still on you."[10]

However, African Americans also recognize that Lincoln, however reluctant and ambivalent, set in motion with the Emancipation Proclamation the processes that inevitably brought slavery to an end, something his two immediate successors might not have done. James Buchanan probably and Franklin Pierce for sure would not have waged a war to preserve the union, ceding to the southern states the right of secession. Lincoln's greatness therefore derives from his unwavering commitment to the preservation of the Union by any means necessary, including a half million dead and the confiscation of $3 to 4 million in the property of slaveholders. Concerned that the Emancipation Proclamation might at some point be declared unconstitutional, he urged the adoption of the second Thirteenth Amendment, which he signed (Lincoln was the first and only president to sign amendments, since it is not constitutionally required).

Second, Lincoln, throughout his career, was unwavering in his commitment to the idea that slavery was morally unjustifiable. Writing in 1864 he said, "I am naturally anti-slavery. If slavery is not wrong, nothing is wrong. I cannot remember when I did not so think and feel."[11] Finally, some African Americans understand that Lincoln's ambivalence and reluctance on slavery were dictated by the political imperatives of winning national office and the war and by his fidelity to the racist Constitution he was sworn to preserve and protect. This view of Lincoln is perhaps best summed up by Frederick Douglass. In an 1876 speech unveiling a monument to Lincoln, he told a largely white audience, "[Y]ou are the children of Lincoln, we are at best his stepchildren." Douglass went on to say that "viewed from the genuine abolition ground, Mr. Lincoln seemed tardy, cold, dull and indifferent, but measuring him by the sentiment of his country, a sentiment he was bound as a statesman to consult he was swift, zealous, radical and determined."[12]

Conservative ambivalence toward Lincoln is related among some to his decision to wage what some refer to as the "war of northern aggression" in which the north not only sought to destroy slavery but also "the precapitalist, conservative, and agrarian southern way of life."[13] In this view the southern states had a sovereign right to secede, and Lincoln in waging the war acted in a dictatorial and unconstitutional way.

Other conservatives view Lincoln's use of presidential power as setting a dangerous precedent for expansion of presidential power,[14] and as the source "of contemporary statist liberalism and equalitarian excess that modern conservatism opposes."[15] Finally, some conservatives, most notably Wilmore Kendall, object especially to Lincoln's claim that when Jefferson used "all men" in the Declaration he indeed meant all men.[16] In some ways, Kendall and these conservatives object as much to what Lincoln said as to what he did. Although Lincoln spoke throughout his career about the natural rights of all men to life, liberty, and the fruits of their labor, in his famous address at Gettysburg he eloquently committed the nation to a "new birth of freedom" that would fulfill Jefferson's promise of equality. In what Wills calls a "clever" and "audacious" assault, Lincoln forever undermines in the mind of the nation the idea that liberty should be denied to some men.[17] For this some conservatives have never forgiven him.[18]

Many conservatives, however, generally view Lincoln as one of them, as a man who acted faithfully and prudentially in the tradition of both Lockean and Burkean conservatism.[19] Lincoln, as we have seen, always rejected abolitionism and after the war commenced he repeatedly rejected the calls of Thaddeus Stevens and Charles Sumner, leaders of the Radical Republican faction in the House and Senate, to turn the war into a fight for the liberation of the slaves. As he repeatedly said, his understanding of the Constitution and the limited powers of the federal government made emancipation impossible except for military necessity. And even then Lincoln acted conservatively, freeing only those enslaved persons in the rebellious states and giving those states four months to rejoin the union and keep their property in slaves.

Lincoln was also solicitous of the Lockean prerogatives of capital. For example, Lincoln, until the Emancipation Proclamation, consistently opposed efforts of his field commanders and the Congress to confiscate property in slaves, threatening in 1862 to veto the Second Confiscation Act unless it was amended to allow slave owners to maintain ownership of enslaved persons. Of this fateful decision—which effectively undermined the Reconstruction idea of forty acres and a mule—Trefousse writes: "In effect, he knocked the teeth out of a movement which would have directed the Republican revolution into channels traditionally followed by revolutions of the past, with the thorough-going economic destruction of a privileged class. By quietly smashing the legislation calculated to start this movement he effectively aborted the revolution. The slaves would be freed and granted suffrage, but the southern aristocracy, except for certain changes wrought by the economic ravages of war itself, would remain a powerful political force."[20]

Trefousse goes on, "That Lincoln should have wanted to block it all shows not only his conservative attitude toward the sanctity of private property, but also his capacity for magnanimity toward the enemy *during* war."[21] By contrast, "Stevens' compassion was always concentrated upon the handicapped Negro, and if there had to be a choice between justice for the black and justice for the white, he unhesitatingly chose the former."[22]

Macpherson describes Lincoln as a "conservative revolutionary," as a "pragmatic revolutionary" who wanted to preserve the union, and finding it militarily necessary to free the slaves he thereby was able to fulfill his long-held personal wish to end slavery.

As a typical capitalist Whig, Lincoln also favored protective tariffs, internal improvements, a national banking system, and an income tax. These reforms established the basis for the hegemony of Lockean laissez-faire capitalism from the 1890s to the 1930s. But Lincoln the conservative capitalist also created the rudimentary infrastructure for a liberal state.[23]

Thus, Lincoln's ideological legacy is ambiguous; part liberal, part conservative; part racist, part antiracist. Because of Booth's bullet we do not know how Lincoln would have addressed the problems of Reconstruction with respect to the status of the emancipated slaves (we do know his idea of colonialization was wholly impractical). However, for the rights of African Americans, Lincoln's murder at the war's end was probably fortunate since Reconstruction probably took a more radical course under his successor than it would have under him.

Reconstruction: Liberalism's Finest Hour

Lincoln was a prudential statesman possessing presidential character and personal integrity.[24] And although he was a white supremacist and racist, Lincoln was never vulgar or malicious. Andrew Johnson lacked all of these qualities; insecure, vain, stubborn, and arrogant, Johnson was probably unfit for the presidency at anytime but for sure in the immediate post civil war period.[25] He was also a vulgar racist, a former slave owner, he opposed secession because he thought slavery was best secured within the union. And he was openly contemptuous of the humanity of Africans and the only American president to express vulgar racism in his official state papers. An example is his veto of an 1866 civil rights bill where he wrote that the legislation would "place every spay-footed, bandy-shanked, thick lipped, flat nosed, wooly-haired ebony colored Negro in the country on an equal footing with the poor white man."[26]

Johnson's lack of presidential character led to a confrontation with Congress and its rejection of his plan for "Presidential Reconstruction" and the imposition after the 1866 congressional elections of the much tougher plan of "Congressional Reconstruction." Presidential Reconstruction involved granting amnesty and restoring civil rights to most of the leaders of the rebellion. The rebels then established state governments that denied blacks voting rights and imposed "black codes," which restored the emancipated to a status almost akin to slavery.[27]

Under congressional reconstruction, led by liberal stalwarts Thaddeus Stevens and Charles Summer, Congress excluded the rebellious states from the union, treating them, as Lincoln almost surely would not have, as conquered territories who had forfeited their rights as states.[28] These states were then divided into five military districts. In order for them to be readmitted to the union, Congress required that they adopt new constitutions allowing blacks to vote and ratify the Fourteenth Amendment. In addition, Congress passed three civil rights bills as well as three enforcement acts, which enhanced the capabilities of the Justice Department to enforce civil rights in the states. The army was authorized to engage in law enforcement activities also, if needed. Finally, the federal government took its first tentative steps toward a welfare state, when it established the Freedmen's Bureau.[29]

Most scholars agree that, as Trefousse writes, "[t]he most notable triumph of this period was the ratification of the 14th Amendment."[30] It was the most notable achievement because it was an assault on one of the institutional pillars of American conservatism, states rights. Friendly and Elliot write that the amendment brought about a "quiet revolution" because "[i]t was if the Congress held a second constitutional convention and created a federal government of vastly expanded powers."[31] Although conservatives in Congress and the states opposed the amendment on federalism grounds, much of the opposition to it was also "deeply racist" as opponents, in both the North and South, argued that equality should not be granted to the "inferior races," including Indians, Chinese, and African Americans.[32]

Although the amendment was soon turned on its head and became the great charter for unregulated laissez-faire capitalism, by the late 1970s it had become what its authors intended, "The Great Charter of Universal Freedom" for all Americans.[33]

In his magisterial *Black Reconstruction: An Essay toward a History of the Part Played in the Attempt to Reconstruct Democracy, 1860-1880*, DuBois portrayed Reconstruction as an attempt by blacks to form a coalition with working-class whites in order to challenge the dominance of the southern planter class; as he wrote, it was "the finest effort to achieve democracy for the working millions which this world had ever seen."[34] This first effort at democracy and equalitarianism in the South lasted less than a decade. It was overthrown in a conservative counterrevolution marked by white terror; a compromised presidential election; and an imperial, racist judiciary intent on the subordination of blacks and the preservation of limited Lockean government and laissez-faire capitalism.

Reconstruction and the Conservative Counterrevolution

The story of the overthrow of Reconstruction is one of the saddest and most familiar in American history.[35] For purposes of this study, I wish to focus on the perversion of the Fourteenth Amendment and the rise of an emergent or incipient congressional conservative coalition of racist, southern Democrats and laissez-faire northern Republican capitalists. Both of these developments are crucial in forging the modern nexus between conservatism and racism, as well as in explaining the emergence of the modern post–New Deal, civil rights era conservative movement.

Going back to the founding, conservatives have viewed the Supreme Court as the "guardian" of racism and Lockean laissez-faire capitalism.[36] The Court began to play this guardian role with respect to racism in *Dred Scott*, its first case dealing with race, and in its first interpretations of the Fourteenth Amendment.

Although the 1873 *Slaughterhouse Cases* had nothing to do with race or civil rights, the decision had a profound impact on the rights of African Americans because it established the precedent that the Tenth Amendment's principles of federalism and states rights would be more important than the Fourteenth's principles of universal freedom and equality.

The cases involved a group of butchers in New Orleans who challenged a state law that gave one company a monopoly on the slaughtering of livestock in the city. They claimed that the law violated several provisions of the Fourteenth Amendment, including its privileges and immunities clause, because it took away their right as citizens to earn a living and therefore their property rights. The Court's 5 to 4 majority disagreed, holding in an opinion by Justice Samuel Miller that the Fourteenth Amendment only prohibited the states from infringing on the privileges and immunities of national citizenship that the Court defined narrowly to include such minor things as the right to protection on the high seas or to use the waters of the United States. In reaching this conclusion, the Court distinguished between two types of citizenship: national, which is conferred by birth or naturalization, and state, which is conferred by residency. While states could not deny persons their limited national citizenship rights, they were free to define and restrict state citizenship rights, notwithstanding the privileges and immunities clause or the Fourteenth Amendment's due process and equal protection clauses. Again, these cases dealt with butchers not blacks, but the Court was aware that its decision would eventually affect African Americans. Indeed Justice Miller wrote that protection of blacks from the "oppression of those who had formerly exercised dominion over [them] . . . was the 'foundation[]' of the Amendment.[37]

Three years later in *Cruikshank vs. the United States* the Court held that the Amendment could not be used to protect blacks from terrorism.[38] In 1872 an estimated 150 to 280 blacks were massacred in Colfax, Louisiana, in the aftermath of a racially divisive election for sheriff.[39] Nine men were arrested under the Enforcement Act of 1870 and changed with conspiracy and murder in order to deprive blacks of their civil rights. Three were convicted and appealed to the Court. The Court reversed their convictions, declaring in an opinion by Chief Justice Morrison Waite that it was the responsibility of the states to punish murder and that the Enforcement Act passed pursuant to Congress' authority to enforce the Fourteenth Amendment did not give it the authority to punish crimes traditionally left to the states. The Court also held that the Amendment only prohibited actions by a state and that the murders in Colfax were committed by private citizens not officials of Louisiana. Finally, disingenuously, the chief justice concluded that even if Congress had the authority to punish crimes against blacks seeking to exercise their civil rights it was first necessary to prove that race was the motivating factor in the massacre, which he said was not mentioned, let alone proven in the case.

It was clear to everyone, however, that these were murders motivated by racism. Indeed, shortly after the decision the *Shreveport Times* in Louisiana published an editorial celebrating the massacre as "the summary and wholesome lesson the Negroes have been taught in Grant Parish . . . by the white men of Grant."⁴⁰ Several years later whites in Colfax placed a plaque on the Grant Parish Court House that read as follows: "On this site occurred the Colfax riot in which three white men and 150 Negroes were slain. This event on April 13, 1873, marked the end of carpetbag misrule in the South."⁴¹

In 1883 the Court declared the Civil Rights Act of 1875 unconstitutional. This act, like the 1964 act, prohibited racial discrimination in access to public accommodations. Congress based its authority to enact the law on the Fourteenth Amendment's equal protection clause. The Court, however, held that the clause only prevented discrimination by state and local governments, not private businesses.⁴² Finally, in the penultimate case of *Plessy vs. Ferguson*, the Court constitutionalized the right of the states to institutionalize racism and white supremacy throughout society.⁴³ The separate but equal doctrine promulgated by the Court in *Plessey* was, of course, a lie. This was made clear three years after *Plessey* in *Cummings vs. Board of Education* where the Court allowed a school district in Georgia to maintain a high school for whites but only offer an elementary education for blacks.⁴⁴

Ironically, the opinion in *Cummings* was written by Justice John Marshall Harlan, the lone dissenter in *Plessey*. Harlan based his decision on principles of federalism, writing that there was no Fourteenth Amendment equal protection issue because "the education of the people in the schools maintained by state taxation is a matter belonging to the respective states, and any interference on the part of federal authority with the management of schools cannot be justified except in the case of a clear and unmistakable disregard of the rights secured by [the Constitution]."⁴⁵ And since there was no right in the Constitution to equality in tax expenditures for education, there was no violation of *Plessey*.

By the beginning of the twentieth century the Court had turned the noblest achievement of the Civil War into an instrument for the oppression of African Americans, on the basis of the conservative principle of federalism. This was done in spite of Justice Samuel Miller's opinion in the *Slaughterhouse Cases* about the unambiguous purposes of the Civil War amendments: "No one can fail to be impressed with the one prevailing purpose found in them all, lying at the foundation of each, and without which none of them would have been suggested; we mean the freedom of the slave race, the security and firm establishment of that freedom and the protection of the newly made freeman and citizen from the oppression of those who had formerly exercised dominion over him."⁴⁶ And of the Fourteenth specifically, Miller wrote, "It is so clearly a provision for the colored race... that a strong case would be necessary for its application to any other."⁴⁷

Contrary to Justice Miller's dicta, the Court at the beginning of the twentieth century did make a strong case to apply the amendment to persons of other races, including those fictional persons called "corporations."

Indeed, until the 1930s the amendment was most often used to protect these nonpersons than any humans.

In 1905 in *Lochner vs. New York*, the Court invalidated a New York state law that limited the hours of bakery workers. The Court held that the state's minimum hours law violated "the general right to make a contract in relation . . . to business which is part of the liberty of the individual protected by the Fourteenth Amendment to the federal Constitution."[48] Using similar reasoning the Court subsequently struck down scores of other state and federal regulatory and redistributive laws. In a word, the Fourteenth Amendment became the guardian of private property and laissez-faire capitalism; a mere Lockean "policeman." Rossiter wryly wrote, "It secured the ends of the individual by protecting his property and standing out of the way of his urge to get more."[49] Macpherson refers to this use of the Amendment as a "successful conservative counterrevolution," a revival of "negative liberty in the form of a weakened national government."[50]

Rossiter describes this successful effort to equate laissez-faire capitalism with liberty as part of the "Great Train Robbery" of American intellectual history; others refer to it as a "perversion" or a "hijacking" of the Fourteenth Amendment. However, in a penetrating constitutional analysis of the role of property in the American tradition, Nedelsky concludes, "Lochner era opinions . . . show an impressive continuity with the Federalist vision of constitutionalism, complete with the rights of property as the central boundary of state power . . . the notion that property was essential ingredients of the liberty the Constitution was to protect, was common to Madison, Marshall and the Twentieth Century advocates of laissez-faire."[51] Rossiter even reluctantly acknowledges, "The laissez-faire conservative, it might be argued, were the true heirs of Locke."[52]

However one interprets the relationship between *Lochner* and Locke—and it is the argument of this study that it is a close one—by the beginning of the twentieth-century laissez-faire capitalism and laissez-faire racism were foundational in American conservatism. To challenge them in a way became un-American. In the 1930s laissez faire capitalism was challenged by the New Deal and in the 1950s and 1960s laissez-faire racism by the civil rights movement. Opposition to the New Deal and the civil rights movement then became foundational in the emergence of the modern conservative movement and the election in 1980 of Ronald Reagan.

Aside from an imperial, racist judiciary,[53] the old order was held together after 1876 by a coalition in Congress of racist white supremacist southern Democrats and laissez-faire northern Republicans. This Faustian alliance between the heirs of the Confederacy and the party of Lincoln exercised its paramount influence from the 1930s to the 1960s, when it successfully blocked or compromised New Deal reform and civil rights legislation.[54] The conservative coalition of this period has its roots insofar as race is concerned in the compromised presidential election of 1876. By the 1890s the Republican Party for all intents and purposes had become the captive of wealthy, corporate interests and had all but abandoned (except for platitudes and minor patronage) the interests of African Americans. Finally, both northern capital and southern racism, although for different reasons, had an interest in states rights and weak national government. Thus, this is another nexus in the foundational relationship between conservatism and racism.[55]

New Deal Liberalism

In *The Conservative Intellectual Movement Since 1945* George Nash writes:

> With rare unanimity the Right believes that the administration of Franklin Roosevelt inaugurated a revolution both in the agenda and structure of American politics. It was the second great crisis in the decline of the Republic [The first was the Civil War—Reconstruction]. In substance this upheaval [was] ... a form of democratic socialism. In structure the political system was profoundly altered: enormous aggrandizement of the President and federal bureaucracy, the steady weakening of Congress, the capitulation of the Supreme Court under pressure in 1937, and of course the shackling of the individual and sapping of the states.[56]

Of Roosevelt and conservatism Rossiter writes simply that he was the "bogeyman of conservatism."[57]

Roosevelt was not the first reform president in American history; however, he was the first to directly challenge key elements of Lockean ideas and institutions and is, more than any other president, responsible for the emergence and endurance of a powerful liberal remnant, even going so far as to rescue the term *liberalism* itself from the stranglehold conservatives had had on it for decades.

Historians frequently refer to challenges to the Lockean legacy as revolutions, as in the "Jeffersonian Revolution," the "Jacksonian Revolution" and the "Roosevelt Revolution." Although none of these presidents brought about real revolutionary transformations, Roosevelt came the closest. Jefferson and Jackson both sought to discipline the power of the propertied elite and extend democracy, but the Jeffersonians themselves were aristocratic or elite in pretensions and wary of governance by the propertyless masses. Jackson, on the other hand, was a democrat (at least insofar as white males) and inaugurated a number of reforms that empowered white working men and attenuated to some extent the disproportionate power of the wealthy. Among the more important of these reforms was the extension of the franchise to virtually all white men, the breaking of the monopoly power of the Bank of the United States and the strengthening of public education. In a word, the Jacksonian revolution did bring to prominence an emphasis on equalitarianism—again for white men—as an important feature of American politics. Nevertheless, Jacksonian democracy did not represent any departure from the fundamentals of Lockean conservatism with respect to the purposes and powers of the national government, federalism, property, or laissez-faire capitalism.

Richard Hofstadter argues that the populist movement of the 1890s was "the first modern political movement of practical importance in the United States to insist that the federal government has some responsibility for the common weal; indeed it was the first such movement to attack seriously the problems created by industrialism."[58] Emerging out of the economic depression of the 1890s, the populist advocated such liberal reforms as debt relief, government ownership or regulation of the railroads and a graduated income tax.[59] Although some white populist for a time sincerely tried to build a biracial, class-based movement, from the outset racism was a major barrier. The Populist Party appealed for black voter support and allowed a few blacks to serve as party leaders, but the Party was eventually undermined as poor whites were persuaded that a vote for the interracial Populists was racial treason.[60] As a result the populist movement eventually fell victim to what Hofstadter called the "Negro bogey."[61] Tom Watson, the movement's most effective leader, turned from advocating interracial solidarity to an extreme form of racism and white supremacy, supporting lynching and the disenfranchisement of blacks.[62] Thus, within a decade populism went from "colored and white in the ditch unite" to "lynch the Negro."[63]

The progressive movement emerged a generation after the populists. Largely, white, urban, and middle class, the progressives did not challenge the Lockean negative state or capitalism. Rather, they attempted to make the state more democratic, honest and efficient and the industrial economy genuinely competitive by attacking monopolies and trusts. There was also a powerful moralistic strain in progressivism in terms of social uplift of the immigrants and their integration into Anglo-Saxon culture.[64] In addition to challenging monopolies, Progressive era governments also imposed quality standards on food, encouraged the initiative and referendum and supported worker rights, including unsuccessfully (because they were voided by the courts) efforts to legislate maximum hours and minimum wages and protections for women and children in the labor force. Thus, the progressives did seek to depart to some extent from the Lockean notion of minimalist government, but "chiefly,"

Hofstadter concludes, "they preferred to keep the positive functions on the part of government minimal, and, where these were necessary to keep them at the state rather than national level."[65]

Progressivism, like populism in the 1890s and Reconstruction in the 1870s, was also undermined by the "Negro bogey." Generally, progressive leaders refused to condemn racism, support black suffrage or antilynching legislation. Indeed, the two progressive presidents—Theodore Roosevelt and Woodrow Wilson—were also two of the more racist and white supremacist presidents of the twentieth century.[66] Although the New Deal too was compromised by fear of the Negro bogey, Franklin Roosevelt's embrace of a positive, interventionist national state was foundational in liberalism's assault on racism and white supremacy in the 1960s.

FDR inaugurated the first full-scale liberal or positive state in American history, replacing the Lockean notion that the state was to leave things alone and the progressive notion that the role of government was merely to provide for a level capitalist playing field with the Roussean idea that the government had a responsibility to provide for the social security of the people. In creating the liberal state, FDR also co-opted or "captured" liberalism as the ideology of the American left.[67] Consistent with the thesis of this study (that Locke's classical liberalism is ideological conservatism), FDR in the 1930s began to use *liberalism* as the label to capture the meaning of his reform program, forcing the outraged defenders of Locke to reluctantly and grudgingly embrace conservatism as their ideological label.

Prior to this time reformers or challengers to the established order used *progressive*.[68] Roosevelt rejected this label because in the past it had been mainly identified with Republicans (Theodore Roosevelt, Robert Lafollette, even Herbert Hoover) and because he wanted to avoid having the New Deal identified with socialism. That is, he wanted to break with laissez-faire capitalism but not with capitalism (he would often say—truthfully—that the purposes of the New Deal were to preserve capitalism). Thus, starting with his 1932 acceptance speech at the Democratic convention FDR referred to the Democrats as "the bearers of liberalism and progress"; subsequently he would describe the Democrats as the "party of militant liberalism."[69]

Conservatives vigorously objected to Roosevelt's symbolic politics. Hoover and the Republicans during the 1930s insisted that the New Deal was socialist or even communist and that they were the true liberals. Meanwhile, since the 1920s the *New York Times* editorialized the "time honored word" had been exploited by "radical and reds."[70] Nevertheless by the early 1940s most conservatives and Republicans had resigned themselves to Roosevelt's capture of the label. They then begin to refer to themselves as "conservatives" and to assert that as an ideology it was superior to liberalism because it reflected the Lockean values of liberty, individualism, and limited government.

Not all conservatives, however, acquiesced to FDR's capture of the label. As late as 1962 Milton Friedman was writing that unfortunately, the enemies of capitalism have appropriated the label 'liberalism' "so that [it] has in the United States come to have a very different meaning in the Nineteenth Century or does today in much of the continent of Europe.... Because of the corruption of the term liberalism, the views that formerly went under its name are now called conservative. But this is not a satisfactory alternative.... Partly because of my reluctance to surrender the term to proponents of measures that would destroy liberty, partly because I cannot find a better alternative, I shall resolve these difficulties by using the word liberalism in its original sense—as the doctrines pertaining to a free man."[71]

Roosevelt's embrace of the label illustrates the importance of symbolism in politics.[72] Recognizing that his policies indeed represented a break with the Lockean tradition but were by no means socialist or communist, he co-opted the then popular symbolism of 'liberal.' Of course, Hartz writes "the defeated wiggery of the Republicans trie[d] to expose the non-Lockean nature of the New Deal, tries to precipitate the moral crisis that would inevitably come if Americans thought they were 'un-American' but it fails. The experimental mood of Roosevelt, in which, Locke goes underground while 'problems' are solved in a non-Lockian way, wins persistently."[73]

"Wins persistently" may be typical Hartzian hyperbole, because what is ironic is that after the ascendancy of the right in the 1980s, the time-honored word has become the dreaded "L" word used to attack Democrats and a label to be avoided by all with national political ambitions. How this came about and its consequences for the fight against modern racism are considered later. But by the 1990s many Democrats had reverted to using 'progressive' to distinguish their ideology from conservatism and from Roosevelt's militant liberalism.

The New Deal

Most historians agree with Hofstadter's contention about the two things that distinguish the Roosevelt revolution from previous reform presidencies. First, the systemic crisis generated by the Depression: "[T]he New Deal episode marks the first in history of reform movements when a leader of the reform party took the reigns of government confronted with a sick economy.... Jefferson in 1801, Jackson in 1829 and after them TR and Wilson, all took over at moments when the economy was in good shape."[74] Second, "[T]he demands of a large and powerful labor movement, coupled with the interests of the unemployed, gave the later New Deal a social democratic tinge that had never before been present in American reform movements."[75]

Thus, the crisis of the civil war and a mobilized antislavery constituency of Radical Republicans usher in the rudiments of the liberal state, and the crisis of the Depression and a mobilized constituency of workers and the unemployed give birth and a tinge of militancy to the ascendant liberal state. And in the 1960s the civil rights movement and the rebellions in the ghettos were to play an important part in the expansion of the liberal state.

The basic contours of FDR's achievements and their limitations are well known, with this period being more thoroughly researched than any except the civil war.[76] The basic reforms included increased regulation of the economy, especially banking, securities, and agriculture; the legal recognition of the bargaining rights of labor; the provision of subsides for housing, public and private; and the *modest* beginnings of Keynesian economics whereby the government would seek to use fiscal and monetary policies to "manage" the economy so as to avoid another depression.

The centerpiece of the New Deal, however, is the Social Security Act of 1935, providing retirement income for the elderly, cash assistance to poor women and children, and unemployment compensation. With this legislation FDR created the American welfare state, which in the context of the near totalitarian hold of Lockean conservatism on the American tradition and its institutional arrangements was indeed almost revolutionary. However, in the context of Western democracies generally this transformation was, as most historians attest, minimalist. Of Social Security William Leuchtenberg, generally sympathetic to FDR, writes:

> In many respects, the law was an astonishingly inept and conservative piece of legislation. In no other welfare system in the world did the state shirk all responsibility for old-age indigency and insist that funds be taken out of the current earnings of workers. By relying on regressive taxation and withdrawing vast sums to build up reserves, the act did untold mischief. The law denied coverage to numerous classes of workers, including those who needed security the most: farm laborers and domestics. Sickness, in normal times the main cause of joblessness, was disregarded. The act not only failed to set up a national system of unemployment compensation but did not even provide adequate national standards.[77]

In addition, virtually all of the New Deal reforms were decisively impacted by the racist bogey so integral to the American liberal tradition. As I will discuss in the next part of this chapter, FDR did almost nothing to attack the racism and white supremacy of the bastardized Lockean tradition. However, it was worse than simple neutrality because he allowed racism to infect nearly every significant New Deal reform. There is an extensive literature on how racism compromised the New Deal, tracing this effect to the saliency of the ideology of white supremacy; the special place of the South in the New Deal coalition; the importance of federalism, the power of the conservative coalition in Congress; and Roosevelt's own temerity and indifference to the plight of African Americans.[78] Although well known to scholars of the period, in the context of this study it is useful to review the connections between racism and conservatism at the ascendancy of the liberal remnant.

The Social Security Act created a two-tier welfare system. The first tier established a social insurance system for unemployed and retired workers. The second tier provided assistance to the blind, elderly, and children from single-parent families. The first system is viewed as an "insurance" program to which all eligible workers are entitled on the basis of their "contributions" (in the form of the Social Security tax). The second system is viewed as a "welfare" program for the poor because they do not make "contributions." Although the African American leadership strongly supported the creation of the welfare state, it just as strongly opposed the creation of the two-tier system.[79] Opposition to the two-tier system arose because the majority of blacks were excluded from the first tier. In order to get the support of members of Congress from the southern states, Roosevelt agreed to exclude the self-employed, domestic servants, clergymen, and nurses from the tier-one insurance program. By excluding these categories of workers, the system excluded 60 percent of all black workers and 80 percent of black women workers while covering 70 percent of whites. This is because in the 1930s black workers were mainly farm laborers or domestic servants. The leaders of both the NAACP and the Urban League engaged in a concerted lobbying campaign, but Roosevelt would not alter the coverage because he feared the exclusion of those workers was the only way he could get a bill through a Congress dominated by the Conservative Coalition. The NAACP and the Urban League also opposed funding the Social Security system on the basis of worker contribution (Actually a flat tax on the covered workers and their employers. It is also the only tax the rich do not pay since the income taxed is capped at upper-middle-class income; today a little more than $100,000), preferring instead financing on the basis of general tax revenue. Roosevelt opposed using general tax revenue because he said it would cost too much and would turn the system into "welfare" or the "dole." However, the income of many covered black workers was at that time too low to pay the Social Security tax. Thus, they too were in effect excluded. The second component of the New Deal welfare state—the National Labor Relations Act—also disadvantaged black workers because it permitted unions to operate "closed shops," which limited employment to members of the union. Black leaders opposed this provision because of concerns that many unions would exclude blacks.

The NAACP proposed an amendment to the act that would have permitted closed shops only when a union did not restrict membership on the basis of race. But this amendment was opposed by the major unions; Roosevelt declined to support it, and it was not adopted. The final component of the welfare state—the Fair Labor Standards Act—established minimum wage and working hours and provided compensation to the unemployed, but this also disadvantaged black workers. First, like the Social Security Act, it excluded domestic and farm labor and was financed on the basis of worker "contributions." Again, black leaders opposed this system, favoring instead a system that covered all workers and was financed on the basis of income and inheritance taxes. Again, Roosevelt opposed this initiative, and it was defeated. The result was the exclusion of the vast majority of black workers from wage and hour protection and unemployment compensation when they lost their jobs. Thus, each of the three components of the early welfare state was based on institutional racism, disadvantaging black workers in general and black female workers in particular. (The provisions excluding domestic and farm labor were not repealed until 1952.)

The exclusion of blacks from the first tier of the welfare state meant that they were relegated to the second tier, which was based on poverty status rather than a guaranteed entitlement. The major tier-two program was the Aid to Families with Dependent Children (AFDC) program, which provided assistance to single-parent families. Unlike the Social Security insurance system, which was a universal program with national standards administered by the federal government, AFDC under the principle of federalism was a joint federal-state program in which eligibility and benefit levels were determined mainly by state and local governments. This allowed the southern states to manipulate eligibility and benefits in order to maintain a cheap supply of black domestic and farm labor. And since farm and domestic labor were excluded by both the Social Security and Fair Labor Standard Acts, blacks and especially black women became heavily dependent on AFDC and were often exploited by the states. Some states in the rural south would simply cut off benefits during cotton-picking season to blacks, while others would sometime deny benefits altogether. And in every southern state AFDC benefits overall were lower for blacks than whites. Throughout the debate on the Social Security Act, black leaders warned that the exclusion of most black workers from the tier-one programs would overtime make them dependent on "welfare," that is, on the tier-two AFDC program.

In order to get the New Deal enacted even in its compromised form, Roosevelt had to get it through a Congress heavily influenced by a coalition of northern Republican laissez-faire conservatives and racist (although to some extent populists) southern Democrats. I discuss Roosevelt's problems with this coalition below, but in addition to Congress he also had to deal with a

Supreme Court still committed to its role as guardian of the Lockean limits on the powers of Congress, of private property, and of federalism.

Bruce Ackerman argues that there have been three transformative periods, "constitutional moments" in American history: the founding era of the Declaration of Independence and the adoption of the Constitution, the Civil War–Reconstruction era, and the New Deal. The New Deal, however, Ackerman argues is unique among those moments, because it was not brought about by formal amendments to the Constitution but by a revolution in constitutional jurisprudence.[80] This jurisprudential revolution was brought about by FDR's famous or, some say, infamous Court packing plan. As the Court seemed poised to strike down many of his key New Deal reforms (including the Social Security Act), Roosevelt rather than going through the long, tedious, and uncertain process of amending the Constitution came up with the scheme to pack the Court with justices of his own. Although Congress eventually rejected the scheme as a transparent attempt to undermine the integrity and autonomy of the Court, the Court itself in 1937 in the famous "switch in time that saved nine" changed course and abandoned its role as the guardian of the negative state and laissez-faire capitalism.[81] The next decade the Court switched thirty-two times; that is, it reversed thirty-two of its earlier decisions and upheld every New Deal statute that was challenged. In effect, the Court repealed the Lockean "herein granted" clause of Article I and using the Commerce Clause granted the Congress almost plenary authority to legislate on any matter that it wished.

Adopting the view that congressional regulatory and social welfare legislation were presumptively constitutional, the Supreme Court did not invalidate another congressional stature until 1995.[82] (By 1995 the Court for the first time since the New Deal had a narrow five-person conservative majority, and under Chief Justice Rehnquist it sought to limit the power of Congress and restore power to the states). FDR's jurisprudential revolution not only removed the Lockean shackles from the government insofar as economic and welfare legislation, but it also laid the groundwork for the debastardization of Locke with respect to race. Leuchtenburg writes that the Court's "expansive reading of the commerce clause would make it possible in the 1960s for the government to tell even the most obscure fried chicken shack that it could not discriminate against African-American patrons because, in the eyes of the judiciary, its two-bit, off-the-beaten track operation was an enterprise in interstate commerce."[83]

The results of Roosevelt's court packing plan are rightly applauded by most liberals. However, it is clear that the means by which he achieved these results were dishonest (he claimed he wanted to increase the Court's size so as to help the aging justices with their workload) and that the results themselves are inconsistent with both Locke and Madison, a viewed shared by critics on the left and right. On the left Nedlesky wrote, "It has been very important for defenders of the New Deal and the Welfare-regulatory state to prove that *West Coast* represented a return to reason and that the Court was wrong to strike down regulatory legislation. But, of course, it is not the legal reasoning of the Lochner era its opponents care about. It is the fundamental challenge that our regulatory-welfare state constitutes a break with our constitutional tradition, a break that the Court tried, but failed to prevent. That is the challenge the opponents have tried to dismiss, and I think we should take seriously."[84] On the right Randy Barnett wrote, "Since the adoption of the Constitution, courts have eliminated clause after clause that interfered with the exercise of government power. This started with the Necessary and Proper Clause ... and culminated in the post–New Deal Court that gutted the Commerce Clause and the scheme of enumerated powers affirmed by the Tenth Amendment.... The Constitution is now lost, it has not been repealed, so it could be found again."[85]

Roosevelt's transparent attempt to undermine the Court also helped solidify opposition to the New Deal and whatever potential it had after 1937 for deeper liberal reforms.[86] Leuchtenburg concludes, "It helped blunt the most important drive for social reform in American history and squandered the advantage of Roosevelt's triumph in 1936."[87] And Hofstadter woefully wrote that FDR paid "a very heavy price ... for his pragmatic attempt to alter a great and sacrosanct conservative institution. The Court fight alienated many principled liberals and enabled many of FDR's opponents to portray him ... as a man who aspired to a personal dictatorship aimed at subversion of the Republic."[88]

One can, however, be sympathetic to Roosevelt's dilemma of trying to use a conservative Lockean government to do liberal Rousseaun things. The Court fight, therefore, was only a minor flare in the overall failure of the New Deal to accomplish more social democratic aims. The conservative coalition in Congress was decisive in blunting liberalism's reach during the New Deal and after,[89] as FDR recognized in his failed attempt in 1938 to purge the party of conservative southern Democrats and his musings later about forming a cohesive liberal party.[90]

Roosevelt's own style of leadership—pragmatic, experimental, ad hoc rather than ideological, systemic, and planned—also undermined the New Deal's reform potential as James Macgregor Burns ably demonstrates. FDR's increasing preoccupation with the coming war in Europe took its toll as well. The spectra that a more direct involvement in production and planning of the economy might result in totalitarianism or the "Road to Serfdom" also haunted New Deal planners as they observed developments in Germany and Italy. Thus, by the end of his second term FDR and his brain trust had abandoned any pretensions they might have had about restructuring the economy and "reached an accommodation with modern capitalism."[91]

The accommodation to capitalism was near inevitable because liberalism is a remnant in a society that remains profoundly and pervasively conservative. FDR and the New Dealers were reform Lockeans not liberated Rousseans. As Arthur Schlesinger Jr. put it in his influential 1949 manifesto, *The Vital Center* (a volume that in its skepticism about central planning resembles Hayek's *The Road to Serfdom*), liberalism was about an activist but limited government that would police the rules of capitalist competition, use fiscal and monetary policies to assure maximum employment, and sustain a welfare state that would provide a minimal level of social security.[92] To attempt to do more, Schlesinger argued, was beyond liberalism's capacities. Although Burns thinks that Roosevelt could have done more, he too admits that ultimately "New Deal objectives ran head on into the absence of a cohesive liberal tradition in America."[93]

Roosevelt's limited reforms, however, were more than conservatism could accept, for they saw FDR as not only capturing a label but as shattering an old order and debasing a tradition. And, like good conservatives, they began to organize a movement of resistance, a movement, to use William F. Buckley Jr's phrase in the publisher's statement in the first issue of *National Review*, to "stand athwart history, yelling stop."[94]

The New Deal and Racism

Liberalism as an ideology in the United States is not necessarily antiracist, but with its embrace of the positive, interventionist national state and its concern with social security it has, unlike conservatism, the potential to be antiracist. Southern racists recognized this potential from the outset of the New Deal, with many openly warning that a powerful liberal state would become a threat to racism in the South.[95] Whether liberals will act on liberalism's antiracism potential will depend on the political realities or the context of the times and the character and the strategic calculations of political leaders. During his long tenure in office FDR made the strategic judgment that the political realities of the 1930s meant that his militant liberalism could not be extended to civil rights. In 1943 he told the NAACP's Walter White, "Had I been permitted to choose them I would have selected quite different ones. But I've got to get legislation passed by Congress to save America. The Southerners by reason of the seniority rule are Chairmen or occupy strategic places on most of the Senate and House Committees. If I come out for the anti-lynching bill now, they will block every bill I ask Congress to pass to keep America from collapsing. I just can't take that risk."⁹⁶ Not only would FDR not take the risk with respect to antilynching legislation, but he—as we have seen—capitulated to southern racists and allowed his New Deal reforms to be compromised.

Roosevelt also failed to confront racism where he could—in his own administration—refusing, for example, to appoint blacks to even minor posts, instead relegating highly competent individuals such as Robert Weaver and William Haste to informal, advisory positions in a so-called black cabinet. These advisory positions were essentially powerless without authority or responsibility, but they provided blacks with unprecedented "access" to the powerful and were symbolic of the embryonic inclusion of a "few black faces in high places," to use Mary Macleod Bethune's phrase. And although there is nothing in the historical accounts, Roosevelt may have decided on informal, advisory appointments rather than formal positions because the latter would have resulted in more southern howls of "Nigger loving New Deal" and probably would not have received Senate confirmation in any event.⁹⁷

Unwilling to face the risk of a massive African American march on Washington, Roosevelt capitulated to A. Phillip Randolph and issued an executive order prohibiting racial discrimination in employment by companies with defense contracts. Executive Order 8802, issued in 1941, also created the Committee on Fair Employment Practices, but the committee was poorly funded and staffed and was not at all effective in ending employment discrimination.⁹⁸ Otherwise, except for a few symbolic gestures (including tolerating his wife's sometimes outspokenness on civil rights), on racism the greatest liberal president in American history behaved as a conservative.

Sitkoff's assessment of blacks and the New Deal still seems about right. The failure of the first liberal government to do more to end the subordination of blacks he write "stained the record of the Roosevelt administration.... The odds against succeeding do not constitute a sufficient excuse for their timidity, half measures and concessions. In moral terms, the horror of racism makes a mockery of lauding anyone as a humanitarian who compromised with its existence as Roosevelt did repeatedly." Yet Sitkoff also was correct when he said, "Those who desired a modification of traditional race relations had to operate in a political system better constructed to impede change than promote innovation."⁹⁹ The Lockean-Madison legacy of conservatism and its institutional manifestations are therefore as much to blame as the timidity of Roosevelt and the New Dealers.

The climate of public opinion on race also was not hospitable to bold antiracism proposals. Although public opinion polling was in its infancy during FDR's tenure, what little we know suggests a profoundly racist white public. The earliest scientific public opinion poll on race was conducted in the late 1930s by the Roper organization. Only 13 percent of whites believed blacks should be free to live wherever they wished, 50 percent of whites believed that whites "should have the first chance" at any job, and 70 percent of whites said blacks were less intelligent than whites.[100]

In this climate even racially liberal New Dealers such as Interior Secretary Harold Ickes and Vice President Henry Wallace generally preferred to deal with racism as an economic problem, arguing that blacks were disproportionately helped by New Deal work and welfare programs, even if they were racially discriminatory. In both the long and short terms, they viewed these programs as the most politically feasible way to address the oppression of blacks. This is an abiding feature of the liberal ideology; it distinguishes between economic and racial liberalism, always giving priority to economic justice for the American people as a whole rather then racial justice for blacks.[101]

But, in a way it is worse. In a footnote in his 1955 article on conservatism Huntington wrote of the American liberal in Europe: "[W]ho extols the United States as the land of freedom, equality, and democracy, and then is asked: 'What about the Negro in the South?' In reply, the American inevitably stresses the magnitude of the social problems involved, the inevitability of gradualness, the impossibility of altering habits overnight by legislative fiat, and the tensions caused by too rapid social change. In short, he drops the liberal language of equality and freedom and turns to primarily conservative concepts and arguments."[102] This conservatism of liberalism on racism testifies to the tenaciousness of the phenomenon in the American mind, in the twenty-first no less than the twentieth century.

The life and career of Arthur Schlesinger Jr. offers an interesting lens through which the liberal outlook on racism may be observed. Schlesinger, as Stephen Depoe writes, is "perhaps the best representative figure of twentieth century American liberalism."[103] The preeminent historian of liberalism, Schlesinger is the author of prize-winning studies of four liberal icons—Andrew Jackson, FDR, and John and Robert Kennedy. Throughout his career he was also a public intellectual, writing popular essays from a liberal perspective on the full array of midtwentieth century issues. Schlesinger was also an activist-intellectual, a founder of the Americans for Democratic Action, the postwar liberal group and assistant to President Kennedy. His *Vital Center* is often referred to as the "manifesto of postwar liberalism." Although he writes of the inevitability of liberalism in the United States, his *Cycles of American History* suggests that it is best understood—as I understand it—as a remnant.[104]

Schlesinger first advanced the idea of cycles in American history in *The Age of Jackson*, where he argued that "American history has been marked by recurrent swings of conservatism and liberalism. During periods of inaction unsolved social problems pile up till demand for change becomes overwhelming. Then a liberal government comes to power, the dam breaks, and a flood of change sweeps away a great deal in a short time. After fifteen or twenty years the liberal impulse is exhausted, the day of "consolidation" arrives, and conservatism once again, expresses the mood of the country, but generally on the terms of the liberalism it displaces."[105]

In his memoirs Schlesinger writes that on reviewing *The Vital Center* from the vantage point of a half century "[i]n domestic affairs I should have paid more attention to the question of racial justice. I do call the treatment of black America 'the most basic challenge to the American conscience' but I wish I had devoted more space to the battle for civil rights."[106] Schlesinger recounts a 1942 tour of the South where he visited a "colored" district in Biloxi, Mississippi, where "I felt that I never imagined such misery and wretchedness in America."[107] But in a statement he writes he would "soon renounce," he concluded nothing could be done to give more power to blacks to improve their wretchedness because "[t]he southern Negro would abuse power even more than the reactionary white. The only hope in the situation lies in activity by southern liberals and this hope is scant. It is very difficult in the war situation to see any steps which might be taken without antagonizing either the conservative whites or radical Negroes. The situation is just bad."[108]

Nevertheless, in *The Vital Center* Schlesinger did call for "an unrelenting attack on all forms of racial discrimination." But he tempered this call for racial liberalism by writing that white southerners had "serious and intelligible reservations about timing and methods."[109] That is, as the Huntington quote above suggests, liberals revert to Burkean notions of gradualism and stability when it comes to dealing with racism. These ideas became the mantras of most post–New Deal liberals on civil rights.[110]

Reportedly in a meeting with A. Phillip Randolph where he was urged to take some action on civil rights FDR responded, "[M]ake me do it." That is, the president told Randolph to bring sufficient pressure on him so that he would have no choice but to act. In the 1960s, African Americans did just that making Presidents Kennedy and Johnson respond with effective civil rights legislation. Their doing so, however, was indeed risky, because it contributed to the unraveling of liberalism and the ascendancy of the conservative movement. These are the subjects of subsequent chapters.

CHAPTER FIVE

African American Thought and the Conservative Remnant

"Manifestly, the ideology has little appeal to anyone discontented with the status-quo" because "conservatism is not just the absence of change. It is the articulate, systematic, theoretical resistance to change."[1] The African American people, with the exception perhaps of the native peoples, have been the most consistently discontented group in the United States. Thus, they and their leaders have been almost "naturally" liberal. That is, they have favored a positive, interventionist national government with the authority to intervene in the affairs of the states and civil society to end racism in the forms of slavery, segregation, and racial discrimination. As a group, disproportionately poor, lacking access to land, housing, education, and employment, African Americans have also favored the positive Roussean state that would have as one of its objectives the creation of an equalitarian society.[2]

For example, in a penetrating insight on the death of Reconstruction, Heather Cox argues that northern whites turned against African Americans not so much because of racism, though racist they were, but more because they "increasingly perceived the mass of African Americans as adherents of a theory of political economy in which labor and capital were at odds and in which a growing government would be used to advance laborers at the expense of capitalists. For these northerners, the majority of ex-slaves became the face of 'communism' or 'socialism,' as opponents dubbed their views.... Northerners turned against freed people after the Civil War because African Americans came to represent a concept of society and government that would destroy the 'free labor world,' that is, a view that assumed that labor and capital had mutually compatible interests. Black citizens, it seemed, threatened the core of American society."[3] Foner makes a similar point about the radicalism of blacks during Reconstruction:

> [T]he rising tax burden fueled opposition to Reconstruction among both planters and yeomen. But blacks embraced the activist, reforming state as a counterbalance to the forces of wealth

and tradition arrayed against them. "They look to legislation" commented an Alabama newspaper "because in the very nature of things, they can look nowhere else." Black lawmakers not only supported appropriations for schools, asylums, and social welfare, but unsuccessfully advanced proposals to expand public responsibility even further, including regulation of private markets and insurance companies, compulsory school attendance, restrictions on the sale of liquor, and even, in Louisiana, the outlawing of fairs, gambling, and horse racings on Sunday.[4]

This black radicalism, or to use FDR's phrase, "militant liberalism," is reflected among the masses of African Americans today. In table 5.1 data from the 1996 General Social Survey are presented comparing black and white opinion on a variety of government programs, even when told a tax increase might be necessary to pay for them. Compared to whites, black opinion is overwhelmingly liberal. Table 5.2 provides opinion on support for the welfare state. Blacks are again overwhelmingly liberal, when compared to whites viewing providing jobs, health, and a decent standard of living as government responsibilities. Table 5.3 shows that among blacks there is even substantial support for socialist ideas such as government ownership of electric utilities, banks, and hospitals. Finally, the table shows that blacks are more likely to agree that it is the government's responsibility to promote an equalitarian society by reducing income differences between rich and poor: 73 percent compared to 44 percent of whites. Kluegel and Smith, after close study of contemporary American opinion on inequality, wrote, "Judged by the black-white gap in beliefs that potentially challenge the dominant ideology, blacks are the group that come closest to being 'class conscious' in the Marxian definition."[5]

These mass sentiments are for the most part embraced by the mainstream of the black intelligentsia and leadership class, including such historical and contemporary figures as Henry Highland Garnett, W. E. B. DuBois, Paul Robeson, Richard Wright, Adam Clayton Powell Jr., Malcolm X, Ralph Bunche, Martin Luther King Jr, Bayard Rustin, Amiri Baraka, A. Phillip Randolph, John Conyers, Jesse Jackson, and Ronald Dellums. For example, Bunche, the Nobel laureate, first black Harvard PhD in political science, first black president of the American Political Science Association, founding chair of Howard University's political science department, and a major contributor to the influential Carnegie-Myrdal project study of race in America, in the 1930s wrote a penetrating critique of the New Deal from a Marxist perspective.[6] Although Bunche subsequently repudiated Marxism, throughout his career he remained a militant liberal. But among the black intelligentsia the allure of Marxism remained. The black historian St. Clair Drake recalled, "By

TABLE 5.1. Racial Differences in Attitudes toward Government Spending on Selected Programs, Even if Tax Increase Is Required (percent in favor)

	Blacks	Whites
Health	87%	64%
Schools	54	25
Retirement Benefits	79	46
Unemployment Benefits	69	21
Culture/Arts	68	31

Source: General Social Survey, 1996, University of Chicago, National Opinion Research Center.

TABLE 5.2. Racial Differences in Attitudes toward the Social Welfare Responsibilities of Government

	Black	White
To Provide Jobs	74%	33%
Health Care	69	33
Assure Decent Standard of Living	70	33
Financial Aid for College	62	30
Decent Housing for All	50	14
Government Should Reduce Income Inequality between Rich and Poor	73	44

Source: General Social Survey, 1996, University of Chicago, National Opinion Research Center.

TABLE 5.3. Racial Differences in Attitudes toward Government Ownership of Selected Enterprises (percent in favor)

	Black	White
Electric Utilities	39%	17%
Hospitals	59	20
Banks	47	18

Source: General Social Survey, 1996, University of Chicago, National Opinion Research Center.

1932 I didn't know any black social scientist who privately or publicly didn't claim to be some kind of Marxist."[7]

However, within black thought there is and always has been enormous ideological diversity. The mainstream media and for the most part mainstream academics in political science have tended to treat black thought as monolithically liberal. But in fact the black community is and, to some extent, always has been the most ideologically diverse in America.[8] In the most comprehensive study of contemporary black ideological diversity and its historical roots, Dawson identified five discrete "ideologies": black nationalism, liberalism, conservatism, feminism and Marxism.[9] Of the five liberalism had the most support at the mass level, conservatism the least.[10] Indeed, conservatism had considerably less support than black nationalism or Marxism.

However, it is clear that historically there are elements of conservatism—Lockean and Burkean—in black thought, even among liberal and radical black thinkers. In this chapter I review these elements of conservatism in what is otherwise a liberal to radical tradition. I also examine the thought of Booker T. Washington and George Schuyler who are generally but wrongly considered conservatives. At the core of their thought one finds accommodationism (or cowardice) as much as conservatism (I postpone until the chapter on neoconservatism discussion of late-twentieth-century black conservatives such as Thomas Sowell and Clarence Thomas).

Classical Black Thought

From its rudimentary beginnings in eighteenth-century petitions and pamphlets to the more sophisticated speeches and writings of Martin Delany, Frederick Douglass, and Martin Luther King Jr., black thought embraced the liberal contract philosophy of natural rights, government by consent of the governed, and the rule of law. In doing so they called for an unbastardized Locke that, in the words of seventeenth-century Philadelphia businessman and revolutionary war veteran James Forten, would include the "Indian and the European, the savage and the Saint, the Peruvian and the Laplander, the white man and the African, and whatever measures are adopted subversive of this inestimable privilege, are in direct violation of the letter and spirit of our constitution."[11] The idea of a bastardized Locke or the broken social contract is succinctly expressed by blacks in a 1774 appeal to the Massachusetts governor and legislature:

> The petition of a grate number of Blacks of this province who by divine permission are held in a state of slavery within the bowels

of a free and Christian Country. That your petitioners apprehend with other men as natural right to our freedoms without being deprived of them by our fellow men as we are free born pepel and have never forfeited this Blessing by any compact agreement whatever.... We therefore beg your Excellency and Honors will give this its deer weight and considerations and that you will accordingly cause an act of the legislature to be passed that we may obtain our natural right to our freedoms and our children be set at lebety.[12]

Douglass' thought was self-consciously and systematically Lockean. As Meyers writes, "the tradition's greatest representative, unequaled in his articulation of the first principles of natural rights liberalism in their application to racial justice in America."[13] In his famous July 4 address he scornfully dismissed those who would violate the contract: "Would you have me argue that man is entitled to liberty? That he is the rightful owners of his body? You have already declared it. Must I argue the wrongfulness of slavery? Is that a question for republicans?... There is not a man beneath the canopy of heaven who does not know slavery is wrong for *him*.... No; I will not. I have better employment for my time and strength that such arguments would imply."[14] Martin Luther King Jr's 1963 "I Have a Dream" oration is premised on the broken social contract, although he used a bounced check analogy: "In a sense we've come to our nation's capital to cash a check. When the architects of our republic wrote the magnificent words of the Constitution and the Declaration of Independence, they were signing a promissory note to which every American was to fall heir. This note was the promise that all men, yes, black men as well as white men, would be guaranteed the unalienable rights of life, liberty and the pursuit of happiness."[15] These selected excerpts from pamphlets and speeches illustrate that from the beginning African Americans, like their European counterparts, imbibed the teachings of Locke's little book and that the commitment to philosophical liberalism knows no color line. It should be clear, however, that this commitment to philosophical liberalism on the part of blacks went hand and hand with a commitment to a positive, centralized state that would have the power to fulfill the terms of the contract.

Modern Black Thought

In some ways modern black thought can be viewed through the life, writings and work of a single man—W. E. B. DuBois—the most influential scholar in the African American tradition.[16] In his *Dusk of Dawn: An Essay toward an Autobiography of a Race Concept*, DuBois wrote, "I think I may say without boasting that in the period 1910 to 1930 that I was a main factor in revolutionizing the attitude of the American Negro toward caste. My stinging hammer blows made Negroes aware of themselves, confident of their possibilities and determined self-assertion. So much so that today common slogans among Negro people are taken bodily from the words of my mouth."[17] DuBois was not boasting, because even beyond the 1930s his writings and activism defined the ideological parameters and contours of debate in black America. Early in his career DuBois remarked, "We face a condition not theory." Therefore, he said any ideology that gave promise of altering the oppressed condition of blacks should be embraced. Earlier in his career in his famous "Conservation of Races" essay he appeared to embrace black nationalism.[18] Later, in the face of Booker Washington's accommodation, he embraced protest liberalism, organizing the Niagara Conference in 1905 and helping to establish the NAACP in 1909. Watching the deteriorating conditions of blacks during the depression, DuBois once again turned to black nationalism, arguing that blacks should develop a separate group economy of producers and consumer cooperatives. After World War II looking back on the limited reforms of the New Deal and impressed by Soviet and Chinese communism, in 1956 he joined the Communist Party and went into exile in Ghana. Although DuBois had embraced socialism as early as 1912, by the 1950s he had become convinced that equality for all men required a complete abandonment of capitalism.

If DuBois is historically the most influential thinker in the African American tradition, Martin Luther King Jr. is the greatest leader in that tradition and one of the four transformative leaders in American history.[19] Although Ronald Reagan was unconvinced, King on religious and philosophical grounds was profoundly anti-Marxist.[20] However, from his earliest sermons he also expressed skepticism about laissez-faire capitalism because it was a system that "took necessities from the masses to give luxuries to the classes."[21] He did not, however, make this skepticism a focus of his work until the last couple years of his life. In those years King, like DuBois, changed his ideology as conditions changed. More precisely, he changed his ideology as he began to focus on the poverty conditions in the northern ghettos rather than conditions in the segregated South. In the last two years of his life King's ideology evolved from militant liberalism toward some inchoate form of democratic socialism.[22]

In fundamental content modern black left/liberal ideologies are shaped by the parameters defined by DuBois during his long career as an activist-intellectual and implemented by King in his much abbreviated career as a political leader.

Black Nationalism: The Residual Stratum in Black Thought

Harold Cruse, in another context, refers to black nationalism as the "residual stratum" in African American thought.[23] The ideology emerges from those thinkers and leaders who came to believe that Locke in America would never be debastardized; that the social contract would always be a racial contract; that to use Dr. King's analogy, America would always "default" on the Lockean "promissory note" insofar as African Americans were concerned.[24] Thus, they have sought self-determination for African Americans either within or beyond the boundaries of the United States.[25]

Beginning self-consciously with Martin Delaney, this residual stratum or rejected (rejected because it has always been embraced by only a distinct minority of black leaders and masses) strain has been espoused by such varied leaders as Bishop Henry M. Turner, Marcus Garvey, Edward Wilmot Blyden, Elijah Muhammad, Malcolm X, Louis Farrakhan, and, of course, DuBois. Black nationalism, particularly what Shelby calls "strong black nationalism" in the form of advocacy of racial separatism, is usually espoused by those who believe that the social contract in America will always be racial.[26] This may be seen in the life and career of Bishop Turner.

Turner, a bishop of the African Methodist Episcopal Church, was named the army's first black chaplain by Abraham Lincoln and after the war served two terms in the Georgia legislature. Disillusioned, angry, and bitter about the betrayal of Reconstruction, Turner embraced a return of blacks to Africa. As long as he could believe in the promise of a debastardized Locke, Turner was prepared to even join forces with the white conservative planter class in the South, opposing the confiscation or sale of their property and supporting literacy and property qualifications for voting.[27] The proverbial straw that broke the camel's back for Turner was the *Civil Rights Cases of 1883*. Turner described the case as a "barbarous decision . . . that absolv[ed] the allegiance of the Negro to the United States."[28] Later, in language similar to that employed in the twentieth century by Malcolm X and Louis Farrakhan, Turner caused a national furor when he said, "I used to love . . . the grand old flag, and sing with ecstasy about the stars and stripes, but to a Negro in this country the American flag is a dirty and a contemptible rag. No star in it can the colored man claim, for it is no longer the symbol of our own manhood rights and liberty. . . . I wish to say that hell is an improvement on the United States where the Negro is concerned."[29]

Even at the nadir of the black condition in America relatively few blacks embraced the uncompromising rejectionist position of Turner. Nevertheless, this rejected strain has had a powerful hold on the black imagination, and it is embraced as an ideology by as much as 15 percent of the black population which significantly exceeds popular support among blacks for conservatism.[30]

Booker T. Washington's "Conservatism"

Booker T. Washington is often viewed as the paradigmatic black conservative in the United States. Washington valorized bourgeois values of individual character, responsibility, and hard work; emphasized the importance of private property and laissez-faire capitalism; and eschewed (at least temporarily) civil rights and racial equality and therefore denigrated the efforts during Reconstruction of the federal government to secure those rights.[31] However, as we shall see in the following sections of this chapter many of these conservative or bourgeois values were embraced by virtually all stripes of black leaders, including quintessential liberals such as Douglass and DuBois in Washington's times and Martin King and Jesse Jackson in the twentieth century. These values are also central in the ideology of black nationalists such as Garvey and Malcolm X. DuBois, for example, in his famous attack on Washington's program in *The Souls of Black Folk* wrote that he "rejoiced" in many aspects of Washington's work but rejected his "adjustment and submission" to the overthrow of Reconstruction and his "practical acceptance of the alleged inferiority of the Negro."[32] Washington's adjustment and submission to the oppression of blacks is what distinguishes his thought from the mainstream of black thinking, and not his embrace of bourgeois values or "triumphant commercialism" to use DuBois' characterization of his embrace of laissez-faire capitalism. Thus his ideology should be understood as accommodationism rather then conservatism.

In *An American Dilemma* Myrdal introduced accommodationism as a construct to study black leadership behavior. According to Myrdal, black leaders confronting the overwhelming power of whites tend to "naturally" or "realistically" accept the system of racial subordination.[33] Accommodation required leaders to accept, not protest, what Myrdal in 1944 referred to as the "subordinated caste" status of blacks. Leaders led only in the context of caste. Changes in the conditions of blacks were to be pursued quietly and incrementally so as not to upset whites and stimulate their resistance. Over time, it was hoped, these quiet, gradual changes would improve the conditions of the group and in the long run alter its subordinate status.

This was the "ideology" pursued by Washington. Faced with white terror—sometimes state sponsored and always with state acquiescence—Washington concluded that the only realistic strategy for blacks was to accept the situation and work out the best deal they could and wait for a better day. DuBois rejected this strategy of accommodation in favor of what he called "manly protest," protest for voting and civil rights because he argued—correctly—that it was "utterly impossible under modern competitive methods for workingmen and property-owners to defend their rights and exist without the right of suffrage."[34]

Washington did not in principle disagree; he simply did not believe—correctly—that blacks at that time could obtain the suffrage DuBois demanded. Thus, he accommodated, but this difference between the two leaders involved strategy not ideology. In the late 1880s in the rural South foremost in Washington's mind was "All those dead Indians" who had resisted or protested rather than accommodated white power. Thus, Washington's conservatism was a product of fear more than principle. In conditions less terrifying—literally terrifying—Washington likely would have embraced DuBois' "protest liberalism." Indeed, secretly, he did exactly that, providing funds and support for efforts to advance the suffrage, civil rights, antilynching activism, and railroad car desegregation.[35] In public, however, he engaged in "Uncle Tomism," begging and pleading, telling demeaning white supremacist "darkey jokes" that flattered and encouraged the most racist of whites. Accommodating conservatism he celebrated the ethos of laissez-faire capitalism and preached to blacks patience, hard work, individual initiative, responsibility, self-help, and Christian character. By practicing these conservative verities Washington argued—wrongly—that blacks would eventually "earn" "full citizenship rights" by proving themselves the equal of whites.[36] "But," Myrdal concludes, "in principle he never gave up the Negro protest against social discrimination."[37] That is, in principle and in secret Washington was a protest liberal.

Washington's thought and behavior, however, are controversial. Some scholars view him as the quintessential Uncle Tom who sold out the interests of the race in order to curry favor with powerful, wealthy racist white men. Others view him as a "pragmatist," a "wizard" who did the best he could to assure the survival of black people in an overwhelmingly hostile environment. However one views Washington—I tend to share the latter view—his thought provides little basis for an authentic, principled, and autonomous black conservatism.

George Schuyler's "Conservatism"

A similar conclusion can be reached regarding George Schuyler, the other major personality in black conservative thought in the United States. Schuyler, the longtime black columnist for the African American newspaper the *Pittsburgh Courier*, in the 1960s became the darling of the white Right because of his caustic attacks on Martin Luther King and the civil rights movement. Throughout this period he engaged in vitriolic criticisms of the civil rights movement, going so far as to justify the use of the fire hoses and attack dogs during the 1963 Birmingham demonstrations.[38] Writing in conservative journals Schuyler argued that the civil rights movement was a radical, communist-influenced movement that threatened system stability.

An ex-socialist, after World War II, Schuyler "reinvented himself" and became the most prominent black conservative in the country.[39] Schuyler in his autobiography explained his conservatism with respect to race by arguing that America, in spite of its racism, was the best place on earth for African people: "My feeling was ... that Negroes have the best chance here in the United States if they will avail themselves of the numerous opportunities they have. To be sure it is not easy being a black man in the United States but it is easier than anywhere else I know for him to get the best schooling, the best living conditions, the best economic advantages, the best security.... Once we accept the fact that there is, and always will be, a caste system in the United States, and stop crying about it, we can concentrate on how best to survive and prosper within the system."[40] In 1948 Schuyler wrote a series of articles titled "What's Good about the South," in which he argued that southerners were kindly and cooperative and the racial situation was tolerable, noting that he encountered black doctors, dentists, and businessmen. Thus, he contended that if blacks worked hard and took advantage of the opportunities available, they would do very well in Mississippi and therefore anywhere else in America.

Schuyler's conservatism on first reading would appear to derive from his satisfaction with the status quo; however, on close reading it appears that he, like Washington, was also worried about those dead Indians. Specifically, he wrote that it was useful to contrast the position of African Americans with what he called the "Amerindian." The "Negro," he wrote, "has been the outstanding example of American conservatism: adjustable, resourceful, adaptable, patient, restrained, and not given to quixotic adventures ... [he] has adjusted himself to every change with the basic aim of survival and advancement. Had he taken the advice of the minority of firebrands in his midst, he would have risked extermination."[41] Of his opposition to black protest, Schuyler was explicit about his fear "not having any illusions about white people per se, I have long been fearful that this [racial agitation] ... might lead to actual civil war which would certainly lead to genocide ... the fate of Amerindians of the eastern United States should not be forgotten."[42] Thus Schuyler's "conservatism" appears to be a product of cowardice, mixed perhaps with a healthy dose of opportunism.

In black America, then, it is difficult to locate a fully developed, principled conservatism among major intellectual or political leaders. Rather, one finds stratagems of accomodationism, cowardice, and opportunism. This is not surprising since it would be difficult for thoughtful blacks to embrace completely conservatism—whether Lockean or Burkean—because they have seen little worth conserving in traditions and institutions organized and maintained on the basis of their denigration and subordination. Change—often radical change—has always been at the core of African American thought.

However, within the broad left-liberal tradition of African American thought one can discern elements of conservatism not muddled by the accommodationism of Washington or the cowardice and opportunism of Schuyler. Although it is only a remnant, within the main body of black thought one finds fragments of conservatism. These conservative fragments include a powerful strain of religiosity; a concern with virtue and individual responsibility; traditional family values; aristocratic pretensions; a concern with private property; and a long and abiding tradition of self-help and moral uplift.

The Conservative Remnant

By some measures African Americans today are the most religious people in the Western world, as indicated by such things as belief in God, in the literal truth of the Bible, in the importance of religion in one's personal life, and frequency of prayer and church attendance.[43] This modern religiosity is likely deeply rooted, going back to slave culture and the belief in deliverance. Although religion is not central to the thought of most black leaders or intellectuals (King and Elijah Muhammad are the obvious exceptions), religion has shown a tenacity and continuity over the years in black culture, and it serves as a bulwark of tradition and stability linking the past, present, and future.

Religion was an inspiration for many of the slave rebellions, a force in the civil rights movement, and it operates to increase voting and other forms of civic participation.[44] Yet, in general, religion in black society has operated as a conservative force working against widespread radicalism and activism,[45] as Locke and Burke would have it, a force for mass quiescence and stability.

Aristocratic pretensions and conservative predispositions toward work, family, and property are integral parts of mainstream black thought. DuBois' aristocracy of talent is probably the best-known example of this conservative tendency, but it is perhaps first and best expressed in the writings of Douglass, and DuBois' mentor, Alexander Crummell.[46] Crummell, clergyman, scholar, and founder of the American Negro Academy, is regarded by August Meier as the "leading Negro nineteenth century intellectual."[47]

Crummell clearly believed in rule by an aristocracy of intellect and property and like Burke and Locke was skeptical of government by the unlearned and unpropertied masses, be they black or white. Moses writes, "Crummell did not advocate majority rule or democratic government for the masses anywhere. He rejected Jeffersonian democracy, not only because of its inherent and inextricable racism. It was obviously unworkable when applied to people who were illiterate, unworldly, economically underdeveloped and politically disorganized—and that included most people of the earth."[48]

Like Washington, Crummell claimed that the newly emancipated slaves lacked the "civilization" necessary to participate in Reconstruction politics and should have been denied suffrage along with poor and illiterate whites until such time as they developed the proper "Christian" character.[49] Crummell, like Locke, would have been quite willing to have property qualifications for the franchise, as long as it was applied without regard to race. Delany and DuBois held similar views.

Related to this most black leaders embraced some version of DuBois' notion of the talented tenth, the aristocratic idea that the race should be led by an elite, by its "college-bred people" who could provide guidance for the ignorant masses. DuBois likely derived this idea of a "saving remnant" from Crummell, but he gave it its most famous and self-conscious articulation. While he believed in equality between the races, DuBois was not an egalitarian; rather he was an avowed elitist with aristocratic pretensions. For example, he wrote in the opening sentence of his 1903 essay "The Talented Tenth." "The Negro race, like all races, is going to be saved by its exceptional men. The problem of education, then, among Negroes must first of all be dealt with by the "talented tenth; it is the problem of developing the best of this race that they may guide the mass away from the contamination and death of the worst, in their own and other races."[50]

In a 1948 address to a gathering of the elite grand Boule of the Sigma Pi Phi, DuBois re-examined the talented tenth thesis, suggesting that he may have put too much faith in the leadership of the elite (who he said as a group might be "selfish, self-indulgent, well-to-do-men, whose basic interest in solving the problem was personal ... without any real care, or certainly no arousing care, as to what became of masses of American Negroes, or to the mass of the people") and too little for the masses who, because they "know life in its bitter struggle," might more naturally produce "real, unselfish and clear-sighted leadership."[51] At this point DuBois was moving toward a definite Marxist analysis; however, he did not abandon altogether his notion of elite leadership, calling in the 1948 address for a "Guiding Hundredth" that would avoid the pitfalls of the tenth by developing a clear agenda and a national organization.

DuBois' aristocratic pretensions and adherence to bourgeois values of hard work, sobriety, and moral values are on full display in *The Philadelphia Negro*, his classic sociological study of the late-nineteenth-century black community.[52] In this work DuBois uses language that sometimes resembles that of today's neoconservatives when they write about poor urban blacks. While he was careful (as today's neoconservatives tend not to be) to identify the sources of lower-class black behavior in the structural properties of racism and poverty, he also identified moral and cultural shortcomings on the part of blacks themselves. Like Glenn Loury today, DuBois castigated Philadelphia's black community for its sexual looseness, crime, substance abuse, preponderance of female-headed households, and general failure to display virtuous behavior.[53] And, like Loury in the 1980s, in the 1890s DuBois argued it was the responsibility of the better class of blacks to serve as "role models" and "uplift the race."[54]

The idea of self-help, the protestant ethic, and the gospel of moral uplift are frequently associated in black thought with putative black conservatives (such as Washington, as well as black nationalists, such as Elijah Muhammad), but as Kevin Gaines shows in *Uplifting the Race: Black Leadership, Politics, and Culture in the Twentieth Century*, this conservative remnant is an integral part of black thought.

Conclusion

In his great history of Western philosophy, Bertrand Russell wrote, "My purpose is to exhibit western philosophy as an integral part of social and political life: not as the isolated speculations of remarkable individuals, but as both effect and cause of the character of the various communities in which different systems flourished."[55] Philosophies and their ideological expressions are, as Marx and Engels, powerfully demonstrated the product of the material conditions under which people live and seldom are the mere products of autonomy. This is no less true for Locke and Rousseau than for Hamilton and Madison or DuBois and Washington. African Americans have been liberal, therefore, because the conditions of their existence have always cried out for a positive state, a positive national state that would first end slavery, then end segregation, and now bring about racial equality. Given these conditions opposition to liberalism becomes the same as racism.

But if Locke had not been bastardized in America, or even if the bastardization had ended with the civil war, given the powerful conservative remnant in black thought the black community *might* today display the same kind of ideological diversity seen among European immigrants that came to this country between the 1880s and 1920s.[56] After the Civil War Douglass gave a speech in Boston titled "What the Black Man Wants." Douglass said, "Justice!" And then in typical Lockean language he said:

> In regard to the colored people, there is always more that is benevolent, I perceive, than just, manifested toward us. What I ask for the Negro is not benevolence, not pity, not sympathy, but

simply justice. The American people have always been anxious to know what they shall do with us.... I have just had but one answer from the beginning. Do nothing with us! Your doing with us have already played mischief with us. Do nothing with us! If apples will not remain on the tree of their own strength, if they are worm-eaten, if they are early ripe and disposed to fall let them fall.... And if the Negro cannot stand on his own legs, let him fall also. All I ask is, give him a chance to stand on his own legs![57]

A "chance to stand on his own legs" has always been at the core of black thinking in the United State. This chance, this opportunity, however, could only come about as the result of a liberal state, a proposition clearly understood by Douglass.[58]

CHAPTER SIX

Racism and the Conservative Intellectual Movement, 1945–1970

In some ways a civil rights movement in the United States is as old as or older than the union. The earliest petitions and pamphlets urging the debastardization of Locke may be understood as the inchoate stirrings of the movement. The abolitionist movement and the slave revolts and rumors of revolts represented the first organized expression of these stirrings and, as discussed in chapter 4, these forces gave rise to the first self-conscious conservative movement in the United States. The ultimate success of the abolitionists in the course of the Civil War and Reconstruction in formally debastardizing the Constitution resulted in a second conservative movement, whose practical result was the rebastardization of the Constitution. This rebastardization of the Constitution resulted in the beginnings of the civil rights movement in the United States.

The starting point of the civil rights movement is usually located in the early part of the twentieth century with the 1905 Niagara Conference, the formation of the NAACP in 1909, and the death of Booker T. Washington in 1915.[1] It is during this period that the basic goals, strategies, and organizational bases of the modern movement for civil rights were developed. At the conference at Niagara, DuBois, William Monroe Trotter, and other African American intellectuals and political activists challenged the dominant accommodationist, anticivil rights philosophy of Booker T. Washington and laid out the alternative civil rights agenda. The goals of the movement were summed up in the Niagara Manifesto: "We shall not be satisfied to take one jot or title less than our manhood rights. We claim for ourselves every single right that belongs to free born Americans, political, civil and social; and until we get these rights we will never cease to protest and assail the ears of America."[2] The manifesto raised specific demands for the right to vote and an end to discrimination in public accommodations, equal enforcement of the law, and quality of education. As for strategy or methods, the manifesto declared, "These are some of the things we want. How shall we get them? By voting where we may vote; by persistent, unceasing agitation, by hammering at the truth; by sacrifice and hard work."[3]

Although the influence of Washington's accommodationism was to continue for some time, in large part as a result of the "hammering" of DuBois in the NAACP's magazine *The Crisis,* a consensus developed among the black intelligentsia and civic, church, and fraternal leadership around the basic goals and strategies of the civil rights movement. The formation of the NAACP provided a centralized organizational vehicle for the movement, and by the time of Washington's death DuBois and his colleagues were well on their way to displacing Washington's accommodationist philosophy. Certainly by the 1930s a civil rights protest consensus had emerged, providing the ideas for the coalition of liberals and labor and religious groups that yielded the enactment of the basic items of the Niagara agenda in the mid-1960s civil rights laws.

The early civil rights movement focused on ideas, particularly the ideas of DuBois, in the pages of *The Crisis*,[4] Lockean ideas and ideas about the promises of equality as articulated by Jefferson and reasserted by Lincoln. Segregation and state-sanctioned inequality the NAACP and its leaders argued were a betrayal of the martyred Lincoln and those honored dead he commemorated at Gettysburg. These ideas alone, however, had few consequences.

From the 1920s to the 1950s the NAACP and other African American organizations also engaged in lobbying and litigation. But these efforts too had few consequences. Thus, there was little conservative reaction, although the seeds of the conservative response were planted during the New Deal as a result of the coming of the positive state and the budding of racial liberalism. A conservative movement did not emerge in reaction to the civil rights movement during its first fifty years because the movement did not present a clear and present danger to the prevailing order. Although ideas do have consequences, the history of the civil rights movement suggests that they do not alone have consequences. Instead, ideas must be linked to powerful movements that challenge existing ideas and power relationships before there is a conservative countermovement.

Brown vs. Board of Education, the fruits of years of litigation, represented precisely that challenge to existing ideas and power relationships in the United States. As we will see later in this chapter, it is difficult to overstate the significance of *Brown* in galvanizing the conservative movement in America. One year later the year-long Montgomery bus boycott brought the civil rights movement from the arenas of ideas, courtrooms, and congressional lobbies to the streets. Predictably, these two developments resulted in the mobilization of reactionary forces and contributed mightily to growth of the conservative movement.

The synchronism of the modern civil rights and conservative movements is clear. Both have their origins in the 1950s, and both challenge prevailing ideas and power relationships.[5] The modern civil rights movement begins with *Brown* and Montgomery. The modern conservative movement begins with ideas, with books. The civil rights movement during the 1950s and 1960s plays itself out on the streets of the cities and the back roads of the South, while the conservative movement plays itself out in the suites and boardrooms of America spreading its ideas through books, journals, foundations, and the media. The civil rights movement was an agent of historical change; the conservative movement was an agent of reaction seeking to stop or reverse processes of social change and maintain or restore the old Lockean order with respect to race, the economy, and the international system.

The synchronism of the two movements continues into the late 1960s and throughout the 1970s with the emergence of the neoconservative variant of conservatism. The neoconservative movement—the subject of the next chapter—emerges partly in response to the successes of the civil rights movement and its turn toward radicalism in the form of black power and the ghetto revolts. Conservatism was a reaction to the formal implementation of a debastardized Locke, while neoconservatism was a reaction to the African American quest for the substantive implementation of Locke or, in a word, for equality. That is, the neoconservatives were responding to the black movement's struggle to deal in a Roussean way with the legacies of the long bastardization of Locke. President Lyndon Johnson stated the case for the Roussean way of dealing with the legacies of Locke's bastardization in his famous 1965 commencement speech at Howard University. "But freedom is not enough. You do not wipe away the scars of centuries by saying: now you are free to go where you want, and do as you desire, and choose the leaders you please. You do not take a person who, for years, has been hobbled by chains and liberate him, bring him up to the starting line of a race and then say 'you are free to compete with others' and still justly believe that you have been completely fair.... We seek not just freedom but opportunity. We seek not just legal equity but human ability, not just equality as a right and a theory but equality as a fact and equality as a result."[6] As will be shown in this and the following chapter, the conservative and neoconservative movements were not purely, or perhaps not even mainly, responses to the civil rights and black power movements. Challenges from other ideas, social changes, movements, and events were "fused" into these movements. However, race and racism were integral in this fusion, both intellectually and politically.

Origins of the Conservative Movement

In 1945 George Nash wrote that "no articulate, coordinated, self-consciously conservative intellectual force existed in the United States."[7] And Diamond wrote that her book was about how a "small clique of post World War II conservative intellectuals" transformed themselves into a "well heeled, grassroots movement representing millions of ordinary citizens."[8] Peter Viereck, a leading postwar conservative intellectual, wrote in 1949 that "conservative ... is a among the most unpopular words in the American vocabulary."[9] In the immediate postwar period, then, conservatism, like liberalism today, was the dreaded "C" word to be avoided by politicians with national ambitions; Viereck wrote that "even Senator Taft prefers the word 'liberal.' "[10] Slowly over the period of the next two decades a conservative intellectual movement emerged, eventually becoming a powerful dissident political movement that effectively displaced the established power structure of the Republican Party and mounted a sustained and substantially effective challenge to the governing liberal remnant.

The conservative intellectual movement as it developed in the postwar period was fused out of three relatively distinct elements. The first were Lockean laissez-faire conservatives who resisted the liberalism of the New Deal. Second were the traditionalists who resisted modernity, industrialism, urbanization, and mass society and wished to return to core Western religious and moral values. Third were militant anticommunists, who were appalled by the accommodation of the Soviet Union, its takeover of Eastern Europe, and the triumph of the communists in China.

The glue that initially held these disparate lines of thinking together, that brought about "fusion," was hostility to communism.[11] Fusionism represented the theoretical imperative to coordinate these disparate elements into a coherent intellectual enterprise. The Lockean conservatives had little in common, for example, with the traditionalists, who tended to be skeptical or downright hostile to the destructively modernizing tendencies of capitalism and its fixation on individualism at the expense of community. Anticommunism, however, was not a source of significant differences and thus could become the basis for philosophical cohesion and movement solidarity. Frank Meyer laid out the intellectual basis for fusion in his 1962 book *In Defense of Freedom*. Meyer discusses communism only in passing in the book, writing that its values were so contrary to those of the West that the only recourse was to crush it by force. Overall, *In Defense of Freedom* is a learned, nicely written critique of what Meyer calls "collectivists" who view freedom in terms of Rousseau equality of material conditions as well as of conservatives (mainly Russell Kirk) who see freedom as living a virtuous life within organic communities.

For Meyer freedom is simply the right of individuals to live unrestrained lives in an ordered society. In other words, the book is an extended essay in defense of Lockean individualism and laissez-faire capitalism.[12]

Thus, in its genesis the conservative intellectual movement was little concerned with race in America.[13] This, however, was to change dramatically with *Brown* and the first stirrings of a mass-based civil rights movement.

The genesis of the postwar conservative intellectual movement is also traced to the publication of a number of influential books beginning in the 1940s. These "notably ill-assorted books" became "the foundation stones" of the philosophical and ideological renaissance of conservatism.[14] Among the works often cited in the pantheon are Richard Weaver, *Ideas Have Consequences* (1948); Ludwig Von Mises, *Human Action: A Treatise on Economics* (1949); Albert Jay Nock, *Memoirs of a Superfluous Man* (1943); Ayn Rand, *The Fountainhead* (1943); Leo Strauss, *Natural Rights and History* (1953); Peter Viereck, *Conservatism Revisited* (1949); Robert Nisbet, *The Quest for Community* (1943); Frederick Hayek, *The Road to Serfdom* (1944); Whittaker Chambers, *Witness* (1952); William F. Buckley Jr., *God and Man at Yale* (1951); Milton Friedman, *Capitalism and Freedom* (1962); and Russell Kirk, *The Conservative Mind* (1953).

These works express the various elements—Lockean conservatism, traditionalism, individualism, and anticommunism—of conservative thought; only a few deal directly with race or racism. Of these books, two standout as canonical: Kirk's *Conservatism in America* and Hayek's *Road to Serfdom*.[15] Friedman's *Capitalism and Freedom*, although not a canonical text, articulates, more so than Hayek for example, the case for laissez-faire Lockean conservatism. Kirk and Friedman's books deal directly with race, although the subject is not central to either work.

Hayek's work appears particularly ill-suited as a canonical text for American conservatism because Hayek explicitly rejects Lockean laissez-faire conservatism and allows for a programmatic agenda not unlike the New Deal. While Hayek argues that socialism and communism constitute roads to serfdom, he does not reject liberalism but what he calls "collectivism." Collectivism Hayck argued inevitably destroys individualism and democracy. Collectivism is "the abolition of private enterprise, of private ownership of the means of production, and the creation of a system of 'planned economy' in which the entrepreneur working for profit is replaced by a central planning body." However, he wrote that it was important "not to confuse this kind of planning with a dogmatic laissez faire attitude," and "[i]n no system that could be rationally defended would the state just do nothing."[16] Thus, Hayek explicitly rejects the Lockean "policemen state" and embraces the Rousseau "welfare state" writing that "there can be no doubt that some minimum of food, shelter, and clothing, sufficient to preserve health and the capacity to work, can be assured to everybody. Indeed, for a considerable part of the population of England this sort of security has already been achieved."[17] He also said that "there is no incompatibility in principle between the states providing greater security in this way and the preservation of individual freedom."[18]

Therefore, rather than embracing the *Lochner*-era negative state and laissez faire conservatism, Hayek's work is consistent with New Deal liberalism, which also rejected the abolition of private property and a planned economy. Indeed, Hayek's *Road to Serfdom* has much more in common with the liberalism of Schlesinger's *Vital Center* than it does, for example, with Friedman's *Capitalism and Freedom*.[19]

Kirk's *Conservative Mind* is also at war with laissez-faire Lockean conservatism and its emphasis on individualism. Kirk's book, which was originally submitted as his doctoral dissertation at Scotland's St. Andrew's University, is a self-conscious effort to use Burkean conservatism to defend the Lockean constitutional tradition in the United States. But he is strongly critical of Lockean "atomistic individualism," believing it should be held in check by Burke's traditions and prejudices and Christian morality. He was similarly skeptical about capitalism's tendency to undermine traditional values and ways of life. His book is a seminal contribution to the intellectual foundations of the conservative movement, widely hailed at the time and viewed today as a classic in American conservative thought.[20] In it he offers a defense of southern racism on barely disguised white supremacist grounds.

In his chapter on southern conservatism, Kirk writes "that while human slavery is bad ground for conservatives to make a stand upon, yet the wild demands and expectations of the abolitionists were quite as slippery a foundation for political decency."[21] Describing "Negros" as "the menace of debased, ignorant and abysmally poor folk," he argued they "must tend to produce in the minds of the dominant people an anxiety to preserve every detail of the present structure, and an ultra-vigilant suspicion of innovation."[22]

Thus, Kirk presents an apologia for racism, slavery and segregation on white supremacist and Burkean principles of tradition and stability. As I will show later in this chapter, Kirk's views were more or less adopted by William F. Buckley, *National Review* and many other conservatives after *Brown*.[23]

Before turning to *Brown*, Buckley, and *National Review*, Friedman's *Capitalism and Freedom* is a classic defense of Lockean laissez-faire capitalism and an attack on the whole New Deal legacy. Contrary to the Left—especially the black Left—Friedman argued that capitalism rather than a barrier to freedom and equality for blacks was structurally the greatest antidote to racism. That is, "The maintenance of the general rules of private property and of capitalism have been a major source of opportunity for Negroes and have permitted them to make greater progress than they otherwise could make."[24]

Thus, the key to moving toward racial equality was the abolition of welfare, public housing, and minimum wage and the adoption of such market-based programs as vouchers for education and housing.

Friedman also opposed all civil rights legislation because "such legislation clearly involves interference with the freedom of individuals to enter into voluntary contracts with one another."[25] Comparing fair employment legislation with the "Hitler Nuremburg laws,"[26] Friedman concluded that the appropriate way to end racism in a free society was for "those of us who believe that a particular criterion such as color is irrelevant is to persuade our fellows to be of like mind, not to use the coercive power of the state to force them to act in accordance with our principles."[27]

George Nash writes, "The civil rights and other minority movements each asserting its rights shocked conservatives."[28] He goes on to conclude that "dismay at the Warren Court was integral to American conservatism."[29] No case was a greater shock or more important in revitalizing the historic nexus between racism and modern conservatism than *Brown*. *Brown* was also an important catalyst in shifting conservatism away from its Burkean distrust of the masses toward an embrace of what came to be known as the silent majority.

Brown shocked conservatives first because it was a Supreme Court decision. Going back to the Federalists conservatives and racists had regarded the Court as near sacrosanct, viewing it as the guardian of laissez-faire capitalism, racism, and white supremacy. Far more than liberal or reform forces, conservatives in American history have embraced judicial review and judicial supremacy.[30] *Brown* upset all of these core assumptions of conservatives about the Court. In addition *Brown* gave symbolic assurance and support to the civil rights movement's bourgeoning challenge in the streets to the racist order. Of *Brown*, Regenery writes that for conservatives "the loss was overwhelming."[31]

Conservatives in 1954 had not recovered from the shock of what they saw as FDR's hijacking of the Court that forced it to abandon its guardian role with respect to laissez-faire capitalism and the limited power of the federal government. Racism, however, was another matter, although the Court in *Caroline Products* had indicated that it was perhaps going to become more solicitous of minority rights. And since the late 1930s it had incrementally begun to strike down racism in jury selection,[32] in housing covenants,[33] and in Democratic Party primaries in the South.[34] Further, with respect to *Plessy*, the Court in a series of cases had first required enforcement of the equality part of the decision in higher education[35] and then in *Sweatt vs. Painter* in 1949 had strongly hinted that segregation in graduate and professional education was presumptively unconstitutional.[36] Moreover, in *Sweatt* the Court had expressly reserved judgment on whether *Plessey* was inapplicable in public education generally.

Brown was nonetheless a shock to conservatives. First, because it was a unanimous decision, suggesting that the issues in the case and the decision itself were unambiguous. Second, the Court did not claim to be guided by the intent of the Fourteenth Amendment, claiming that its intent was "inconclusive" and in any case irrelevant because, unlike in 1868 when the amendment was ratified, "education is perhaps the most important function of state and local government." Third, the decision was based partly on modern psychological and sociological research, conducted by liberal academics, including the African American psychologist Kenneth Clark and Gunnar Myrdal, the Swedish economist.[37] Specifically, based on the Court's reading of the relevant research Warren wrote that legally sanctioned segregation "generates [in black school children] a feeling of inferiority as to their status in the community" that retards their mental and educational development. Finally, the opinion was a near explicit attack on the ideology of white supremacy, suggesting that the only logical basis for school segregation was a belief in black inferiority, a belief which the opinion suggested was rejected by "modern authority."[38]

The decision had an immediate and consequential impact on the conservative intellectual movement and its subsequent manifestation as a powerful political movement. Its first consequence was to draw explicit racists and white supremacists into the movement, requiring a "fusion" of their views with the anticommunists, the traditionalists and the laissez-faire Lockeans. The fusion of racism and white supremacy with the other elements of the conservative intellectual movement was not that difficult. First, a part of the traditionalist values was to some extent a defense of the tradition of racism and white supremacy in the South. Second, many conservatives and liberals alike contended that the civil rights movement was influenced if not controlled by international communism. In chapter 4 I noted Arthur Schlesinger's concerns in this regard, and in *The Mind of the South*, W. J. Cash wrote of "the bogey of the Negro turning communist and staging a Red revolution in the South."[39]

Second, *Brown* suggested to movement leaders that racist whites—north and south—might be mobilized into a racist, rightist bloc or coalition.[40] Nash sums up this un-Burkean turn toward the masses by saying that "the trend toward majoritarianism was enormously stimulated by a series of Supreme Court decisions that aroused not just conservative intellectuals but broad segments of the populace which right wingers could now, at long last, cultivate."[41]

Many conservatives opposed *Brown* on conservative and constitutional principles rather than on the basis of racism or white supremacy. Most also maintained their fidelity to judicial review and supremacy,[42] arguing not that the Court had exceeded its authority but rather simply that *Brown* was wrongly decided—grossly so.[43] Barry Goldwater, for example, in his widely read ideological manifesto *Conscience of a Conservative* and his syndicated newspaper columns attacked *Brown* on purely constitutional grounds:

> It so happens that I am in agreement with the *objectives* of the Supreme Court decision as stated in the *Brown* decision. I believe that it is both wise and just for negro (sic) children to attend the same schools as whites, and that to deny them this opportunity carries with it strong implications of inferiority. I am not prepared, however, to impose that judgment of mine on the people of Mississippi or South Carolina. . . . I have great respect for the Supreme Court as an institution, but I cannot believe I display that respect by submitting abjectly to abuses of power by the Court, and by condoning its unconstitutional trespass into the legislative sphere. . . . I am therefore not impressed by the claim that the Supreme Court's decision is the law of the land. The Constitution, and the laws "made in pursuance thereof" are the "supreme law of the land." The Constitution is what its authors intended it to be and said it was—not what the Supreme Court says it is.[44]

Similarly Robert Bork, the conservative movement's leading jurisprudential scholar, objected to the Civil Rights Act of 1964 on conservative constitutional principles, calling the landmark legislation "unsurpassed ugliness."[45] Bork, like Friedman, said the core principle at stake in any civil rights law was individual liberty of persons to do with their property as they wished, including denying access to persons because of their race.[46] However, he also wrote, "It is also appropriate to question the practicality of enforcing a law which runs contrary to the customs, indeed the moral beliefs, of a large portion of the country."[47] But some in the conservative intellectual movement rejected *Brown* on both conservative and explicitly racist and white supremacist principles.[48] Foremost among these was William F. Buckley considered below, but aside from Buckley the most influential racist, white supremacist critic of *Brown* was James J. Kilpatrick. Kilpatrick, the editor of the *Richmond Time Dispatch* and subsequently a nationally syndicated columnist and national television news commentator, on the basis of his 1962 book *The Southern Case for Segregation*, became a regular contributor to *National Review* and "one of its more or less 'official' spokesmen on constitutional issues and civil rights."[49]

Kilpatrick's book is divided into three parts. The first is the standard conservative attack on *Brown*. Here Kilpatrick argues that the courts should interpret the Constitution and its amendments strictly in terms of the intent of the framers. The framers of the Fourteenth Amendment did not intend to abolish school segregation; thus, under federalism, Kilpatrick argued, it was up to each state to decide the question. Finally, constitutionally, he argued the decision was a case of blatant judicial activism based on social and psychological theories rather than sound constitutional principles.

The second part of the book is an analysis of the future. Here Kilpatrick suggests that racial segregation is legally and constitutionally dead, noting that the *Brown* desegregation principle had been applied to cases involving golf courses, courthouses, and other public places. However, given this inevitability, he urges "patience"; desegregation can come only "slowly, cautiously, voluntarily" at "some time in the future."[50] This he calls the "doctrine of gradualism." Further, he predicts that *Brown* notwithstanding, the South would likely maintain near "total segregation" in elementary and secondary education because "the intimate, personal and prolonged association of white and Negro boys and girls in public schools, in massive numbers, as social equals, is more than community attitudes will accept."[51]

Rather than accept school desegregation Kilpatrick predicted the complete withdrawal and abandonment of the public schools by whites. Among the reasons whites would likely never accept school desegregation, Kilpatrick wrote, they simply were "appalled by the sexual mores and violent attitudes of some Negro pupils."[52] Writing that these mores and attitudes and the low performance of blacks on the IQ test may be innate, he concluded, "If these Negro characteristics *are* innate, the white southerner sees nothing but disaster to his race in risking accelerated intermingling of blood lines."[53] Kilpatrick also predicted that whites would never allow their children to be taught by blacks, and therefore the likely result of *Brown* would be the wholesale firing of black teachers and principals.

Segregation will also likely be maintained in the protestant churches; and he wrote that "whatever the Supreme Court may do . . . to the miscegenation laws, ostracism, swift and certain awaits those who cross the marital line."[54] In public accommodations such as hotels, restaurants, and other quasipublic places "doors that have closed will open one by one."[55] And, "A South that once would have regarded these innovations with horror will view them first with surprise, then with regret, at times distaste and at last with indifference."[56]

Thus Kilpatrick foresaw and grudgingly accommodated the gradual southern acceptance of the inevitable. However, in the third part of the book, he presents a forthright white supremacist defense of racism. Echoing the antebellum ideas of Fitzhugh Kilpatrick, he wrote "[O]over a thousand years, the Negro race, as a race, has failed to contribute significantly to the higher and noble achievements of civilization as the West defines that term . . . [F]rom the dawn of civilization to the middle of the twentieth century, the Negro race, as a race, has contributed little more than a few grains of sand to the enduring monuments of mankind."[57]

Kilpatrick also displays the paternalism typical of antebellum slaveholders and their apologists, writing that "what is so often misunderstood outside of the South is that delicate intimacy of human beings, whose lives are so intimately bound together.... In plain fact, the relationship between white and Negro in the segregated South, in the country and city, has been far closer, more honest, less constrained, than such relationships generally in the integrated North." He then goes on to write of his fondness as a boy for "two Negroes who served my family for more than twenty years." He refers to the two servants as "Lizzie" and "Nash."[58]

On whether "Negro" inferiority is innate, Kilpatrick professes to be agnostic, but in any event he thinks the question is irrelevant: "In terms of the problems immediately at hand, the question of whether the Negro's shortcomings are 'innate' seems to me largely irrelevant anyhow. The issue is not likely to be proved to the satisfaction of either side any time soon; it may not be susceptible of proof at all. Whether these characteristics are inherited or acquired, they *are*."[59]

Kilpatrick's book was severely criticized in the liberal media, partly because of its open espousal of by then discredited white supremacist and racist dogmas. Since at least the publication of Myrdal's work liberal scholars and journalists accepted the proposition that the Negroes' alleged inferiority was a product of environmental conditions, specifically, their environment of racial oppression. Kilpatrick sneeringly dismisses this view, writing that "one inquires, why pray has it taken so long for the Negroes innately equal potentialities to emerge, the answers trail off into lamentations on the conditions under which the Negro has lived. The fault, if there is any fault, is held not to be in men's genes, but in their substandard housing."[60]

Although Kilpatrick's book was dismissed by liberals, it was passionately embraced by many in the conservative intellectual movement, including Buckley, the movement's most prominent and influential public intellectual.[61]

William F. Buckley Jr. and the Fusion of Racism in the Conservative Intellectual Movement

Of Buckley, Hodgson writes that he "is probably the most important single figure in the whole history of the revival of conservatism in late twentieth century America."[62] And Nash writes, "To a very substantial degree, the history of reflective conservatism in America after 1955 is the history of the individuals who collaborated in—or were discovered by—the magazine William F. Buckley founded."[63] Buckley, through *National Review*, the journal he founded in 1955, is generally credited more than any other person with making fusion a success, providing a forum and the intellectual leadership that facilitated unity among Lockean laissez-faire conservatives, the traditionalist, and the anticommunists. Although less acknowledged, Buckley also must be credited with making racism and white supremacy integral parts of modern postwar conservatism.[64]

In 1951 Buckley, fresh out of Yale, published *God and Man at Yale*, a caustic polemic castigating the Yale faculty for its anti-Christian, collectivist liberalism. The book caused a sensation in conservative intellectual circles, became a *New York Times* bestseller, and almost overnight made Buckley a leading popularizer of a militant conservatism. (For more than three decades Buckley was the only conservative with a nationally televised program, broadcast on PBS). Four years later, with the help of a subvention from his father and other wealthy patrons, he founded *National Review*, which quickly became the principal organ of the conservative movement in the United States. In its inaugural issue Buckley, who from the outset exercised near complete editorial control, wrote that the magazine would stand "athwart history yelling stop." Stop the transgressions of the New Deal's "collectivism." Stop the spread of Communism; indeed role back the Communist advances in Eastern Europe and elsewhere.[65] Then, after *Brown*, stop the advance of the movement for civil rights and racial justice.

Throughout the 1950s and early 1960s Buckley and *National Review* opposed the civil rights movement and the decolonialization struggles in Africa on explicit white supremacist grounds. For example, in a 1957 editorial entitled "Why the South Must Prevail" Buckley wrote:

> The central question that emerges—and it is not a parliamentary question or a question that is answered by merely consulting a catalog of the rights of American citizens, born equal—is whether the white community in the South is entitled to take such measures as are necessary to prevail, politically and culturally, in areas in which it does not predominate numerically? The sobering answer is Yes—the white community is so entitled because, for the time being, it is the advanced race. It is not easy, and it is unpleasant, to adduce statistics evidencing the median cultural superiority of white over Negro: but it is fact that obtrudes, one that cannot be hidden by ever-so-busy egalitarians and anthropologists. The question, as far as the White community is concerned, is whether the claims of civilization supersede those of universal suffrage. The British believe they do, and acted accordingly, in Kenya, where the choice was dramatically one between civilization and barbarism, and elsewhere; the South, where the conflict is by no means dramatic, as in Kenya, nevertheless perceives important qualitative differences between its culture and the Negroes', and intends to assert its own.

> *National Review* believes that the South's premises are correct. If the majority wills what is socially atavistic, and then to thwart the majority may be, though undemocratic, enlightened. It is more important for any community, anywhere in the world, to affirm and live by civilized standards, than to bow to the demands of the numerical majority. Sometimes it becomes impossible to assert the will of minority, in which case it may give way, and the society will regress; sometimes the numerical minority cannot prevail except by violence: then it must determine whether the prevalence of its will is worth the terrible price of violence.[66]

In *Up from Liberalism* (the title is a deliberate play on Booker Washington's *Up from Slavery*) Buckley's most systematic exposition of his ideology (although it is little more then a callow polemic), he rejected the idea of the innate inferiority of blacks, writing, "There are no scientific grounds for assuming congenital Negro disabilities. The problem is not biological, but cultural and educational."[67] Nevertheless, he argued that African peoples everywhere were inferior to Europeans everywhere and that liberal advocates of equality and universal suffrage were undermining standards of civilization.[68]

Finally Buckley suggested that the civil rights movement might represent a challenge to property-centered laissez-faire capitalism. In an observation evocative of critics of black suffrage during Reconstruction, Buckley writing of why southern blacks should be denied the franchise said one reason was economic (the other was educational; blacks he argued would likely seek to integrate the schools, which would lower "intellectual and moral standards.") Of the economic reason he wrote, "The Negroes in the South comprise, generally speaking, the lowest economic class. Given plenipotentiary political power, Negroes would be likely to use it to levy even further (Negro facilities are for the most part paid for by dollars taxed from whites) against the propertied class—which is, by and large, composed of whites. I believe it is a man's right to use his political influence to protect his property; but one should be plain about what one is up to, as not all Southerners are."[69]

In Africa Buckley argued that to accede to African demands for independence would result in a "return to barbarism."[70] Frequently, he ridiculed the African independence movements and their leaders, telling *Esquire* in a 1961 interview that Africans would be ready for independence "when they stopped eating each other," and in a speech that year he called the Congolese people "semi-savages."[71] *National Review* during the 1950s and 1960s published a large number of articles deprecating the humanity of Africans and calling for their continued domination by any European peoples willing to continue to bear the white man's burden.[72]

Not all of *National Review*'s contributors defended the South on racist and white supremacist principles; many invoked principles of federalism and the limited reach of federal authority.[73] Also, Buckley carefully avoided association with vulgar southern racists such as George Wallace and Mississippi governor Ross Barnett, but in the final analysis in the struggle for civil rights Buckley and *National Review* lined up on the side of southern racist and white supremacist. Conservatism and racism, in other words, for Buckley and his circle were almost always the same. Similarly, opposition to the decolonialization of Africa, like opposition to the debastardization of Locke, was sometimes couched in terms of political stability and Communist subversion, but the consequences were nevertheless support for racism and advocacy of the ideology of white supremacy.

Buckley was not only an important and influential public intellectual; he was also a politically engaged partisan. In 1961 the Young Americans for Freedom (YAF) was organized under his personal tutelage at his house in Connecticut. YAF became the young shock troops of the 1964 Goldwater insurgency.[74] Buckley was close to Goldwater strategically and personally (his brother-in-law, Brent Bozell, ghost wrote Goldwater's book, and Goldwater wrote the forward to *Up from Liberalism*); Buckley wrote that he considered Goldwater the magazine's "most prominent constituent."[75] Ronald Reagan proclaimed *National Review* his "favorite magazine" and was said to be in "awe of Buckley's intelligence."[76]

In 1965 Buckley ran a quixotic campaign for major of New York. Having no wish to win (when asked what would he do if he won, he quipped, "I would demand a recount"), he ran in order to demonstrate to conservatives that they could attract white "ethnic" votes,[77] by appealing to their fiscal conservatism, fear of blacks, and concerns about crime and welfare. Described by the *New York Times* as a campaign based on bigotry and racism,[78] Judis concluded that in its "contours although not its size Buckley's coalition perfectly anticipated the northern urban coalition that Ronald Reagan would create in 1980 and 1984 and that would allow him to carry New York City."[79]

Rossiter labeled Buckley's ideology as "ultraconservatism," and not really conservatism but a "dangerous radicalism."[80] Of Buckley and his crowd, Rossiter wrote they must be judged "reactionaries" because "in their indignation over the trends of the past quarter century they are seeking purposefully to roll back the social process to 1948 or 1932 or even, if we can believe what some of them say, to 1896." [81]

Although the ultraconservatives moderated their views between the Goldwater insurgency in 1964 and Reagan's election in 1980, this kind of conservative racism was an integral component of the movement—adjusted to the exigencies of changing circumstances—that came to power in 1980. Buckley celebrated this event as a guest of honor at the inaugural and as a frequent companion and confidant of the president.

CHAPTER SEVEN

Racism and Neoconservatism, 1968–1980

Modern conservatism after 1945 was a reaction to the New Deal, modernity, international Communism, and the beginnings of the protest phase of the civil rights movement. Neoconservatism or the men and women who became neoconservatives generally supported the New Deal, modernity, *Brown*, and the early civil rights protest. Cold war liberals, they viewed the civil rights struggle as part of the campaign against international communism. These erstwhile liberals (and in some cases radicals) embraced conservatism when the civil rights movement turned toward radicalism, as a reaction to the black power movement;[1] the ghetto revolts;[2] and Martin Luther King's increasing radicalism as manifested in his opposition to the Vietnam War and his call for "a radical restructuring" of the economy in order to achieve a more equalitarian society.[3]

Neoconservatism was also a response to Lyndon Johnson's Great Society or, more precisely, to its War on Poverty and affirmative action, policies that were viewed as dangerous steps toward an equalitarianism that threatened to undermine core Lockean values. Thus, like traditional postwar conservatism, neoconservatism emerged in the 1960s partly as a response to the black struggle for equality.

But like traditional conservatism neoconservatism was a fusion of reactions by some liberals to multiple developments of the 1960s and early 1970s. My focus is on the role of race and racism. But neoconservatism was also a reaction to the campus rebellions that began at Berkeley in 1964, to the adversarial youth counterculture, and to the antiwar and feminist movements.

Also like traditional conservatism, neoconservatism was first an intellectual movement premised on the Weaverian notion that ideas have consequences, consequences, that is, if they are well financed and publicized and have access to the suites of power. The neoconservatives also drew on some of the same intellectual resources as the conservatives, including Burke and Leo Strauss. But ultimately they too were Lockeans defending a debastardized Locke against liberal, Rousseanlike challenges. Like their traditional counterparts, as conservatives they were sometimes breathtakingly inconsistent, attacking the elites of the culture while pandering to the masses.

This majoritarian element of neoconservatism was in sync with the efforts of conservative politicians such as George Wallace, Richard Nixon, and Ronald Reagan to awaken and politically mobilize the "Silent Majority" that was "unyoung, unpoor, and unblack" in a backlash against the forces of social change.[4]

Neoconservatism's intellectual assault on the black quest for equality can be traced through an examination of its ideas about equality generally and its specific attacks on the welfare state, affirmative action, and the War on Poverty. Although these ideas were generally expressed in race-neutral language, they often had a specifically racial and at times white supremacist component. In both its race-neutral and race-specific components neoconservatism and racism in effect became the same. Finally, the neoconservative movement and the election of President Reagan helped to give rise to a small but vocal group of black neoconservatives who, unlike Booker Washington and George Schuyler, were not required to embrace conservatism because of fear of extermination.

I examine each of these aspects of the neoconservative movement in this chapter; however, before doing so, I should note that traditional conservatism as expressed in the pages of *National Review* was not silent in response to the civil rights movement's turn toward radicalism. Rather, after its grudging accommodation to the civil rights reforms enacted in the mid-1960s, it resurrected the Reconstruction era ideas of Andrew Johnson, the Supreme Court, and Booker Washington.

In the *Civil Rights Cases of 1883* Justice Joseph Bradley wrote: "When a man has emerged from slavery, and by the aid of beneficent legislation has shaken off the inseparable concomitants of that state, there must be some stage in the progress of his elevation when he takes the rank of a mere citizen, and ceases to be the special favorite of the laws, and when his rights as a citizen, or a man, are to be protected in the ordinary modes by which other men's rights are protected."[5] In his 1866 veto of the *Freedmen's Bureau Act,* President Johnson wrote, "The idea on which the slaves were assisted to freedom was that on becoming free they would be a self-sustaining population. Any legislation that shall imply they are not expected to attain a self-sustaining condition must have a tendency injurious alike to their character and their prospects."[6] In his plan to achieve full citizenship for the Negro, Booker T. Washington in 1899 urged blacks to establish businesses and acquire property, while recognizing that their condition could not be elevated by "artificial methods" or a "mere battledore and shuttlecock of words."[7]

Several contributors to *National Review* in the late 1960s embraced these themes. For example, in a 1967 editorial *National Review* gave a cautious endorsement to black power, contending that racial integration was impossible and that black power, stripped of its radical rhetoric, could be a philosophy for black self-help and separate development within the confines of the ghettos. Jeffrey Hart argued that the disabilities faced by blacks in the ghettos were not—as the Kerner Commission suggested—caused by racism but rather were the results of a cultural "lag" among blacks manifested in their lack of "coherent" institutions, ethnic solidarity, stable families, and entrepreneurial capabilities. The solutions he suggested were a regimen of Friedmanlike reforms (changes in welfare to encourage work, elimination of minimum wage, rent controls, etc.) and efforts to encourage black solidarity and separatism. Ultimately he suggested that the solution was "hard work and discipline" in the tradition of Booker Washington.[8]

National Review's contributors also warned that the civil rights movement's shift toward radicalism was genuine and represented a threat to the system and should be repressed. Meyer warned that the civil rights movement was shifting toward revolutionary agitation in pursuit of a program of "confiscatory socialism" and that it should be forcefully repressed.[9] And Buckley wrote in *The Jeweler's Eye* that King's planned poor peoples campaign would cripple the nation's capital and that this "incipient revolution" demanded repression. "Repression" he wrote was "an unpleasant instrument, but it is absolutely necessary for a civilization that believes in order and human rights. I wish to God Hitler and Lenin had been repressed."[10]

Meanwhile, a small group of liberal intellectuals, mainly Jewish, observing these developments were, to use Irving Kristol's phrase, "mugged by reality" and began to bring the sophisticated tools of modern social science and the polemical skills of the New York literati to the task of blunting the impact of the black movement.[11] Ultimately, they were to be much more consequential intellectually and politically than the crowd around Buckley at *National Review*.

Origins of Neoconservatism

Irving Kristol, often referred to as the "godfather" of the neoconservative movement, defined it as an "impulse" or "persuasion" emerging out of the academic-intellectual world, provoked by disillusionment with contemporary liberalism.[12] As I indicated, this disillusionment had several sources, but prominent among them was the turn toward substantive or Roussean equality on the part of the federal government and the civil rights movement. These "right-wing liberals," to use George Nash's phrase, were intent on stopping any efforts by the federal government to bring about a racially equalitarian society.[13] They were especially repelled by President Johnson's argument that the Lockean notion of equality of opportunity was not enough, given the centuries of Locke's bastardization. Rather, the president at Howard University had said, "[W]e seek not just equality as a right and a theory but equality as fact and equality as a result." Although many other influences shaped the neoconservative movement, its hostility to government efforts to promote racial equality was perhaps central to its domestic concerns.[14]

The neoconservatives invoked Burkean principles of aristocracies of merit, skepticism about social change, stability, and moderation as intellectual weapons in the war against the equalitarian impulses of the 1960s and 1970s.[15] Ironically, however, they saw as their principal adversaries not the masses but their fellow academics and intellectuals, whom they derisively referred to as the "new class." This new class of liberal intellectuals, neoconservatives argued, was willing to risk the stability of society in pursuit of their vision of racial equalitarianism. Echoing William Buckley's famous quip that he would rather be governed by the first two thousand names randomly selected from the Boston telephone directory than the Harvard faculty, Kristol argued that neoconservatives should rely on the common sense of the people rather than the "unwisdom of its governing elites" in politics, the judiciary, the universities, and the media.[16] Kristol was referring of course to the common sense of white people, and it seems not to have occurred to him that he and his colleagues were an integral part of the very governing elite he disparaged.[17]

Neoconservatism was therefore an intellectual movement in search of a mass constituency that would allow it to capture power through the democratic process. But it was first an intellectual movement, a movement of ideas deliberately designed to shape public opinion, campaigns, and elections and the making of public policy. Unlike traditional conservatism, neoconservatism cannot boast of any number of seminal books. Indeed, in reading the neoconservative corpus one is hard pressed to find a single intellectually significant book or even journal article. Rather, most of the writings are shallow polemics without enduring intellectual or academic value.[18]

Most scholars agree on a consensus list of the major contributors to the origins and maturation of neoconservatism in America. In addition to Kristol, virtually all students of the movement would include on this list Norman Podhoretz, Nathan Glazer, Edward Banfield, James Q. Wilson, Midge Decter, Aaron Wildavsky, and Gertrude Himmelfarb, Daniel Bell, the cofounder with Kristol of *The Public Interest*, is also sometimes included, although from the beginning he contended that he was not a conservative of any sort, neo or otherwise. Daniel Patrick Moynihan is also sometimes included, although he, while a consummate intellectual and political opportunist, never abandoned liberalism and for all of his career was a passionate advocate of various and sundry strategies to achieve racial equality.[19]

Neoconservatives and their ideas have had and continue to have consequences. This, however, is because they and their ideas have been well financed by what Saloma calls a" labyrinth" of conservative corporate donors, philanthropists, and foundations.[20] Blumenthal tells an interesting story of how money can make intellectuals and their ideas consequential. Charles Murray in the 1970s was an unknown scholar in Iowa, whose principal claim to fame was an obscure pamphlet written for the Heritage Foundation titled "Safety Nets and the Truly Needy," which argued that welfare caused poverty. However, according to Blumenthal, William Hammett, president of the Manhattan Institute, saw Murray as a " 'nobody' who could be somebody" and therefore raised more than $100,000 to allow him to turn his ideas on welfare and poverty into a book ($25,000 was raised by Kristol from the Olin Foundation). After Murray completed the book (*Losing Ground: American Social Policy, 1950–1980,* Basic Books, 1984), ten thousand dollars was raised to sponsor a two-day conference on the book with the participation of some of the nation's leading scholars, liberal and conservative, of social welfare policy. Finally, to bring Murray to the attention of the public a major book tour with lectures and radio and television interviews was set up by the institute. Blumenthal wrote, "In just months, Murray was transformed from a 'nobody' into an intellectual star" ... although the book was beset with errors and omissions."[21]

Conservative donors helped fund and sustain *The Public Interest*, which over the years provided a patina of social science legitimacy to the assault on government social policies (turning the idea of the unintended consequences into almost a law of social policy in the United States) as well as a forum for the popular consumption of academic research. *Commentary*, the journal of the American Jewish Committee, also was transformed (edited by Podhorez) into a forum for a systematic assault on the civil rights and black power movements and the Great Society. Many of the neoconservatives found well-funded perches in the labyrinth of conservative think tanks, which gave them ready access to the national media and to the corridors of power in Washington.[22] And once Ronald Reagan became president many were inhabitants of these corridors. Meanwhile mainstream African American intellectuals and their ideas were marginalized and relegated to the fringes of public discourse;[23] while at the same time new cadres of black conservative intellectuals were subsidized in order to discredit the black intellectual and political establishment and legitimatize in the broader community neoconservative ideas about race.[24]

In the following pages I examine the neoconservative attack on the post–civil rights era quest for racial equality. The assault on racial equality was not the only element of the neoconservative domestic agenda. However, it along with its use of traditionalism as an ideology facilitated a fusion with more traditional conservatives, and their ideas together were used to mobilize the "common sense" of white people in an antiblack equality majority electoral coalition.[25]

Equality and Affirmative Action

Neoconservatism, like traditional conservatism going back to Locke and Burke, sees a fundamental incompatibility between liberty and equality. That is, any effort by the state to achieve an equalitarian society must inevitably infringe on the liberty of some, especially the some with wealth and property.[26] In this view they are undoubtedly correct; the Lockean view of the framers that you could have "liberty and justice" for all is at war with the idea that individuals should have the liberty to accumulate and use the unlimited wealth of their labor and pass it on to their descendants, while others are at liberty to live in poverty.[27] Thus, equalitarianism going back to Rousseau has always accepted this tension between liberty and equality as an inevitable part of the redistribution of wealth that is the objective of democratic politics. Conservatives have always claimed that in the contest between the two liberty was more important than equality. Neoconservatism contributes nothing new to this centuries old debate about economic liberty and social justice.

In the 1960s, however, as the quest for equality in the United States was increasingly racialized, the neoconservatives did make a distinctive contribution to the war against equality. As I indicated in chapter 5, African American thought from at least Reconstruction has contained a powerful equalitarian impulse, and African American public opinion has favored government policies to reduce income inequality between rich and poor. In the late 1960s these African Americanist views on equality were not limited to intellectuals and a silent black public. Rather, they were attached to a powerful social movement led by Dr. King and linked to violent disorders in the ghettos and an ascendant radicalism represented by the black power movement. Dr. King contended that the objectives of his poor people's campaign was to elevate the conditions of all poor Americans, but everyone knew this was only incidental; the real objective of the campaign was to close disparities in income and life chances between blacks and whites. That is not to create an equalitarian society per se but rather a society where race did not predict one's employment, income, or life chances. This objective of racial equality King understood, however, would likely require a radical restructuring of the economy. Bayard Rustin, neoconservatism's favorite black intellectual, understood this relationship between racial equality and radicalism. Although Rustin, a long-time democratic socialist, opposed King's methods, he supported his objectives.[28] That is, Rustin in strategy sessions with King argued that the goals of the poor people's campaign were more likely to be achieved through "politics" rather then "protest."[29]

In a 1965 article that was later to become famous and, ironically, originally published in *Commentary*, Rustin wrote, "I believe that the Negro's struggle for equality in America is essentially revolutionary. While most Negroes—in their hearts—unquestionably seek only to enjoy the fruits of American society as it now exists, their quest cannot *objectively* be satisfied within the framework of existing political and economic relations."[30] Rustin went on to argue that the civil rights movement was evolving into a "full-fledged social movement" concerned not merely with removing the barriers to full opportunity but with achieving the *fact* of equality."[31] Rustin was explicit and detailed in the pages of *Commentary* about the revolutionary implications of this next phase of the black movement, writing:

> [T]he term revolutionary, as I am using it does not connote violence; it refers to the qualitative transformation of fundamental institutions, more or less rapidly, to the point where the social and economic structure which they comprised can no longer be said to be the same. The Negro struggle has hardly run its course; and it will not stop moving until it has been utterly defeated or won substantial equality. But I fail to see how the movement can be victorious in the absence of radical programs for full employment, the abolition of slums, the reconstruction of our educational system, new definitions of work and leisure. Adding up the cost of such programs, we can only conclude that we are talking about a refashioning of our political economy.[32]

If this radical turn toward equalitarianism on the part of the civil rights movement, black power radicalism, and ghetto revolts was not enough, the neoconservatives were equally alarmed—perhaps more so—that the views of Rustin were getting a favorable hearing in some quarters of the Johnson administration and were being fueled by the "rising expectations" of the poor as result of the War on Poverty. Finally, elements of the "new class" were providing intellectual legitimacy to these dangerous developments.[33]

The neoconservatives responded with the usual right-wing nostrums about the limited role of government (and increasingly its limited capabilities), but with respect to racial equality they began to articulate the notion that the inequality between blacks and whites was not structural (in the sense of being caused by racism or chronic unemployment) but rather was psychological or cultural. It was not the fault of "white racism" as suggested by Myrdal in the 1940s or the Kerner Commission (with its new class staff) in 1968; nor was it the fault of flaws in capitalism but rather black-white inequality as it was manifested in the ghettos was the fault of black people themselves. By the time of Reagan's election with the massive outpouring of writings on the so-called black underclass—writings by liberal/Left as well as conservative and neoconservative scholars—this idea had become dominant in Washington policy circles.[34]

But this line of thinking about the ghetto poor has its origins in the writings of influential neoconservative intellectuals. First and perhaps most important was Edward Banfield's widely read and reviewed 1968 book *The Unheavenly City*, which established the parameters for neoconservative understanding of race, class, and poverty. Banfield's work used as a point of departure Oscar Lewis' theory that the ethnic ghettos (in Lewis' case Mexican American and Puerto Rican) of America are characterized by a culture of poverty. However, he rejected Lewis' notion that this culture was generated as a response and adaptation to structural deficiencies in capitalism and inadequacies in the welfare state.[35] Instead, Banfield contended that the culture of poverty observed in American cities was rooted in complex psychological processes, writing that "extreme present orientedness, not lack of income or wealth is the principal cause of poverty in the sense of the culture of poverty."[36] Banfield carefully avoids any discussion of race or ethnicity as casual or correlated with this present-oriented psyche, although the urban lower class that he writes of is disproportionately black and Latino. However, his theory bears striking similarities to the work of Edward Rossin, an early twentieth-century white supremacist. In a 1901 article Rossin argued that Europeans, what he called the more "energetic races," were future oriented, valuing foresight and the capacity to defer gratification, while blacks and others "live from hand to mouth taking no thought of tomorrow."[37] Banfield does not cite this work.

Related to this kind of neoconservative thinking about race, class, and inequality, in his 1978 paean, *Two Cheers for Capitalism*, the godfather himself in an argument that anticipates by two decades Charles Murray and Richard Herrnstein's *The Bell Curve* wrote: "Human talents and abilities, as measured, do tend to distribute themselves along a bell-shaped curve, with most people clustered around the middle, and with much smaller percentages at the lower and higher ends.... Moreover it is a demonstrable fact that in all modern, bourgeois societies, the distribution of income is also roughly along a bell-shaped curve, indicating that in such an "open" society inequalities that do emerge are not inconsistent with the [Lockean] bourgeois notion of [natural] inequality."[38] Aside from the Great Society's War on Poverty (discussed below), the principal policies to close the equality gap between blacks and whites was court-ordered busing for purposes of school desegregation and affirmative action in access to employment, higher education, and government contracting. Nathan Glazer led the attack on these programs. Although busing was a flawed policy as a remedy to the fundamentals of educational disparities between blacks and whites, it was effective in some parts of the country and might have been more so if the Supreme Court had allowed cross-district busing between city and suburb.[39] Glazer, however, presented an unnuanced assault, viewing busing as just another new class social experiment that was educationally irrelevant and socially and politically disruptive.

Glazer's 1975 work *Affirmative Discrimination: Ethnic Inequality and Public Policy* was the first book-length attack on affirmative action. From a chaste Lockean perspective affirmative action for sure raises novel and difficult philosophical, constitutional, and policy questions. But for blacks in the immediate aftermath of the abolition of more than two hundred years of a bastardized Locke, these questions likely seem disingenuous and opposition to affirmative action as a means to remedy past wrongs and move toward a more racially equalitarian and just society seems perverse, if not racist.[40] And from the perspective of a Burkean conservative interest in stability and harmony; affirmative action is a most effective and relatively costless mechanism for integrating blacks into elite institutions and thereby contributing to racial peace and stability.[41]

In addition to arguing that affirmative action undermined the Lockean commitment to individual rights, Glazer and other neoconservatives argued that in the post–civil rights era racism was no longer a major barrier to black access to education and employment; that affirmative action did very little to assist lower income blacks; that it fueled resentment among lower-middle-class white "ethnics"; and that it devalued the achievements of successful blacks who were all viewed as "affirmative action babies." Finally, there was the question of whether it was good for Jews. Jews have historically been disadvantaged by anti-Semitic quotas at elite institutions, and there was concern that they might be disadvantaged by the use of quotas for affirmative action purposes. Daniel Patrick Moynihan stated this concern bluntly: "If ethnic quotas are to be imposed on American universities and similarly quasipublic institutions, it is Jews who will be driven out."[42]

Neoconservatism as an ideology has its origins in a number of developments of the 1960s, and the movement has diverse personalities with distinctive approaches to these developments, but as Sara Diamond writes, what unified them was an "evolving critique of fellow liberals['] view that the state essentially had a role to play in effecting greater social equality."[43] The neoconservatives may not have been animated by racism (although certainly there appears elements of white supremacist thinking in some of their writings), but their ideological concerns about the tensions between liberty and equality, their devotion to an abstract, chaste Locke while ignoring the consequences of its long racial bastardization, and their wariness about the disruptive effects of government efforts to achieve racial equality made neoconservatism and racism in the late 1970s essentially the same.

The Great Society as the Neoconservative Bogeyman

Most neoconservatives, unlike the traditional conservatives, supported the centerpieces of President Johnson's Great Society reforms, including civil rights, federal aid to education, and Medicare. These programs were in their view merely an extension of New Deal liberalism. Aside from civil rights, the core of these reforms was the provision of medical care to the elderly and the poor funded on the basis of a payroll tax. Like Social Security, these were universal, entitlement programs that ostensibly would be paid for by the recipients. In other words, they were classic New Deal liberalism in that in principle they did not involve the redistribution of income or any radical restructuring of the health care industry.

What the neoconservatives could not abide was the Great Society's War on Poverty, because unlike Medicare the War on Poverty was specifically designed to deal with the problem of racial inequality. That is, the programs were aimed at addressing the disproportionate incidence of poverty in the rural South and the urban ghettos. Although African American leaders were not involved in the design or implementation of the war, many scholars view it as a natural outcome of the civil rights movement. John Donovan in his account of the war's origins writes that it was a "prime example of [legislation] drafted principally for the poor Negro although public discussion of the program has seldom been completely candid in acknowledging this fact . . . but the urgent necessity of an all out attack on the pathology of the dark ghetto dictated the prime objective of the war on poverty."[44]

The 1965 Watts riot and the subsequent rebellions in other cities added to the sense of urgency.[45] Because of the near universal hostility to the war among conservatives in Congress and diminution of attention and resources because of the war on Vietnam, which began at about the same time the War on Poverty was not, to use Dr. King's phrase, "even a good skirmish."[46] The initial 1964 budget for the war (specifically for the Office of Economic Opportunity [OEO], the lead agency in the war) was $750 million, in 1965 $1.5 billion and in 1967 the president requested $1.75 billion. But in 1966 OEO was already funding projects at an amount projected at nearly $2 billion. Thus, within two years the war was being underfunded, in part because of the need to shift funds to fight the war on Vietnam. As a result, the War on Poverty came to end before it really began.[47]

Nevertheless, neoconservative intellectuals targeted the War on Poverty with vengeance, making it the major example of the "failed policies of the 1960s," a refrain used over and over by Reagan in his 1976 and 1980 presidential campaigns. As Kristol wrote in a retrospective on neoconservatism, "[W]e were especially provoked by the widespread acceptance of left-wing sociological ideas that were incorporated into the war on poverty."[48]

The neoconservatives initially made their case against the war in two seminal articles, one by Glazer and the other by Wildavsky.[49] These ideas had consequences so that by the time of Reagan's election they were orthodox not only among conservatives but among most liberals as well.

In his 1971 article Glazer argued that partly because of the "revolt of the blacks," the nation faced a "crisis in social policy." In attempting to deal with the problem of black poverty, Glazer contended that government was making things worse by breaking down "traditional mechanisms" for addressing social problems such as the family, church, and neighborhood. Thus, "our efforts to deal with distress themselves increase distress."[50] Second, the war was contributing to a "revolution of rising expectations" and a revolutionary "demand for equality" that the government was incapable of satisfying.[51]

The government was incapable of satisfying the demand because of the limitations of resources, the lack of knowledge, and the complexity of the problem. Overall, Glazer said that much of black poverty was, he thought, cultural, mainly, the breakdown of male responsibility for the family. Government could do little about this. Rather, what was required was a return on the part of blacks to "traditional practices and restraints" regarding work, sexuality, and family.[52] Government efforts to intervene with welfare or other antipoverty policies not only would not work; the evidence Glazer suggested was that they were likely to be perverse, to make things worse. This became the neoconservative mantra on social policy; because of the "law of unintended consequences," government should do nothing, because to do anything ran the risk of inevitably making things worse. This, then, would contribute to more dissatisfaction with government which in turn would raise expectations further leading to more new class social experiments in an endless cycle of demands. This in the end would ultimately undermine the economy and society.

Wildavsky in "Government and the People" reenforces the Glazer thesis about the limits and unintended consequences of social policy. Of the War on Poverty, he wrote that "no previous government had ever attempted to do for this sector of the population—those whom Marx called the "lumpen proletariat"—what the American government set out to do. Yet nobody knew *how* to go about it either."[53] Arguing elsewhere that the conditions of blacks were improving while the rhetoric of dissatisfaction was increasing,[54] Wildavsky concluded that the federal government should abandon efforts to address the problems of the "severely deprived" because, "[t]he escalation of demands together with the lack of knowledge of solutions meant a multiplication of programs, each under or over-financed, each justified by the notion that it was somehow an experiment that would prove something."[55]

Instead of government action the neoconservatives joined the traditional conservatives in insisting that the problem of black poverty was best left to the market, the state and local governments, the family, and the neighborhood. In this way, at least, responsibility for failure would be dispersed, and the federal government would no longer be burdened by demands it could not satisfy and should not attempt to satisfy.[56]

Again, by the time of Reagan's election to the presidency these neoconservative ideas were commonplace; indeed Reagan incorporated many of them into his rhetoric and into his approach to governance. Bill Clinton in his 1992 campaign and in his approach to governance also embraced these ideas. These ideas did have consequences that resulted in a virtual abandonment of any efforts by the federal government to remedy the results of two hundred years of institutionalized racism. In this way too neoconservatism and racism in consequences, perhaps also unintended, became the same.[57]

Black Neoconservatives

In chapter 5, I showed that African American thought and opinion have been characteristically liberal and left, with conservatism at best being a remnant or at worse the product of cowardice and fear. After the election of Reagan to the presidency, a new, relatively small group of black intellectuals and political leaders emerged who *might* be authentically or autonomously conservative.[58] Certainly in the post–civil rights era fear or cowardice should not be a motivating factor in their embrace of conservatism. However, I emphasize *might* be autonomous or authentic because some in this group might have been manufactured, created by the conservative labyrinth in order to put a black face on neoconservative ideas, to provide a shield against the argument advanced in this book that in America conservatism and racism are the same.[59] In other words—and I cannot know this—some of those blacks who embraced neoconservatism in the 1980s may be partly, like Schuyler, intellectual and political opportunists.[60] However, since we cannot know this, we have to assume that their conservatism is autonomous. That is, with the successful formal or legal debastardization of Locke in the 1960s these individuals may not be dissatisfied with their status or the status of blacks in the post–civil rights era, just as in the post War II era as a result of their inclusion in elite institutions many Jewish intellectuals became satisfied with their status and embraced neoconservatism. Of autonomous conservatism as a type, Huntington writes that it "is not necessarily connected with the interests of any particular group, nor, indeed, is its appearance dependent upon any specific historical configuration of social forces. Conservatism is an autonomous system of ideas which are generally valid. Whether or not a particular individual holds these values high depends not on his social affiliation but upon his personal capacity to see their inherent truth and desirability. Conservatism, in this sense, is, as Russell Kirk says, simply a matter of will and intelligence."[61]

Prior to the 1980s the most prominent African American associated with neoconservatism was Bayard Rustin, a major strategist of the civil rights movement and a confidant of Dr. King. But as indicated earlier, Rustin was a democratic socialist. However, he was, like his white neoconservative counterparts, resolutely hostile to black power, the ghetto revolts, and the movement's general tendency toward "infantile" radicalism in the late 1960s and 1970s.[62] And, as I indicated earlier, he was also opposed after the passage of the Voting Rights Act to the continual use of mass protests by blacks.

In the 1980s several outspoken, unabashed conservatives gained widespread attention in the national media. This group included, among others, Thomas Sowell, Walter Williams, Glenn Loury, Shelby Steele, and Clarence Thomas.

In general, the core principles of Sowell and Williams' thought are in an adaptation and application to race of the ideas of Milton Friedman. Both economists in their writings argue that limited government, laissez-faire capitalism, and individual responsibility and initiative in education, the labor market, and entrepreneurship are sufficient to address the post–civil-rights-era problems of blacks. In other words, as Reagan said in his first inaugural, for Sowell and Williams, "government is the problem, not the solution" to the problems of black America.[63]

Sowell also added a specific cultural component to his argument, contending that throughout the world certain ethnic groups have developed certain cultural attributes that predispose them to success in bourgeois, capitalist societies.[64] In the United States native born blacks tend to lag behind whites (and West Indian immigrants) because they lack these attributes, and in the post–civil rights era this cultural lag rather than racism explains the persistence of racial inequality.[65] Given this cultural explanation Sowell, like Glazer and Wildavsky, argues that government social policies cannot much change things and indeed are just as likely to make them worse.

Glenn Loury, also an economist, in a series of articles in *The Public Interest* and other journals also argued that in the post–civil rights era, poverty in black America was increasingly caused by cultural deficiencies among blacks themselves.[66] A black ghetto-specific culture predisposed blacks within it to engage in "immoral" behavior—promiscuous sex, bearing children out of wedlock, crime, drug abuse—that made it difficult for individuals and neighborhoods to succeed in America. Thus, what was required was not government social reform from outside the community but moral reform by blacks to confront what he called the "enemy within." Thus, he condemned black leadership for agitating for affirmative action and new social policies while neglecting its major responsibility to lead a campaign of moral reconstruction of the ghettos.

Shelby Steele makes a similar argument while also castigating white liberals for their "guilt" complex and black liberals for their "cult of victimhood."[67] White liberal guilt results in support for sentimental but unworkable social programs, while the cult of victimhood results in blacks blaming whites, racism, or the system for their conditions rather than taking responsibility for their own culpability.

With the exception of Loury, each of these individuals is categorically opposed to affirmative action as is Justice Clarence Thomas.[68] Scott Gerber in his study of Thomas' jurisprudence describes the justice as a philosophical Lockean committed to a jurisprudence of "originalism." That is, Thomas is unswervingly committed to the principles of Locke as they are embodied in the Declaration of Independence and the Constitution.[69] Thus, adhering to a chaste Locke, he writes that *any* consideration of race by the government in policy allocations is "categorically prohibited by the Fourteenth Amendment."[70]

Thomas is also apparently committed to Calhoun era jurisprudence on federalism and Lochner era jurisprudence on the Commerce Clause. In *U.S. Term Limits Inc et al. vs. Thornton et al.* Thomas in a long dissenting opinion wrote that each state could limit the terms of its members of Congress because "the ultimate source of the Constitution's authority is the consent of the people of each state, not the consent of the undifferentiated people of the nation as a whole.... The Constitution simply does not recognize any mechanism for action by the undifferentiated people of the nation."[71] In his opinion for the five-person majority Justice John Paul Stevens rejected Thomas' analysis, concluding that "the framers envisioned a uniform national system." He wrote that Thomas' opinion "would seem to suggest that if the Constitution is silent about the exercise of a particular power—that is, where the Constitution does not speak expressly or by necessary implications—the federal government lacks the power and the states enjoy it.... Under the dissent's unyielding approach, it would seem *McCulloch* was wrongly decided. Similarly, the dissent's approach would invalidate our dormant commerce clause jurisprudence."[72]

In conclusion, whether autonomous or manufactured there is nothing intellectually new or interesting about black neoconservative thought as the foregoing indicates or as is indicated in their own self-conscious statement of the "axioms" of the thought.[73] Rather, it is simply traditional conservative or neoconservative ideas applied to the problem of race in America. The fact that these principles are applied to race by blacks does not, of course, disturb the conclusion that they are in effect racist.

Conclusion

Neoconservatism—at least for the short run—has been one of the most successful intellectual movements in modern American history. With ideas of little intellectual consequence but with access to wealth, the suites of power, and the prestige media, neoconservative intellectuals were able to discredit and delegitimize the second Reconstruction, the second effort to foster a racially equalitarian society. Many of the ideas they employed against racial equalitarianism in the 1970s were the same or similar to those employed in the 1870s during the first Reconstruction.

I do not contend that the neoconservatives were racists or even white supremacists. I will grant for the most part that at least most were not racists. However, in their disparaging of the most limited, tentative, halting steps to achieve a racially just society—to repair the damages caused by the long bastardization of Locke—they contributed ideas that in their consequences were racist.

Ideas, however, even well-funded ones do not have consequences unless they are attached to or co-opted by powerful, mobilized constituencies. George Wallace helped to mobilize a racist, rightist bloc in the 1960s and 1970s. In the 1968 election Richard Nixon described this bloc as part of the "silent majority." Neoconservatism as an ideology that claims to draw its inspiration from Burke, to its lasting shame, pandered to this majority, while its new class rhetoric was "a reactionary slander on America's most thoughtful and concerned citizens."[74] By the time of the election of Reagan to the presidency a new "fusion" had occurred on the right. Traditional conservatives had made a grudging accommodation to the New Deal, and the 1960s civil rights reforms and the neoconservatives had embraced traditional conservatism's views on the primacy of the market, the states, and mediating institutions (family, church, neighborhood), while rejecting any further federal intervention to achieve a more equitable or just society.[75] Except on foreign policy, this fusion persists today and continues to shape ideas, politics, and policy.[76]

In the final chapters of this book I discuss how these fused ideas came to power in 1980 and their impact on governance on race from 1981 until the end of the Reagan presidency and beyond.

CHAPTER EIGHT

The Ascendancy of Ronald Reagan and the Parts Played by Ideology and Race

This chapter examines the ascendancy of the conservative movement to national power, with the election of Ronald Reagan in 1980. The seeds of Reagan's election were first planted in the 1948 presidential election, replenished in 1964, and became fully flowered in 1968. By 1972 the fruits that would result in the 1980 election outcome were there for the harvesting.

Little of the history I will recount here will be new to those familiar with postwar presidential elections, nor do I offer in this chapter a systematic history of presidential elections from 1948 to 1980. Rather, I want to show the relationship between racism and conservative principles in understanding presidential politics. As I have tried to show in the previous chapters, conservatism as an ideology in the United States, whether expressed by intellectuals such as Milton Friedman or William Buckley or politicians such as Barry Goldwater or Ronald Reagan, is the same as racism. That is, a strict adherence to the principles of the ideology necessarily results in the maintenance of the subordination of African Americans.

Numerous scholars have pointed to the significance of racism in the conservative ascendancy to national power between 1964 and 1980.[1] I will discuss some of this work in the course of this chapter; however, the main point expressed here is that "it's the ideology, stupid." That is, conservatives used racism to win elections, rather than attempting to win elections in order to formulate racist policies.[2] This is not to imply that the conservatives who took control of the Republican Party were racists. Most probably were not, and even if they had been, the "norm of racial equality" had by that time made explicit racist appeals unacceptable.[3] Rather, appeals to antiblack sentiments became just one among many ways for conservatives to accomplish their strategic objective of winning elections. Winning those elections on the basis of conservative principles, however, if those principles were implemented was tantamount to racism.

Conservatism and Racism: "It's the Ideology, Stupid"

Interestingly, as I was preparing the first draft of this chapter, a squabble emerged in the national press over whether Reagan was a racist. Paul Krugman, one of the *New York Times'* liberal columnists, started the contretemps. In a column titled "Seeking Willie Horton" Krugman wrote, "Reagan didn't begin his 1980 campaign with a speech on supply side economics, he began it—at the urging of young Trent Lott—with a speech supporting states' rights delivered just outside Philadelphia, Mississippi, where three civil rights workers were murdered in 1964."[4] Krugman contended this was a deliberate attempt to signal to white racists that he was on their side and was part of a Republican strategy going back to the 1960s to build a conservative majority on the basis of racism. A couple of weeks later David Brooks, the *Times'* conservative columnist, responded with "History and Calumny," writing that the attack on Reagan was a slur; that the decision to speak in Philadelphia was a result of Reagan's "famously disorganized campaign staff"; and that "[i]n reality, Reagan strategists decided to spend the week after the Republican convention courting African American voters. Reagan delivered a major address at the Urban League, visited Vernon Jordan in the hospital where he was recovering from gunshot wounds, toured the South Bronx and traveled to Chicago to meet with the editorial boards of *Ebony* and *Jet* magazines."[5] But Brooks also acknowledged, "It's callous, at least, to use the phrase 'states rights' in any context in Philadelphia. Reagan could have done something wonderful if he had mentioned civil rights at the fair. He didn't. And it's obviously true that race played a role in the G.O.P's ascent," Nevertheless, Brooks concluded, it is a "distortion" to conclude that "Reagan opened his campaign with an appeal to racism."[6]

Several days later Bob Herbert, the *Times'* African American columnist, weighed in, writing, "Reagan was the first presidential candidate ever to appear at the fair, and he knew exactly what he was doing when he told that crowd 'I believe in states rights.' ... Throughout his career Reagan was wrong, insensitive and mean spirited on civil rights and other issues important to black people. There is no way for the scribes of today to clean up that dismal record."[7] A few days later Lou Cannon, a sympathetic biographer of Reagan, wrote an op-ed in the *Times* contending that "Reagan was not a racist" and that the Philadelphia speech was a "southern stumble" by an "undisciplined candidate" that probably cost him votes among moderate northern whites without increasing his support among conservative southern whites.[8] In order to make his case that Reagan was not a racist, Cannon recounted several frequently told Reagan stories (see below) about Reagan's black friends and Reagan's family's long-standing opposition to racism. Krugman got the last word: "Reagan's defenders protest furiously that he wasn't personally bigoted. So what? We're talking about his political strategy. His personal beliefs are irrelevant."[9]

Just as Reagan's friends express outrage at the suggestion he was a racist, Reagan himself, throughout his career vehemently denied the charge and also expressed outrage at the mere suggestion that he had any sympathy with racism or was in any way antiblack. In his presidential memoirs Reagan wrote, "The myth that has always bothered me the most is that I am a bigot who somehow surreptitiously condones racial prejudice.... Whatever the reason for this myth that I am a racist, I blow up every time I hear it."[10] In order to show his antiracist bona fides Reagan repeatedly told stories from his youth about the antiracist attitudes and behavior of his father; how his brother's best friend was black; how he brought black playmates to his house; how his best friend was black; how when a local hotel refused to serve black friends he took them home for the night; and how as a young sports caster he had spoken out against segregation in baseball. Summarizing these anecdotes, Reagan wrote that he was willing to "weigh my fight against bigotry and prejudice against that of most civil rights advocates, because I was doing it when there was no civil rights fight."[11]

Reagan continued this pattern of denial once he became president. In 1983 Benjamin Hooks, the NAACP head charged that no administration in thirty years had "demonstrated as much determination as President Reagan to roll back hard-won gains of black Americans." Over the objections of his staff, Reagan wrote a letter to Hooks, saying, "Ben, there is (sic) no facts to substantiate such charges and they are a distortion of the actual record as well as my own position on these matters.... Ben if it was only possible to look into each other's hearts and minds, you would find no trace of prejudice or bigotry in mine."[12] Similarly, when Justice Thurgood Marshall in a television interview with Carl Rowan called Reagan a racist he was invited to the White House for one of Reagan's storytelling sessions. After the meeting Reagan wrote in his diary, "I literally told him my life story, how there was no prejudice in me. I gave examples of my relations with minorities as a young man in school, as a sports announcer, as governor. I think I made a friend."[13]

At the 1988 Gridiron dinner Reagan, sipping wine, told Rowan that he was not the enemy of poor and black people and that Rowan "had never really understood me on this racism business." Later Reagan invited Rowan to lunch at the White House: "Carl, I suggested this meeting... because I had a feeling often that you didn't have the straight thing on me and racism and so forth.... Carl, I was on the side of civil rights years before anyone ever used the term 'civil rights.' "[14] Reagan then defended his administration's civil rights record (citing data that Rowan wrote "was so erroneous as to be laughable") and then told him the familiar stories about his youthful antiracist activities. When Rowan asked him about opening his campaign in Philadelphia, Reagan responded, "I don't even remember doing that."[15]

Although Reagan perhaps protested too much and too often,[16] it is the argument of this chapter that his antiblack policies derive not from his racial views but from his ideology. That is, it was Reagan's doctrinaire, principled Lockean conservatism that resulted in racist policies and practices. This conservatism required him to oppose any use of government power to secure civil rights for black people because to do so violated core conservative principles of limited government, individual liberty, or states' rights.

Reagan and Lockean Conservatism

Virtually all students of Reagan agree that he was one of the most ideologically committed persons—if not the most ideologically committed—ever to reach the presidency.[17] Reagan was a "movement conservative," an integral part and representative of the postwar conservative movement whose ideas had consequences in the formative stages of his ideological evolution from New Deal liberalism to conservatism.

Reagan's critics and even some of his admirers have portrayed Reagan as an intellectually incurious, banal, laid back, "amiable dunce," who comprehended little more than what was on his carefully prepared cue cards.[18] But Hugh Heclo writes that "though he was not a thinker's idea of a thinker ... Reagan was a man of ideas born out of life experiences."[19] Over the years of his career Reagan in his speeches, newspaper columns, radio commentaries, and constant storytelling articulated a coherent political philosophy and ideology. Indeed, few American presidents (excluding the founding generation) have articulated and sought to advance as Reagan did policies based on a set of well-developed and internally consistent principles. And as the several volumes of recently published Reagan speeches and radio commentaries indicate, Reagan's ideas were Reagan's.[20] Or rather Reagan's ideas were Locke's. Although there is no evidence of Reagan having read Locke, his ideas were quintessentially Lockean, although he most often refers to Jefferson and the founding generation.[21] But Heclo is correct while "moderns might object," in his understanding of the relationship between the people and the government, "Reagan was simply being true to the Lockean tradition of American liberalism."[22]

Perhaps the best treatment of the Lockean principles embedded in Reagan's thought is Andrew Busch's *Ronald Reagan and the Politics of Freedom*.[23] Busch begins by writing, "First and foremost Reagan was more consistently and self-consciously grounded in the philosophy of the founders than any president since the New Deal."[24] Of the Lockean ideas advanced by Reagan, none is perhaps more central than his view on the sanctity and inviolability of private property. In a 1986 speech Reagan described the possession of private property as "one of the most important civil rights, the most fundamental protection of the individual and the family against the excessive and always growing demands of the state."[25]

To protect this right Reagan, like Locke, argued throughout his career that the powers of government had to be strictly limited to its policeman role as a means to uphold the natural rights of individuals to acquire and dispose of their property as they wished. Constitutionally, throughout his career Reagan advanced the notion of "original meaning" to make the case that the federal government should be kept within its Lockean limits as spelled out in the original intent of article I, section 8.

Reagan therefore rejected the ideas of positive rights or the positive state. Instead, he celebrated freedom and individualism; the Lockean tradition of the freedom of the self-reliant, self-made man who, without the constraints of government, is allowed to succeed or fail on his own initiative. In Reagan's America if the government was kept within its boundaries, most Americans could succeed, and for those who could not, then, that too was an inevitable byproduct of freedom. These principles of the sanctity of private property, limited government, individual freedom, and initiative for Reagan became the basis for his support of a virtually unregulated laissez-faire capitalism with a minimalist, if any, welfare state. (He would have allowed for a temporary social "safety net" for the "truly needed" but at the state and local levels rather than by the federal government.)

Federalism, writes Busch, was the "constitutional lodestar" of Reagan's ideology, a moral and political commitment to states' rights as a major impediment to power of the state. Finally, although Reagan was not personally pious (he rarely attended church), he constantly extolled the values of religion in American life.[26] Heclo goes so far as to conclude that "religious convictions about America's meaning...lay at the heart" of what he calls Reagan's "sacramental vision."[27]

Most American politicians, even liberals, give lip service to Lockean ideas and values, but for Reagan they were central to his rhetoric because he really believed "we have strayed a great deal from our founding fathers' vision of America.[28] This straying Reagan locates in the New Deal. Although Reagan had voted for Roosevelt and Truman, by the time of his conversion to conservatism in the 1950s he was repeatedly saying that the New Deal was based on fascism.[29]

The civil rights movement also represented, for Reagan, a straying away from the conservative vision of the founders; thus, he could oppose the civil rights laws of the 1960s, telling David Broder that he was in "complete sympathy with the goals and purposes of the 1964 and 1965 Acts" but opposed both of them because the federal government simply did not have the authority to "trample" on the rights of the states and individuals.[30] In California Reagan supported Proposition 14, an initiative to overturn a California law prohibiting racism in the sale of housing. On this proposition his opposition could not be based on principles of limited federal power and states' rights. So, he invoked property rights, the inviolability of property of rights. Thus, he declaimed, "There is a limit as to how far you can go through the law. You cannot benefit one person by taking away the freedom of others. I believe that the rights to dispose of; and control one's own property is a basic human right, and as governor I will fight to uphold that right."[31]

On conservative principles Reagan opposed affirmative action and the Great Society's antipoverty initiatives. Here he invoked Lockean ideas about individualism, self-reliance and entrepreneurship. In his memoirs Reagan wrote, "I opposed quotas in employment, education, and other areas. I consider quotas, whether they favor blacks or whites, men or women, to be a new form of discrimination as bad as the old ... *any* quota system based on race, religion or color is immoral."[32]

As an alternative to the Great Society, Reagan in 1966 proposed something he called "The Creative Society," which required individual initiatives, self-help and private enterprise as the routes to overcome the bastardization of Locke and achieve an equalitarian society.[33] For blacks crippled by the legacy of two centuries of government sanctioned racism, Reagan nevertheless argued government could not be a means of redress. Could not because as he told the NAACP in 1981 "massive amounts of government aid and intervention have failed to produce the desired results."[34] And then acknowledging that the federal government had a "proper function" in bringing about civil rights, Reagan extolled the virtues of laissez-faire capitalism in bringing about substantive equality (he did not, however, in this speech acknowledge his earlier opposition to this "proper function" of government). "Now, you wisely learned to harness the Federal Government in the hard pull toward equality, and that was right, because guaranteeing equality of treatment is government's proper function. But as the last decade of statistics I just read indicated, government is no longer the strong draft horse of minority progress, because it has attempted to do many things it's not equipped to do. I ask you if it isn't time to hitch up a fresh horse to finish the task. Free enterprise is a powerful workhorse that can solve many problems of the black community that government alone can no longer solve."[35]

Thus, a powerful case can be made that Reagan and the conservative movement's racism was not the product of the ideology of white supremacy; of racism in the sense of the wish to maintain the status of blacks as a subordinate group or of racial animus on Reagan's part. Rather, Reagan was simply a representative of old fashioned Lockean ideas. For blacks of course this is a distinction without a difference. Indeed, other things being equal, a racist liberal or radical would probably do more to advance the interests of blacks than nonracist conservatives like Reagan or Milton Friedman.

In a methodological appendix to *An American Dilemma* Myrdal identified "certain tendencies toward scientific bias" in the study of the "Negro." Of the several biases identified (he calls them "scales"), Myrdal described ideology as the "master bias," more important than one's biases in favor of or against the South or the Negro.[36] That is, ideology—how an individual locates himself on the "scale of radicalism-conservatism"—is more important in the advance of Negro freedom and equality than how one locates himself on the "scale of friendlessness toward the Negro." This is so Myrdal suggests because a liberal or radical is more likely to propose equalitarian government programs; to, for example, provide health insurance and full employment. And even—as the New Deal experience reviewed in chapter 4 shows—social welfare programs designed and implemented on a racist basis are better for blacks than no social welfare programs at all.

Reagan was not just conservative—Eisenhower and Gerald Ford were conservatives. Reagan was an ideologically committed conservative, an ultraconservative, a movement conservative, a part of a movement that since the 1950s had sought to challenge existing power relationships within the Republican Party and ultimately to challenge governing ideas and power relationships in the society that had been ascendant since the New Deal. Not only was Reagan a product of the movement, from 1964 to his election in 1980, but he was also its most articulate and popular spokesman. As Burnham puts it he was its "charismatic prophet."[37]

The Conservative Movement and Reagan

Movement conservatives viewed the nomination and election of Eisenhower and Nixon as triumphs of the Eastern liberal establishment and internationalist wing of the Republican Party over its traditional Midwestern conservative faction. Eisenhower's two terms of "Modern Republicanism" deeply disappointed conservatives, first, because the Eisenhower administration embraced the New Deal rather then seeking to dismantle it and second because the administration embraced the idea of peaceful coexistence with the Soviet Union rather than confrontation. The failure of the administration to come to the aid of the Hungarians when they revolted against Soviet domination in 1956 was particularly disturbing. Many on the right used the slogan "Better dead than red" to express their preference for war rather than accommodation with the "evil empire." Nixon's visit to the Soviet Union and Eisenhower's invitation to Soviet leader Khrushchev to visit the United States suggested to conservatives that there was little difference between Eisenhower and what they viewed as the cowardly appeasement of the Truman foreign policy.

Conservatives in the movement had always been wary of Nixon, viewing him as part of the party's liberal establishment. This wariness became outrage when Nixon in 1960 acquiesced to Nelson Rockefeller's demand that the party adopt a relatively liberal platform on domestic and foreign policy, including a strong civil rights plank. This plank called for "aggressive action to remove the remaining vestiges of segregation in all areas of national life."[38] Referred to by Goldwater as the "Munich of the Republican Party," this agreement did as much to spark the conservatives' efforts to take over the party as did any other single event.[39] While movement conservatives supported Nixon against Kennedy, the support was half-hearted. *National Review*, for example, editorialized that Nixon was simply the lesser of two evils.[40]

A year after Nixon's defeat Brent Bozell wrote of the frustrations of movement conservatives with their status as a "captive" faction within the Republican Party, while at the same time suggesting that the movement should seek to wrest control of the party from the Nixon-Rockefeller establishment. In a passage that, ironically, reflects the situation of blacks in the post–civil rights era Democratic Party (see chapter 10) Bozell wrote:

> For eight years, the movement has necessarily been on the leadstring of the left with Eisenhower Republicans in power, conservatives were, from every point of view a captive faction. They could protest, but there was no requirement on anyone to listen. They could counsel, but could not develop any direction of their own. They could plot, but as long as the GOP—their natural vehicle to power—was still running and was in the opposition's hands, any direct bids for power were bound to fail. Worse still, they could not even build; for powerful forces among them fostered the down-the-line support of Republican leadership as a lesser evil. Now [election of Kennedy] the movement is provisionally emancipated. What it does and where it goes are essentially matters of its own choosing.[41]

The movement's capture of the party beginning with the Goldwater insurgency was based on multiple issues—anti-Communism, antigovernment spending, opposition to trade unions, and finally a revival of traditionalism and conservative, evangelical Christianity—but racism was at the outset central to the movement's strategy to capture the party and win the presidency.[42]

Nixon and Rockefeller had calculated in their 1960 agreement that strategically an embrace of civil rights would win more black votes in the important states of the Northeast and Midwest than they would gain by appealing to whites in the South. Goldwater and movement strategists rejected this approach.

William Rusher, *National Review's* publisher and an early supporter of the Goldwater insurgency, argued in a 1963 essay that the Democratic Party was vulnerable in the South to the appeals of conservative Republicans because of growing white resentment about the Kennedys' embrace of civil rights. Rusher wrote that since the Civil War the Democrats had "run with the hares down South on the race issue, while riding with the hounds up North—nominating loudly integrationist presidential candidates while calmly raking in, on locally segregationist platforms, 95 percent of all Senate and House seats . . . south of the Mason-Dixie line."[43] Rusher's *National Review* essay was one of the earliest articulations by a conservative intellectual of the southern strategy of appealing to whites on the basis of racism.[44]

Clifton White, the architect of the Goldwater insurgency, writes that "no one on our National Draft Goldwater Committee, not even our staunchest supporters in the Deep South, ever suggested Senator Goldwater run on a segregationist platform. If they had, I'm positive the Senator would have angrily rejected the idea."[45] But White concluded: "Nonetheless, we had to face political realities. I recognized that any conservative candidate—even a dedicated integrationist—would have great difficulty making inroads in the North. . . . This region . . . is largely controlled by Democratic big-city machines. In a Presidential election even a middle-of-the-road Republican stood a good chance of getting clobbered in these states, as Dick Nixon discovered to his everlasting dismay in 1960. The only hope the Republican Party had of counterbalancing this tremendous handicap was to win the Southern states."[46] White emphasizes that this did not mean the conservative movement was writing off the black vote. On the contrary, he writes that the Draft Goldwater Committee set up specialized committees to mobilize the black vote "on the assumption that Negroes, like members of all other so-called minority groups, were above all else Americans interested in the future of their country. . . . [a]nd would reject the polarizing approach of the left, which seeks to deal with them as a mass voting bloc, and that many of them would embrace the true equality of conservatism, which welcomes Negroes, like all citizens, as individuals worthy of respect. Personally, I still hope that some day not in the distant future the Negro community will awaken to the fact that white liberals are merely using Negros support to promote their socialistic schemes."[47]

However, as Goldwater famously put it in a 1963 speech to Georgia Republican activists, since the Republicans were never going to win back the black vote, the party "ought to go hunting where the ducks are."[48]

Goldwater and White's southern strategy outraged Rockefeller, the leader of the party's liberal faction. On July 14, 1963, he issued his "Bastille Day Declaration." In this statement Rockefeller accused the conservative movement of a "transparent" plan to "erect political power on the outlawed and immoral basis of segregation and to transform the Republican Party into a sectional party of some of the people.... A program based on racism or sectionalism would not only... defeat the Republican Party but destroy it altogether."[49]

In spite of Rockefeller's protests, Goldwater was easily nominated at the 1964 Republican Convention, winning 883 of the 1308 delegates (he won 97 percent of the southern delegates). When Rockefeller rose to address the convention he was booed and jeered at by the delegates for more than a half hour before he could begin to speak, and the convention decisively rejected a liberal civil rights plank 877 to 409.

At the convention the movement's capture of the party—what White called "the great Republican revolution of 1964"—was complete. The party's once powerful liberal faction had been soundly defeated, and the conservative movement had effectively taken control of the party.[50] Although the movement would not consolidate its control until the nomination of Reagan in 1980, after 1964 delegates to Republican conventions were basically the same as those who nominated Goldwater.[51]

White, Rusher, and others in the draft Goldwater insurgency adamantly reject then and now the idea that the conservative takeover was based on racism. In his account of the conservative ascendancy Rusher completely ignores the role of race or racism,[52] while White writes that support for Goldwater among southern whites was not because of his opposition to civil rights. Rather, "It was more his willingness to accept the South as partner with an equal share in working out the nation's destiny that appealed to a group of people who for a century had been treated as poor and undesirable relations in the American family."[53]

No serious scholar of the ascendancy of the conservative movement in the Republican Party in 1964 or to the presidency in 1980 concludes that it was only because of racism (see the studies cited in note 1), although the *New York Times'* Paul Krugman comes close to this conclusion in his book.[54] Rather, racism was among several factors contributing to the movement's success. Racism was perhaps not even the major factor. But it cannot be—as many conservative intellectuals are inclined to do—dismissed as having no role or only a minor or inconsequential one.[55] Geoffrey Hodgson seems to me to have it about right concerning the multiple factors involved in the conservative ascendancy: "The business class's inevitable resentment of unions, taxation, regulation and the power of government generally was one effective recruiting source for conservative efforts. The fear of communism, foreign and domestic, aroused by events between 1945 and 1963 contributed a new and potent source of converts. But the evidence strongly suggests that racial prejudice and resentment against the civil rights revolution also powerfully reinforced conservative ranks."[56]

While attention often focuses on the special role of the South in relationship to racism and the conservative ascendancy, in the early 1960s the seeds of the so-called northern white backlash that in the 1980s would flower into the Reagan Democrats can also be observed. Clifton White indicates that in 1963 he received a "private study" that alerted him to a growing white backlash in the big cities of the North "against the obvious excesses of certain elements in the civil rights movement."[57] White wrote, "It was an issue we made no plans to exploit. But it was there nonetheless and it was helping turn thousands in the 'nationality' groups against the Kennedy administration and the Democrat big city machines."[58]

In late 1964 the private became public when David Danzig published in *Commentary* a widely read article titled "Rightists, Racists, and Separatists: A White Bloc in the Making." In this article Danzig, associate director of the American Jewish Committee, wrote that the "harm Negroes are doing their own cause in the north by adopting extremist tactics like school boycotts and rent strikes . . . has become a respectable cover for opposition to integration itself, once it begins to loom as an open possibility in the local school, neighborhood or union."[59] In cities throughout the North he contended Italian, Jewish, Irish, and Polish Americans—what White referred to as the "nationality groups"—were beginning to rebel against government efforts to promote equality in education, housing, and employment. Foreseeing the possibility that these groups might form a coalition with southern racists and traditional conservatives, Danzig wrote that "the old conservative slogans that served in the fight against the New Deal and the welfare state—'federal tyranny,' 'preservation of the Constitution,' 'American individualism'—are being applied to the civil rights struggle and used as a new rallying point cry for right-wing support."[60] As a result he concluded that "in 1964, the year of the Civil Rights Act, the Negro is more exposed to social reaction within the white communities than he has been at any time since Reconstruction."[61]

This incipient rightist-racist coalition was overwhelmed by Lyndon Johnson's landslide defeat of Goldwater in 1964. White woefully wrote, "By November 1964 the 'white backlash' was a seemingly dead issue, drowned in the great pounding wave of 'peace vs. war' and buried under the comforting illusory promises of the Great Society."[62] White was too pessimistic; the white backlash was wounded perhaps but far from dead. Even in 1964 George Wallace had shown its life by winning more than a third of the Democratic primary vote in Maryland (43 percent), Wisconsin (34 percent) and Indiana (30 percent). And in 1968 Nixon successfully exploited the backlash against the "excesses" of the civil rights and black power movements and forged an enduring coalition between racists and rightists throughout the country. By 1980 these northern nationality groups were referred to as "Reagan" Democrats.

Scholars of social movements in the United States and elsewhere frequently refer to the role of students and young people in the mobilization process. Certainly, there is an extensive popular and scholarly literature on the role of SNCC, SDS, and related student groups in the civil rights, black power, and antiwar movements. However, the role of students in the conservative movement has been overlooked, although as Cliff White and others have pointed out, Young Americans for Freedom (YAF)—the largest conservative student organization—was indispensable to the success of the Goldwater insurgency, members of which were later important organizers for Reagan. (In 1969 Reagan was selected YAF's honorary chairman.)[63] With more than twenty-eight thousand members YAF was larger than SNCC, SDS, the Black Panthers, and the Weathermen combined.[64]

YAF was founded in 1960 at the estate of William Buckley. Its founding document, the "Sharon Statement" (after Sharon, Connecticut, the location of the Buckley estate), was a militantly Lockean document. It declared that the *only* purposes of government were to maintain internal order and provide for the national defense and that whenever it strayed beyond these "rightful functions," it threatened order and liberty.[65] Andrew wrote, "Sharon embraced the doctrine of laissez faire with a vengeance."[66] The brief, one-page statement was also militantly anti-Communist, declaring that only a policy of victory over Communism could secure American freedom.

Virtually all white and largely northern, from the outset YAF showed little concern for civil rights.[67] It opposed the civil rights laws of the 1960s on familiar conservative constitutional principles, individual liberty, states' rights, and the limited powers of the federal government. In addition, some in YAF thought the civil rights movement was "tinged with communism."[68] In any event, the young conservatives in YAF, like many of their elders around *National Review*, were willing to stand athwart civil rights for blacks on the basis of Lockean conservative principles, making for these idealistic young people conservatism and racism the same.

Race and the Party System: The Mobilization of Bias

Since the founding of the Republic the aim of party and governing elites has been to keep issues of race off the partisan and policy agendas, as a means to maintain the subordinate position of blacks. Indeed, as indicated in chapter 2, the two-party system itself was established and maintained in part for this very purpose. The incentive structures of this system make it extremely unlikely that either of the two parties will be willing to risk its capacity to govern by taking on the controversial job of fighting for racial equality. Thus, it has been in only rare and brief instances that race has been at the center of American politics, occasioned either by crisis or the calculations of short-term advantage by one of the parties. Usually it has been the more racially conservative party that has seen an advantage in making race an issue as a means to partisan advantage over the more racially equalitarian party. This advantage is sought by either implicit or explicit appeals to the racist and white supremacist sentiments of the white electorate. Generally, however, both parties have preferred silence on race, ignoring the subordination of blacks while campaigning on the economy; war and peace; or personalities, scandals, and corruption.

Political scientists refer to this process of systematically excluding certain issues from partisan and policy agendas as the mobilization of bias or the nondecision-making process. E. E. Schattsneider writes, "All forms of political organization have a bias in favor of some conflicts and the suppression of others because organization is the mobilization of bias. Some issues are organized into politics while others are organized out."[69] Bachrach and Baratz refer to this phenomenon as nondecision making, when elites succeed in excluding discussion of issues viewed as detrimental to the system's interests.[70] In other words, party elites work together to prevent certain issues from being considered by the public.

In a two-party system the leaders of the parties always wish to emphasize issues that hold together their coalition while dividing the opposition. In the United States in those rare instances when race is on the agenda, it normally operates to disadvantage the more racially equalitarian party, and thus it is always in that party's interest to get rid of the issue as quickly as possible and return to the status quo. That is, when race becomes an issue even the racially liberal party tends to become conservative.

From the first presidential election in 1788 until 1860 race was a nondecision in American politics, a period of seventy-two years. From 1860 until 1876, a period of sixteen years, race was more or less, directly or indirectly, on the national agenda. Then, from 1876 until 1964, a period of eighty-eight years, the issue was again off the agenda except for a fleeting appearance in 1948. From 1964 until the election of Bill Clinton in 1992, a period of eighteen years, race was again directly or indirectly on the partisan and policy agendas.[71]

For all except about thirty-six years, then, race was a nondecision in American politics. Conservatives have been in the saddle for most of American history in both parties, and they used the Constitution and various and sundry strategies and compromises to avoid having to make decisions about freedom and equality for the colored race.

The conservative, Lockean constitution was, as discussed in chapter 3, instrumental in this mobilization of bias. The racially motivated Electoral College effectively disempowered any parties that would challenge the two-party duopoly and its silence on race. The Three-fifths Clause gave southern slaveholders and racists disproportionate power in the House and the Electoral College. And for a time the selection of senators on the basis of place rather than people gave the slaveholders a veto over any decisions on race. As a result of these conservative constitutional devices southern racists effectively controlled the presidency, the Congress, and the Supreme Court until 1861.

As a result of the expansion of the country into the West, these delicate constitutional balances became wobbly, and the issue of slavery threatened to disrupt the nondecision-making process by undermining the disproportionate power of the slaveholders. Party leaders fashioned a series of compromises between 1820 and 1850 designed to maintain the old order,[72] but to no avail, so in 1860 for the first time race became the major issue in a presidential election.

Race, not racism, was the issue of the 1860 election. Lincoln and the newly formed Republican Party were not racial equalitarians. On the contrary, they were racists and white supremacists committed only to the prevention of the territorial expansion of slavery. This was too much, however, for the southern slaveholders who having already lost the balance of power in the Senate feared that the Republican Party platform would, as Lincoln often said, put slavery on the road to eventual extinction. So, as Lincoln said in his second inaugural, "The War Came."

Not only did the war come, but with the war came also the destruction of one of the two existing major parties, and for a time the issue of racial justice moved from nondecision to decision in American politics.

The Demobilization of Bias I: Racism and Conservatism in Reconstruction Presidential Elections

In her excellent study of the history of the use of racism and white supremacy in American presidential elections *The Race Card*, Tali Mendelberg writes, "Racial appeals appeared prominently on the American political scene with the rise of the national party system of the 1860s, and intensified with the shock of emancipation. The parties positioned themselves on the issue of political rights for African Americans, with Democrats to the right, Republicans on the left."[73] Although the Republican Party in the immediate aftermath of the civil war fought for the rights of blacks, Mendelberg writes that the political culture of the time required the Republicans to at the same time conform to the ideology of white supremacy or what she calls the "norm of inequality." Throughout the Reconstruction era campaigns the racial appeals of both parties were consistent: blacks were an inferior people. These Reconstruction era appeals, which endure until the present, "drew on deeply rooted stereotypes, fears and resentments... African Americans were portrayed as having a proclivity toward three evils: sexual immorality, criminality and the desire to subjugate whites, and economic dependency and laziness."[74]

Immediately after the war the Republicans and most northern whites were willing to embrace civil rights for blacks *in the South* as fitting punishment for the treasonous behavior of the southern slaveocracy. However, in the face of violent southern resistance and the extension of the civil rights laws to the North, the first white backlash emerged, and the Republican Party quickly began its retreat from racial equalitarianism.[75]

This retreat was couched in terms of the principles of Lockean conservatism as well as the precepts of racism and white supremacy. For example, in 1872 Horace Greely running, ironically, as the "liberal" Republican challenger to Grant (with Democratic support) invoked conservative principles of individualism, limited government, federalism, laissez-faire capitalism, and the virtues of self-help. Rhetoric about the moral deficiencies of blacks was also prominent during the 1872 campaign. Finally, Reconstruction policies to ensure black civil rights and improve their social and economic well-being were denigrated by liberal Republicans and southern Democrats as "failed experiments" that had increased taxes in wasteful government spending.[76]

With the disputed election of Hayes in 1876 the conservatives captured control of the Republican Party and the national government until 1932. Between 1860 and 1932 the Republicans won fourteen of nineteen presidential elections (Wilson and Cleveland's two terms are the exceptions), controlled the Senate sixty-two of these seventy-two years, the House forty-six, and for thirty-eight years both the House and the Senate were under Republican control.

With this control the party's interest in race disappeared, and the two-party system returned to normalcy—the mobilization of bias or nondecision making on race. This silence on the continued subordination of blacks was to continue, with the exception of 1948, until the 1960s civil rights era. But when the issue returned to the national politics the ideology of white supremacy and its norm of racial inequality had been displaced by the "norm of racial equality," which required parties and candidates to adhere to chaste Lockean principles about the dignity and worth of all men.[77] This meant that the conservative party in order to win on the basis of race had to use implicit racial appeals.[78] It also meant that appeals on the basis of conservative principles would become more important in maintaining the racial order.

The Mobilization of Bias: Presidential Elections 1948–1960

Race briefly reentered partisan politics in 1948 after seventy-two years of silence as a result of several factors, some idiosyncratic to this particular election and several of enduring consequences for shaping postwar partisanship on race.

The first of the idiosyncratic factors was the death of FDR and Truman's ascension to the presidency. The second was the third-party challenge of Henry Wallace and the progressives. The third was Phillip Randolph's threat of a disruptive march on Washington to protest segregation in the military.

The enduring factors include the growing influence of the black vote in the pivotal electoral college states of the Northeast and Midwest; the coming of the cold war conflict between the United States and the Russia for the "hearts and minds" of the colored world; and the emergence of a small but important faction of race liberals inside the Democratic Party.

African Americans had opposed the dumping of Vice President Henry Wallace and his replacement by Truman in 1944. Although Wallace as secretary of agriculture had an indifferent record on race, as vice president he cultivated a reputation of racial liberalism.[79] However, Truman was a cautious centrist, balancing recognition of the forces of racism and white supremacy in border state Missouri while also attempting to secure the black vote in Kansas City and St. Louis. Black delegates at the Democratic Convention were perhaps Wallace's strongest supporters, and the *Pittsburgh Courier* denounced the selection of Truman as an "appeasement of the South."[80] The historian Rayford Logan called it "a tragic blow to the cause of liberalism and democracy," and Walter White referred to it as "the debacle at Chicago."[81]

Thus, as when LBJ assumed the presidency after the death of JFK, Truman felt constrained to prove his liberal bona fides on civil rights. In the case of both Truman and Johnson this was somewhat ironic since neither Kennedy nor Roosevelt had particularly strong civil rights records. Nevertheless, both were deeply admired in the black community at the time of their deaths for the little they had done on civil rights. Truman, therefore, had to address this reality as he struggled to carry on FDR's legacy.

Wallace's third-party left-liberal challenge also threatened to siphon off the support of black and other liberal voters. The Progressive Party convention adopted a relatively liberal platform on foreign and domestic issues, including civil rights. Blacks were also fully included as convention delegates and prominent leaders such as DuBois and Paul Robeson were featured in convention proceedings.[82]

In addition to the Wallace challenge Phillip Randolph was once again threatening to disrupt the Capitol in protests of segregation in the armed forces, including urging African American men to refuse induction. By issuing the executive order prohibiting segregation in the armed services, Truman was able to simultaneously avert Randolph's march and shore up his electoral support among black voters who otherwise might be attracted to Wallace.[83]

By 1948 the black vote was a factor to be reckoned with in the North. Fortuitously for blacks, Henry Lee Moon, the NAACP publicist, published *Balance of Power: The Negro Vote in 1948*. In this slim volume (of which Walter White conveniently had an autographed copy delivered to the president), Moon wrote:

> The Negro's influence in national elections derives not so much from its numerical strength as from its strategic diffusion in the balance-of-power and marginal states whose electoral votes are generally considered vital to the winning candidate. In the 1944 elections there were twenty-eight states in which a shift of 5 percent or less of the popular vote would have reversed the electoral votes cast by these states. In twelve of these, with a total of 228 electoral votes, the potential Negro vote exceeds the number required to shift the states from one column to the other. Two of these marginal states—Ohio with 25 votes and Indiana with 13—went Republican. The ten remaining states—New York, New Jersey, Pennsylvania, Illinois, Michigan, Missouri, Delaware, Maryland, West Virginia and Kentucky—gave to Mr. Roosevelt 190 electoral college votes essential to his victory. The closeness of the popular vote in the marginal states accented the decisive potential of the Negro's ballot.[84]

Moon's book was soon followed up by a long memorandum to Truman from Clark Clifford, his principal campaign strategist. Clifford told the president that the Negro vote today holds the balance of power in presidential elections for the "simple arithmetical reason that the Negroes are geographically concentrated in the pivotal, large and closely contested states such as New York, Illinois, Pennsylvania, Ohio, and Michigan. . . . As always, the South can be considered safely Democratic."[85]

Civil rights was also increasingly perceived in the State Department as a "Cold War imperative." That is, racism and the ideology of white supremacy at home, the president was told, was undermining the nation's standing and credibility and providing the Soviet Union with a powerful propaganda tool to use against the United States in the emerging Cold War.[86] This view was constantly impressed on the president by the leaders of the NAACP.

Finally, a small but growing faction of white racial liberals in the party was pressuring the president. Hubert Humphrey was one of its leaders, and at the 1948 Democratic Convention in a militantly liberal speech he said, "The time has come for the Democratic Party to get out of the shadow of states rights and walk forthrightly into the bright sunshine of civil rights."[87]

The convention as a result of Humphrey's speech and leadership and over the objections of President Truman adopted the strongest civil rights plank of any major party since Reconstruction.

As a result of the confluence of these short- and long-term forces Truman was forced to do what his predecessor had declined to do for thirteen years—take the risk of adopting a liberal position on civil rights and alienating southern racists and white supremacists. In addition to desegregating the military, Truman appointed the Committee on Civil Rights, a liberal interracial panel to investigate and make recommendations; and became the first president to address the NAACP.

In his memorandum to the president Clifford had minimized the risks, writing that "the South can be considered safely Democratic." It was not. Immediately after the adoption of the procivil rights platform, southern Democrats led by South Carolina Governor Strom Thurmond walked out of the convention and organized the States' Rights Party, "Dixiecrats," as a fourth party to contest the election.

Truman seemed doomed to defeat; challenged on the left and right flanks of his party, the pundits and pollsters predicted an easy victory for the Republican nominee, New York Governor Thomas Dewey. Dewey, with a relatively liberal civil rights record, was endorsed by most black newspapers; however, he took the election and the black vote for granted and played down his civil rights record during the campaign. Berman concludes by saying that "if a sizeable number of blacks had opted for Dewey or Wallace in any two or three key states of California, Illinois and Ohio Dewey would have won."[88] Thurmond carried four Deep South states (South Carolina, Mississippi, Alabama, and Louisiana). Thurmond clearly was a racist and white supremacist, but throughout the campaign he downplayed racism and emphasized conservative, Calhounian principles of limited government and states' rights.[89] In other words, the Dixiecrats' campaign of 1948 blended conservative and racist precepts, planting the seeds for the full flowering of this nexus in the campaigns of conservative presidential candidates in 1964 and thereafter.

Looking back on the 1948 election a year later Arthur Schlesinger was optimistic about the prospects for racial liberalism in future presidential elections. He said, "The strengthened civil rights plank in the Democratic platform helped President Truman win the election . . . if one is to judge by the subsequent election returns they signified temper tantrums rather than a cry of conscience against civil rights; for where Truman and the neo-confederate Thurmond were on the same ticket, Truman ran ahead two to one."[90] However, southern white support for the Democrats declined from 75 percent in 1944 to barely 50 percent in 1948.

Schlesinger, therefore, was engaging in wishful analysis. Rather than encouraging racial liberalism in the Democratic Party, the 1948 election had the opposite effect. The memory of 1948 became a mountain of despair for liberals rather than a stone of hope. Chappell writes, "Liberal survivors of the 1948 struggle, considering electability the sine qua non of all liberal hopes, took great pains to avoid alienating southern Democrats after the election."[91]

President Truman led the way in this liberal retreat. Although he continued from time to time during his second term to rhetorically advance the cause of civil rights, he refused to invest any political resources in trying to enact legislatively the recommendations of his Committee on Civil Rights (abolition of the poll tax, antiynching legislation). Rather, he reached out to reconcile and accommodate southern conservatives in order to overcome the divisions of 1948 in preparation for 1952 and to enact the rest of his domestic agenda. In addition, foreign policy and the Korean War became preoccupations of the president.

By the end of Truman's time in office, the Democratic Party, like the racially liberal Republican Party in the 1870s, preferred nondecisions, silence on race, rather than to continue the risky path of continuing to pursue racial justice.

The Elections of 1952 and 1956

In 1952 both parties wanted General Eisenhower to be their nominee, and both wished to curry favor with the growing black electorate while not antagonizing the white South. Eisenhower elected to seek the Republican nomination, and after a bitter intraparty battle between the party's liberal-moderate and conservative factions won the nomination, defeating Ohio senator Robert Taft. Taft, the conservative icon, had taken positions on civil rights somewhat more advanced than Eisenhower's. While both candidates opposed legislation mandating fair employment practices, Taft supported abolition of segregation in public accommodations and antipoll tax and lynching legislation. On each of these Eisenhower was either noncommittal or opposed.

Meanwhile, the Democrats nominated Adlai Stevenson, the urbane governor of Illinois. Although a hero to liberal intellectuals and reformers, Stevenson's positions on civil rights were no more advanced than Eisenhower's. Haunted by the memory of 1948, Stevenson's principal concern was maintaining the unity of the party. Fearing that a strong civil rights stance would lead white southerners to support Eisenhower or form another Dixiecrat party, Stevenson took a moderate position on civil rights.[92] Stevenson, for example, opposed the use of federal authority to compel school desegregation or fair employment practices. Generally, he counseled gradualism on race, contending that time and patience were the keys to bringing about change in southern race relations.[93] To further appease southern whites, Stevenson selected Alabama senator John Sparkman as his running mate. Although a supporter of FDR's New Deal economic reforms, Sparkman was also a committed white supremacist and segregationist.

Stevenson's equivocations on civil rights to some extent reflected his own "conservative background" and personal sympathies with southern whites.[94] But they also mirrored general liberal ambivalence on race as reflected in the positions taken by ADA.[95] Thus, in 1952 and 1956 both candidates took similar moderate positions on race, and the issue did not play a major role in either campaign. African Americans voted overwhelmingly for Stevenson in both elections (although in 1956 Eisenhower may have received as much as 40 percent of the black vote), while Eisenhower carried several southern states (including Virginia, Tennessee, Florida, and Texas) and became the first Republican to win a majority of the white southern vote.

Eisenhower's presidency made modest advances in civil rights, including desegregation of military posts and the elimination of segregation in the District of Columbia and federal facilities. Eisenhower also signed the Civil Rights Acts of 1957 and 1960. Although largely symbolic, these laws were the first civil rights legislation enacted by Congress since Reconstruction.[96] Perhaps Eisenhower's most important contribution to the civil rights cause was the appointment of Earl Warren as chief justice. Eisenhower later expressed regret about the appointment of the liberal Warren, and after the *Brown* decision he refused to endorse it and privately expressed opposition.

During the 1952 campaign both Eisenhower and Stevenson had said they were opposed to the use of federal power to compel desegregation. But when Arkansas Governor Orval Faubus blatantly used the state's National Guard to defy a court order to desegregate Little Rock's Central High, Eisenhower *reluctantly* sent in the army to compel compliance.[97] This was a landmark development, marking the first time the army had been used to secure the rights of blacks since Reconstruction.

Nevertheless, as the 1956 election approached, both parties engaged in calculated ambiguity on civil rights.[98] Harlem's Democratic congressman Adam Clayton Powell Jr. and several black newspapers endorsed Eisenhower for reelection, viewing his record on race as superior to Stevenson's.

The Election of 1960

Arguably, Richard Nixon had a better record on civil rights than John Kennedy.[99] Nixon certainly was no Lockean conservative on race or the welfare state. That is, he never questioned the constitutional authority of the federal government to enact the welfare state or to pass legislation prohibiting discrimination in employment or public accommodations. Yet as Garry Wills wrote of Nixon in *Nixon Agonistes* (in many ways the best book on Nixon),

"He is the least 'authentic' man alive, the late mover, the tester of responses, submissive to the 'discipline of consent.' There is one Nixon only, though there seems to be new ones all the time—he will try to be what people want."[100] Nixon, in other words, was the consummate political opportunist. All democratic politicians are political opportunists; it is a necessary part of the craft. And this is probably even more true for presidential aspirants in the United States whom Lord Bryce aptly described as "timid in advocacy... infertile in suggestion... always listening for the popular voice, always afraid to commit himself to [a] point of view which may turn out unpopular."[101] Yet Nixon, as we shall see later in this chapter, of postwar presidential candidates was in a class by himself.

Kennedy, however, had little knowledge of, interest in, or concern about black people. Schlesinger suggests that Kennedy's views on race were influenced by his acceptance while at Harvard of the "Dunning School" interpretation of Reconstruction, which taught that blacks were mentally incapable of exercising the civil and political rights conferred on them after the civil war, and that the South was unjustly treated during Reconstruction.[102] One gets a sense of Kennedy's view of Reconstruction in his profile of Edmund Ross (the senator whose vote prevented Andrew Johnson's removal from office). Kennedy wrote that "the event in which the obscure Ross was to play such a dramatic role, was the sensational climax to the bitter struggle between the President, determined to carry out Abraham Lincoln's policies of reconciliation with the defeated South, and the more radical Republican leaders in Congress, who sought to administer the downtrodden Southern states as conquered provinces which had forfeited their rights under the Constitution.... Andrew Johnson, the courageous, if untactful Tennessean who had been the only Southern member of Congress to refuse to secede with his state, had committed himself to the policies of the Great Emancipator.... Meanwhile, Kennedy described Thaddeus Stevens as "the crippled fanatical personification of the extremes of the Radical Republican movement."[103]

As a senator Kennedy had voted with the liberal bloc on civil rights, but he was not a leader on the issue. As he contemplated running for president as soon as he was elected to the Senate in 1952, he too was haunted by the memory of 1948. Therefore, his principal strategic concern was maintenance of the Democratic Party coalition.

As the 1960 election got under way both Kennedy and Nixon adopted cautious, centrist positions on civil rights: Nixon because he hoped he could maintain at least the near 40 percent of the black vote Eisenhower received in 1956, and Kennedy because he wanted to at least match Stevenson by winning the support of both of blacks and southern whites (his selection of Lyndon Johnson as his running mate was part of this delicate coalition maintenance effort).

Race was, therefore, not a major issue in the campaign, both candidates preferring nondecisions. However, Kennedy's sympathetic call to Martin Luther King Jr.'s wife after her husband's imprisonment in a Georgia jail may have affected the outcome of the election. Mrs. King, fearing for Dr. King's safety, called both Nixon and Kennedy asking for their assistance. Nixon refused, but Kennedy called Mrs. King, and his brother Robert, the campaign's manager, later called the judge in Georgia in an attempt to secure King's release (although he thought his brother's initial call was a strategic error because of its likely negative impact on white southerners). As a result of the Kennedys' intervention, Martin Luther King Sr. endorsed Kennedy, and the Sunday before the election, flyers were distributed at black churches describing the incident. Many observers believe that in the extremely close election the incident may have shifted enough black votes in enough states to cost Nixon the election.[104]

In *A Thousand Days*, Schlesinger wrote, "Historians of the Twenty-first Century will no doubt struggle to explain how nine-tenths of the American people, priding themselves every day on their kindliness, their generosity, their historic consecration of the rights of man, could so long have connived in the systematic dehumanization of the remaining tenth—and could have done so without not just a second but hardly a first thought. The answer to this mystery lay in the belief, welling up from the depths of the white unconscious, in the inherent and necessary inferiority of those of darker color."[105]

Schlesinger wrote this as the introduction to his discussion of President Kennedy's ambivalence on civil rights. Like FDR, once he assumed the presidency, Kennedy did not wish to take the risk of alienating southern racists and white supremacists by embracing the cause of civil rights. As he explained to Martin Luther King and Roy Wilkins, "nobody needs to convince me any longer that we have to solve the problem, not let it drift on gradualism. But, how do you go about it? If we go into a long fight in Congress, it will bottleneck everything else and still get no bill."[106] Later when Joseph Rauh of ADA urged him to propose legislation, Kennedy replied, "No, I can't go for legislation at this time. I hope you have liked my appointments. I'm going to make some more, and Bobby will bring voting suits and we will do some other things."[107] When Rauh asked the president whether he wanted ADA to bring some liberal pressure on civil rights as it was doing on economic issues, Schlesinger wrote, "Kennedy replied emphatically, banging his hand on the desk: No, there's a real difference. You have to understand the problems I have here."[108]

As the freedom rides, sit-ins, and mass demonstrations mounted during his first two years, Kennedy was more concerned about their Cold War consequences than he was about the injustices they were designed to highlight. However, as the militancy of the protests increased, particularly after the King-led demonstrations at Birmingham in 1963, Kennedy was also consumed by fear that protests could grow into a "general uprising" and that the nation's "cities might be engulfed in riots."[109] Thus, Kennedy decided to act because King made him do it.

In June 1963 George Wallace kept his campaign promise and "stood in the school house door" to block the admission of two black students to the University of Alabama. Kennedy, against the advice of his staff, decided in response to go on national television to make a speech on civil rights. The hurriedly prepared address is the most eloquent and forthright ever given by a president.[110] Describing racism and white supremacy as morally wrong and constitutionally unjustifiable, Kennedy recounted statistical data on the subordinate social and economic status of blacks and the daily indignities black men faced because of their "dark skin." Then he asked his fellow whites, "[W]ho among us would be content to have the color of his skin changed and stand in his place?"[111] Several weeks after the speech Kennedy sent Congress what would become the Civil Rights Act of 1964, moving, Schlesinger wrote, "to incorporate the Negro revolution into the democratic coalition."[112] Five months later the president was dead, shot down in broad daylight in downtown Dallas, Texas.

When Vice President Johnson became president he was willing to take the risks. As a southern politician with national ambitions Johnson had taken a moderate, centrist position on civil rights. However, he claimed that in his heart he had always been a militant liberal on civil rights, and to the extent that one can know, this appears to be the case.[113] Claiming that his moderation on the issue was due to the constraints of his Texas constituency, Johnson was liberated by his ascension to the presidency. In explaining his militant liberalism on civil rights Johnson, with a twinkle in his eye, told James Farmer, the head of CORE, "To quote a friend of yours 'free at last, thank God Almighty, I'm free at last.' "[114]

Within two weeks of taking office, Johnson invited his old friend and mentor, Richard Russell, to the White House. Russell, the highly respected senator from Georgia, was the recognized leader of the racist and white supremacist forces in the Senate.[115] When the conversation turned to the civil rights bill Johnson said, "Dick, you've got to get out of my way. If you don't I am going to roll over you. I don't intend to cavil or compromise." Russell responded, "[Y]ou may do that, but it's going to cost you the South, and cost you the election." To which Johnson replied, "If that's the price I have to pay, I'll pay it gladly."[116]

Johnson personally did not pay the price, winning election to the presidency by one of the largest margins ever recorded. However, he well understood that his party would eventually pay the price. On the evening of the signing of the civil rights bill Johnson told Bill Moyers, "I think we just delivered the South to the Republican Party for a long time."[117] The white South was lost for a long time because in 1964 race moved from nondecision to decisions, from the margins to the center of American partisan and policy agendas where it was to remain in some fashion until 1992.

Johnson's quip to Moyers, whether he realized it or not, reflected the historical lesson of Reconstruction: the racially liberal or equalitarian party is vulnerable to a conservative, white backlash in the two-party system. Liberals recognizing this vulnerability since Reconstruction had tried to keep the issue off the agenda. In 1963 African Americans shattered this mobilization of bias and forced reluctant presidents to act. The conservative reaction was swift and predictable.

The Demobilization of Bias II: Racism and Conservatism in Civil Rights Era Presidential Elections

The Election of 1964

Race was at the center of the 1964 election, but not the campaign. Neither Goldwater nor Johnson wanted to emphasize the issue; therefore they rarely spoke about it, and civil rights was not the subject of campaign ads by either party. Race was central to the campaign, nevertheless, because of Goldwater's southern strategy and his decision to vote against the Civil Rights Act of 1964.

When Goldwater decided to run for president, he assumed he would be running against Kennedy. Given the animosity toward the Kennedys in the South, Goldwater and his strategists assumed that he would have a good chance of carrying the South and perhaps winning. With Johnson's ascension to the presidency, Goldwater and his strategists felt that as a southerner Johnson would carry the South and thus there was little hope of victory.[118]

Goldwater's vote on the Civil Rights Act was central to the campaign's fading hopes of carrying the South. One of only six of thirty-three Senate Republicans to oppose the bill (compared to twenty-one Democrats; all except one from the South), Goldwater was careful to craft his speech on the basis of conservative principles. In his June 18, 1964, speech on the Senate floor, Goldwater began by noting that he had voted for the Civil Rights Acts of 1957 and 1960 and that he supported all but two of the provisions of the pending bill. Those provisions—banning discrimination in public accommodations and employment—Goldwater said were flatly unconstitutional: "I find no constitutional basis for the exercise of federal regulatory authority in either of these areas; and I believe the attempted usurpation of such power to be a grave threat to the very essence of our basic system of government, namely, that of a constitutional republic with regard to private enterprise in the area of so-called "public accommodations" and in the area of employment—to be more specific, Titles II and VII of the bill."[119]

Limited government, laissez-faire free enterprise, and the sanctity of private property—with this language Senator Goldwater's speech shows the ineluctable relationship between racism and conservatism in America.[120]

Goldwater addressed civil rights only one other time during the campaign, in an October 16 speech in Chicago.[121] Written by Claremont political scientist Henry Jaffa and chief-justice-to-be William Rehnquist, Goldwater ordered that it be "purged of any taint of racism."[122] The core of the speech titled "Civil Rights and the Common Good" invoked the conservative principle of individual freedom and liberty, the individual liberty of free men to engage in, without government interference, racist behavior if they wished. "Our aim" Goldwater said "as I understand it, is neither to establish a segregated society nor to establish an integrated society. It is to preserve a free society.... It is often said that only the freedom of a member of a minority group is violated when some barriers keep him from associating with others in his society. But this is wrong! Freedom of association is a double freedom or it is nothing. It applies to both parties who want to associate with each other.... We must never forget that the freedom to associate means the same thing as the freedom not to associate."[123]

Perlstein describes the speech as a "popular sensation," and it gave Goldwater strategists some reason to believe that it might help to turn the tide of the election.[124] This was not to be. Goldwater lost the election in one of the largest landslides in American history, winning just 38.5 percent of the popular vote and 52 electoral votes. His stance on civil rights may have played some part in Goldwater's massive loss, but if it did, it was a minor part. Goldwater lost because he was successfully (and to some extent accurately) portrayed by the Johnson campaign as a right-wing radical who would dismantle the New Deal, destroy trade unions, and get the country into a nuclear confrontation with the Soviet Union.

Goldwater did, however, win six states including his home state and five Deep South states (South Carolina, Louisiana, Georgia, Alabama, and Mississippi). From this conservative movement strategists could take heart because it demonstrated there was a base on which to build—a racist base for sure, but a base nonetheless.[125] As George Will later quipped, "Goldwater won the election of 1964. It just took sixteen years to count the votes."[126] And this base was not just in the South, as Wallace's performance in the 1964 Democratic primaries indicated. Wallace's campaign in 1964 was a demagogic fusion of racism and traditional conservative principles—anticommunism, traditionalism, states' rights, and religiosity. This was a potent combination in the long run ascendancy of conservatism because the Alabama governor was the "alchemist... that laid the foundation for the conservative counterrevolution that reshaped American politics in the 1970s and 1980s."[127]

There is a near political science consensus on the significance of the 1964 election in reshaping the partisan relationship between racism and conservatism in the United States. Carmines and Stimson, who pioneered in studying this race-based partisan shift, show that during the 1950s and early 1960s, the key issue that distinguished liberals from conservatives centered on the New Deal. During this period, such attitudes had no correlation with issues of race. Beginning with the 1964 election, however, this pattern began to change. Race increasingly became the key issue that divided left and right sides of the political spectrum and organized peoples' attitudes on a variety of other issues—including what by then were closely associated questions of social welfare policy. By 1972, this transformation was complete. Race was now the central issue cleavage in partisan politics.[128]

Finally, the 1964 election produced Ronald Reagan.[129] Indeed, Reagan is probably the only person who came out of the Goldwater insurgency with an enhanced national reputation that in two years would result in his election as governor of California. Reagan achieved this status with "The Speech," the election eve, nationally televised address he gave in support of Goldwater's candidacy. Goldwater's aides objected to the speech (describing it as "emotional" and "unscholarly"), but at Reagan's urging Goldwater watched it and gave the go ahead.[130] Essentially a boiler plate attack on the New Deal as an assault on property and freedom,[131] the speech was a repackaging of the standard speech Reagan had been giving for years while lecturing for General Electric. It was a sensation, however, and immediately made Reagan the new national leader of the conservative movement.

Immediately after the election a small group of ultraconservative California businessmen recruited Reagan to run for governor in 1966.[132] Reagan won an overwhelming victory against the liberal incumbent Edmund G. "Pat" Brown (California's last unambiguously liberal governor). Reagan's victory was made possible by the same forces that animated the neoconservative movement—opposition to the growing size of welfare, the student protests at Berkeley, the youth counterculture, the antiwar movement, and the Watts riot.[133] Although race was not a central issue in the campaign, Reagan's opposition to the state's fair housing law certainly appealed to antiblack sentiments in the state.[134]

Within ten days of his election Reagan gathered his staff at his home to discuss running for the presidency in 1968.[135]

The Election of 1968

The two-party system's mobilization of bias against partisan and policy nondecisions on race completely collapsed in 1968. Theodore White writes of this bias and the 1968 election: "American politics at home had, for years, been similarly guided by the hidden polarity of race. But from 1965 to 1968 they were to become increasingly visible."[136] And Mendelberg writes with respect to the 1968 election, "The stage was set for the first racial appeal in American history to win a presidency."[137]

Unlike in 1960, in 1968 Nixon had given up on the possibility of winning any significant share of the black vote. Thus, like Goldwater, he decided to go hunting where the ducks were, among racist whites. The record is ambiguous as to whether Nixon was a racist, but he was Nixon and therefore prepared to embrace whatever policy or position postures the circumstances required, which sometimes required racist postures and sometimes antiracist policies.[138] Nixon, however, unambiguously embraced white supremacist sentiments, frequently using *nigger* in private and telling aides that social welfare programs were wasted on blacks because they were "genetically inferior to whites."[139] This, however, did not matter because Nixon was prepared to support social programs for blacks—the Family Assistance Plan, affirmative action—if he saw political advantages in doing so. But he would also use racism if that was politically advantageous, telling John Ehrlichman, "The key voter blocs to go after are Catholics, organized labor and the racists."[140]

What had changed in 1968 was not Nixon but the political climate, which had changed in two ways. First, Wallace was determined to break the two-party system's silence on race by running as an independent candidate. Second, the incipient backlash against the civil rights movement had fully developed by 1968 as a result of the movement's turn toward radicalism and violence.

The riots that began in Watts in 1965 and continued throughout the country until 1968 increased the size and intensity of the backlash. Many liberals saw the riots—as the Kerner Commission concluded—as products of "white racism" (Vice President Humphrey said after Watts that if he had to live in the conditions of the ghetto he might riot).[141] Many African Americans saw the riots as legitimate expressions of protest or rebellion against the oppressive conditions of the ghettos. Indeed, a "riot ideology" quickly developed that interpreted the riots as legitimate expressions of black protest.[142] J. Edgar Hoover viewed the riots as the beginnings, perhaps, of black revolution.[143] They were not viewed this way by conservatives or by the overwhelming majority of whites. Rather, these violent outbursts were viewed as criminal behavior, "Rioting Mainly for Fun and Profit" as Edward Banfield titled the chapter in *The Unheavenly City*.

The view was also shared by elements within the liberal establishment. Theodore White in his analysis evoked post-Reconstruction stereotypes about black savagery and criminality. In *The Making of the President, 1968*, he described the rioters as a "handful of hoodlums," a "small handful of barbarians," and argued there was "no real rationale for the riots except rage—blind, primitive, generations—deep, reasonless, subduable only by force from outside."¹⁴⁴ Wallace in his campaign explicitly appealed to these sentiments, while Nixon, as Mendelberg ably demonstrates, did so implicitly.¹⁴⁵ That is, knowing that he could not "out Wallace Wallace" on race given the norm of equalitarianism in 1968, Nixon resorted to implicit appeals to antiblack sentiments.¹⁴⁶

Nixon won the election with 43.4 percent of the popular vote to Humphrey's 42.7 percent and Wallace's 13.5 percent (Nixon captured 301 electoral votes, Humphrey 191, and Wallace 46). Although the outcome was one of the narrowest in American history, Nixon knew that in the normal party system it was a landslide because the Wallace vote was a Nixon vote. Obsessed with Wallace from the time he became president, Nixon focused on strategies to keep Wallace out of the 1972 election.

Wallace's electoral votes came from the same states Thurmond had carried in 1948 and Goldwater in 1964. Looking at these results Theodore White concluded that the Deep South was now "probably a racist bloc,"¹⁴⁷ a racist but also a conservative bloc. White southerners are the most conservative part of the electorate, individualistic in world view, Lockean with respect to the role of the government, laissez-faire capitalist, and highly religious.¹⁴⁸

The Election of 1972

The election of 1972 was one of the most extraordinary in American history insofar as ideology is concerned. George McGovern's campaign was the most liberal ever conducted by a major party nominee, with the possible exception of William Jennings Bryan's 1896 campaign. On bread and butter, black and white, war and peace, and "right and wrong," McGovern was a "militant liberal," to use FDR's phrase.¹⁴⁹ But when FDR ran in 1932 he did not campaign as a militant liberal. Instead, he presented himself as a cautious, budget balancing centrist. Similarly, when LBJ ran in 1964, although clearly liberal, he positioned himself as a centrist, consensus builder in contrast to Goldwater's extremism.

McGovern, on the other hand, was an unreconstructed, unabashed Roussean liberal whose advanced liberalism, as Miroff's fine study shows, unequivocally embraced the "equalitarian demands of the previously excluded."¹⁵⁰ His "liberal redistributive economic agenda" included a guaranteed job, a minimum income, and a highly progressive income and estate tax with the rate reaching as much as 100 percent on the wealthiest Americans.¹⁵¹ In addition to these broad reforms McGovern's platform had specific components targeted toward racial equalitarianism, including busing for purposes of school desegregation, affirmative action, and "[f]ull enforcement of all equal opportunity laws, including federal contract compliance and federally regulated industries and giving the Equal Employment Opportunity Commission adequate staff and resources and power to issue cease and desist orders promptly. The platform vastly increased efforts to open education at all levels and in all fields to minorities, women and other under-represented groups."[152] Finally as an "old fashioned anti-imperialist liberal" McGovern called for an immediate withdrawal from Vietnam and large-scale cuts in the defense budget.

McGovern's campaign, unlike that of any other Democratic nominee, was a genuine grassroots insurgency that challenged the Democratic Party establishment and brought blacks and other previously excluded groups into the party. This grassroots insurgency character of the campaign was symbolized at the convention by the ouster of the Illinois delegation headed by Chicago mayor Richard Daley and its replacement by one co-led by Jesse Jackson. Feminists, gays, lesbians, countercultural youth, and antiwar activists were also important constituents in McGovern's coalition.

If McGovern was the last unreconstructed liberal nominated by the Democratic Party, Nixon may have been the last liberal president.[153] Movement conservatives were highly critical of Nixon's liberalism with respect to both domestic and foreign policy. In foreign policy detente with the Soviet Union, the opening to China and arms control were viewed as appeasement. And Cliff White described Nixon's domestic policies as "patently socialistic schemes."[154] These schemes included the Family Assistance Plan, SSI (providing income for the disabled and the elderly) indexing social security to inflation, and expanded federal regulation of the environment and the workplace. Nixon also presided over the implementation of affirmative action—the most far reaching racially equalitarian policy of the post–civil rights era.[155]

Although Nixon's policies did to a significant extent represent advanced liberalism, in the course of the campaign he labeled McGovern as a radical liberal on domestic policy and in foreign policy as "soft on communism" and weak on national defense. These attacks on McGovern, however, were made first and most effectively by Senators Humphrey and Henry Jackson, his Democratic primary opponents. By the time of the fall election, the outcome was a foregone conclusion. Ironically, both Nixon and McGovern agree on one of the key factors determining the outcome—the attempted murder of George Wallace, which made it impossible for him to mount a second third-party challenge.

McGovern cites Wallace's shooting as one of the "handful of events" that "played the largest role in his defeat."[156] And Nixon told H. R. Halderman, his chief of staff, immediately after the Democratic Convention to call Billy Graham to get him to pressure Wallace not to run as an independent, "which would surely elect McGovern."[157] Throughout, Nixon said the "main key for us is too keep this a two way race."¹⁵⁸ In addition to soliciting the help of Graham, Nixon ordered an investigation of Wallace and his associates and secretly funneled money to Wallace's 1971 gubernatorial opponent.¹⁵⁹

Nixon in all likelihood would have won the 1972 election even if Wallace had run as an independent. Given the prosperous state of the economy (artificially induced by the wage and price controls and an accommodating Federal Reserve policy) and the promise of peace in Vietnam Nixon likely would have defeated any Democratic nominee. But McGovern's enhanced Roussean, equalitarian agenda and the lacerating of him as a cultural radical suggests that he lost by a larger margin than would have Senators Humphrey, Jackson, or Edmund Muskie. (Pennsylvania's liberal Republican senator Hugh Scott memorably labeled McGovern the triple "A" candidate—Acid, Amnesty, and Abortion.) This is because McGovern's advanced liberalism was probably too advanced for the Lockean American political culture, a subject to which I return in the concluding chapter.

McGovern lost by one of the largest margins in history, winning only 37.5 percent of the vote. Nixon won forty-nine states, all except Massachusetts. McGovern also won the largely black District of Columbia, leading William Buckley to quip that he carried "Harlem and Harvard." Race played a minor role in the outcome of the election (although McGovern's support of busing was used against him). Foreign policy and the economy were the decisive issues, although the emergent right and wrong issues also played a role.

The election left the Democratic Party in disarray, divided into three roughly equal factions—a racist bloc represented by Wallace, a centrist New Deal liberal bloc headed by Humphrey and Jackson and McGovern's advanced liberal faction, which at its core was African American.

By 1980 the racist bloc had defected to the Republicans. This still left the Democrats with "rampant identity confusion" because "[f]earing the price McGovern paid for carrying the liberal label, the Party picked non-liberals or liberals who adopted disguises."¹⁶⁰ From 1948 to 1968 liberal Democrats were haunted by the memory of the 1948 election. From 1972 until 2008 they were haunted by the memory of 1972.

When Goldwater lost by a landslide in 1964, the conservative movement was available to continue his cause and succeeded sixteen years later in electing one of its own to the presidency. Given that there was no comparable liberal movement (and the black movement was rapidly becoming coopted), there was no Reagan to continue McGovern's insurgency. Instead there was Bill Clinton, who, ironically, started his political career as a young McGovernite. Unfortunately for liberalism, Clinton was no Reagan and therefore rather than embrace McGovernism, he repudiated it. Indeed, *McGovernism* became shorthand for derision, used even against Democratic candidates who were not liberal. Jimmy Carter, thus, became a "southern fried McGovern" and Clinton himself a "counter-cultural McGovernik."[161]

The Election of 1976

Reagan almost defeated Gerald Ford for the Republican nomination in 1976. After losing the first series of primaries and caucuses, Reagan made a stunning comeback in North Carolina and then went on to win most of the southern, western, and mountain state contests. At the convention the final delegate vote was 1,187 for Ford and 1,070 for Reagan, making this one of the closest nomination fights in history (Reagan actually won a majority of the primary votes by a narrow margin of 50.7 to Ford's 49.3).[162]

Ford's succession to the presidency after Nixon's resignation did not ease movement conservative concerns that had been long festering under the Nixon administration. Ford was not a movement conservative. Rather, he was a traditional Midwestern conservative somewhat like Robert Taft (except for Taft's isolationism). Movement conservatives were disappointed that Nixon had not selected Reagan to replace the disgraced Spiro Agnew as vice president, but they were outraged when Ford selected not Reagan or some other movement conservative but instead the hated Nelson Rockefeller.

Conservatives also objected to Ford's equivocations on abortion, his support of the Equal Rights Amendment, but especially his continuation of détente and arms control with the Soviet Union and his retention of Henry Kissinger as secretary of state. The disenchantment with Ford was so powerful among conservatives that William Rusher advocated the formation of a third party that would be unambiguously conservative.[163] Rusher proposed that this new party nominate a Reagan-Wallace ticket. The evidence indicates that Reagan briefly considered joining a ticket with the racist, white supremacist governor but abandoned the idea as impractical.[164]

Meanwhile, the Democrats nominated Jimmy Carter, the one-term, born again, evangelical Christian governor of Georgia. Although early in his career Carter did not challenge racism and white supremacy,[165] by the time he was elected governor he had reconciled himself to the civil rights revolution. Appointing blacks for the first time to statewide offices and hanging a portrait of Dr. King in the Georgia capitol, Carter fashioned himself as a New South liberal on civil rights. Endorsed both by Martin Luther King's father and George Wallace, Carter captured the nomination by presenting himself as an honest, cautious, fiscally conservative moderate "new Democrat."

As a native son, Carter was able to win ten of the eleven southern states (all except Virginia) in a biracial coalition that garnered 43 percent of the white vote and 90 percent of African Americans.[166] Endorsed by the Rev. Pat Robertson and other Christian evangelical leaders, Carter's religiosity and his emphasis on moral values made him appealing to some southern whites who since 1964 had been inclined to vote for Wallace or the Republican nominee.

The economy was the major issue during the campaign.[167] Stagflation—the unprecedented combination of high unemployment and high inflation—was used by Carter as the "misery index" to assail Ford's economic performance. Watergate and Ford's pardon of Nixon were also issues used by Carter to promise to restore trust in government. (Throughout the campaign he promised that he would never lie to the country to contrast himself with Nixon.)

Race was not an issue in the 1976 election. Both candidates took stands against mandatory busing, but neither wanted busing or any other race-related concern to be an issue. After Carter made remarks suggesting he supported ethnic segregation in housing, in order to repair the damage, he reluctantly endorsed the full employment bill sponsored by the Congressional Black Caucus. Generally, however, both candidates reverted to the traditional two-party nondecisions approach to dealing with race.

Carter won the election by the narrowest of margins: 50.1 percent to 49.9 and 297 to Ford's 240 electoral votes. The key to his victory clearly was his capacity to carry his native South, something he was able to do to a degree no Democratic nominee had done since JFK.

The Election of 1980

Fundamentally, the 1980 Reagan campaign represented a consolidation of the gains made for the Republican Party on the basis of race since Goldwater's 1964 campaign and the Nixon campaigns of 1968 and 1972. In 1964 the realignment of the parties on the basis of race commenced with Goldwater's vote on the Civil Rights Act of 1964, with the economically liberal Democrats also becoming the party of racial liberalism while the economically conservative Republicans became also the party of racial reaction. By using implicit, color-coded appeals to antiblack sentiments, Nixon in 1968 reinforced the linkages in the public mind among racism, ideology, and party. Thus, when Reagan became the Republican nominee in 1980 as the conservative prophet it was strategically unnecessary for him to use even implicit appeals to racism. Nixon had completed that work; thus all Reagan had to do was make his appeals on the basis of ideology and partisanship.[168]

Reagan, however, had not been languishing in California while Nixon was at work. On the contrary, throughout this period, Reagan "ducked in and out of the one-horse towns referred to in Southern idiom as wide-places-in the-road ... sipping bourbon and branch water" and spreading the conservative gospel. Not getting in newspapers or on television, Reagan—the glamorous movie star in this "living room chitchat and one on one politics" was building a grassroots base of support for what Nixon was doing more visibly at the national level.[169] Thus when he easily won the nomination to challenge Carter's reelection in 1980, he had already personally laid the groundwork to defeat the native son president on his own turf.

The 1980 election was the classic retrospective election.[170] That is, it was a referendum on the presidency of Jimmy Carter.[171] Looking at Carter's four-year performance, he was almost certain to lose to any reasonably competent alternative. Reagan's advisors understood this and first sought to shield him from the media where he was prone to gaffes that suggested he might not possess either the character or competence to be president.[172] Second, his advisors carefully crafted and Reagan studiously memorized a classic retrospective appeal that he used with devastating effect against Carter during their only debate:

> Are you better off than you were four years ago? Is it easier for you to go and buy things in the stores than it was four years ago? Is there more or less unemployment in the country than there was four years ago? Is America as respected throughout the world as it was? Do you feel that our society is as safe, that we're as strong as we were four years ago? If you answer to all of those questions yes, why then I think your choice is very obvious as to who you'll vote for. If you don't agree, if you don't think that this course we've been on for the last four years is what you would like to see us follow for the next four years, then, I could suggest another choice that you have.[173]

Reagan could raise these retrospective questions because Carter faced the electorate with perhaps the worst economic performance of any president since Hoover. The misery index that he had so effectively employed against Ford four years earlier had nearly doubled, with unemployment at 7 percent and inflation at 12.4 percent. In international affairs Carter appeared bewildered by the Soviet invasion of Afghanistan and as election day approached, the nation had been humiliated for nearly a year as the Iranian government held U.S. diplomats as hostages. A botched attempt to rescue the diplomats reinforced Carter's image as an indecisive, bumbling commander-in-chief. In domestic policy this image was reinforced by his sending several different budgets to Congress in the course of the year.

Carter's muddling moderation on domestic issues (especially his failure to support national health insurance) had led Senator Edward Kennedy, the leader of the party's liberal faction, to challenge him for the party's nomination. Although Carter easily defeated Kennedy, he was clearly weakened by the challenge.

Carter tried to portray Reagan as a radical, ultraconservative who would undermine Social Security, threaten international peace, and encourage racism, but the genial, smiling Reagan was able to deftly deflect any serious consideration of these issues in the media. Instead, Carter was frequently portrayed as mean spirited, insincere, and divisive. For example, when Carter (speaking at Martin Luther King's church) took Reagan to task for opening his campaign in Mississippi and invoking states' rights in his speech, the *Washington Post* came to Reagan's defense in a sharp editorial attack:

> Mr. Carter has abandoned all dignity in his round-the-clock attack on Mr. Reagan's character and standing, jumping (in a most sanctimonious tone of voice) for "offenses" similar to many Mr. Carter himself has committed, and most recently, concluding from all this that Mr. Reagan is a "racist" and a purveyor of "hatred." This description doesn't fit Mr. Reagan. What it fits, or more precisely, fits into, is Jimmy Carter's miserable record of personally savaging political opponents (Hubert Humphrey, Edward Kennedy) when ever going got rough. . . . Jimmy Carter, as before, seems to have few limits beyond which he will not go in the abuse of opponents and reconstruction of history.[174]

Race was not a salient issue during the campaign. Except for the contretemps about the Philadelphia visit, there was little discussion of explicit race issues such as busing or affirmative action or of implicit race issues such as welfare or crime. On race both candidates engaged in nondecisions. The issues were the economy and competence. Reagan won on both. However, Reagan's votes in the election, North and South, came disproportionately from those who expressed antiblack sentiments; thought the civil rights movement was moving too fast; were opposed to busing; and thought blacks should look to themselves rather than government to alleviate their condition.[175] Reagan made no direct appeals to these sentiments. Instead, he invoked the familiar Lockean, conservative verities of limited government, states' rights, individualism, and free market capitalism.

Reagan won decisively, 50.9 percent of the popular vote to Carter's 41.2 percent and 6.6 percent for John Anderson, the Republican turned independent. The margin in the Electoral College was equally impressive, 489 to 49. Reagan was especially strong in the South and the intermountain West, but Carter carried only five states: Georgia, Minnesota (the home of his vice president), West Virginia, Maryland, and Hawaii. In addition, the Republicans picked up twelve Senate seats, in the process defeating several of that body's leading liberals, including Senator McGovern. This was the largest Republican gain since 1946 and the first time it had held a Senate majority since 1952. And while not winning the House, Reagan's coattails did result in the gain of thirty-three seats.

The economy and foreign policy were the dominant issues cited as the most important by 56 and 32 percent of the electorate respectively,[176] while social issues of any kind (including race) were cited by only 7 percent of the voters compared to one-third in 1972.[177] Although Reagan was perceived as the more conservative candidate, only 11 percent of voters said they voted for him because he was "the real conservative."[178] Overall, there was no shift to the right except on defense spending. Indeed, Ladd concludes that the electorate was more conservative on the issues in 1976 than it was in 1980.[179] And while Carter was the most unpopular president since the end of World War II, poll data indicate also that "Reagan was the least popular candidate to win the presidency in that same period."[180]

The 1980 election it is clear was not a mandate for Reagan's conservative agenda.[181] The 1980 election, Burnham writes, "was not an ideological election but neither was the 1932 election."[182] Yet the 1980 election in some ways was the most important since 1932. This is because after existing for so many years in the political wilderness, the conservative insurgency that began in the 1950s had elected its prophet to the presidency. And mandate or not, the movement was intent on using Reagan's presidency to implement as much of its agenda as political circumstances permitted.[183] After all, as President Kennedy quipped after his narrow victory, "one vote is a mandate."

Although by the time of the 1980 election blacks, like other Americans, were dissatisfied with Carter's performance, they nevertheless gave him near 90 percent of their vote.[184] In early 1980 Carter's approval rating among blacks was 30 percent compared to 29 percent among whites. Thus, African Americans in 1980 were not voting for Carter but against Reagan, against Reagan because although they were dissatisfied with the performance of the most conservative Democratic president since Grover Cleveland, they were even more opposed to the prophet of the conservative movement taking his place.

Blacks, Burnham concluded after the election, "were more nearly isolated now than they have been since at least the beginning of the civil rights revolution of the 1950s. If the country really does go conservative, they lose."[185] Isolated and exposed, the only recourse blacks had to prevent the ascendant conservatives from using the presidency to roll back the liberal, racially equalitarian gains of the 1960s and 1970s was, as Holden put it "to discover means of leveraging within the legislative process."[186] In the next chapter, I examine how successful this leveraging was during the Reagan presidency.

CHAPTER NINE

The Reagan Presidency and Race

Walter Dean Burnham's observation quoted near the end of the last chapter suggesting that as a result of Reagan's election blacks were isolated and that if the country really went conservative they would lose in an implicit endorsement of the thesis of this study about the relationship of conservatism to racism. Fears about a racist backlash were certainly widespread in the black community as Reagan prepared to take office. O'Reilly writes that "of all the predictions made about the Reagan administration . . . the notion of an imminent assault on the civil rights gains of the 1960s was perhaps the most common."[1] Many observers compared the ascendancy of Reagan in 1981 to the election of Rutherford B. Hayes in 1876 and the end of Reconstruction. Laughlin MacDonald, a prominent voting rights attorney, writing shortly after Reagan took office, concluded, "It is not an exaggeration to say that minorities stand perilously close to where they were in 1877, when the nation, grown weary of the race issue, agreed to let local officials deal with voting rights as they saw fit."[2]

Yet it is the conclusion of this chapter and the scholarship generally on the Reagan administration and race that while the administration did attempt to roll back some of the civil rights progress of the 1960s, these efforts generally failed. While the administration did not have much success in its attacks on civil rights policies and programs specifically, it did have some successes—although not unqualified—on issues indirectly related to race—welfare and poverty. In this chapter I analyze the reasons for this disjuncture between administration failures on civil rights and its successes in cutting back racially equalitarian welfare and antipoverty policies.

This chapter first examines civil rights policies. Specifically, I study the administration's failed attempt to weaken the Voting Rights Act; its efforts to diminish enforcement of the Civil Rights Act of 1964 through its support of the Supreme Court's decision in the Grove City case; and its efforts to dismantle affirmative action through revision of Executive Order 11246. I also look at two closely related race issues, the Martin Luther King Jr. holiday legislation and the congressional enactment of sanctions on the racist apartheid regime in South Africa.

In the second part of the chapter I examine the administration's attack on those policies designed to bring about a more racially equalitarian society with respect to social and economic status. This is done primarily through analysis of the president's budgets, especially the first one, submitted in 1981, which substantially reduced outlays for the poor. I also examine administration efforts to reform welfare.

In both civil rights and social welfare policies the administration did not pursue an overtly racist agenda. Rather, it pursued an ideologically conservative agenda. The results of this ideologically driven agenda on race, if it had been successful, would have been racist. That is, it would have resulted in less protection of civil rights of African Americans, and in the case of social welfare policies, a less racially equalitarian society. The post-Reconstruction administrations did not always pursue overtly racist agendas. They too frequently relied on the conservative verities of the free market, limited government, states rights, and individual initiative and self-reliance. But we now know all too well that this conservatism in its consequences for the newly freed slaves was the same as Andrew Johnson's overt racist agenda.

The Reagan Presidency and the Constraints of Power

The American presidency is an office of great majesty and power, combining as it does in a single office the symbolic majesty of a monarch and the substantive power of a chief magistrate. Elected independently of the legislature, serving a fixed term, and removable only in extreme circumstances, the American president is an executive with extraordinary constitutional powers.

In the American system of separated powers, however, the president's powers are sharply constrained in one famous formulation reduced to little more than the power to persuade.[3] This is particularly the case in domestic policy as Wildavsky sought to demonstrate in his classic essay "The Two Presidencies."[4] While in diplomatic and military affairs presidents were often able to have their way; in domestic affairs they were not because they were frequently unable to "persuade" the Congress, interest groups, media or public. Thus, any American president, even with the "mandate" of a Reagan or FDR, usually has difficulty in enacting a domestic reform agenda. This is because presidents operate within constitutional and institutional constraints of divided and fragmented power in a system built on the Lockean-Madisonian principle that "gridlock is good."

In addition to these inherent constraints on domestic presidential power, each president enters office with a specific set of institutional constraints, a specific constellation or correlation of power, and the "climate of expectations" coming out of the elections.

When Reagan became president. the debastardization of Locke as a result of the 1960s civil rights revolution had been institutionalized. Hugh Davis Graham labels this process of institutionalization of the civil rights movement "quadrilateralism," the routinization of the civil rights policy-making process as a consequence of the "capture" of the relevant congressional committees, bureaucracies, and judiciary by the civil rights lobby.[5] This process has historically characterized policy making in the United States. First, there is the initial controversy and debate about the law itself, then a period of consolidation, and finally institutionalization as interest groups, the bureaucracy, the courts, and congressional committees work out a modus oprandi in the day-to-day conduct of business. For the most part this occurred during the Nixon administration, which signaled a bipartisan consensus on civil rights.

Thus, by 1980 even William Buckley and the *National Review* crowd had accommodated the civil rights revolution, much as they had earlier grudgingly accommodated the New Deal revolution. Further, avowedly racists and white supremacists had virtually disappeared from mainstream public spaces. Public opinion had also undergone a decisive transformation. By 1980 even white southerners embraced the principle of equality under law and a desegregated society.[6] And there was little support in public opinion for old fashioned white supremacist sentiments; for example in 1963, 31 percent of whites agreed with the statement that blacks were an inferior people, but by 1981 only 10 percent agreed.[7]

However, scholars of post–civil rights era racism caution that while the data show a clear decline in racist and white supremacist attitudes, hostility toward blacks among whites had by no means disappeared. Instead, these scholars contend that racism has become less overt, more subtle, and more difficult to document. This new, more subtle opinion on race has been labeled "symbolic racism," "modern racism," "racial resentment," or "laissez faire racism."[8] What this research shows is that by 1980 white Americans in their attitudes toward blacks were not racist but Lockean. That is, they were resentful or hostile to blacks not because they believed they were inferior or wished to subordinate them, but rather because they were committed to basic or core Lockean values, especially individualism. According to these scholars white Americans prize self-sufficiency and individualism and believe that blacks lack these values. Sniderman summarizes the research by saying that "white Americans resist equality in the name of self-reliance, achievement, individual initiative, and they do so not merely because the value of individualism provides a socially acceptable pretext but because it provides an integral component of the new racism."[9] In this Lockean construct blacks according to whites are not genetically inferior or cursed by God, and equality could be achieved if only they would work hard and act responsibly. As a function of Lockean values, Sears writes that the new modern post civil rights era racism is a product of the "finest American values."[10]

When Reagan entered the presidency the climate of expectations was such that he could not—dared not—embrace even a hint of old fashioned white supremacy. By 1980 even Strom Thurmond and George Wallace had embraced the norm of equality. But Reagan and the conservatives and neoconservatives who joined the administration could and did embrace Lockean laissez-faire racism and attempted to thwart any government initiatives to achieve substantive equality between the races.

Reagan's ascendancy to the presidency represented the arrival of the conservative movement's prophet. But the Washington in which the prophet arrived was not the conservative Promised Land. The government was divided, with the House of Representatives controlled by the Democrats. Although in 1981 the Democratic Party in the House still had an influential faction of conservative southerners, it was dominated by liberals. In the Senate the Republican majority of fifty-three was split between a movement conservative faction of thirteen, twenty-five traditional conservatives, and a faction of fifteen moderate-liberals representing the remnant of the Rockefeller wing of the party.[11] Persuasion, therefore, was going to be necessary if the movement's agenda was to become law.

Finally, by the 1980s African Americans had developed a considerable lobbying presence in Washington. As late as the 1960s with the exception of the NAACP and to a lesser extent the Urban League and an even lesser extent Martin Luther King's Southern Christian Leadership Conference, there was little organized black influence in Washington.[12] By the time Reagan arrived in the capitol, African Americans had developed a diversified and increasingly sophisticated lobbying presence.[13] Although as Pinderhughes shows, the black lobby, when compared to its white counterpart, had multiple issue agendas and was not well funded, but it did have access to legislative and bureaucratic decision makers and the capabilities to influence civil rights legislation and its implementation.[14]

In addition to the NAACP and the Urban League, the black lobby's most effective voice in Washington was probably the Leadership Conference on Civil Rights (LCCR). Founded in 1949 by A. Phillip Randolph, Arnold Aronson, a Jewish labor activist, and Roy Wilkins of the NAACP, by 1980 LCCR was a coalition of more than one hundred black, labor, Jewish, and other ethnic and religious minorities. During the 1960s Clarence Mitchell, the NAACP's Washington lobbyist, also headed LCCR, but by 1980 it was ably led by Ralph Neas, a white former Capitol Hill staffer. Although there were some tensions in the coalition between the various groups, on basic civil rights law the LCCR was a unified bloc.[15]

The Congressional Black Caucus, with more than twenty members, was an internal lobbying bloc in the House, and the Joint Center for Political and Economic Studies, a think tank founded in 1969, provided research and technical support. In 1977 TransAfrica was formed to lobby on issues related to Africa and the Caribbean. Finally, on civil rights and social welfare issues, the black lobby frequently worked with the established liberal-labor lobby, especially ADA and the AFL-CIO.

During his presidency Reagan became known as the great communicator. As he attempted to deal with questions of race and poverty during his two terms, he had to call on these communication skills to persuade a reluctant Washington establishment to go along. On issues of welfare and poverty, he was somewhat successful, first, because unlike civil rights the lobby for poor people in Washington was virtually nonexistent. The poor themselves find it difficult to sustain an organized presence in Washington,[16] and the groups that attempt to speak for the poor tend to be weak and resource dependent.[17] But equally important, unlike civil rights, the Lockean "notion of self-reliance also delegitimates collective action by the poor viewing the poor as responsible for their own poverty and hinders efforts to organize middle-class support for issues of social justice."[18] On welfare reform, for example, Mink writes, "[It] did not bear directly on the lives of most middle class feminists, and so they did not mobilize their networks and raise their voices.... [and] when they did enter the debate... they echoed policymakers['] claims that 'real welfare reform is to be found in the patriarchal family economy and mothers' work outside the home."[19]

The Congressional Black Caucus, the Urban League, and the NAACP did lobby for the poor, but voting rights and affirmative action were their priorities. As a result, anticipating a likely assault by Reagan on welfare and poverty programs, in 1981 the Center on Budget and Policy Priorities was established. Funded by charitable and philanthropic contributions, the center was the most effective lobby for poor people throughout Reagan's tenure.

Presidential Character in the Reagan Presidency

Although James David Barber's psychological theory of the presidency has been rightly criticized on theoretical, methodological, and practical and predictive grounds, it is also rightly praised for calling much-needed attention to the importance of personality and character in the exercise of presidential power.[20] In Barber's typology Reagan was a "passive" president ("receptive, compliant, other directed"), while Paul Quirk refers to Reagan as a "minimalist" president, that is, as "one who requires little or no understanding of specific issues and problems and instead can rely almost entirely on subordinates to resolve them."[21] The only recent minimalist president in Quirk's view, Reagan's "chairman of the board" style of leadership accommodated his "disinclination to do much reading or sit through lengthy meetings." Thus, Reagan would "personally establish the general policies and goals of his administration, select cabinet and other key personnel who shared his commitments, then delegate broad authority to them so they could work out the particulars."[22]

Although some Reagan scholars dismiss this minimalist view of the president's character, the research reported in this chapter on the Reagan White House decision making processes tend to confirm the view noted by Boyarsky as early as Reagan's gubernatorial years: "Reagan was not a tough boss. He was more the relaxed chairman of the board, placing complete confidence in subordinates to whom he delegated authority. Proposals usually came from below instead of originating with him."[23] And Sloan concludes that in the presidency Reagan was "uninterested in how things got done ... rarely sought information ... and was willing ... to be minutely managed and scripted by his staff."[24] Indeed, Reagan himself when asked about his work habits quipped, "It's true hard work probably never hurt anybody, but I figured why take a chance."[25]

All modern presidents, given the variety and complexity of the problems that confront the United States, are dependent on staff, the multiple offices and persons that constitute the institutional presidency.[26] But again observers of the Reagan presidency write of a "pattern of staff supremacy"; of "the stunning power of the White House staff" and "the most centralized and staff-dominated presidency in history."[27] Staff dependency of this sort, however, does not necessarily mean an absence of presidential leadership in achieving his goals. "A minimalist president," Quirk reminds us "can exercise his powers as expansively as any."[28]

For a minimalist president to succeed, however, depends to a much more substantial degree on the commitment of his staff to his agenda and its competence than would be the case for "active," "self-reliant" presidents. In Reagan's case especially it would depend on the extent to which the cabinet and staff were committed to his movement conservative ideology. But "By definition movement activists do not hold state power, and even under a like-minded regime they are unlikely to be satisfied. Such was the case for the conservative movement under the Reagan-Bush administrations."[29]

Kessel concluded no differences existed between Reagan's ideology and policy preferences and those of his staff, writing, "His beliefs are their beliefs. His conservatism their conservatism."[30] However, his conclusion is based on interviews with senior White House staff conducted during 1981 and 1982 in which individuals were simply asked whether they agreed with Reagan's domestic and foreign policy preferences. Not surprisingly all said they were in complete agreement. But if one examines the backgrounds of the senior

White House staff, one finds relatively few movement conservatives. For example, of the acknowledged "core staff" in the first term—James Baker, Michael Deaver, Edwin Meese, and William Clark (the National Security Advisor), only Meese is recognizable as a movement conservative. Baker was a traditional conservative, Clark a technocrat, and Deaver a public relations specialist more concerned with marketing the president than with ideas. In the second term the White House chiefs of staff—Don Regan and Howard Baker—were a technocrat and a traditionalist Republican, respectively.

Similarly, of Reagan's fifteen cabinet-rank appointees in 1981, only two are identifiable as movement conservatives or neoconservatives (James Watt at Interior and UN Ambassador Jeanne Kirkpatrick). Most were constituency-oriented technocrats (Drew Lewis at transportation, Don Regan at treasury) or traditionalist Republicans, and Richard Schweiker at Health and Human Services and Samuel Pierce (the only black in the cabinet) were identified with the Rockefeller remnant of liberalism.[31]

While the cabinet and senior White House staff were not identified with movement conservatism, the administration made a systematic effort (directed by Meese) to make appointments to the second-level White House staff and the subcabinet on the basis of the "litmus of Reaganite conservative ideology.... They are ideologically committed. There is no allegiance to the department, but to the Oval Office or the conservative cause."[32]

This pattern of conservative ideological litmus tests for the subcabinet characterized appointments to the civil rights bureaucracies, including William Bradford Reynolds as assistant attorney general for civil rights, Clarence Pendleton as chair of the Civil Rights Commission, and Clarence Thomas as head of the Equal Employment Opportunity Commission.

To summarize, Reagan entered the presidency with what movement conservatives considered a mandate for change, including change in the liberal civil rights, welfare, and antipoverty policies of the 1960s and 1970s. Change, however, would not be easy. Apart from the inherent weaknesses of the presidency in bringing about major changes in domestic policy, the conservative movement's prophet faced a changed climate of expectations on race with the norm of racial equalitarianism making any overt racist or white supremacist policies illegitimate. He also confronted a House controlled by liberal Democrats and a Republican Senate where moderate traditionalists rather than movement conservatives constituted the party majority. By 1981 the African American lobby had developed considerable leverage in legislative and bureaucratic processes, as a result of the institutionalization of the civil rights movement. And while the movement's prophet had won the election, he felt constrained to staff the senior levels of the administration with technocrats or traditional conservatives, relegating movement conservatives to subordinate staff and subcabinet positions.

As a minimalist, staff-driven president, it would take extraordinary exertions on Reagan's part to deinstitutionalize civil rights and bring about major civil rights reforms. For the most part Reagan did not exert this kind of activist leadership, and as a result—at least partly—the conservative movement's hopes of rolling back the civil rights gains of the 1960s and 1970s were largely dashed. However, the debastardization of Locke with respect to civil rights gave rise to laissez-faire racism, which in the name of Lockean values of individualism and self-reliance delegitimatized the welfare and antipoverty programs relevant to dealing with the legacies of Locke's long bastardization. Partly as a result, Reagan had somewhat more success in reforming welfare and dismantling or cutting back on policies designed to ameliorate racialized poverty.

Civil Rights

The Voting Rights Act

The Voting Rights Act of 1965 was passed partly in response to the protests at Selma lead by SNCC and Dr. King, but only partly. In early 1965 President Johnson wanted to pass the strongest voting rights act as soon as possible. In a January 15, 1965, phone conversation with King, Johnson told him that voting rights was the "core" civil right and that a voting rights bill would be the "greatest breakthrough, bigger than the 1964 Act." He then urged King to find and "publicize the worst examples of voting registration injustices" as a means to put pressure on Congress to act. In a sense, then, Johnson invited the protest at Selma, and he effectively used it to get Congress to swiftly pass the legislation, telling the Congress and the nation, "We Shall Overcome" in his post Selma address proposing the bill.[33]

The principal objective of the act was simply to secure the rights of African Americans to vote. Since the end of Reconstruction as a result of an amazingly effective series of stratagems (poll taxes, literacy tests, multiple ballot boxes, single month registration periods, etc.) as well as economic intimidation and terrorism, African Americans throughout the South were disenfranchised. For example, in Louisiana African American registered voters declined from a high of 130,444 in 1897 to 5,320 in 1910.[34] The purpose of the Voting Rights Act was to put an end to these stratagems and end the terror and intimidation at once.

The act, among other things, suspended literacy tests and other qualifications used to discriminate against blacks and authorized the Justice Department to send registrars to any state where literacy tests had been used and less than 50 percent of eligible voters were registered. Most controversially, section 5 of the act required approval of the Justice Department or the U.S. Court of

Appeals for the District of Columbia of any changes in voting practices or qualifications in states covered by the act. Reagan opposed the act in 1965, describing it (especially section 5) as "humiliating to the South." Reagan and other conservative critics of the act described it as patently unconstitutional, representing an unprecedented and unwarranted federal intervention into the affairs of the states. This view of the act's section 5 was also shared by Justice Hugo Black who, after William O. Douglass, was the Court's foremost liberal. Black, a southerner, in his dissent in *South Carolina vs. Katzenbach* wrote "Certainly if all the provisions of our Constitution which limit the power of the federal government and reserve other powers to the states are to mean anything, they mean at least the states have the power to pass laws and amend their Constitutions without first sending their officials hundreds of miles away to beg federal authorities to approve them."[35] Nevertheless, the Congress and the Supreme Court overwhelmingly approved the act, and by 1980 southern blacks were registering and voting at about the same rate as whites.[36]

The act, however, was a temporary, five-year remedial measure. In 1970 Congress renewed it for five years. Bowing to southern entreaties, Nixon in 1970 sought to amend the section 5 requirement that states "preclear" changes in their election laws with the Justice Department or the District of Columbia Appeals Court. The Congress rejected these amendments and passed a simple extension, with a nationwide ban on literacy tests. In 1975 Congress again extended the act for five years and this time extended its protection to language minorities. In 1970 and 1975 liberals on the White House staff and in the Congress (led by Senate Republican Leader Hugh Scott of Pennsylvania) persuaded Nixon that the principled and politically expedient thing to do was avoid a racially divisive fight on voting rights.[37]

Meanwhile, a series of Supreme Court decisions starting with *Allen vs. Board of Education* in 1969 held that the act not only prohibited states from denying the right to vote to minorities but from using any practice or procedure that "diluted" the impact of their votes.[38] In other words, the Court held that Congress intended to guarantee not just formal but substantive equality; not just the right to vote but the right by minorities to cast ballots that gave them the opportunity to elect candidates of their choice. Conservative and neoconservative critics of *Allen* and its progeny argued that these decisions were a radical departure from the intent of Congress and that they in effect granted blacks an "entitlement" to "proportional representation" and were a form of affirmative action that categorized "individuals for political purposes along racial lines and sanction[ed] group membership as a qualification for office."[39]

Given conservative and neoconservative hostility to affirmative action and the president's views on the legislation when it was enacted, critics and supporters alike expected a major effort at reform, specifically section 5's preclearance requirement. The critics were emboldened when the Supreme Court in 1980 in *City of Mobile vs. Bolden* significantly undermined its minority vote dilution jurisprudence. In *Bolden* the Court held that the Fifteenth Amendment as well as the Voting Rights Act required plaintiffs to prove not only that a challenged practice or procedure diluted minority voting, but also that this was the intent of those who adopted it or kept it in place.[40] Voting rights scholars and lawyers argued that the intent standard would make it virtually impossible to win vote dilution cases, because it was difficult to prove what was in the minds of those who adopted a practice or procedure.[41] Thus, in seeking renewal of the act for the fourth time, the civil rights lobby wished to amend it in order to reverse the Court's *Bolden* decision. At the outset of the Reagan administration, then, the stage was set for the first major test of wills on civil rights.

Although it was clear that an early administration posture on renewal of the Voting Rights Act would be necessary given its expiration in 1982, the White House staff apparently did not start work on developing a position until the Spring of 1981. The Voting Rights Act contrasted with the administration's development of its posture on welfare reform, which began before the president's inauguration (discussed later in this chapter).

Meanwhile, working closely with LCCR and other civil rights organizations, Congressman Peter Rodino, chairman of the House Judiciary Committee, and Senator Charles Mathias, a liberal Republican member of the Senate's Judiciary Committee, introduced a bill to extend the act for twenty-five years with an amendment to overturn *Bolden*. The amendment to section 2 of the act prohibited nationwide any practice or procedure that had the *results* of denying or abridging the right to vote on account of race or color. Referred to the judiciary's subcommittee on the Constitution chaired by Don Edwards, a liberal California Democrat, the Rodino-Mathias bill was quickly drafted and unanimously approved in the subcommittee and in the full committee with one dissenting vote.[42] In addition to amending section 2, the committee also voted to extend section 5 indefinitely.

Congressman Henry Hyde, the ranking Republican on the subcommittee and a traditional Midwestern conservative from Illinois, accepted the amended section 2 but proposed an amendment to section 5 that would have allowed the covered states to "bail out" of the requirement that they preclear changes in election procedures with the Justice Department or District of Columbia Appeals Court. Instead, Hyde proposed that states be allowed to go into their local federal district courts and show that preclearance was unnecessary because they no longer engaged in racial discrimination. The committee rejected the Hyde amendment, and the House soon thereafter passed the committee bill with a veto-proof majority of 385 to 24 (with 30 abstentions).

The early House consideration of extension of the act got the attention of the White House staff, and the administration started to develop its position. Conservatives in the administration were clearly opposed to the retention of section 5 (unless it had a bailout provision) and to the amended section 2. However, the staff was divided with some members arguing that the administration could not afford to appear to be against voting rights for minorities. As Michael Uhlman, the staff liaison on the legislation, wrote in an October 1981 memorandum, "The political given is that the President must be postured as favoring extension of the Act's special provisions."[43]

On May 6, 1981, the senior White House staff (Baker, Meese, Martin Anderson, and Fred Fielding) met to consider the administration's position on the legislation and concluded that section 5 should be repealed, that to the extent possible the provision covering language minorities should be dropped, and that consistent with *Bolden* a showing of "purposeful discrimination" should be necessary to prove any violation of the act. [44]

Southern conservatives led by Strom Thurmond, Jesse Helms, and Mississippi congressman Trent Lott were particularly adamant on Section 5. In a letter to the President Thurmond transmitted a copy of a long report written by South Carolina senator Sam Ervin "The Truth Respecting the Highly Praised and Constitutionally Dubious Voting Rights Act," in which he argued that section 5 was an unconstitutional bill of attainder.[45] And in a memorandum to Meese Uhlman wrote, "We should at all cost resist compromise which would allow a finding of a Fifteenth Amendment violation on the basis of mere effects."[46]

More moderate members of the administration, however, took the opposite view. For example, Melvin Bradley, the senior African American on the staff, urged a simple extension as did HUD secretary Pierce.[47] Elizabeth Dole, then assistant to the president for public liaison, also wrote in favor of extension, warning of the negative political consequences of antagonizing "the growing number of Hispanics in key states."[48] Even Martin Anderson, who thought there was a "lot wrong with the current law" nevertheless urged a four-year extension for "political/symbolic reasons."[49] Writing of these political/symbolic reasons in a memorandum to Attorney General William French Smith Uhlman wrote, "I am sensitive to the controversy. . . . But I am sensitive also to the fact . . . that the spirit which informs the Act is a mark of the nation's commitment to full equality."[50]

Thus, the administration was divided, and when the attorney general presented his long-delayed report to the president its recommendations were ambiguous. It made little reference to section 2, while urging that the southern states be given some options of a bailout from section 5.[51]

The minimalist, staff-driven president was, therefore, confronted with a deeply divided administration. In addition, Congressman Hyde urged support for the House bill, writing, "If you move quickly, you may be able to broaden your constituency by eliminating a fear which plagues the black community most: that the time will soon return when they [are] literally unable to vote.... Or made to feel that they have no meaningful impact whatsoever on their destiny."[52] Richard Wirthlin, the president's pollster, reported majority support for extension of the act even among southern whites, 53 percent compared to 65 percent among black southerners.[53]

Aside from a handful of new right conservatives in the Congress, there was little organized opposition to the House bill. Abigail Thernstrom and Patrick Buchanan wrote op-eds opposing the legislation and the conservative *Washington Times* editorialized against it.[54] But the overwhelming majority of the academic community, the bar and mainstream media strongly supported the House bill. In addition, it was recognized even at this time by some of the White House staff that the legislation might in the long run help conservatives by placing minorities in a handful of districts thereby facilitating the election of conservative Republicans in the South.[55] Also, it was understood that while the civil rights lobby was focusing on the Voting Rights Act, it had fewer resources to devote to the administration's budget which was its top priority.[56]

On October 6 the president announced his position on the bill: support for a ten-year extension, a liberal section 5 bailout standard, but no position on the amended section 2. This was a compromise position, supported by the Justice Department but opposed by Meese and other conservatives in the administration.

In December the Senate began consideration of the House bill. Already sixty-one senators (including twenty one Republican and eight southern Democrats) had announced their support for the bill. In the Senate the Judiciary Committee was chaired by Thurmond, but he ceded management of the legislation to Orrin Hatch, chair of the Subcommittee on the Constitution. A fervent new right movement conservative, Hatch focused his attention on section 2, which he argued mandated affirmative action quotas in the election process. The Republican Senate leadership, however, did not want a prolonged debate on this racially charged issue, particularly since in the midst of Senate deliberations the Bob Jones controversy erupted. By granting tax exemptions to schools practicing racial discrimination, the administration in Bob Jones appeared to be giving taxpayer aid to unreconstructed racists and white supremacists. This brought further pressure on the administration and Senate leaders to quickly resolve the voting rights issue. Eventually, Senator Bob Dole brokered a compromise that reinforced the House bill's disclaimer that nothing in section 2 "establishes a right to have members of a protected class elected in numbers equal to their proportion in the population." The bill passed the Judiciary Committee seventeen to one and the Senate eighty-five to eight. The president signed it on June 29, 1982. In signing the act's extension for twenty-five years the president said, "[T]his measure is as important symbolically as it is practically. . . . It securely protects the right to vote while strengthening the safeguards against representation by forced quotas."[57]

In signing the extension of the act for twenty-five years the president disappointed and angered movement conservatives by failing to repeal or significantly modify section 5 and neoconservatives by embracing section 2's results test. The outcome of this first test of wills between the administration and the civil rights lobby confirmed the changed climate of opinion on racism in the United States, the power of the civil rights lobby, and the continuing significance of the liberal remnant in the Republican Party. It also established the pattern that would structure the outcome of the other major civil rights disputes during Reagan's tenure.[58]

The Grove City Case

The Grove City case was the longest and most intense civil rights dispute of the Reagan presidency. Grove City College is a small, private institution in Pennsylvania, affiliated with the United Presbyterian Church. Committed to Christian values, the college in order to protect its autonomy and avoid federal intervention in its religious education refused to accept any federal aid. Its students, however, received federal loans and grants.

In 1977 the college refused to sign routine forms sent by the Department of Health, Education, and Welfare certifying it would comply with Title IX *of the Education Amendments Act of 1972.* Title IX prohibits discrimination on the basis of sex by any educational program or activity receiving federal assistance. The Carter administration quickly moved to cut off all federal assistance to Grove City students. In 1980 a federal district court ruled that grants to students did constitute assistance to the college, but the government could not cut off assistance to the students to force its compliance with Title IX. The Carter administration appealed, and the Third Circuit Court of Appeals reversed the district court, ruling that assistance to students could be cut off in order to compel the college's compliance with the law. Grove City appealed, and the case was pending before the Supreme Court when Reagan assumed the presidency.

Reagan's Justice Department reversed the position of the Carter administration. While it agreed that indirect aid to students did require Title IX compliance, and the government could therefore cut off loans and grants, it rejected the appeals court's judgment that the college itself was the recipient of the funds. Rather, it argued that only the college's financial aid office was the recipient, and therefore aid could only be terminated to that "specific program or activity." In a six-to-three decision the Supreme Court adopted the position of the Reagan administration, ruling that Title IX limited the termination of funds to the specific program or activity receiving the assistance and not the entire institution.[59] The administration adopted this narrow reading on the basis of two conservative ideological principles. First, the reach of federal regulatory authority should be limited. Second, religious institutions should be given special protections from federal interference on First Amendment grounds. Finally, the administration argued that this narrow, specific approach was the intent of Congress when it crafted Title IX.

The Civil Rights lobby viewed the Grove City decision as a threat not only to enforcement of Title IX but also to Title VII of the Civil Rights Act of 1964, which requires the cutoff of federal funds to institutions engaged in racial discrimination. Led by LCCR, the civil rights lobby argued that it did not make sense to allow an institution to discriminate in one activity or program while continuing to receive federal support for all its other activities or programs. On the contrary, LCCR argued that discrimination in any program or activity, whether it received direct federal assistance or not, should result in termination of all federal assistance to the entire institution. LCCR also noted that the Grove City decision reversed nearly twenty years of practices by the civil rights bureaucracies, which had always required institution-wide termination of federal assistance if discrimination was found in any of its programs or activities.

Using essentially the same strategy it had used in 1981 and 1982 to secure renewal of the Voting Rights Act, the LCCR quickly prepared draft legislation to overturn the Court's decision. The coalition to reverse Grove City, however, was much broader than the voting rights coalition. It included women (directly affected by Title IX), the elderly, and the disabled. This was because the proposed "Civil Rights Restoration Act" applied the institution-wide mandate not only to enforcement of Title IX and Title VII of the Civil Rights Act of 1964, but also to section 504 of the Rehabilitation Act of 1973 (dealing with the disabled) and the Age Discrimination Act of 1973.

In April 1984 (two months after the Court's decision) the Civil Rights Restoration Act was introduced in the House. Three months later it passed the House by a veto-proof margin of 375 to 32. Shortly before House passage Faith Ryan Whittlesey, the White House staff person on the legislation, received a memorandum from J. Douglas Holladay describing the situation as a "real mess" because for conservatives Grove City was a "major achievement" but saying that the president would "likely be forced into the unfortunate position of supporting the [House] bill."[60]

The administration was able to avoid this mess until 1986 because the legislation was referred in the Senate to the Labor and Human Resources Committee, chaired by Senator Hatch, who, recognizing the House bill had overwhelming support in the Senate, simply refused to allow it to be reported to the floor. In 1986 the Democrats took over the Senate, and Edward Kennedy became chair of the committee. An original cosponsor of the bill (which had fifty-eight cosponsors), Kennedy was committed to enacting the legislation as quickly as possible. At this point the administration recognized the bill had veto-proof majorities in both Houses.

The White House was divided on whether Reagan should face the political realities and sign the bill and avoid an embarrassing override of his veto. However, the staff wanted to avoid further allegations that the president was "insensitive to civil rights and women," but the president was under pressure from conservatives who argued that he had already capitulated to the civil rights lobby on voting rights and affirmative action.[61] In addition, the business community was overwhelmingly opposed to the bill as was the conservative religious community. Reagan himself was said to have been "particular[ly] concerned at the threat he believed the Act posed to religious freedom."[62]

In a last ditch effort to avoid a veto, the White House decided to support a compromise, substitute bill introduced by Wisconsin Republican Congressman James Sensenbrenner. Sensenbrenner's substitute represented a major reversal of the administration's position, since it too included the institution-wide mandate. However, it somewhat loosened the requirements for business compliance and expanded exemptions for some religious institutions. Nicholas Laham, a conservative critic of the administration's handling of civil rights throughout its eight years, concludes that the "administration had no choice but to abandon its previous policy" and accept the Sensenbrenner substitute because "no members of Congress, however conservative, want[ed] to be perceived as indifferent, if not antagonistic, to the cause of civil rights."[63]

The House rejected the Sensenbrenner substitute and passed the legislation overwhelmingly in its original form. Reagan vetoed it. His veto message was accompanied by the Sensenbrenner substitute, which he proposed as alternative legislation. In the message he wrote that the bill sent to him "would vastly and unjustifiably expand the power of the federal government over the decisions and affairs of private organizations, such as churches, synagogues, farms, businesses, and state and local governments. In the process, it would place at risk such cherished values as religious liberty."[64] Although Reagan personally went to the capitol to lobby Republicans to sustain his veto, it was overridden in the House 292 to 23 and in the Senate 73 to 24.

The Grove City case represented a major legislative defeat for Reagan, one of the few times a veto was overridden. In this four-year test of wills with the civil rights lobby the president was unable to make good on his promises to his conservative constituencies. At least, however, in this case he tried, even risking damage to his political standing by vetoing legislation certain to be overridden. In the next case, however, he did not even try, because he could have satisfied his conservative and neoconservative friends with a simple "stroke of the pen" that would have revoked federally mandated affirmative action.

Affirmative Action

In the course of his constant quest for the presidency Reagan frequently implied that with the stroke of a pen he would end affirmative action, which he often described as a quota system. For example, in a 1980 speech he said that "we must not allow the noble concept of equal opportunity to be distorted into federal guidelines or quotas which require race, ethnicity, or sex—rather than ability and qualifications—to be the principal factor in hiring or promotion."[65] If there was any issue, then, that conservatives had high expectations that the Reagan presidency would act on, it was affirmative action, particularly since the president could act on his own authority.

Neoconservatives in the 1970s contended in relentless attacks that affirmative action represented a fundamental violation of the Lockean principle of individualism, that people should be treated as individuals and not as members of groups. Thus, affirmative action represented affirmative racism. African American leaders viewed affirmative action as a modest means to remedy the wrongs of three hundred years of racism and, what is more important, as an effective bureaucratic tool to assure compliance with the nondiscrimination provisions of the 1964 Civil Rights Act.

When Nixon issued Executive Order 11246 in 1971 its purpose was not remedial but rather to assure nondiscrimination in employment, by requiring employers to develop affirmative action plans with "goals and timetables" for hiring, training, and promoting African Americans, women, and other minorities. Subsequently the order became the model for affirmative action programs in government contracting, higher education, and employment. Conservative critics of the order argued that the goals and timetables were little more than euphemisms for quotas and a racial "spoils system." Thus, when Reagan became president the stage was set for what many considered the most important civil rights conflict since the 1960s.

Unlike the voting rights and Grove City cases, public opinion was on the side of the antiaffirmative action forces. Public opposition, however, depends on the type of program and policy. Polling began on the issue in the 1970s, and the polls have consistently shown that both whites and blacks support affirmative action programs that do not involve preferences or quotas.[66] A 1978 poll, for example, found that 91 percent of blacks and 71 percent of whites agreed with the statement: "After years of discrimination it is only fair to set up programs to ensure that women and minorities are given every chance to have equal opportunities in education and employment." A 1990 poll found that 96 percent of blacks and 76 percent of whites supported the general proposition that "affirmative action programs that help blacks get ahead should be supported." However, when affirmative action policy is defined specifically in terms of "preferences" for minorities, support declines dramatically among both blacks and whites. From 1970 to 1996, white support for preferences has never exceeded 20 percent, and among blacks it has rarely exceeded 50 percent. A 1984 poll found that only 10 percent of whites and 23 percent of blacks agreed with the statement: "To make up for past discrimination, women and minorities should be given preferential treatment in getting jobs and places in college as opposed to mainly considering ability as determined by test scores." And in 1996, when the public was asked in the University of Chicago's General Social Survey whether because of past discrimination blacks should be given preferences in hiring or promotion, only 10 percent of whites and 50 percent of blacks said yes.

There is, therefore, support among whites for the abstract or general principle of affirmative action to assure equal opportunity, but there is hardly any support for preferences as a tool to implement the principle. Among blacks opinion is about equally divided. It is probable that some of the overwhelming opposition to preferences for blacks is rooted in white supremacist or racist thinking, but some of it is also rooted in the Lockean ideal of individualism and the related principle of meritocracy. Similarly, black opposition is probably also a reflection of their adherence to the idea of individual merit and achievement, which affirmative action preferences appear to contradict. Thus, if opponents could frame the issue as being about quotas and preferences rather than nondiscrimination and equal opportunity, they could count on significant public support.

Also, unlike voting rights and Grove City there was more of an organized antiaffirmative action constituency, although it was divided. While most academicians and intellectuals probably supported affirmative action as modeled after 11246, there was an influential bloc of neoconservative scholars who were outspoken opponents. In addition the so-called colorblind coalition included politically well-connected movement conservative organizations as well as elements of the business and Jewish communities.[67]

The business and Jewish communities, however, were divided. The Chamber of Commerce and the Associated General Contractors supported major revisions in 11246, while the National Association of Manufacturers and the Business Roundtable continued to support it. Among Jews, the Anti-Defamation League supported revision of the order, but the American Jewish Committee opposed any changes in it that would bar the use of goals and timetables as long as quotas were prohibited.

Thus while the colorblind coalition of movement conservatives, neoconservatives, Jews, and business was not monolithic, it did serve as a "critical counterweight to the civil rights community in providing the President the critical support he needed to sustain his planned reforms,"[68] counterweights that for the most part did not exist in the voting rights and Grove City cases.

However, like Grove City and voting rights, there was support among traditionalist conservatives and moderates in the administration and Congress for retention of Nixon's order. This support was based partly on a sincere commitment to the purposes of the order but also on concern that any attempt to change it would be portrayed as racist or anticivil rights, which would undermine the party's appeal to minorities and women. There was apparently also some concern that an attack on affirmative action might adversely affect the president's chances for reelection; therefore, it was decided to postpone any action until after the 1984 election.

After Reagan was reelected, Meese, who with Patrick Buchanan was the most militant critic of affirmative action, became attorney general and Don Regan, the treasury secretary, switched jobs with James Baker and became White House chief of staff. Shortly after assuming his position, Meese sent to the White House a comprehensive set of recommendations proposing to revise 11246 "to prohibit the use of quotas and numerical goals and timetables on the part of firms that contract with the federal government."[69] In addition, the Department of Justice package included numerous draft documents, a presidential letter to members of Congress, letters to newspapers, talking points for the White House press secretary, and letters to Republican congressional leaders asking for their support. Clearly Meese and his Justice Department colleagues planned for rapid implementation of the recommendations and a massive public relations campaign.

Instead of transmitting the recommendations to the president, Regan on October 22, 1985 (seven months later), convened a meeting of the White House Domestic Council to consider what, if any, recommendations should be sent to the president.[70] The council was deeply divided. Joining with Meese and Buchanan (by now White House communications director) in favor of the revisions was Bradford Reynolds, the acting associate attorney general; Clarence Pendelton, chair of the Civil Rights Commission; Education Secretary William Bennett; and Clarence Thomas, chair of EEOC. The opposition was led by William Brook, the secretary of labor (the department responsible for administering the order), and included Secretary of State George Shultz (who was labor secretary in the Nixon administration when 11246 was adopted); James Baker; Elizabeth Dole, now transportation secretary; and HUD secretary Pierce.[71]

The divided council decided to send Reagan four options (1) revised language strengthening the existing ban on quotas, (2) allow federal contractors to voluntarily use goals and timetables, (3) a complete ban on the use of goals and timetables, and (4) no changes in the existing order.[72]

Although it is not completely clear from my review of the records at the Reagan library, apparently given the divisions in the council Regan decided not to submit any options to Reagan.[73] Given the minimalist, staff—driven president, Regan's actions in effect killed any chance for reform. In addition to opposition within the administration, Regan was also aware of widespread opposition in Congress. By June of 1986 69 senators and 182 representatives had publicly announced their opposition to any changes in the order, and many had sent personal letters to the president. Opposition was almost unanimous among Democrats, and among those publicly opposed to any revisions were Republican congressional leaders Bob Dole and Bob Michaels.

Democratic Congressmen Augustus Hawkins and Don Edwards joined with Republican Congressman James Jeffries to draft a bill codifying the order into a federal stature, thus reversing the anticipated Reagan revisions and removing it from the stroke of any future president's pen. New York's Republican congressman Hamilton Fish wrote the president that he foresaw "an extraordinary bipartisan coalition of representatives and senators" forming to pass the bill.[74] Even Georgia senator Mack Mattingly, a new right movement conservative, wrote Reagan urging him not to revise the order because of his fear that congressional legislation would be passed that "would go further than the current system. It is conceivable that it would go beyond goals and timetables to include rigid quotas, a system which I, like you, oppose."[75] Although Reagan might have had the votes in the House to sustain a veto of legislation, the battle would have divided his cabinet and his party in Congress and inevitably left a larger scar of racism on his legacy.

In the speech prepared by the Justice Department for Reagan's delivery on national television announcing revocation of the order, Reagan would have invoked Lockean values in a direct attack on the Roussean principles articulated by President Johnson in his 1965 Howard University address:

> Those who point toward "equal results" ... have put into place permanent policies, permanent definitions of "discrimination" that judge the wrongfulness of conduct—whether on the part of employers or landlords or communities or schools or business establishments—on the basis of whether they have the proper proportions and numbers of [members of minority] groups. ... This is discrimination pure and simple. ... Purely and simply, affirmative action as it has developed in this country has nothing whatsoever to do with civil rights; affirmative action is in violation of every traditional value of civil rights. ... Racial quotas and racial preferences are inconsistent with every value that underlies our constitutional republic. Even if we have not always lived up to

this ideal, it has always been an ideal with enlightened Americans; with the advent of affirmative action, this ideal has been called into question as never before.[76]

Reagan, of course, did not deliver the speech, deciding not to decide he decided to maintain a policy he had unwaveringly opposed since its inception. Although Regan may have formally kept the Domestic Council's options off Reagan's desk, Reagan knew of the dispute as it was widely reported in the press.[77] And at a February 11, 1986, press conference Reagan while acknowledging that he was waiting for the council's recommendations nevertheless said he intended to eliminate the use of quotas.

How does one account for Reagan's failure to keep his promise? In a brief conversation with Martin Anderson at the Reagan library I posed this question to him. He responded that Reagan had two overarching goals: tax cuts and reductions in the size of the domestic budget, and the expansion of the military. All else, Anderson said, he generally left to the staff.[78] This is also Graham's view of Reagan's lack of leadership on affirmative action and civil rights generally: "In fields such as civil rights policy, which did not make Reagan's short list of crucial import, this meant being occasionally persuasive, but more often being disengaged, incurious, ill-informed, inconsistent . . . 'being Reagan' in the affirmative action debate meant avoiding a bloody and possibly losing battle, saving chits to cash in on the great, short-listed policy conflicts such as tax cuts and defense buildup. Whichever Reagan was the real Reagan, the result was a passive and inattentive president in the affirmative action debate."[79]

Meese rejects the Anderson-Graham arguments that Reagan was inattentive on affirmative action and other civil rights issues. Rather, he contends that Reagan understood that most of these issues had been created "*by rulings of the federal courts*" (his emphasis) and that "the long term institutional solution" was "restoring the constitutional rule of law."[80] Meese writes that Reagan battled throughout his tenure to "reshape the judiciary through a rigorous process of interviews and background checking."[81] Reagan appointed almost half the federal judiciary, including eighty-three appellate judges and three Supreme Court justices. Reagan also elevated movement conservative William Rehnquist to the post of chief justice. Under Rehnquist the Court in a series of 5-to-4 decisions substantially undermined the scope of affirmative action,[82] and under Chief Justice John Roberts, a lower level White House assistant to Reagan, the Court may be poised to declare any use of race by the government unconstitutional.[83]

In addition to being a minimalist president, Reagan was also a rhetorical president sometimes giving primacy to rhetoric over substantive policy making. Muir writes, "The key to the Reagan administration is its rhetorical character.... He set out to define a philosophy of freedom, to distinguish it from a philosophy of equality and plant it in the soul of the nation."[84] Thus, it is argued that Reagan's strident rhetoric against affirmative action throughout his career helped to undermine its legitimacy and contributed to solidifying public opposition and thus put it on the road to eventual extinction.[85]

Nevertheless most conservative scholars are sharply critical of the President's failure to make reforms in civil rights policy, especially his failure to revise 11246.[86] Lahman, for example, writes of Reagan's "confused, contradictory positions on affirmative action" and that the president on affirmative action was a "self-serving politician who was willing to sacrifice his conservative philosophical beliefs in order to protect the interests of the Republican Party, especially its moderate wing, whose members shared the same liberal views on civil rights as their Democratic counterparts."[87] Thus, like many conservatives Lahman concludes, "Having survived the most conservative administration in modern history affirmative action gained new legitimacy."[88]

The legitimacy and political viability of affirmative action were to some extent confirmed when movement conservatives took control of both houses of Congress in 1995. In 1996 Speaker Newt Gingrich urged the reform of affirmative action rather than its elimination, arguing that it would be politically irresponsible and potentially damaging to the party's majority status to repeal affirmative action before a better policy was developed to replace it.[89] In 1998 both the Republican-controlled House and Senate rejected amendments to a transportation bill that prohibited the use of a 10 percent "goal" in the allocation of contracts to minority- and female-owned businesses. The amendment was rejected in the Senate 58 to 37 and in the House 225 to 194. Several weeks later the House defeated by even larger margins an amendment prohibiting colleges and universities receiving federal funds from using affirmative action in their admission policies. Although the amendment was supported by Gingrich and the rest of the Republican leadership, fifty-five Republicans joined 193 Democrats to defeat it.[90]

It appears, then, that the conservative movement is looking to the Supreme Court's conservative majority to take the lead in the elimination of affirmative action. A decision by the Court framed with Lockean principles would, given the saliency of constitutionalism, have more legitimacy than a similar decision by a Republican president or Congress and would be less damaging politically.

South African Sanctions and the Martin Luther King Jr. Holiday

Although these two cases are somewhat different, they share one thing; most of the documents relevant to administration decision making were classified. Under the Presidential Records Act of 1978 access to records of former presidents are to be made available twelve years after the expiration of their terms. Former presidents or their designees may, however, assert "constitutionally based" privileges to exempt the release of certain documents. These include the "state secrets" privilege, which allows the withholding of military, diplomatic, or national security documents. Under this privilege virtually all of the decision-making correspondence and memoranda concerning South Africa are classified, leaving mostly routine correspondence and cover letters in the open files.[91]

Although it is likely that after twenty years much of the classified material on South Africa could be released without prejudice to national security, the state secrets privilege is a plausible basis to withhold documents. Not so with records regarding the Martin Luther King Jr. holiday.

In November 2001 President George W. Bush issued Executive Order 13233, allowing former presidents or their representatives to withhold presidential records for as long as they wish without explanation or justification. The order also allowed a sitting president to block the release of former presidents' records even if the former president has no objections to the release. When President Bush issued the order it was speculated that he did so in order to protect his father from the release of embarrassing information from his service as vice president.

Pursuant to Bush's order, Reagan's representatives withheld records about the King holiday decision-making process. In January 2005 I filed a Freedom of Information Act request for presidential records regarding the King holiday. In April 2007 I was informed that the papers had been processed and were available at the Reagan library. However, twenty-six pages of the documents were withheld. These pages included memoranda among Melvin Bradley, Edwin Meese, Edwin Harper, and others. The King papers do not fall under any constitutional or statutory privilege and the Presidential Records Act clearly required their release. In 2009, thanks to President Barack Obama, they were released.

In any event, in trying to trace the administration's decision making on these two issues, unlike the issues examined earlier, I was initially handicapped by lack of access to relevant documents.[92] However, in his first days in office President Obama revoked Bush's order. I received the twenty-six withheld pages in April 2009, permitting a full analysis of the archival record on the King holiday.

South African Sanctions

The United States was integrally involved with the economic development and political consolidation of the racist, white supremacist South African state.[93]

American corporations were involved in commerce, and South African political leaders looked to the United States as a model for how to subordinate and control African people, drawing particular inspiration from Booker T. Washington's philosophy.[94] Despite this close relationship between the regimes, U.S.–South Africa relations were generally not a part of policy discussions in the United States. Black churches in their missionary work in South Africa protested the treatment of black South Africans as did the NAACP, but generally the plight of Africans in Liberia, the Congo, and Haiti were of more concern to black leaders than the situation in southern Africa.[95]

The advent of the cold war changed the perspective of U.S. policy makers, as they came to view mineral-rich South Africa as a strategic resource and ally against the expansion of Communism in the region. Thus beginning with the Truman administration the United States and South Africa became strategic allies.[96] The Eisenhower administration signed a mutual defense pact with the regime and defended it diplomatically at the UN. Meanwhile, U.S. businesses continued to engage in profitable commerce and racists and white supremacists and the conservative movement defended the regime as a bastion of Western civilization in the midst of African backwardness.

President Kennedy appointed a number of liberals sympathetic to the freedom aspirations of Africans to diplomatic posts, including Undersecretary of State Chester Bowles and Assistant Secretary for Africa G. Mennen Williams. But his administration and that of President Johnson maintained the close economic, diplomatic, and security relationships with the regime. The developing civil rights movement and the decolonialization struggles brought sharp criticism of South Africa at the UN, but both Kennedy and Johnson resisted any thoughts of a break in relations or the imposition of sanctions, as called for by SNCC and CORE in the 1960s.[97]

In typical Nixon fashion, his policy toward southern Africa was based on hypocrisy. In 1969, Henry Kissinger submitted to Nixon National Security Study Memorandum 39. It included five options for dealing with southern Africa, ranging from closer association with the racist regimes to complete disengagement. Nixon approved option two. Dubbed "the Tar Baby Option," it called for public opposition to the regimes but a secret policy of closer economic and political ties.[98] The tar baby option was premised on the study's conclusion that "the whites are here to stay and the only way that constructive change can come about is through them."[99]

By 1976 opposition to the policy at home and abroad led Kissinger to abandon this policy of secret "constructive engagement" and forthrightly embrace an antiracism posture.[100] Thus, in the 1976 "Lusaka Declaration" he said that "racial Justice" was a "dominant issue of our age" and that the racist Rhodesian regime would face "unrelenting opposition" from the insurgents.[101]

Of South Africa he said there was still time to dismantle apartheid peacefully, but "[t]here is a limit to that time—a limit of far shorter duration than was generally perceived even a few years ago."[102]

American conservatives led by Jesse Helms, Patrick Buchanan, and Reagan bitterly attacked the Lusaka Declaration. Reagan campaigning in the 1976 primaries called it a betrayal of American interests that would result in a massacre in Rhodesia.[103]

The Carter administration's emphasis on human rights and the appointment of Andrew Young as UN ambassador led to increased attacks on South Africa. In 1977 Vice President Mondale met in Geneva with South Africa president P. W. Botha and urged him to undertake reforms leading to the full inclusion of blacks in the political process.

UN ambassador Young believed that Africa, including South Africa was his portfolio and that he had a special mandate to participate in the shaping of policy. In his public diplomacy, Young caused consternation among conservatives in America and whites in South Africa by prioritizing the freedom of Africans, while downplaying the Soviet threat. In administration deliberations Young was allied with Secretary of State Cyrus Vance, while Zbigniew Brzezinski, the national security advisor, took the traditional cold war view that the major threat to U.S. interests in the region was the Soviet-Cuban presence. Glen Abernathy concludes that partly as a result of Young's influence, the administration "set in motion" a policy to achieve "a peaceful transformation of South Africa toward a biracial democracy . . . while forging elsewhere a coalition of moderate black leaders to stem continued radicalization and eliminate the Soviet-Cuban presence from the continent."[104] Other scholars are not so sure about the change in policy or of Young's influence. Gaddis Smith, for example, concludes that there was no change in basic policy and that Young was fired as UN ambassador less because of his unauthorized meeting with Palestinian diplomats" but more generally because his philosophy was contrary to the administration's new direction. African policy now reflected more concern with meeting Soviet influence and less with African issues per se."[105]

In 1976 when Reagan challenged Ford for the nomination, he criticized the Kissinger policy in southern Africa because of its alleged downplaying of the Soviet threat. And in 1980 he criticized Carter for his human rights focus in southern Africa and emphasized the primacy of the Soviet threat as the lodestar of his foreign policy in the region.[106] This view was shared by Reagan's principal foreign policy advisors, including William Clark, Jeanne Kirkpatrick, and Chester Crocker, the assistant secretary of state for Africa. Reagan's views were undoubtedly shaped by his reading of *National Review* over the years, which in its pages had constantly emphasized the threat of Communism and downplayed, even denigrated, the freedom aspirations of Africans. Thus, as he prepared to assume office a closer engagement with the white supremacist, apartheid regime could be anticipated.

Organized African American interest in the liberation of South Africa and Africa generally goes back to the antebellum era and was a part of the agenda of black civil rights organizations from their inception. The decolonialization of Africa was a focus of the several Pan African Conferences led by DuBois beginning in 1900, and it was a major aim of Marcus Garvey's Universal Negro Improvement Association. In 1937, Ralph Bunche and Paul Robeson, among others, organized the Council on African Affairs to protest European colonialism, and it was followed in 1952 by the American Committee on Africa. Although these two organizations engaged in multiple lobbying activities, they were not a major presence in Washington.[107] The NAACP and the other civil rights organizations had ending domestic racism as their major priority and thus could devote little of their limited resources to Africa. Once the civil rights laws were enacted, these groups focused on lobbying for their effective implementation, while also shifting attention to the problem of poverty among African Americans. The 1960 Sharpeville massacre, in which South African authorities killed dozens of blacks and wounded nearly two hundred, sparked nationwide protests but did not result in sustained, organized pressure for a change in U.S. policy. Thus, for the most part U.S.–South Africa policy was developed and implemented with little input or influence by African Americans until the formation of TransAfrica in 1977.

The successful debastardization of Locke in the United States helped to change the climate of opinion on global racism, making it, to use the favorite word of the Reagan administration "repugnant" to all but the most unreconstructed conservatives such as Jerry Falwell and Jesse Helms. This more liberal climate of opinion was an important resource once African Americans mobilized to change U.S.–South African policy.

The mobilization began in earnest with the formation of TransAfrica in 1977. TransAfrica developed out of a 1976 conference of the Congressional Black Caucus convened to explore ways that blacks could influence the Ford administration's policy toward white-ruled Rhodesia. The conference, convened by Congressmen Charles Diggs and Andrew Young, concluded that there was little blacks could do to alter administration policy toward Rhodesia or Africa generally. After the conference the caucus concluded that this problem could only be corrected by the establishment of a black organization devoted exclusively to lobbying on African policy. A Black Caucus statement declared that "the conspicuous absence of African Americans in high level international affairs position[s] and the general subordination, if not neglect, of African and Caribbean priorities could only be corrected by the establishment of a private advocacy organization."

Unlike the Council on African Affairs, which was a radical organization influenced by Communist sympathizers, such as DuBois and Robeson, TransAfrica was a resolutely mainstream, liberal organization.[108] Well funded and ably lead by Randall Robinson, a Harvard-trained lawyer and former congressional staffer, the group was well positioned when Reagan took office to exercise influence in support of the liberation struggles in southern Africa.

Reagan appointed Chester Crocker, an Africanist scholar at Georgetown's Center for Strategic and International Studies, as assistant secretary of state for Africa. Crocker's appointment was opposed by Jesse Helms and other congressional conservatives because he was viewed as too sympathetic to the concerns of African peoples.[109] The White House was generally unconcerned with Africa, leaving day-to-day conduct of policy to Crocker. Although Crocker did not break with the policy of past administrations, the rhetoric changed with the problem of Soviet influence in southern Africa given more emphasis. Crocker also openly established the Nixon policy of "constructive engagement" in which the United States, while condemning apartheid, attempted to engage the South African government as a means to blunt the perceived Soviet threat. Crocker believed that over time this policy of engagement rather than confrontation would nudge the government toward reform of its racist structures.[110] In developing this policy Crocker writes that he attempted to avoid "the twin poles of movement conservatism and liberal and black ... [groups.] [T]hese power blocs had very different agendas from ours. They had no incentive to work with the State Department on anything. Their role was to protest, raise funds, gain national attention, and thereby expand their base for future battles."[111]

The Crocker-Reagan policy went largely unchallenged during most of Reagan's first term. However, in 1984 the South African government promulgated a new constitution, which created a trilateral, segregated parliament that gave limited rights to "coloreds" and Indians but excluded Africans from any share in power. This action triggered violent protests by black South Africans and the declaration of a state of emergency by the government. Televised worldwide, these protests made apartheid a national concern and suggested that the Reagan policy of constructive engagement was a failure.

Shortly thereafter TransAfrica organized what became known as the Free South Africa movement. This movement involved a successful campaign to persuade universities and state and local governments to withdraw investments from companies with businesses in South Africa. By 1986 twenty-one states and more than one hundred cities had joined the disinvestment campaign. In addition, beginning the day after Thanksgiving, TransAfrica organized a series of celebrity arrests at the South African embassy. Politicians, athletes, and entertainers conducted sit-ins and were arrested. This "political theater" received favorable, national media coverage.[112] As a result of the protest "South Africa emerged as one of the most prominent and divisive foreign policy debates" of Reagan's tenure,[113] and "one of Reagan's most important foreign policy defeats."[114]

Reagan suffered this defeat because, as Crocker puts it, rather than a problem in foreign policy, South Africa became a "new civil rights front."[115]

Reagan was defeated on this new civil rights front for the same reasons he was defeated on the domestic civil rights fronts: a divided administration confronted a powerful black lobby and a bipartisan congressional coalition that was unwilling to support "officially sanctioned racism."[116]

In June 1985 the House passed by voice vote a bill introduced by California Congressman Ronald Dellums, which imposed sanctions on South Africa by cutting off almost all U.S. economic ties. Although the Republican Senate did not consider the bill, it was clear that sentiment was growing for some kind of sanctions legislation.

Robert McFarlane, the national security advisor, conveyed these sentiments to South African president Botha in a June 1985 meeting in Geneva. In his notes of the meeting McFarlane reported that Botha had agreed to begin "good faith" negotiations with black leaders and take steps toward inclusion of blacks in the political process "short of one man, one vote," which Botha claimed leading blacks "acknowledge that [sic] is impossible now."[117] McFarlane conceded that Crocker and the State Department's Africa experts were skeptical about Botha's intention, but wrote that "while not an expert, I must say that if Botha is as convincing to blacks as he was to me, he has a good chance of bringing it off."[118] He then indicated that he explained to Botha "the President's vulnerability on the issue" because of "the primitive understanding of the strategic stakes in our Congress and public at large.... I went over the pending legislative measures and the likely future of successful enactment and possible override were they to be vetoed and made clear that the President would not necessarily be swayed from a veto just because of the prospect for an override."[119]

In 1986 the South African government declared a second state of emergency in an attempt to repress the two-year-long rebellion sparked by the adoption of the new constitution. The police and military repression, televised on the evening newscasts, recalled the repression of the civil rights protesters in the 1960s. Like the protests at Birmingham and Selma, the brutal repression of South Africa's blacks galvanized opposition to the regime and increased calls for the imposition of sanctions.

As early as the winter of 1984 the Conservative Opportunity Society, a small group of Republican members of the House led by Newt Gingrich, had sent a letter to the South African ambassador threatening to vote for sanctions unless the violence ended and steps were taken to dismantle apartheid.[120]

In June 1985 the House overwhelmingly passed with the support of fifty-six Republicans a sanctions bill. In order to avoid Senate passage, Bob Dole, the majority leader, and Richard Lugar, chair of the Foreign Relations Committee, persuaded a reluctant Reagan to issue an executive order imposing limited sanctions. The Reagan order banned the import of South African gold coins, restricted bank loans, limited technology exports, and codified the "Sullivan Principles."[121] Conservatives in and out of the administration opposed Reagan's order, but in the end it had little impact on the situation in South Africa, so pressure mounted for more comprehensive sanctions. Finally Dole, Lugar, and Senator Nancy Kassellbaum, the chair of the Africa Subcommittee, informed the president that they were prepared to follow the House and enact legislative sanctions.

The administration was divided. Crocker and the State Department argued for a conciliatory approach,[122] while Jeanne Kirkpatrick, CIA director William Casey, and Patrick Buchanan favored a hard-line rejection of any accommodation with Congress and "open alignment with South Africa."[123] This hard-line approach coincided with Reagan's view, shaped by his militant anti-Communism and his insensitivity to the plight of oppressed blacks, whether in the American South or South Africa. As Crocker gingerly puts it, "Sadly, Reagan failed to convey a sense of outrage on racial issues."[124]

Crocker writes, "We lost the sanctions debate on July 22, 1986."[125] On this date Reagan gave a speech to the World Affairs Council in which he rejected sanctions and for all intents and purposes aligned the United States with the South African white supremacists. In order to avoid a Senate vote and possibly attract enough votes to sustain a veto, the State Department drafted a conciliatory speech in which the president opposed the House bill as "punitive" but nevertheless did not rule out in principle legislative sanctions if South Africa did not move to dismantle apartheid.[126] Reagan rejected the State Department draft and instead turned to Buchanan to draft an alternative. In what Crocker describes as a "stridently polarizing message" and "vintage Afrikaner—speak,"[127] Reagan on national television praised the South African government for "dramatic changes" and called Nelson Mandela's ANC a "terrorist organization" and concluded, saying that "the South African government is under no obligation to negotiate the future of the country with an organization that proclaims a goal of creating a communist state and uses terrorist tactics and violence to achieve it."[128]

The Buchanan-Reagan speech's flat out embrace of the South African racists created a firestorm of criticisms, and Republican leaders, facing elections in several months, quickly passed the Comprehensive Anti-Apartheid Act of 1986.[129] Reagan's veto was easily overridden, 317 to 13 in the House and 78 to 21 in the Senate. Although this was a major foreign policy defeat for Reagan, Republicans saw it as a test of the party's position on racism, as Dole said at the time, "this has become a domestic civil rights issue."[130]

The Martin Luther King Jr. Holiday

The legislation making Dr. King's birthday a national holiday was also a domestic civil rights issue on which President Reagan once again found himself out of touch with the mainstream of his party. Unlike South Africa, on this issue Reagan capitulated rather than face a certain override of his veto.

Four days after King was murdered Michigan congressman John Conyers introduced legislation to make his birthday a national holiday. Reagan was opposed to honoring King. He had, of course, opposed King's civil rights work, but he was even more opposed to King's outspoken opposition to the Vietnam War and his poor people's campaign with its Rousseau equalitarian objectives. And like many movement conservatives of the 1950s and 1960s, Reagan believed—apparently sincerely—that King may have been a Communist or a Communist sympathizer or "dupe."[131] Nevertheless, by the time Reagan became president the momentum to enact the legislation was growing, and it was clear that Congress might pass it, perhaps, with enough votes to override a veto.[132]

In January 1983 anticipating likely congressional action, the White House designated Melvin Bradley, the most senior African American on the staff, to investigate the situation and prepare alternatives to a legal holiday.[133] The designation of Bradley as the lead staffer on the issue was unusual, since on most race-related issues considered by the White House, Bradley was not included in the staff deliberations.[134]

On February 7 Bradley transmitted his "Options Paper on the Martin Luther King Jr. Holiday" to Edwin Harper.[135] It laid out a balanced presentation of the views of the supporters and opponents without offering a recommendation. But it suggested that the president might propose as an alternative to a legal, national holiday the "Personal Option Approach," where Congress would enact legislation that would permit federal employees to select a day on which to honor historical figures leaving the option to the individual employee as to whom to honor. An "American Heroes Day" was also proposed, in which Congress would designate a list of heroes to be honored on a designated national "day of recognition." Bradley also wrote that opponents of the legislation believed King's "place in history was not beyond reproach" because of his antiwar activities, his opposition to the Goldwater candidacy, and his advocacy of the admission of "communist China" to the UN, as well as the fact that "[h]is positions and activities also had an influence on increased social spending and heavy-handed government regulation."[136] Bradley wrote that King's supporters contended "whatever may have been Dr. King's political activities, it would appear that for most Americans they are obscured by an overpowering symbol of hope, freedom, justice, peace, brotherhood, self-sacrifice and the pursuit of legitimate ends through nonviolent means."[137]

Finally, Bradley estimated that the creation of the holiday would cost the federal government "approximately $210 million" and that "the fall-off in the production of goods and services in the private sector during that week and the loss in gross national product could be substantial."[138]

At this point the paper trail essentially ended as the correspondence among Meese, Bradley, and other White House aides from January 1983 until the president signed the bill on November 1983 was withheld pursuant to Bush's executive order.

However, an interesting letter and document were available in the initially released papers. On November 16, 1983, shortly before the House voted 338 to 90 to approve the holiday, Charles Brennan, a former assistant FBI director, wrote a letter to Reagan opposing the bill. The letter was accompanied by a document purporting to describe King's excessive drinking, Communist sympathies, and "degenerate sexual urges."[139] Brennan claimed that "virtually everything in his report" was "gleaned from the book entitled "*The FBI and Martin Luther King, Jr*. The author is no redneck. He is a political science professor and, ironically, is supportive of King. But, facts are facts, and even the author could not gloss over them."[140] However, Brennan went on to write, "It was the muck the FBI collected. It was not the FBI's most shinning hour. . . . The point is the muck is there."[141] John Roberts (now the chief justice) recommended to the White House Counsel that a "noncommittal letter" of thanks be sent to Brennan and the documents be referred to the Office of Policy Development, "which will presumably be reviewing the policy questions of whether to support a King holiday."[142] On November 3, 1983, Bradley wrote presidential assistant Jack Svahn, "I believe it is very important that we be able to demonstrate that the President's position on the King Holiday proposal is not influenced by this kind of correspondence." In his own hand Svahn wrote, "Mel—It isn't."[143]

In his history of secrecy in the American government Moynihan concluded that most of the documents classified or withheld from the public should not have been and that instead of a "culture of openness" there was in the government the "routinization of secrecy" without logic or apparent purpose.[144] This certainly appears to be the case with the twenty-six pages of the King holiday papers withheld by Reagan operatives. Most of the pages are duplicates of material found in the previously open files. The rest are exchanges among a staff desperately seeking to find some alternative to the national holiday for King that was inevitably going to pass both houses of Congress with overwhelming bipartisan majorities.

Reflecting this inevitability, Joe Wright wrote Meese, "There are no apparent favorable indicators," and "given the evident political consequences of any decision to oppose the House bill . . . should in my opinion be fully explored with the President himself."[145] A principal reason there were no favorable indicators Wright told Meese was because "many conservatives have adopted the King Holiday as a 'safe' means of showing symbolic support for civil rights."[146]

Nevertheless, until the Senate vote White House staffers were busy considering possible alternatives to what was viewed as "an ill-conceived piece of legislation."[147] Perhaps the most bizarre proposal was recommended by Tom Gibson in a memorandum to Craig Fuller. Gibson recommended revoking the Columbus Day holiday and then subjecting it and the King holiday to a congressionally mandated national referendum.[148] Finally, Bradley proposed exploration of the possibility of a Sunday observance of the holiday and "earmark[ing] the 235 million in annual savings to the pursuit of one or more of Dr. King's goals."[149] Among the goals to be pursued were special training for the hardcore unemployed, an adult literacy program, a program to deal with the "deterioration" of the black family structure, and a possible civilian conservation corps.[150] "The advantage of this alternative," Bradley wrote, "is that it trades off a matter of symbolic importance in return for concrete needed gains for black Americans."[151]

These alternatives were, however, nothing more than wishful, desperate musings. The Senate passed the bill 78 to 22, and on November 2, 1983, in the presence of Dr. King's widow and other veterans of the civil rights movement Reagan signed it. A month earlier, however, in a press conference he could not resist the urge to slander Dr. King. During the Senate debate Jesse Helms, leader of the Senate's movement conservatives and the bill's most obdurate opponent, had called for the opening of the FBI files on King, claiming they would prove that King was a Communist or at least a Communist sympathizer. When asked about Helms' allegations, Reagan, to the consternation of his aides, responded, "We will know in about 35 years, won't we"? He was referring to the time for opening the files. He then went on to say, "I don't fault Senator Helms' sincerity with regard to wanting the records opened. I think he is motivated by a feeling that if we are going to have a national holiday named for any American, when it's only been named for one American in all our history up until this time, that he feels we should know everything there is to know about the individual."[152]

The Prophet Confronts a Consensus on Civil Rights

Reagan assumed the presidency sixteen years after the Congress, over his objections, enacted the Civil Rights Act of 1964. By 1980 there was a bipartisan consensus that the revolution should not be reversed, indeed should be modestly extended. President Reagan disagreed and during his tenure attempted to weaken the Voting Rights Act, limit enforcement of the 1964 act, and considered revoking affirmative action. On each of these issues Reagan confronted a bipartisan consensus that forced him to retreat. When he did not retreat his vetoes were easily overridden. The debastardization of Locke made racism unacceptable at home. Thus South Africa's racism became a domestic civil rights issue, and Reagan suffered perhaps the worst foreign policy defeat of his presidency when the Congress overrode his veto of sanctions legislation. And as best we can tell, Reagan wanted to veto the King holiday legislation but declined to do so because he would have been overridden and left isolated with unreconstructed movement conservatives like Jesse Helms and Patrick Buchanan (As a columnist, Buchanan urged a veto of the bill).

In 1987 the Senate rejected Reagan's nomination of Robert Bork to the Supreme Court. The conservative movement's most eminent legal scholar was rejected in part because of his opposition to the 1964 Civil Rights Act, as senators throughout the debate recalled his writing that the legislation was "unsurpassed ugliness."

Reagan's setbacks on civil rights also demonstrated the influence of the civil rights lobby on national policy making. A popular and ideologically committed president was nevertheless defeated time after time by a relatively resource-poor minority group. Matthew Holden Jr. captures the significance of this phenomenon when he writes: "The necessary implication is that a racial minority, that is also a political minority, is notably exposed if it can not discover means of leveraging within the legislative process. It is apparent that no group in American society can withstand steady, recurrent hostility from the presidency. The reason simply is that there are too many forms of discretion within the scope of the executive. But a group that possesses a significant position in the legislative process has means by which to exact from an administration a high price for adverse action."[153] This is precisely the situation that blacks confronted during the Reagan presidency: a hostile president but a significant position in the legislative process that allowed them to leverage it on civil rights so that Reagan found, to use Holden's phrase "the game [was] not worth the candle."[154]

On issues of welfare and poverty blacks had less leverage in the legislative process. Reagan, therefore, had somewhat more success in his attacks on programs for the poor. This relative lack of leverage in the legislative process, however, is less important than the fact there is no consensus on poverty and welfare policy in the United States. While a racially bastardized Locke has been repudiated, the chaste Locke of limited government, individualism, and self-reliance remains dominant. And when this chaste Locke is intertwined with laissez-faire racism it weakens those who would challenge a determined reform-minded president.

Welfare and Antipoverty Policies, 1981–1987

Reagan's principal domestic priority was not civil rights reform but to reduce taxes, decrease spending on the welfare state, and reduce the regulatory role of the government.[155] This hostility to taxing and spending was at the core of Reagan's philosophy. It is related to the conservative movement's belief in as much of unfettered capitalism as accommodation to the New Deal will permit. Unfettered capitalism is, then, related to the Lockean hostility to government efforts to create a more Roussean, equalitarian society.

These beliefs for movement conservatives took precedence over the traditional conservative belief in balanced budgets. Deficits in effect became a way to "starve the beast." The beast is the welfare state, and movement conservatives believed that sharp reductions in taxes (coupled with, in Reagan's case, massive increases in military spending) would starve the beast by reducing the amount of money Congress could appropriate for domestic programs. This has been the implicit, unstated policy of the Republican Party since the Reagan presidency. This strategy was given philosophical support by Milton Friedman, who argued that budget deficits were preferable to surpluses or balanced budgets because deficits were the only means available to contain the public's desire for an ever-growing welfare state.[156]

The phrase "starve the beast" is usually associated with Grover Norquist, the head of the Washington-based Americans for Tax Reform (founded in 1985 at the urging of Reagan). However, in his memoirs Reagan embraced the metaphor, writing, "I have always thought of government as a kind of organism with an insatiable appetite for money, whose natural state is to grow forever unless you do something to starve it. By cutting taxes, I wanted not only to stimulate the economy but to curb the growth of government and reduce its intrusion into the economy.[157]

Although American values and attitudes are ambivalent and inconsistent with respect to the welfare state and equality, in general they share what McClosky and Zaller call the "Lockean settlement."[158] That is, they support the Roussean Social Security program and other major New Deal welfare programs and the Great Society's Medicare/Medicaid programs and are even willing to see these programs expand to include, for example, national health insurance. But they also support the Lockean "logic of opportunity syllogism,"[159] which holds as its major premise that opportunity for economic advancement is available to all who are willing to work. Thus, where one ends up in the social and economic hierarchy depends on individual talent and initiative. Therefore, efforts by the government to attack inequality are viewed by the public with skepticism. As Kluegel and Smith put it, adherence to this "dominant ideology . . . generally disposes people toward conservative attitudes toward inequality related public policy."[160]

The Lockean settlement also predisposes Americans to be hostile toward the poor, believing that their poverty is a result of personal not institutional failure. Therefore, the government's responsibility is minimal. In Europe where a "Rousseau settlement" is more pervasive citizens view the government's responsibility quite differently. In a 1991 poll respondents were asked to agree or disagree with the statement: "It is the government's responsibility to take care of the poor." Seventy percent of Russians and Spanish agreed, nearly two thirds of the French, Italian and British but only 23 percent of Americans.[161]

In addition, Americans have always distinguished between "the worthy and unworthy or the deserving and undeserving poor."[162] The unworthy or undeserving are the able-bodied individuals who fail to provide for themselves and their families, while the worthy are those who are poor through no fault of their own, such as the elderly and the disabled. Reagan would use this distinction throughout his career referring to the worthy as "the truly needy."[163]

White Americans support the welfare state but they hate welfare. In his 1999 book Martin Gilens asked *Why Americans Hate Welfare*? Although his analysis is complicated, in the end his conclusion is that Americans hate welfare because they associate it with black people, and believe in the old white supremacist stereotype that blacks prefer welfare to work.[164] The 1992 General Social Survey found that 47 percent of whites believed that African Americans are lazy and 59 percent that blacks would prefer to live on welfare than work. And those whites (44 percent) who believed that the majority of people on welfare were black also believed that most people on welfare were undeserving because they did not wish to work. By contrast, the 18 percent who believed that most people on welfare were white believed recipients were worthy or deserving and were on welfare due to "circumstances beyond their control."[165]

Neoconservative intellectuals throughout the 1960s and 1970s reinforced these stereotypes, as did Reagan in his "welfare queen" and "young buck" rhetoric.[166] In 1984 Charles Murray published his influential broadside arguing that welfare unfairly transferred resources from the productive, demoralized recipients and should be abolished or drastically cut. This he argued would force people to work and in the long run would make them prosperous and happy (see chapter 7).

Thus, when Reagan took office it was assumed that he would "wage war on welfare"[167] as well as on those Great Society–related programs in housing, employment, and education whose objectives were to bring about a more racially equalitarian society.

The largest and most expensive welfare programs are Social Security and Medicare. The principal beneficiaries of these programs are the deserving poor, white, elderly, and disabled. With widespread public support and a powerful Washington lobby (the American Association for Retired Persons), Social Security and Medicare are referred to as "the third rail" in American politics; touch them and you are dead politically. Although Reagan ideologically would have liked to wage war on Social Security by making cuts, privatizing it, or making it voluntary, he knew the political climate and the influence of the elderly lobby would likely lead to defeat. Being a political realist Reagan, much to his budget director's despair, refused to attack or propose major cuts in Social Security. As Stockman woefully wrote, the Reagan revolution was supposed to have returned the government to its Lockean policeman role "a spare and stingy creature, which offered even handed justice and no more." But "Reagan had no business trying to make a revolution because it wasn't in his bones. He was a consensus politician, not an ideologue.... His conservative vision was only a vision."[168]

With Social Security off the table, that left only welfare for the undeserving poor and those programs designed to meliorate the bastardization of Locke. As we have seen these programs did not have a powerful lobby, and the political climate was hostile to them. If white Americans recognized the legacies of Locke's bastardization on the incidence of poverty among blacks, like Reagan, they did not wish the government to try to deal with them. Rather, "To most white Americans the fact that blacks make up a disproportionate share of the poor because of past discrimination (if this fact is recognized at all) does not constitute a problem in need of solution, because most white Americans do not believe that poverty itself presents any structural limits to opportunity.[169]

Since the beneficiaries of the non–Social Security and Medicare welfare programs (aid to poor women and their children, housing, food stamps, and Medicaid) are disproportionately black, Reagan's war on welfare became in its effects a war on blacks. Conservatism's war on welfare in its consequences became the same thing as racism.

Welfare Reform

If one judges by the hour and half January 6, 1981, meeting at Blair House between the president-elect and his senior advisors, welfare reform was a top priority of the incoming administration. In addition to Reagan, the nine persons in attendance included James Baker; Secretary of Health and Human Services designee Richard Schweiker; Robert Carlson, Reagan's California welfare director; and Martin Anderson, a senior policy advisor and the author of an important conservative manifesto on welfare.[170] At this meeting Carlson presented a briefing book with thirty-six issues for discussion and presidential approval for submission to Congress.[171]

At the core of the recommendations were proposals to create a series of block grants for the principal federal welfare programs for the poor, including AFDC, low-income energy assistance, and Medicaid. In addition, Carlson proposed that the thirteen categorical nutrition programs (food stamps; school lunch; summer feeding; the women, infants and children program; etc.) be consolidated into a comprehensive nutrition program. Under each of these proposed block grants the states were given "complete discretion over eligibility requirements, they could best determine priorities for truly needy families and design systems which could be financed with block grants."[172]

In addition, a series of other cost-saving measures were proposed, including limiting eligibility for AFDC to families with income at or above 150 percent of a states' needs standard (poverty level) and denying eligibility to children eighteen and above who were attending school. Stringent work requirements were also recommended, including requiring recipients attending college to work, revamp[ing] and mandating that all states establish "workfare" programs to assure that all AFDC recipients "perform useful tasks in the public sector when private sector jobs are unavailable, and to provide valuable job experience which can help recipients obtain private sector jobs."[173] These recommendations were in line with three conservative principles: states rights, cost cutting, and workfare. Workfare was based on the notion, articulated by Anderson and other conservative welfare analysts, that "enormous benefits discouraged work and therefore eligibility should be restricted, caseloads reduced, benefits cut and work should be mandatory."[174]

Although Reagan, with slight modifications, approved each of the thirty-six recommendations, they were not in 1981 submitted to Congress as comprehensive welfare reform. It is unclear as to why; however, Anderson suggests that welfare reform, like everything else, had to take a back seat to the priorities of tax cuts and the military buildup, and some staffers worried that the proposals would make the administration "appear mean and cruel to the poor."[175] However, as discussed below through its budget and administrative regulations, the administration was able to reduce welfare caseloads and grant states more options to require AFDC recipients to work.

In his 1986 State of the Union address Reagan made welfare reform an urgent priority of the administration, and under the direction of Attorney General Meese he appointed a task force to study the problem and make recommendations. In a February 5 radio address to the nation Reagan spoke of a "gathering crisis" in our "inner cities . . . especially among the welfare poor" caused by the "growing percentage of babies born out of wedlock."[176] Reagan blamed the crisis on "misguided welfare programs" and the Great Society, telling the nation, "From the 1950s on poverty in America was declining. American society, an opportunity society, was doing its wonders. Economic growth was providing a ladder for millions to climb out of poverty and into prosperity.

In 1964 the famous war on poverty was declared and a funny thing happen. Poverty, as measured by dependency, stopped shrinking and then actually began to grow worse; therefore, you could say, poverty won the war."[177]

In July 1987 the president announced the creation of an Interagency Low Income Opportunity Advisory Board, headed by Charles Hobbs, assistant to the president for policy development. The individuals consulted by the board included Charles Murray, Midge Decter, Walter Williams, and Thomas Sowell. The board presented its recommendations to the president in December 1986. Unlike the Blair House recommendations, Hobbs' report avoided block grants and focused mainly on tightening eligibility and a mandatory work requirement.[178]

Meanwhile in Congress the Democrats were proposing the 1962 AFDC-UP program (AID to Families with Dependent Children—Unemployed Parent) be made mandatory for all states. Under this program two parent families with children qualify for welfare if the "principal wage earner" is unemployed. Optional under current law (in 1987 twenty-one states had adopted the program), the Democrats argued that the failure to pay benefits to intact families promoted the breakup of families. Although Reagan in his radio address had lamented the impact of welfare on the breakup of families as "the most insidious effect" of the system, the administration opposed making AFDC-UP mandatory because it would increase costs and expand the number of recipients. In a compromise worked out between Senators Moynihan and Dole AFDC-UP was made mandatory, and participation in training or work programs was required of all able bodied recipients with children over the age of three.

Conservatives in and out of the administration urged the president to veto the bill, claiming that instead of decentralizing the system the mandatory AFDC-UP further centralized power in Washington while expanding the cost and coverage of the program. In a memo to Ed Feulner Stuart Butler wrote that the bill was a "disaster" because it "would raise welfare expenditures; raise benefit levels; expand welfare eligibility; micro manage welfare and restrict work programs. In stark contrast to the whole thrust of the Administration's proposals, they fail to decentralize welfare in any meaningful way."[179] But Feulner wrote, "President Reagan will face a very unpleasant choice—either veto a bipartisan welfare bill and be denounced as anti poor, or sign it and expand the welfare state."[180]

Reagan signed the bill. A July 15, 1988, memorandum for the president from Ken Cribb, Joe Wright, and Chuck Hobbs urged the president not to veto the legislation. Hobbs' signature on the memorandum was likely crucial, since he was the major architect of the administration's welfare strategy. The memorandum conceded that conservative "criticisms are certainly significant," and the "bill is not the welfare reform bill we would sign onto if we had our druthers.... But the most important forward step, and the one best understood by the public, is the establishment for the first time in federal law of the principle that someone able to work for their welfare must do so."[181]

The Family Support Act of 1988 signed by Reagan was far short of the kinds of radical reforms envisioned by the president in his January 1981 Blair House meeting. Except for the requirement that one parent in a two-parent family work in a public- or private-sector job for at least sixteen hours a week, the act did little to alter the system.[182] Substantively, then, the president's efforts to reform welfare fared only a little better than his efforts to reform the nation's civil rights laws. But, again the Reagan presidency was also a rhetorical presidency. The president's rhetoric throughout his presidency—indeed throughout his career—had sought to delegitimatize welfare and stigmatizes its recipients as lazy, shiftless welfare queens and young bucks.[183] Busch concludes that this rhetoric and the modest reforms of the 1988 Act, therefore, "served as a way station to the more fundamental reforms enacted in 1996."[184]

In 1992 Bill Clinton responded to Reagan's rhetorical legacy and to the perception that Reagan and Bush had won in the 1980s because conservatives had successfully portrayed Democrats as the liberal "give away party; giving white tax money to blacks and poor people."[185] Thus, in his 1992 campaign Clinton pledged to "end welfare as we know it." His strategists had told him that in order to win back the "Reagan Democrats" in the key battleground states of the Midwest (Ohio, Pennsylvania, Illinois, and Michigan), he would have to adopt a tough antiwelfare position. In television ads that ran in Ohio and Pennsylvania Clinton pledged to limit assistance to two years and force people to work. Clinton also used Reagan-like rhetoric, attacking teenage pregnancy and out-of-wedlock births as evidence of the lack of "individual responsibility" and "family values."

Clinton's campaign rhetoric and ads suggested that people would be cut off welfare and forced to find a job, period. In fact, his proposal, based on the work of David Ellwood (a Harvard public policy professor who became a top advisor in the first two years of the administration) involved a broad program of expanded social services including job training, healthcare, childcare, and public-sector jobs.[186] This proposal, which had the support of the Congressional Black Caucus, liberals, and children's advocacy groups, would have cost more than the existing welfare system, an estimated $30 billion. For almost two years Clinton delayed sending a bill to Congress, focusing in his first year on the budget deficit and in the second on national health insurance. Meanwhile, his staff was working on ways to scale back the expensive Ellwood plan. In late 1994 Clinton submitted his plan, but it was too late for Congress to act before the election.

When the Republicans won a majority in both houses in 1994, they took Clinton's campaign pledge seriously and attempted to enact the recommendations discussed by Reagan and his aides at Blair House in 1981. Three times Congress passed bills ending the sixty-year-old federal welfare system, including food stamps, Medicaid, and AFDC, transferring them as block grants to the states. Clinton vetoed the first two bills (forcing deletions in the third bill of the Medicaid and food stamp block grant provisions), but as the 1996 presidential election got underway, Clinton signed the bill.[187]

In a series of long, learned, passionate speeches opposing the bill, Senator Moynihan said the bill signed by Clinton raised the spectra of Victorian workhouses and women and children living on the streets, concluding that it represented the "most regressive event in social policy of the twentieth century."[188] Most of the president's senior policy advisers opposed the bill, and three resigned in protest when Clinton signed it.[189] Yet Clinton was told by his principal campaign strategist—Dick Morris—that if he vetoed the bill, Robert Dole, the Republican nominee, would use the veto to undermine his support among Reagan Democrats.[190]

The bill Clinton signed passed both houses of Congress overwhelmingly, but with the support of only two of the then 39 members of the Congressional Black Caucus. Just as Clinton signed the bill at least partly for political reasons, many of the liberal Democrats voted for it for the similar reasons. Here is Democratic New York Congressman Gary Ackerman explaining his vote: "It was not a happy decision. This is a bad bill but a good strategy. In order to continue economic and social progress, we must keep President Clinton in office. And we are in striking distance of a majority in the House in this year's election. We had to show America that Democrats are willing to break with the past, to move from welfare to workfare. Sometimes to make progress and move ahead, you have to stand up and do wrong. If we take back the House, we can fix this bill and take out some of the draconian parts."[191]

Thus, Reagan got his radical welfare reform bill; it just took fifteen years. The bill signed by Clinton amended Title IV of the Social Security Act of 1935 to, among other things, abolish the federal government's guarantee of aid to poor women and their children and transferred authority to the states, limited assistance to five years, denied benefits to unmarried mothers under eighteen, and, with a few exceptions, required adult recipients to work.

At the time the legislation was passed Senator Moynihan and others worried that it would throw millions of women and children into destitution once the time limits expired. However, during the prosperous 1990s, welfare recipients were able to keep those jobs, and studies indicate they were able to keep jobs during the high unemployment of 2000–2003. However, many former recipients did not find work, and many of those employed were working at jobs with wages and benefits too low to support families. Ten years after, the impact of the legislation on the well-being of poor black women and their children is still not clear. Rebecca Blank, dean of the University of Michigan's

Gerald R. Ford School of Social work, summarizes what we know about the law's consequences a decade later: "While there is a lot of evidence that work has increased and that earnings on average rose more than benefits fell, the translation of these facts into a definitive statement of well-being is hard to make. More women are working and poor, rather than nonworking and poor [but] we do not . . . have enough data on the long-term effects of these behavioral changes on children or families to yet make definitive pronouncements on the long term successes and failures of welfare reform."[192]

However one assesses the impact of the legislation, its enactment during the Clinton presidency represents a major triumph for Reagan and the conservative movement.

Budget and Antipoverty Programs

"President Reagan," writes Sheldon Danziger, "reformed welfare by cutting the budget."[193] In the 1981 budget, federal domestic spending was cut by more than $31 billion. Nearly 70 percent of these cuts were in programs for poor people, although they constituted only 18 percent of domestic income security programs.[194] Unable to cut Social Security, Reagan's 1981–1982 budget cut AFDC and other means-tested programs by 54 percent, job training by 81 percent, housing assistance by 47, and legal services for the poor by 28 percent.[195] In addition Washington virtually "abandoned the cities," with huge cutbacks in operating grants to state and local governments.[196] As *Newsweek* observed on the day these cuts were being enacted, "The Great Society, built and consolidated over fifteen years, was shrunk to size in just 26 hours and twelve minutes of floor debate."[197]

The Reagan cuts had a disproportionate impact on blacks. While this was not necessarily the intent, the impact of Reagan's budget was institutionally racist.[198]

In the 1982 midterm elections the Democrats picked up twenty-six seats in the House and thereafter blocked any further major cuts in welfare and antipoverty programs, and even restored some programs to their 1981 levels.[199] Martin Anderson concludes, "It is commonly believed that federal spending on social welfare programs [was] slashed during the presidency of Ronald Reagan. It was not. Spending on social welfare increased surely and steadily, perhaps more than Reagan would have liked, but nevertheless it did increase."[200]

Nevertheless, within the limits of the Washington policy process the administration was able to pursue its ideological agenda and cut back and limit the growth of racially equalitarian social policies.[201] As Sloan concludes, under Reagan, "For the first time since the New Deal, the federal government ceased attempting to constrain the propensity of capitalism to generate inequality."[202]

In addition, the president's starve-the-beast strategy and his antitax rhetoric created a "deficit trap" that made the enactment of such programs after he left office all the more difficult.[203]

This is perhaps the most important legacy of the ascent of the conservative movement's prophet to the presidency: the foreclosed opportunities for further progress toward a racially just society. The efforts of movement conservatives to reverse the civil rights gains of the 1960s were for the most part not realized. And although cuts were made by Reagan to programs designed to help poor blacks in 1981 and 1982, to some extent they were reversed in later years. But after Reagan's ascendancy no president has been willing to once again undertake the difficult task of trying to use the government to bring about the full incorporation of blacks into society by undertaking another war on poverty. The legacy of the conservative movement on race then comes down to, as Sara Diamond writes, to "what might have been": "On race matters in the United States one can only imagine what progress might have been made absent the longevity of the racist right. Though ultimately unsuccessful in its goals, the segregationist movement's strength left an enduring mark on partisan politics as the Republicans and eventually the Democrats, too, made themes of racial division central to their campaigns. The indirect effect of the organized racist right was to leave policymaking stalled at the phase of ending formal segregation, and to hinder redress of continuing and pervasive racial injustice."[204] After the Reagan victories in the 1980s the racially equalitarian Democratic Party, like its Republican counterpart in the 1880s, repudiated its commitment to pursue racially liberal equalitarian policies. It did so because many of its elites, again like their Republican counterparts in the 1880s, came to believe that a commitment to racial equalitarianism undermined the party's capacity to win elections. In the concluding chapter of this book this Democratic capitulation is examined, and the might-have-been question is explored further. I also, to quote Myrdal shortly before his death, express my "worried thoughts" about the future.[205]

CHAPTER TEN

Conclusion

After the ascendancy of Ronald Reagan, his landslide reelection, and the election of his vice president to succeed him, influential Democratic Party elites came to believe that the party could not recapture the presidency unless it disassociated itself from the interest of African Americans. From 1968 to 1988 issues related to race occupied an important place in national elections. Historically, when race is an issue the racially liberal or equalitarian party loses. In this situation the liberal party naturally moves initially to take a more conservative position on race and then to the mobilization of bias in order to remove the issue from partisan competition. As shown in chapter 8, for all but about forty years this mobilization of bias in the party system was the norm, interrupted only by the brief Reconstruction era and the period from the 1960s to the 1980s.

In some ways this mobilization of bias was not just against the party's racial liberalism but against the kind of advanced liberalism in domestic and foreign policies embraced generally by the party when it nominated McGovern in 1972. But to party elites race was believed to be at the core of the party's electoral vulnerability.

The drum beat for the mobilization of bias began shortly before the 1984 election and increased in intensity after 1988. In 1984 Hamilton Jordan, President Carter's chief political strategist, wrote an article in the *New Republic*, the liberal opinion journal, arguing that the Democratic Party was too liberal to win national elections and that in order to become more competitive it had to become more conservative. Jordan traced the party's liberalism to its capture by "special interests," labor, feminists, but especially blacks.[1] Just prior to the 1988 election Harry McPhearson, a former Johnson administration functionary, wrote an op-ed in the *New York Times* titled "How Race Destroyed the Democratic Coalition," in which he contended that the party's identification with blacks put it at risk of becoming a permanent minority in presidential elections.[2] The *Times* itself in its postmortem on the 1988 election raised similar concerns.[3] In 1991 Thomas Edsal, a *Washington Post* reporter, with his wife, Mary, published an article in *Atlantic Monthly* simply called "Race," where these arguments about the crippling effects of blacks on the post–civil rights era Democratic Party presidential coalition were synthesized.[4] Later in a best-selling book, clearly written to influence the 1992 election, Thomas Edsal once again invoked the specter of race destroying the Democratic Party. He argued that in order to win the presidency Democrats should deemphasize issues of racism, poverty, civil rights, and affirmative action and instead focus on the concerns of the white middle class in terms of lower taxes, opposition to quotas, and a tough approach on welfare and crime.[5]

These published lamentations had their counterparts in internal polling and strategic studies by the Democratic National Committee (DNC). After the 1984 election the DNC commissioned several studies to determine why the Democrats lost the presidency. One was conducted by Stanley Greenberg, Clinton's 1992 pollster. It pointed directly to the party's identification with blacks as the source of the problem. Based on a series of focus-group interviews with "Reagan Democrats" in Macomb County, a Detroit suburb, Greenberg argued that the reason these white middle- and working-class voters turned against the Democrats was because of their "distaste" for blacks and because of their association of the party with "them." Greenberg wrote, "These white Democratic defectors express a profound distaste for blacks, a sentiment that pervades almost everything they think about government and politics.... Blacks constitute the explanation for their [Reagan Democrats'] vulnerability and for almost everything that has gone wrong in their lives, not being black is what constitutes being middle class, not living with blacks is what makes a neighborhood a decent place to live. These sentiments have important implications for Democrats, as virtually all progressive symbols have been redefined in racial and pejorative terms."[6] Implicit in Greenberg's report was the notion that if the party was to win the presidency it would have to distance itself—at least symbolically—from blacks and their interests and present itself—again at least symbolically—as the party of the white middle class. This notion was made explicit in a report prepared by Milton Kotler and Nelson Rosenbaum for the DNC. In 1985 DNC chair Paul Kirk, a protégé of Senator Edward Kennedy, paid a private consultant firm more than $250,000 for a study of what the party might do to win in the future. The study, reportedly the largest research project ever undertaken by the party, was based on a series of focus-group interviews and a national survey of more than five thousand voters. Kotler and Rosenbaum concluded that the Democrats needed to "de-market" the party to the social and economic "underclass" and focus instead on the concerns of the middle class. Like the Greenberg study, this report concluded that among southern whites and northern urban "ethnic" voters the party was perceived as taking money from hardworking whites and giving it (in the form of welfare) to lazy, undeserving blacks.[7] The study was distributed to a number of party leaders, and the reactions of some to its language and tone were so negative that Kirk refused to release it and reportedly ordered all but a few copies destroyed.

Finally, the Progressive Policy Institute, the research arm of the Democratic Leadership Council (DLC), the organization of white conservative and centrist Democrats formed in 1985 (see later), published *The Politics of Evasion*. The study, widely publicized, made in a more scholarly way the same points made in the Greenberg and Kolter and Rosenbaum studies. In some ways it became a kind of political bible of the party's more conservative elements, finding its way into the strategy, rhetoric, and proposals of Bill Clinton, a DLC founder and chairman.[8]

Although these calls for the abandonment of liberalism have their roots in the reaction of party centrists and conservatives to the McGovern insurgency, it was the ascendancy of Reagan that was the major impetus for the party's shift to the right.

Reagan as a "Reconstructive" President

In his innovative study of the presidency Skowronek concludes that substantively, unlike other reconstructive leaders (Jefferson, Jackson, Lincoln, and FDR), Reagan accomplished very little. Indeed, he concludes Reagan "fell far short of the mark in revitalizing national government around his priorities and opening a more productive course for development.... [He] proved far less successful than the New Deal in reconstructing American government. The institutional commitments of the liberal regime though battered and starved, were not decisively dislodged, and their 'entitlements' would continue to determine the range of political possibilities." However, like other reconstructive presidents "Reagan closed off a prior course of development" and "changed the terms and conditions of national politics."[9]

For these reasons, it is only somewhat hyperbolic to refer to the "Reagan Revolution" to characterize his presidency, or to refer to the president as the "Roosevelt of the Right."[10] Reagan's greatness as a leader is in what might have been, the closed off opportunities for liberal, activist government that otherwise might have remained available. Reagan accomplished this partly by "forging a long-term political coalition capable of advancing the claims of liberty against the powerful coalition whose values were equalitarian and economic security."[11] Or as Berman puts it "like no other politician since Franklin Roosevelt he made very good use of language and sentiment to tap into the wellspring of traditional beliefs and values, which were associated with an old fashioned patriotism, on the one hand, a commitment to free markets and individual opportunity, on the other."[12]

FDR co-opted the word *liberal* and used it to legitimatize the regulatory and welfare functions of government, thereby transforming the context of ideological, political and policy debates in the United States. Reagan did the opposite. He discredited liberalism, and to some extent delegitimatized the idea of using government to bring about a more equalitarian society. In doing so, like Roosevelt, he brought about a similar transformation in the context of ideological, political, and policy debates.

Reagan's attack on liberalism had a specifically racial component. First, it sought to delegitimatize the black quest for racial justice through recurrent attacks on the "failed" government programs of the 1960s, the welfare state, and affirmative action. Second, it reframed the policy debate on race from an emphasis on the responsibilities of government to a focus on the shortcomings of blacks themselves in terms of the absence of individual responsibility, "family values" and community self-help.

In general, this conservative transformation has been remarkably successful. Liberalism has been substantially discredited (at least among white elites and publics), becoming the dreaded "L" word to be avoided by politicians with national ambitions.[13] Policy debate in general and on race in particular has indeed shifted to the right; race matters are now more frequently discussed in terms of black irresponsibility, and white mass opinion appears to some extent to have both shaped and followed this elite framing of ideology and policy debates.

It is these contextual transformations that Democratic Party elites had to grapple with as they sought to regain majority status.

The Democratic Leadership Council, Bill Clinton, and the Mobilization of Bias, 1988–1992

The DLC, the organization of centrist and conservative party leaders formed in 1985, was made up of "the most organized and successful challengers to the prevailing liberalism of the post-1968 Democratic Party."[14] And early on the DLC identified Bill Clinton as the candidate to carry its neoliberal philosophy to the White House. Al From, its executive director and driving force, recognized Clinton's potential as a national leader and tried to recruit him as DLC chair, telling him in a 1989 visit to Arkansas, "[I] have a deal for you, if you take the DLC chairmanship, we will give you a national platform, and I think you will be the next president of the United States of America."[15] Once he became president, Clinton "served a pivotal if ironic role in the post Reagan era. In order to win in the relatively conservative environment nurtured by Reagan, Clinton had to adopt numerous themes from the 1980s... [H]e gave a bipartisan stance and turned [the themes] from topics of intense debate into new positions of the national consensus."[16]

At the core of the DLC's effort to remake the Democratic Party and fashion an alternative to liberalism was its concern about the party's perceived racial liberalism, but in its 1990 "New Orleans Declaration: A Democratic Agenda for the 1990s," it embraced the full scope of Lockean verities: "traditional American values," "belief in individualism," a "strident defense of the two parent family," and a "neo-Jeffersonian emphasis on state and local initiatives."[17] The Declaration also declared that instead of focusing on "redistribution of wealth," the Democrats should work to establish a "free market . . . which in turn would promote economic growth."[18] The document also proposed spending cuts rather than tax increases to balance the budget and called for an end to "welfare paternalism."[19] These ideas are consistent with longstanding conservative movement ideas; however, the DLC described them as "progressive" and a "new formula for activist government."[20] Indeed, some students of the DLC view its agenda as a "liberal-leaning platform couched in soothing centrist rhetoric for a party unable to do so and one that has considerable appeal to the party's liberal base."[21]

In this view the DLC's "progressivism" was an effort to develop a winning strategy that would allow the party to pursue liberal ends by conservative means. Traditional liberals were not convinced. Arthur Schlesinger described the DLC as a "quasi-Reaganite faction" whose public philosophy would be a "disaster" for liberalism.[22]

In many ways the DLC resembles the ironically named liberal Republican Party faction led by Horace Greely during Reconstruction. Its aim was to win elections, by any ideological means necessary. That is, DLC members may have been "closet liberals," embracing centrism or neoliberalism as means of political survival rather than conviction.[23] This would appear to be especially the case with the young former McGovernite Bill Clinton. In this sense Clinton and the DLC were simply accommodating the party to the historical fact of liberalism's remnant status in American politics, a remnant that can only be advanced in times of crisis or by stealth.

The DLC and Race

In its early years the DLC attracted a handful of black members, including Congressmen Bill Gray and John Lewis and Los Angeles mayor Tom Bradley. But as the group began to move further right in the late 1980s, most African Americans (and traditional white liberals such as Congressman Dick Gephardt) began to disassociate themselves from the organization.

The proverbial straws that broke the camel's back were the DLC's increasingly hard-line Reaganite position on affirmative action and its decision not to invite Jesse Jackson and George McGovern to address its 1991 Cleveland conference. All of the prospective 1992 Democratic presidential candidates were invited except Jackson and McGovern. From said Jackson was not invited, although he had twice before addressed the conference because he was a "hindrance to the party's electoral future," and he and McGovern represented" the old, big government, taxing wing of the party ... [T]hey are not reformers."²⁴

The DLC for a time waffled on affirmative action but in 1990, it took a Reagan-like "unequivocal stand against quotas." While affirming affirmative action in principle, the DLC adopted the language of Reagan's undelivered 1985 speech on affirmative action, declaring, "[W]e oppose discrimination of any kind—including Quotas."²⁵

As a result of the Jackson flap and the DLC's hardening position on affirmative action, a "racial backlash" developed among black leaders. Congressman Gray said the decision not to invite Jackson had "racial overtones." Calling on From to resign, Gray said his allegations that the party was beholden to special interests was a "Republican charge" that "mouths right-wing Republican attacks" and From and the DLC's positions on civil rights "sound like David Duke." Gray also specifically rejected the canard "that those who would help the poor are somehow the captive of special interests."²⁶ Meanwhile, Jesse Jackson came to Cleveland to protest, suggesting the DLC was racist and conservative.²⁷

From did not resign, and Clinton, running on the DLC platform, in 1992 was overwhelmingly supported by blacks in the primaries and general election. On welfare, crime, and affirmative action Clinton as president pursued the DLC agenda, while declining to consider any policies or programs to deal with racialized poverty. Nevertheless, blacks remained his most loyal and enthusiastic bloc of voters.²⁸

The embrace of Clinton by blacks in spite of his embrace of Reaganite positions on race and poverty demonstrates the captive status of blacks in the post-Reagan Democratic Party.²⁹ To paraphrase Brent Bozell from chapter 8 blacks were necessarily on the lead-strings of the right during Clinton's presidency. As a captive faction, they could protest, but no one was required to listen. Worse still, they could not even build a powerful independent force of their own because powerful forces among them fostered the down-the-line support of Democratic leadership as a lesser of two evils.

Whither the Future of Liberalism and Racial Liberalism

Most scholars—as I have for the most part in this work—trace the collapse of liberalism to events of the 1960s and the ascendancy of the conservative movement and its prophet. But C. Wright Mills in his enduringly instructive 1950s book, *The Power Elite,* traces liberalism's declining fortunes to the ideology's remnant status in the American tradition. Describing the United

States as "a conservative country without a conservative tradition," Mills wrote that liberalism in the 1950s was a "decayed and frightened" ideology, which "over the past century.... has been undergoing a moral and intellectual decline of serious proportion."[30] Mills traced this decline to FDR's failure to develop a liberal party or nurture a liberal movement. Mills wrote, "The New Deal left no liberal organization to carry on a liberal program; rather than a new party, its instrument was a loose coalition inside an old one, which quickly fell apart so far as liberal ideas are concerned."[31] FDR recognized this dilemma for liberalism within the Democratic Party in his unsuccessful attempt to purge the party of its more conservative elements. He also toyed with the idea of forming a liberal party, but toying was all he did, leaving the liberal remnant without either movement or party.

For Mills, this Rooseveltian failure left liberal ideas and programs gridlocked in the "semi-organized stalemate" characteristic of the Lockean-Madisonian constitutional system.[32] This stalemate was broken, and the liberal moment flourished—briefly—as a result of an unusual set of circumstances: the assassination of President Kennedy, the ascendancy of a skilled legislative strategist in President Johnson, an unusually large Democratic congressional majority as a result of Goldwater's landslide loss, and a powerful African American social movement that inspired other groups to seek a more equalitarian society. But President Johnson knew very well that this liberal hour would be brief; therefore, he sought to get as much done as quickly as possible knowing the semi-organized stalemate would soon return liberalism to its remnant status.[33]

Mills might have anticipated the events of the 1960s, but writing in the McCarthyite 1950s he saw "radicalism defeated and radical hope stoned to death," and liberalism in its "imbroglio with the noisy right" had no defense against the conservative establishment or what Mills called "the petty right . . . political shock troops."[34] Given these conditions Mills probably would not have been surprised that the noisy, petty right—thanks to Buckley, Friedman, Goldwater, and Reagan—has become respectable and the militant liberalism espoused by FDR has become the dreaded "L" word.

So what is the future of the Democrats, the liberal remnant, and its racially liberal residual? In spite of or perhaps possibly because of the DLC's and Bill Clinton's transformative work, the two parties are pretty evenly balanced in national politics (with a slight advantage to the Republicans in presidential elections), and short of some catastrophe they are likely to remain so for the foreseeable future. Some scholars, however, suggest that demographic and cultural changes point toward "an emerging Democratic majority."[35] Thus, it is possible that another liberal hour may be on the horizon. Another liberal hour, however, does not necessarily mean a racially liberal time. The next liberal hour, like the first, may on questions of race and poverty be unwilling to take the risks. This is the impression one gets from reading recent liberal manifestos, none of which addresses in any direct way racialized poverty. For example, Paul Krugman's various proposals to achieve greater equality—with national health insurance as the centerpiece—are mainly devoted to enhancing the status of the beleaguered middle class. He has nothing to say about the poor in general or the ghettoized poor specifically.[36] And Paul Starr in *Freedom's Power: The True Force of Liberalism* discusses income inequality, health care, energy, environment, the debt, and deficits but nothing about the glaring problems of ghetto poverty or institutional racism in employment, health, housing, and the criminal justice system.[37] Both Starr and Krugman also propose tax increases—on the wealthy—but they, like most post-Clinton Democrats, do not propose spending the money on the poor. The liberal intellectuals of the age of Reagan, like Galbraith and Schlesinger in the age of Roosevelt, do not see black people and their problems.

Meanwhile, "the inner cities," as Berman writes, "continue[d] to rot away."[38] As a result of the civil rights revolution and the Great Society, a solid black middle class exists in black America as well as a stable albeit unsteady working class. But anywhere from a quarter to a third of African Americans remain mired in poverty. This concentrated poverty in urban ghettos in the Reagan era was labeled an "underclass," a term that was partly employed to denigrate poor blacks.[39] The idea of an urban underclass also ignores the problems of concentrated poverty among blacks in the rural South.[40] Whether these persons are called "poor people" or an "underclass" and whether they live in an inner city or in a rural southern hamlet the central problem is jobs—the lack of work with sufficient wages to sustain families.

At least since the publication of Moynihan's famous 1965 report on the Negro family, serious and sympathetic students of the plight of poor blacks have identified joblessness—especially male joblessness—as central to the disabilities of ghetto life.[41] When work is not available crime increases, marriages are dissolved or never formed, children perform less well in school, health declines, mortality is higher, and substance abuse increases.[42] This is why this problem was the principal focus of Dr. King at the time of his death and why after the civil rights revolution African American leaders made full employment the centerpiece of the "black" agenda. Ultimately, the black lobby was able to pressure the Congress and President Carter to enact the Humphrey-Hawkins "Full Employment and Balanced Growth Act of 1978." But by the time it was passed—at President Carter's insistence—it had been so watered down that the *New York Times* called it a "cruel hoax on the hard core unemployed holding before them hope—but not the reality—of a job."[43]

Today in many of the nation's inner cities the black male unemployment rate is estimated at more than 50 percent,[44] 70 percent of children are born out of wedlock, the high school dropout rate is 35 to 50 percent, a third of young men are incarcerated or on parole, and violence is chronic. In some areas of many cities the government is failing in its first responsibility—to protect the lives, liberties, and property of its citizens. In many places the conditions are near Hobbesian in that "there is no place for industry because the fruit thereof is uncertain: and consequently no culture of the earth ... nor use of commodities ... no commodious buildings ... no arts, no letters, no society; and which is worst of all, continued fear, and danger of violent death."[45]

But McClosky and Zaller write:

> Many members of the opinion elite, moreover, regard the existence of a sizeable underclass of impoverished citizens as a standing indictment of the economic system that produced them. When, as a result of normal swings in the nation's mood and voting tendencies, some of these liberally inclined elites come to power, they will attempt to mobilize public support for a renewed assault on poverty and cultural deprivation that the private enterprise system has been unable to eliminate on its own. In view of the widespread equalitarian values we have been able to document in this study there is reason to believe such appeals for economic reform will meet with considerable success.[46]

There is substantial support among Democratic Party elites for government assistance to improve the social and economic conditions of blacks, which increased after the election of Reagan. In response to the question, "Should the government provide aid to blacks to improve their economic and social position, or should blacks help themselves?" in 1984 57 percent of Democratic Party elites selected government aid; in 1992, 75 percent. However, among rank-and-file Democrats the percent supporting government assistance declined form 41 percent in 1984 to 33 percent in 1992. Among Republican elites support more than doubled between 1984 and 1992, from 12 to 27 percent. But among the rank and file it declined from 21 to 12 percent.[47] In general, as Stanley Feldman and John Zaller show there is more congruence on opposition to the welfare state among conservative Republican elites and masses than there is in support among liberal Democratic elites and masses. This again is because liberalism is the remnant, therefore, conservatives can easily justify their antiwelfare attitudes by appealing to Lockean values. Liberals, however, are conflicted. They too are committed to the Lockean settlement but also to the Roussean idea that the government should reduce inequality.[48]

But even in another liberal or Roussean moment, it is likely that blacks will have to make the Democratic president—even an African American— respond to their specific concerns, as Randolph did in the 1930s and 1940s and as King did in the 1960s. But—and this is my greatest worry—given the ongoing integration or incorporation of talented young blacks into systemic institutions and processes there may be no Kings or Randolphs around to make them do it; to bring the inevitably necessary pressure on liberals. After all, a young man named Barack Obama concluded he could make a greater contribution to racial justice as a politician than as a community organizer.

Notes

Introduction

1. This is the first study to systematically explore this relationship between conservatism and racism. But Gunnar Myrdal hinted at it in a methodological appendix in *An American Dilemma*, although he was dealing with the problem of ideological biases in social science research on race. Nevertheless he wrote in a footnote, "These ideological tendencies are biased in a static and do-nothing (laissez-faire) conservative direction, which, in the main, works against a disfavored group like the American Negroes," *An American Dilemma: The Negro Problem and Modern Democracy* (New York: Harper and Row, 1944, 1962), 1036. Ronald Walters pursues the relationship by defining the "radical aspect" of the conservative movement as "white nationalism" intent on using "both unofficial power and the official power of the state to maintain white supremacy by subordinating blacks and other non-whites." See *White Nationalism, Black Interests: Conservative Public Policy and the Black Community* (Detroit: Wayne State University Press, 2003), 26.

2. Interview with Kevin Phillips, "Forum," KQED Radio, San Francisco, April 4, 2006.

3. Myrdal, *An American Dilemma*, pp. 12–13.

4. Kelly Miller, "Radicals and Conservatives," in *Radicals and Conservatives and Other Essays on the Negro in America* (New York: Schocken Books, 1908, 1968), 25.

5. Jay Sigler, *The Conservative Tradition in American Thought* (New York: Putnam, 1969), 4.

6. George H. Nash, *The Conservative Intellectual Movement in America* (New York: Basic Books, 1976), 199.

7. Eugene Genovese, *The Southern Tradition: The Achievements and Limitations of American Conservatism* (Cambridge: Harvard University Press, 1994), 2.

8. Richard Weaver, *Ideas Have Consequences* (Chicago: University of Chicago Press, 1948); and his *The Southern Tradition at Bay: A History of Postbellum Thought* (New Rochelle, NY: Arlington House, 1968).

Chapter 1

1. References to conservatism in America as the remnant, an illusion, or a thankless persuasion are in Albert Jay Nock, "Isaiah's Job," in William F. Buckley Jr.

ed., *American Conservative Thought in the Twentieth Century* (Indianapolis: Bobbs Merrill, 1970), 509-22; M. Morton Auerbach, *The Conservative Illusion* (New York: Columbia University Press, 1959); and Clinton Rossiter, *Conservatism in America: The Thankless Persuasion* (New York: Vintage Books, 1955).

2. Bruce Frohnen, Jeremy Beer, and Jeffrey O. Nelson, eds., *American Conservatism: An Encyclopedia* (Wilmington, DE: Isis Books, 2006), x.

3. Alan Brinkley, "The Problem of American Conservatism," *The American Historical Review* (April 1994): 409, 412, 415. For an argument that scholarship on conservatism is more extensive than Brinkley suggests, see Leo Riboffo, "Why Is There So Much Conservatism in the United States and Why Do So Few Historians Know Anything about It?" *American Historical Review* 99(1994): 438-79.

4. Phillip Abbot, "Still Louis Hartz, After All These Years: A Defense of the Liberal Society Thesis," *Perspectives on Politics* 3 (2005): 93-109.

5. See Auerbach, *The Conservative Illusion*; Rossiter, *Conservatism in America*; Bernard Crick, "The Strange Quest for an American Conservatism," *Review of Politics* 17(1955): 361-63; and Samuel P. Huntington, "Conservatism as an Ideology," *American Political Science Review* 51(1957): 454-73.

6. See Auerbach, *The Conservative Illusion*, where he traces the "transcendental" value of conservatism to Plato's idea of "harmony." Modern conservatism also attempts to locate the ideology's core principles in Western political thought prior to the writings of Machiavelli, Hobbes, Locke, and Rousseau. See, for example, Leo Strauss, *Liberalism, Ancient and Modern* (New York: Basic Books, 1968); John Murley, ed., *Lee Strauss, the Straussians and the American Regime* (Lanham, MD.: Rowman and Littlefield, 1999); and Shadia Drury, *Leo Strauss and the American Right* (New York: St. Martin's, 1997).

7. Huntington, "Conservatism as an Ideology," p. 457. Brinkley also writes, "Conservatism is not an 'ideology' with a secure and consistent internal structure" and that it lacks "consistency and clarity." See "The Problem of American Conservatism," p. 414. While Huntington contends that conservatism lacks a substantive ideal, he lists six principles—derived from Burke—where he contends there exists "substantial agreement" among conservative writers.

8. Karl Mannheim, "Conservative Thought," in *Essays on Sociology and Social Psychology*, by Karl Mannheim, ed. Paul Kecskemeti (New York: Oxford, 1953). Mannheim distinguishes conservatism from traditionalism. Although traditionalism can become consciously conservative in times of ideological conflict, generally, it is little more then a "tendency to cling to vegetative patterns, to old ways of life which we may consider as fairly ubiquitous and universal. Traditionalism is not therefore necessarily bound up "with political or other sorts of conservatism" (p. 95). On this distinction see also David Allen, "Modern Conservatism: The Problem of Definition," *The Review of Politics* 43(1981): 582-604.

9. Mannheim, "Conservative Thought," p. 95.
10. Ibid., p. 115.
11. Huntington, "Conservatism as an Ideology," p. 455.
12. Ibid., p. 671.
13. Ibid., p. 459.
14. Ibid., p. 456.

15. Ibid., p. 465.
16. Ibid., p. 460.
17. Ibid., p. 471.
18. Ibid., p. 457.
19. Ibid., p. 459.

20. Article I, section 9, prohibiting Congress from ending the slave trade before 1808 and limiting any tax on imported slaves to ten dollars; article V prohibiting any amendment to the Constitution that would alter the 1808 date or the ten-dollar tax; article IV, section 2, requiring the northern states to return slaves who escaped to freedom back to their bondage in the South; and article I, section 2, the Three-fifths Clause.

21. Donald Robinson, "The Constitutional Legacy of Slavery," *National Political Science Review* 4 (1994): 11.

22. Wilma King, *Stolen Childhood: Slave Youth in Nineteenth-Century America* (Bloomington: Indiana University Press, 1995). Of this bastardization of Locke Alexis de Tocqueville wrote that the "atrocities" of American slavery were so unparalleled as "suffice to show that laws of humanity have been totally perverted," see *Democracy in America*, vol. 1, ed. Phillip Bradley (New York: Vintage Books, 1945), 395.

23. Jill Lepore, *New York Burning: Liberty, Slavery, and Conspiracy in Eighteenth-Century Manhattan* (New York: Vintage Books, 2005).

24. Stokely Carmichael and Charles Hamilton, *Black Power: Politics of Liberation in America* (New York: Vintage Books, 1967), 3–4.

25. Pierre Van den Berghe, *Race and Racism: A Comparative Perspective* (New York: Wiley and Sons, 1967), 11.

26. See George M. Fredrickson, *White Supremacy: A Comparative Study in American and South African History* (New York: Oxford, 1981), 70, 73. More generally see Winthrop Jordan, *White over Black: American Attitudes toward the Negro, 1550–1812* (Baltimore: Penguin Books, 1968).

27. In my own work on post–civil-rights-era racism—where racist behavior is not rationalized on the basis of attitudes or ideology—I found the Carmichael and Hamilton definition especially useful. Indeed the definition (or something akin to it) is near indispensable for experimental research on institutional racism. See Robert C. Smith, *Racism in the Post Civil Rights Era: Now You See It, Now You Don't* (Albany: State University of New York Press, 1995), chs. 1–2, 4.

28. Hegel and Kant are quoted in Errol Henderson, "Navigating the Muddy Waters of the Mainstream: Tracing the Mystification of Racism in International Relations," in Wilbur Rich ed., *African American Perspectives on Political Science* (Philadelphia: Temple University Press, 2007), 351–52. More generally see Charles Mills, *The Racial Contract* (Ithaca, NY: Cornell University Press, 1997).

29. Forrest Wood, *The Arrogance of Faith: Christianity and Race in America from the Colonial Era to the Twentieth Century* (New York: Knopf, 1990).

30. George Fredrickson, *The Black Image in the White Mind: The Debate on Afro-American Character and Destiny* (New York: Harper and Row, 1961).

31. Thomas Jefferson offered one of the first pretensions of scientific proof of black inferiority to whites, where like Hegel and Kant, he concluded that blacks lacked moral and reasoning capacities. See his *Notes on Virginia*, ed. William Peden (Chapel

Hill: University of North Carolina Press, 1954), 162–63. Generally on these pretensions see Stephen Gould, *The Mismeasure of Man* (New York: Norton, 1981); Rhett Jones, "Proving Blacks Inferior: The Sociology of Knowledge," *Black World* 21 (July 1967): 9–22; and Elazar Barkan, *The Retreat of Scientific Racism in Britian and the United States between the World Wars* (Cambridge: Cambridge University Press, 1992).

32. Joe R. Feagin, *Racist America: Roots, Current Realities and Future Reparations* (New York: Routledge, 2000).

Chapter 2

1. C. B. Macpherson, *Political Theory of Possessive Individualism* (New York: Oxford University Press, 1962), 194.

2. The classic statement of Locke as a liberal is of course Louis Hartz, *The Liberal Tradition in America: An Interpretation of American Political Thought since the Revolution* (New York: Harcourt, Brace, and World, 1955). See also Rogers Smith, "Beyond Tocqueville, Myrdal and Hartz: The Multiple Traditions in America" *American Political Science Review* 87(1993): 549–66. Smith contends that liberalism is only one of three traditions in American thought and practice and is not hegemonic as Hartz argued. Liberalism, Smith argues, exists alongside republicanism and racism ("ascriptive hierarchy") in often conflicting and contradictory ways in the American political tradition. See also his comprehensive statement of his argument in *Civic Ideals: Conflicting Visions of American Citizenship in U.S. History* (New Haven: Yale University Press, 1997). As discussed in note 75, I do not see the sharp distinction Smith posits between liberalism and republicanism.

3. Hartz, *The Liberal Tradition*, p. 11.

4. Douglas Brinkley, *The End of Reform: New Deal Liberalism in Recession and War* (New York: Knopf, 1995), 8.

5. Gary Gerstle, "The Protean Character of American Liberalism," *American Historical Review* (September 1994): 1045.

6. Clifford Girvetz, *The Evolution of Liberalism* (New York: Collier Books, 1950, 1963); and Paul Starr, *Freedom's Power: The True Force of Liberalism* (New York: Basic Books, 2007), 1–3.

7. It is not my purpose here to get into the intellectual argument about the origins of the state or the nation-state and the difference between state and government. Of course no one accepts the contract theory of the state (not even the contract theorists themselves) as anything other than a useful philosophical "imaginative project," but beyond that there are still considerable contestations. See Jon Migdal, "Studying the State," in Mark Lichbach and Alan Zuckerman, eds., *Comparative Politics: Rationality, Culture and Structure* (Cambridge: Cambridge University Press, 1997); Hugh Selton-Watson, *Nation and States: An Enquiry into the Origins of Nations and the Politics of Nationalism* (Boulder, CO.: Westview, 1977); and Margaret Levi, "The State of the Study of State," in Ira Katznelson and Helen Milner, eds., *Political Science: State of the Discipline* (New York: Norton, 2002). Although not very much read and wrong on many particulars Frederick Engels, *The Origin of the Family, Private Property and the State* (New York: International, 1993), is still worthy of study.

8. Social scientists have not been able to reach consensus, with definitions of ideology ranging from the classic understandings of Marx and Mannheim to contemporary arguments among political science survey researchers. See W. B. Gallie, "Essentially Contested Concepts," *Proceedings of the Aristotelian Society* 56(1956): 167-98. See alsoTerry Eagelton where he lists seventeen relatively distinct definitions of ideology in his *Ideology: An Introduction* (London: Verso, 1991).

9. The idea of the social contract has been traced back to the work of the Manegold of Lautenbach, an eleventh-century Austrian monk, who wrote that if a king "violates the contract under which he was elected, disturbing and confounding that which he was established to set order, then the people is justly and reasonably released from obligation to obey him"; see Michael Lessnoff, ed., *Social Contract Theory* (New York: New York University Press, 1990). I write "free men" because each of the major contract theorists—Hobbes, Locke, and Rousseau—contended that only men were involved in the contracting process that created the state. On this sexism in liberal philosophy, see Susan Okin, *Women in Western Thought* (Princeton: Princeton University Press, 1979); Carol Pateman, *The Sexual Contract* (Stanford: Stanford University Press, 1988); and Arlene Saxonhouse, *Women in the History of Political Thought* (New York: Praeger, 1985).

10. Hartz, *The Liberal Tradition in America*, pp. 60–51. Hartz goes on to write, "There was a frontier that was veritable state of nature. There were agreements, such as the Mayflower Compact that were . . . social contracts" (p. 61).

11. Ibid., p. 62.

12. Smith, *Civic Ideals*. See also Uday S. Mehta, "Liberal Strategies of Exclusion," *Politics and Society,* 18 (1990): 427-54.

13. See chapter 5.

14. Hobbes' views, although distinct, are closer to Locke than to Rousseau's. For a relevant comparison of Hobbesian and Lockean views, see Macpherson, *Political Theory of Possessive Individualism*.

15. Karl Mannheim,"Conservative Thought," in Peter Kecskemeti, ed., *Essays in Sociology and Political Psychology* (New York: Oxford, 1953), especially pp. 116–18.

16. Wilmore Kendal, *The Conservative Affirmation* (Chicago: Regenery, 1963), ch. 5, "The Social Contract: The Ultimate Issue between Liberalism and Conservatism." See also his *Basic Symbols of the American Political Tradition* (Baton Rouge: Louisiana State University Press, 1970).

17. On Kendall see John Murley and John Alvis, eds., *Willmore Kendall: Maverick of American Conservatives* (Lanham, MD: Lexington Books, 2002).

18. Engels, *The Origin of the Family, Private Property and the State*, chs. 3–7.

19. Jean Jacques Rousseau, *Discourse on Inequality* (New York: Oxford University Press, 1994), 46.

20. Ibid., p. 47.

21. Ibid., p. 59.

22. Ibid., p. 54.

23. Ibid., p. 66.

24. Ibid., p. 67.

25. Ibid., p. 85.

26. Jean Jacques Rousseau, *The Social Contract* (Chicago: Henry Regenery, 1954), 170.

27. Ibid., p. 51.

28. Ibid., p. 29.

29. Ibid., pp. 31–32.

30. Ibid., pp. 99–100.

31. Ibid., p. 100.

32. Ibid., p. 152.

33. Ibid., p. 149. Rousseau argued that a really democratic government would require a small state where citizens could get to know each other; simplicity of mores, a high degree of equality, and finally "no luxury at all or very little.... It corrupts the rich by making them possessive and the poor by making them covetous" (p. 101).

34. On Rousseau's unwavering sexism, see Pateman, *The Sexual Contract*, p. 101; Okin, *Women in Western Thought*, p. 148; and more generally Joel Schwarz, *The Sexual Politics of Jean Jacques Rousseau* (Chicago: University of Chicago Press, 1984).

35. Critics of Jefferson's idea of equality as he expressed it in the Declaration often accused him of suffering from the French disease or being "unduly influenced by the French school of thought." Carl Becker, *The Declaration of Independence: A Study in the History of An Idea* (New York: Vintage Books, 1922, 1970), 27.

36. Thomas Peardon, "Introduction," *The Second Treatise of Government* (Indianapolis: Bobbs-Merrill, 1952), p. xi.

37. Ibid., pp. 5–8.

38. Ibid., pp. 12–13.

39. Ibid., pp. 17–18. This belief in a divine command to mix labor with land helps to explain why Europeans felt little hesitation, indeed might have felt obligated, to take the land of the native peoples of America, because Locke observed they left the land wild and uncultivated, without agriculture or industry. In doing so, they were violating God's command.

40. Ibid., p. 21.

41. Ibid., p. 28. Although their approach to Locke emerges from markedly different philosophical and ideological perspectives, Leo Strauss agrees with Macpherson that Locke's ideas constitute the philosophy of emergent capitalism. See *Natural Rights and History* (Chicago: University of Chicago Press, 1953), 234–51.

42. Ibid., p. 29.

43. Macpherson, *Political Theory of Possessive Individualism*, p. 198.

44. Ibid., p. 207.

45. Locke, *The Second Treatise of Government*, p. 71.

46. Ibid., p. 79.

47. Quoted in Macpherson, *Political Theory of Possessive Individualism*, p. 233. In his initial description of the origins of the state Locke describes the conduct of "a few degenerate men," which makes life untenable in the state of nature (a few criminals among a vast majority of good and decent men). However, as Macpherson notes, he later writes that the state of nature is "very unsafe, very insecure ... full of fears and continual dangers.... What makes the state of nature unlivable ... is not the viciousness of the few but the disposition of the 'greater part' to depart from the law of reason" (pp. 240–41). Macpherson describes these contrasting views as "the central contradiction" in Locke's theory.

48. Macpherson, *Political Theory of Possessive Individualism*, p. 223. Locke thought that in addition to repression by the state, the deluge of the poor could be checked more efficiently by pietistic Christianity or as he put it by "a few simple articles of belief 'that laboring and illiterate man may comprehend'" (p. 224).

49. Ibid., p. 222. Macpherson notes that modern day commentators tend to excuse Locke's harsh views on the treatment of the poor by reference to the standards of his times.

50. Ibid., p. 252.

51. Ibid. See also Martin Seliger, *The Liberal Politics of John Locke* (New York: Praeger, 1968), 285–86.

52. Jerome Huyler, *Locke in America: The Moral Philosophy of the Founding Era* (Lawrence: University Press of Kansas, 1995), 338.

53. Ibid., quoting from Locke's 1697 essay "On the Reform of Poor Laws."

54. Ibid., p. 159.

55. Ibid. It should be noted that Locke was also opposed to government subsidies or welfare for business enterprises as well.

56. Cedric Robinson, "Slavery and the Platonic Origins of Anti-Democracy," *National Political Science Review* 5 (1995), 24.

57. Gregory Vlastos, "Slavery in Plato's Thought," in M. I. Finley (ed.), *Slavery in Classical Antiquity* (New York: Barnes and Noble, 1960), 137, 147.

58. Benjamin Jowet, trans., *Aristotle's Politics* (New York: Random House, 1953), 13. See generally Mavis Campbell, "Aristotle and Black Slavery," *Race* 25 (1974): 285–86.

59. Rousseau, *The Social Contract*, pp. 6, 15.

60. Hobbes rejected slavery but wrote that one man might acquire dominion over another as a result of conquest in war. He describes this, however, as a master-servant relationship rather than slavery because the conquered has through a covenant a moral obligation to his master, whereas an enslaved person has no such obligation but may "justly" escape, capture, or kill his or her master. Thomas Hobbes, *Leviathan*, intro. John Plamentaz (New York: World, 1966), 199.

61. Bernard Bailyn, *The Ideological Origins of the American Revolution* (Cambridge: Harvard University Press, 1967), 233–44.

62. Quoted in James Farr, "So Vile and Miserable: The Problem of Slavery in Locke's Thought," *Political Theory* 14 (1986): 263. Locke was a wealthy man, a member of the English elite employed by the nobility and recognized as one of the intellectual leaders of the British reform movement. In addition to his investments in slavery and the slave trade, he had extensive holdings in mortgages and loans. See Macpherson, *The Political Theory of Possessive Individualism*, p. 253.

63. Farr, "So Vile and Miserable."

64. Ibid., p. 278.

65. Ibid.

66. Ibid., p. 270.

67. Ibid., p. 271. Farr, rather unconvincingly, argues that the correct understanding of Locke's just war theory of slavery is as an attack on "theories of royal absolutism" (p. 281).

68. Bailyn, *The Ideological Origins of the American Revolution*.

69. Ibid., p. 244.

70. I use "bastardization" as a term of art rather than as a technical social science concept. But Professor William Strickland at the University of Massachusetts, Amherst, suggests that with some refinement it might be elevated to conceptual status if understood as "the contrary use of an idea, concept, philosophy or event to further a political point of view absolutely at odds with the intent or meaning of the concept, idea, philosophy or event in question." Personal communications, April 9, 2009.

71. One is almost tempted to say dishonest, but see Farr, "So Vile and Miserable," pp. 381–85, for his argument that for Locke "the shores of Africa were out of sight and out of mind."

72. My San Francisco State colleague Professor James Martel concludes I am too generous in my assessment of Locke and his relationship to racism. He writes that Locke's epistemological writings have "categories of human beings who have no functional capacity to reason. Although Locke contends that every man is born with the ability to reason, most never achieve more than a bare modicum of reason and hence do not enjoy the same rights and privileges as those who do. It's an easy step to include racism in this mix and I think that is exactly what has happened. Thus 'all men are created equal' but the unreasonable are not really men so the application of equal rights to white people does not necessarily contradict the exclusion of blacks in Lockean theory. So, I don't think there is a 'good Locke' that has been bastardized. He is just a bastard." Personal communications, April 23, 2009. Professor Martel has written extensively on the social contract theorists and the classical liberal tradition; see his *Love Is a Sweet Chain: Desire, Autonomy and Friendship in Liberal Political Theory* (New York: Routledge, 2001) and *Subverting the Leviathan: Reading Thomas Hobbes as a Radical Democrat* (New York: Columbia University Press, 2007).

73. William Freehling, "The Founding Fathers and Slavery," *American Historical Review* 97 (1972): 83.

74. Ibid.

75. I do not wish to get involved in the intellectual wrangle between the Lockeans and the classical republicans on the relative influence of each tradition during the founding era or in the subsequent development of the political culture and institutions of the United States. Suffice it to note that I do not see a sharp distinction between Lockean philosophical or ideological liberalism and republicanism. Rather, I tend to agree with Steven Dworetz that "[t]he antithesis between these two traditions is neither historically nor theoretically sound." See *The Unvarnished Doctrine: Locke, Liberalism and the American Revolution* (Durham, NC: Duke University Press, 1990), 191. But to the extent there is a conflict Locke wins. See Huyler, *Locke in America*; Mark Hulling, *The Social Contract in America: From the Rebellion to the Present* (Lawrence: University Press of Kansas, 2007); and Ronald Pestritto and Thomas West, eds., *The American Founding and the Social Compact* (Lanham, MD: Lexington Books, 2003). See also Daniel Rogers, "Republicanism: The Career of a Concept," *Journal of American History* 79 (1992):11–38.

76. Becker, *The Declaration of Independence*, p. 27.

77. *The Federalist Papers*, intro. Clinton Rossiter (New York: New American Library, 1961), 301.

78. The constitutional straightjacket on the power of Congress to address national problems was not effectively removed until the Constitution was informally amended during the New Deal and the Warren Court's era of judicial activism in the 1950s and 1960s. See chapters 4 and 6.

79. See Charles Beard, *An Economic Interpretation of the Constitution* (New York: Free, 1913, 1965); and Robert Brown, *Charles Beard and the Constitution: A Critical Analysis and Interpretation* (New York: Norton, 1965).

80. The president, vice president, senators, judges, and justices of the courts were unelected. For members of the House article I, section 2 indicates that citizens shall be qualified to vote by each state on the basis of the qualifications for voting for the lower house of its legislatures. Most states used property ownership as qualification (among white men), and Dahl estimates that at the time of the revolution nationwide probably fewer than 60 percent of white men could vote. See *How Democratic Is the American Constitution?* (New Haven: Yale University Press, 2003), 198. Dahl derives his estimates from Alexander Keyssar, *The Right to Vote: The Contested History of Democracy in the United States* (New York: Basic Books, 2000).

81. On the Constitution's antidemocratic biases, see also Daniel Lazare, *The Frozen Republic: How the Constitution Is Paralyzing Democracy* (New York: Harvest Books, 1997); and Woody Holton, *Unruly Americans and the Constitution* (New York: Hill and Wang, 2007).

82. Dahl, *How Democratic Is the American Constitution?* pp. 97–119.

83. In the first congressional elections in 1788 five southern states gained fourteen House seats or a bonus of 48 percent, allowing them to reach near parity with the eight larger northern states. Over the nine censuses and reapportionments from 1778 to 1860, the mean bonus percentage of seats for the southern states was twenty-five. In the Electoral College the mean bonus in votes for the southern states was 17 percent. See Hanes Walton Jr. and Robert C. Smith, *American Politics and the African American Quest for Universal Freedom* (New York: Longman, 2006), 10–12. The Three-fifths Clause was abolished after the Civil War. Ironically, however, this resulted in an increase in the power of southern racists and white supremacists, because the emancipated blacks were now counted as whole persons, but from the 1870s to 1970s most of them were not allowed to vote.

84. Garry Wills, *Negro President: Jefferson and the Slave Power* (Boston: Houghton Mifflin, 2003), is a provocative discussion of the influence of the slave power on early American politics. See also Leonard Richards, *Slave Power: The Free North and Southern Domination, 1780–1860* (Baton Rouge: Louisiana State University Press, 2000).

85. Henry Jaffa, *American Conservatism and the American Founding* (Durham: Carolina: Academic, 1984).

86. Russell Kirk, *The Conservative Mind: From Burke to Santayana* (Chicago: Regnery, 1953), 110.

87. Ibid., p. 113.

88. Clinton Rossiter, *Conservatism in America* (New York: Vintage Books, 1955), 79, 104, 141. See also Jennifer Nedelsky in *Private Property and the Limits of American Constitutionalism* (Chicago: University of Chicago Press, 1990), arguing that laissez-

faire capitalism was at the center of Madison's conservative "property based tradition of constitutionalism" and the judiciary's role was to safeguard this tradition. I discuss this matter in greater detail in chapter 3 on the New Deal.

89. Peter Viereck, *Conservatism Revisited: The Revolt against Revolt, 1815-1949* (New York: Scribners, 1949), 21.

90. Jeffrey Myers, *Frederick Douglass: Race and the Rebirth of American Liberalism* (Lawrence: University Press of Kansas, 2008), 127-37.

91. *The Federalist Papers*, no. 47, p. 78.

92. Of course the separation of powers sometimes worked to the advantage of African Americans in their struggle for equality, as, for examples, in the 1860s when the Congress was sympathetic while the other two branches were hostile or indifferent or in the 1950s when the Supreme Court took the lead while the Congress and presidency were indifferent or deadlocked. But this has been rare, and it has been even rarer when all three branches at the same time have been committed to equality for blacks. Indeed, this has only been the case for several years during the 1960s.

93. William Riker, *Federalism: Origins, Operation and Significance* (Boston: Little, Brown), 140. Of course, like the separation of powers, federalism could at the margins work to the advantage of blacks by allowing them during slavery and segregation to leave the more oppressive southern states for the less oppressive northern part of the country.

94. Donald Robinson, *To the Best of My Ability: The Presidency and the Constitution* (New York: Norton, 1987), 82.

95. Paul Frymer, *Uneasy Alliances: Race and Party Competition* (Princeton, NJ: Princeton University Press, 1999).

96. Robinson, *Slavery in the Structure of American Politics*, p. 435.

97. Isaac Kramnick, *The Portable Burke* (New York: Penguin Books, 1999), ix.

98. Dworetz argues that the religious or "theistic" Locke is more central than Strauss and Macpherson's bourgeois Locke in understanding his philosophy and its influence during the founding era. See *The Unvarnished Doctrine*, especially chapter 5. See also Hulling, *The Social Contract in America*, pp. 30-33.

Chapter 3

1. M. Morton Auerbach, *The Conservative Illusion* (New York: Columbia University Press, 1959), 79.

2. Ibid.

3 Samuel Huntington, "Conservatism as an Ideology," *American Political Science Review* 51 (1951): 454-73.

4. Huntington identifies four "manifestations" of conservatism in the Western world: (1) the response of the church and other medieval institutions to the development of a centralized state, (2) the reactions to the French Revolution, (3) the response to the rise of the industrial working class, and (4) the reaction in the American South to industrialism and abolitionism. Ibid., pp. 462-66. As we shall see in chapter 6 the

rise of the modern conservative movement in the United States was partly a reaction to the gathering challenge of the civil rights movement in the 1950s.

5. Harvey Wish, *George Fitzhugh: Propagandist of the Old South* (Baton Rouge: Louisiana State University Press, 1943), 96.

6. Don Fehrenbacher, *Constitutions and Constitutionalism in the Slaveholding South* (Athens: University of Georgia Press, 1989), 49. See also Daniel Mulcare, "Restricted Authority: Slavery Politics, Internal Improvements, and the Limitations of National Administrative Capacity," *Political Research Quarterly* 61 (2008): 671–85.

7. W. J. Cash, *The Mind of the South* (New York: Knopf, 1941). These elements generally are agreed on by students of the South. Kirk, for example, lists the following: (1) a preference for the slow process of natural change, (2) a deep affection for agricultural life and a contempt for trade and manufactures, (3) assertive individualism, (4) "sensitivity about the Negro Question," and (5) localism. See Russell Kirk, *The Conservative Mind: From Burke to Santayana* (Chicago: Regnery, 1953), 151, 153–54. Some of the elements of the mind of the South have been documented in empirical or survey research. See J. S. Hurlbert, "The Southern Region: A Test of the Hypothesis of Cultural Distinctiveness," *The Sociological Quarterly* 30 (1989): 245–66; John Reed, *Southerners: An Essay on the Social Psychology of Sectionalism* (Chapel Hill: University of North Carolina Press, 1983); and Reed, *The Enduring South* (Lexington: Lexington Books, 1972).

8. Cash, *The Mind of the South*, p. 168.

9. Ibid., pp. 129, 310.

10. "Negro bogey man" is Richard Hofstadter's phrase, which he used in describing how racism undermined the populist and progressive movements; see *The Age of Reform* (New York: Vintage Books, 1955), 4–7.

11. Barrington Moore Jr., *Social Origins of Dictatorship and Democracy: Lord and Peasant in the Making of the Modern World* (Boston: Beacon, 1966).

12. Louis Hartz, *The Liberal Tradition in America* (New York: Harcourt, Brace, and Jovanovich, 1955), 147. See also Auerbach, *The Conservative Illusion*, p. 147.

13. Wish, *George Fitzhugh*, p. 157.

14. Ibid., p. 195.

15. Ibid.

16. Quoted in James McPherson, *Abraham Lincoln and the Second American Revolution* (New York: Oxford University Press, 1991), 50.

17. Wish, *George Fitzhugh*, p. 36.

18. Ibid., p. viii. In his essay on Fitzhugh in *American Conservatism: An Encyclopedia* (Wilmington, DE: ISI Books, 2006), 314, Mark Henrie writes that "ex-Marxist historian Eugene Genovese responded to the collapse of communism by aggressively championing the insights of Fitzhugh. Genovese saw in Fitzhugh the best foundation in the American tradition on which to construct a needed antiliberal critique of alienation and anomie within bourgeois society," (p. 314).

19. John C. Calhoun, A Disquisition on Government and Selections from the Discourse (Indianapolis: Bobbs-Merrill, n.d.), vii.

20. Henry Jaffa, *A New Birth of Freedom: Abraham Lincoln and the Coming of the Civil War* (Boulder: Rowman and Littlefield, 2000), 420, 428, 429, 439.

21. "UnBurkean reasons" because Burke was opposed to slavery, describing it as "an incurable evil" that should be "utterly" abolished. In the meantime he urged humane treatment, "civilization," and gradual emancipation. See his 1792 "Sketch of a Negro Code," in Isaac Kramnick, ed., *The Portable Burke* (New York: Penguin Books, 1999), 183–84.

22. John C. Calhoun, *A Disquisition on Government*, p. 45.

23. Jaffa, *A New Birth of Freedom*, p. 439.

24. Ibid., p. 44.

25. John Randolph, another important southern conservative thinker, also rejected natural rights and the social contract and advocated a militant laissez-faire capitalism where the government's role was limited to that of policeman. Randolph argued that any effort by positive law to improve society was "a menace to liberty." "Give me fifty speeches no matter how dull or stupid," he said, "rather then one positive law on the stature book." Quoted in Kirk, *The Conservative Mind*, pp. 158–59.

26. John C. Calhoun, *A Disquisition on Government*, p. xxii.

27. Interestingly, when Lani Guinier, the African American legal scholar, suggested the possible use of Calhoun's theory to protect the African American minority interest in state legislatures and Congress in the 1990s President Clinton labeled her "antidemocratic" and withdrew her nomination to be the assistant attorney general for civil rights. See Guinier, *The Tyranny of the Majority: Fundamental Fairness and Representative Democracy* (New York: Free, 1995).

28. Jaffa, *A New Birth of Freedom*, p. 435.

29. Auerbach, *The Conservative Illusion*, p. 119.

30. John Crowe Ransom, *I'll Take My Stand: The South and the Agrarian Tradition by Twelve Southerners* (New York: Smith, 1951).

31. Richard Weaver, *Ideas Have Consequences* (Chicago: University of Chicago Press, 1948); Weaver, *The Southern Tradition at Bay: A History of Post Bellum Thought* (New Rochelle, NY: Arlington House, 1968).

32. For a recent example of how writers in the tradition try to downplay or ignore racism, Eugene Genovese in his valorization of southern culture as the bulwark against liberalism and modernity in America writes, "I have not dwelt upon the racist legacy of the southern...." See *The Southern Tradition: The Achievements and Limitations of American Conservatism* (Cambridge: Harvard University Press, 1994), 9.

33. Weaver, *The Southern Tradition at Bay*, pp. 259–69.

34. Of the twelve essays in *I'll Take My Stand*, two dealt explicitly with race. Frank Lawrence Owsley's "Irrepressible Conflict" is an explicitly racist and white supremacist track that defends slavery and segregation, while Robert Penn Warren's "Briar Patch" is an enlightened essay, especially for the times, calling for equal protection of the laws for blacks and the joining together in unions of black and white workers.

35. Clinton Rossiter, *Conservatism in America* (New York: Vintage Books, 1962), 231.

36. V. O. Key, *Southern Politics* (New York: Vintage Books, 1949), 5.

37. Rossiter, *Conservatism in America*, pp. 246–47.

Chapter 4

1. The concepts of the 'negative' and 'positive' states are derived from Isaiah Berlin's essay "Two Concepts of Liberty," in Berlin, *Four Essays on Liberty* (New York: Oxford, 1970), 118–72.

2. Louis Hartz, *The Liberal Tradition in America* (New York: Harcourt Bruce, 1955), 11. Hartz also writes, "Ironically, 'liberalism' is a stranger in the land of its greatest realization" (p. 11). Here Hartz is clearly confusing ideology and philosophy. To his credit he acknowledges that he is using terms "broadly" and that liberalism is a "vague," "clouded" term with all sorts of modern reform connotations (pp. 3–4).

3. H. W. Brand argues that war—specifically the cold war—was a necessary condition for the success of postwar liberalism. Without war or some kind of national emergency Americans are, he contends, hostile to the positive, liberal state. See *The Strange Death of American Liberalism* (New Haven: Yale, 2001).

4. This enduring impact of African Americans on American political development is a principal organizing framework in Hanes Walton Jr. and Robert C. Smith, *American Politics and the African American Quest for Universal Freedom* (New York: Longman, 2007).

5. Lerone Bennett is probably the most uncompromising African American critic of Lincoln. See *Forced into Glory: Abraham Lincoln's White Dream* (Chicago: Johnson, 2000).

6. Letter to Horace Greeley, *Abraham Lincoln: Collected Works*, vol. 5: 388–89.

7. Evidence of this is Lincoln's support for the first Thirteenth Amendment. Adopted by Congress in March 1861, this proposed amendment would have prohibited any future amendment granting Congress the authority to interfere with slavery in any state. It was hoped by the northern states that this amendment would preserve the union. In order to show his support Lincoln took the unprecedented step of signing the amendment. See Mark Brandon "The 'Original' Thirteenth Amendment and the Limits to Formal Constitutional Change," in Sanford Levinson, ed., *Responding to Imperfection: The Theory and Practice of Constitutional Amendment* (Princeton: Princeton University Press, 1995).

8. See Hans Trefousse, *The Radical Republicans: Lincoln's Vanguard for Freedom* (Baton Rouge: Louisiana State University Press, 1945). See also Eric Foner, *Free Soil, Free Labor: The Ideology of the Republican Party before the Civil War* (New York: Oxford).

9. Quoted in Donald Fehrenbacher "Only His Stepchildren: Lincoln and the Negro," *Civil War History* 12 (1974): 307.

10. Ibid.

11. Abraham Lincoln "The Prerogative Theory of the Presidency," in Harry Bailey, ed., *Classics of the American Presidency* (Oak Park, IL: Moore, 1980), 33.

12. *The Life and Times of Frederick Douglass Written by Himself*, intro. Rayford Logan (London: Collier Books, 1892, 1962), 485, 489. Lincoln believed that if slavery was limited to the South this would eventually result in its gradual elimination.

13. Bruce Frohnen, "Civil War" in Bruce Frohnen, Jeremy Beer, and Jeffrey O. Nelson, eds., *American Conservatism: An Encyclopedia* (Willington, DE: ISI Books, 2006), 156.

14. Until the 1970s conservatives viewed presidential power as inherently liberal while Congress was considered the naturally conservative institution, representing the states and local interests. See James Burnham, *Congress and the American Tradition* (Chicago: Regenery, 1959).

15. Herman Belz, "Abraham Lincoln," in Frohen, Beer, and Nelson, eds., *American Conservatism: An Encyclopedia*, p. 517.

16. Wilmore Kendall, *Basic Symbols of the American Democracy* (Baton Rouge: Louisiana State University Press, 1970).

17. Gary Wills, *Lincoln at Gettysburg: The Words That Remade America* (New York: Touchstone, 1992).

18. M. E. Bradford, "How to Read the Declaration of Independence: Reconsidering the Kendall Thesis," *The Intercollegiate Review* (Fall 1992): 46–47.

19. This view is usually associated with Henry Jaffa, *A New Birth of Freedom: Abraham Lincoln and the Coming of the Civil War* (Lanham, MD: Rowman and Littlefield, 2000).

20. Trefoussee, *Radical Republicans*, p. 167.

21. Ibid.

22. Ibid.

23. Richard Bensel, *Yankee Leviathan: The Origins of Central State Authority in America, 1857–1877* (New York: Cambridge University Press, 1990).

24. I am using "presidential character" with the meaning suggested by James David Barber, although Lincoln hardly fits his psychological approach or typology. See Barber's *Presidential Character: Predicting Performance in the White House* (Englewood Cliffs, NJ: Prentice-Hall, 1972).

25. See, for example, Albert Castel, *The Presidency of Andrew Johnson* (Lawrence: University Press of Kansas, 1979). See also David Stewart, *Impeached: The Trial of President Andrew Johnson and the Fight for Lincoln's Legacy* (New York: Simon and Shuster, 2009). In addition to a fine character analysis of Johnson, Stewart's work demolishes the canard, advanced by John F. Kennedy (in *Profiles in Courage*) among others, that Johnson's impeachment was unjustifiable, and those who supported him were courageous. Kennedy's view is discussed in chapter 8.

26. Quoted in Linda Faye Williams, *The Constraints of Race: Legacies of White Skin Privilege and the Politics of American Social Policy* (College Park: Pennsylvania State University Press, 2003), 25.

27. See Eric Foner, *Reconstruction, America's Unfinished Revolution, 1863–77* (New York: Harper and Row, 1988), ch. 5.

28. Lincoln would not likely have taken this view because he consistently argued that the southern states had not left the union and indeed could not leave the union. Thus, his policy would probably have been more akin to Johnson's than to the Congress. What he would have done in the face of the black codes and white terror we cannot know.

29. Paul Cimbala and Randall Miller, eds., *The Freedmen's Bureau and Reconstruction: Reconsiderations* (New York: Fordham University Press, 1999).

30. Trefoussee, *Radical Republicans*, p. 405.
31. Fred Friendly and Martha Elliot, *The Constitution: That Delicate Balance* (New York: McGraw-Hill, 1984), 18.
32. William Nelson, *The Fourteenth Amendment: From Political Principle to Judicial Doctrine* (Cambridge: Harvard University Press, 1988), 96.
33. Walton and Smith, *American Politics and the African American Quest for Universal Freedom*, pp. 30–32.
34. W. E. B. DuBois, *Black Reconstruction* (New York: Athenaeum, 1935, 1969), 88.
35. See Foner, *Reconstruction*; DuBois *Black Reconstruction*; and Rayford Logan, *The Betrayal of the Negro: From Rutherford B. Hayes to Woodrow Wilson* (London: Collier Books, 1965). On the compromised presidential election of 1876 that symbolized Reconstruction's end, see C. Vann Woodward, *Reunion and Reaction: The Compromise of 1877 and the End of Reconstruction* (Boston: Little, Brown, 1951). On the terrorism at the core of the end of Reconstruction, see Allen Trelease, *White Terror: The Ku Klux Klan Conspiracy and Southern Reconstruction* (New York: Harper and Row, 1971).
36. G. Edward White, *The Constitution and the New Deal* (Cambridge: Harvard University Press, 2000).
37. *The Slaughterhouse Cases*, 16 Wall (83 U.S.) 26 (1873).
38. *U.S. vs. Cruikshank*, 91 U.S. 542 (1876).
39. Charles Lane, *The Day Freedom Died: The Colfax Massacre, the Supreme Court and the Betrayal of Reconstruction* (New York: Holt, 2008).
40. Quoted in John R. Howard, *The Shifting Wind: The Supreme Court and Civil Rights from Reconstruction to Brown* (Albany: State University of New York Press, 1999), 104.
41. Ibid.
42. *The Civil Rights Cases of 1883*, 35. CT. 18(1883).
43. *Plessey vs. Ferguson*, 163 U.S. 537(1896).
44. *Cummings vs. Board of Education*, 175, U.S. 528 (1899).
45. Ibid.
46. *The Slaughterhouse Cases*.
47. Ibid.
48. *Lochner vs. New York*, 198 U.S. 45.
49. Clinton Rossiter, *Conservatism in America* (New York: Vintage Books, 1955), 139.
50. McPherson, *Abraham Lincoln and the Second American Revolution*, p. 145.
51. Jennifer Nedelsky, *Private Property and the Limits of American Constitutionalism* (Chicago: University of Chicago Press), 228.
52. Rossiter, *Conservatism in America*, p. 153.
53. For a critique of judicial supremacy, see Larry Kramer, *The People Themselves: Popular Constitutionalism and Judicial Review* (New York: Oxford University Press, 2004).
54. Although James Patterson traces the informal formation of the coalition to the late 1930s, its historical roots with respect to race clearly go back to the end of

Reconstruction. See Patterson's "A Conservative Coalition Forms in Congress, 1933–39," *Journal of American History* 52 (1966): 757–72.

55. On how the separations of powers and the commitment to federalism on the part of the Republican Party helped to undermine Reconstruction, see W. R. Brock, *An American Crisis: Congress and Reconstruction* (New York: MacMillan, 1963); and Les Benedict, *A Compromise of Principle: Congressional Republicans and Reconstruction* (New York: Norton, 1974).

56. George Nash, *The Conservative Intellectual Movement in America Since 1945* (New York: Basic Books, 1976), 213.

57. Rossiter, *Conservatism in America*.

58. Richard Hofstadter, *The Age of Reform* (New York: Vintage Books, 1955), 61.

59. C. Vann Woodward, *Tom Watson: Agrarian Rebel* (New York: Oxford 1938, 1963).

60. Gerald Gaither, *Blacks and the Populists Revolt: Ballots and Bigotry* (Tuscaloosa: University of Alabama Press, 1977).

61. Hofstadter, *The Age of Reform*, p. 61.

62. Woodward, *Tom Watson*.

63. The quote is from John Herbert Roper, *C. Vann Woodward, Southerner* (Athens: University of Georgia Press, 1987), 121.

64. Hofstadter, *The Age of Reform*, chs. 4–5. See also Gary Gerstle, "The Protean Character of American Liberalism," *American Historical Review* 99 (1994): 1043–72.

65. Hofstader, *Age of Reform*, p. 305.

66. Kenneth O'Reilly, *Nixon's Piano: Presidents and Racial Politics from Washington to Clinton* (New York: Free, 1995), ch. 3.

67. Ronald Rotunda, "The 'Liberal' Label: Roosevelt's Capture of a Symbol," *Public Policy* 17 (1968): 377–48.

68. Gerstle, "The Protean Character of American Liberalism."

69. Rotunda, "The Liberal Label," p. 393.

70. Ibid. Interestingly, the first time the *New York Times* reported a political group using the label 'liberal' was in 1921 when it reported that the president of the Liberal League of Negro Americans urged Negroes in New York City to arm themselves.

71. Milton Friedman, *Capitalism and Freedom* (Chicago: University of Chicago Press, 1962), 5–6.

72. The classic statement is Murray Edelman, *The Symbolic Uses of Politics* (Urbana: University of Illinois Press, 1964).

73. Hartz, *The Liberal Tradition in America*, p. 260.

74. Hofstadter, *The Age of Reform*, p. 305.

75. Ibid., p. 308.

76. Aside from Arthur Schlesinger's three volumes *The Age of Roosevelt* (New York: Houghton Mifflin, 1957, 1959, 1960), see James MacGregor Burns' still insightful *Roosevelt: The Lion and the Fox* (New York: Harcourt Brace, and World, 1956); William Leuchtenburg, *Franklin D. Roosevelt and the New Deal* (New York: Harper and Row, 1963); and more recently see David Kennedy, *Freedom from Fear: The American People in Depression and War, 1929–1945* (New York: Oxford, 1999); and Jean Edward Smith, *FDR* (New York: Random House, 2007).

77. Leuchtenburg, *Franklin D. Roosevelt and the New Deal*, p. 132.

78. Harvard Sitkoff, *A New Deal for Blacks: The Emergence of Civil Rights as a National Issue* (New York: Oxford, 1978), 39–41, discusses FDR's indifference and temerity. On how racism compromised major elements of the New Deal program, see Jill Quadagno, *The Color of Welfare* (New York: Oxford, 1994); Michael Brown, *Race, Money and the American Welfare State* (Ithaca: Cornell University Press, 1999); Linda F. Williams, *The Constraints of Race: Legacies of White Skin Privilege and the Politics of American Social Policy*; Ira Katznelson, *When Affirmative Action Was White: An Untold History of Racial Inequality in Twentieth Century America* (New York: Norton, 2005); and Charles and Dana Hamilton, *The Dual Agenda: Social Policies of Civil Rights Organizations from the New Deal to the Present* (New York: Columbia University Press, 2002).

79. Hamilton and Hamilton, *The Dual Agenda*.

80. Bruce Ackerman, *We the People: Transformations* (Cambridge: Harvard University Press, 1991).

81. It is not clear that FDR's plan was directly responsible for this switch because in the relevant case (*West Coast Hotel vs. Parrish*, 300, U.S. 379 1937) the decision had been reached (although not announced) before the president sent his proposal to Congress. In *Parrish* the Court for the first time revoked its Lochner era jurisprudence and upheld a state minimum wage law. A year earlier it had declared a similar law unconstitutional.

82. In *United States vs. Lopez* (slip opinion # 913–1260, 1995) the Court declared unconstitutional a federal law, based on the Commerce Clause, prohibiting the possession of a firearm in a school zone. Since *Lopez* the Court has declared several other Commerce Clause based statures unconstitutional, including parts of the Violence against Women Act. The Court's conservative majority is clearly unhappy with the Roosevelt revolution in Commerce Clause jurisprudence but likely because of precedent (and the popularity of the legislation) it will not seek a conservative counterrevolution but see John Noonan, *Narrowing the Nation's Majority: The Supreme Court Sides with the States* (Berkeley: University of California Press, 2002).

83. William Leuchtenburg, *The Supreme Court Reborn: The Constitutional Revolution in the Age of Roosevelt* (New York: Oxford, 1995), 162. As the Court abandoned its guardian role with respect to private property, it began to gradually see its role as guarding the rights of minorities as symbolized by Justice Harlan Stone's famous footnote four in *United States vs. Caroline Products* (304 U.S. 144, 1938). In this note Stone wrote that laws impinging on the rights of minorities required a "more exacting judicial scrutiny" than other laws. See Robert Cover, "The Origins of Judicial Activism in the Protection of Minority Rights," *Yale Law Journal* 91 (1982): 1287–1316.

84. Nedelsky, *Private Property and the Limits of American Constitutionalism*, pp. 229–30.

85. Randy Barnett, *Restoring the Lost Constitution: The Presumption of Liberty* (Princeton: Princeton University Press, 2004), 3.

86. The bulk of the opposition to the Court plan was based on the principle of the independence and integrity of the Court. But southern politicians, bar associations, and editorial writers also expressed opposition in terms of defending the Court's guardian role with respect to racism. After 1937 in spite of Roosevelt's essential quiescence

on race he was often vilified in the southern press. A favorite epithet was the "Nigger Loving New Deal," Sitkoff, *A New Deal for Blacks*, pp. 113-14.

87. Leuchtenburg, *The Supreme Court Reborn*, p. 157.

88. Hofstadter, *The Age of Reform*, p. 312.

89. Ira Katznelson, Kim Geiger, and Daniel Kryder, "Limiting Liberalism: The Southern Veto in Congress," *Political Science Quarterly* 108 (1993): 283-304.

90. Roosevelt frequently mused about trying to realign the parties along ideological lines creating in his words "two real parties—one liberal, the other conservative," but he never devoted much effort and organization to the endeavor except for some secret conversations with Wendell Willkie during the 1944 campaign. Burns, *The Lion and the Fox*, pp. 402, 466-67. In 1936 he did abolish the two-thirds rule for presidential nominations, effectively ending the southern veto over the process. On FDR's party reform efforts see Sidney Milkis, "FDR and the Transformation of Partisan Politics," *Political Science Quarterly* 100 (1985).

91. Alan Brinkley, *The End of Reform: Liberalism in Recession and War* (New York: Knopf, 1995), 269.

92. Arthur Schlesinger Jr., *The Vital Center* (Cambridge, MA: Riverside, 1949, 1962).

93. Of the absence of this liberal tradition or the pervasiveness of Lockean conservative values Brinkley writes that "much of the American electorate welcomed (even expected) assistance from governments in solving their own problems but nevertheless remained skeptical of state power and particularly of efforts to expand and concentrate it." *The End of Reform*, p. 17.

94. In 1955 when *National Review* began publishing hostility to Roosevelt, and the New Deal was in some conservative quarters as strong as it was in the 1930s. Eisenhower's seeming acceptance of much of the New Deal during the 1952 campaign was a powerful stimulus to the emergence of the Buckley-Goldwater-Reagan style of conservatism.

95. Sitkoff, *A New Deal for Blacks*, pp. 102, 108.

96. Walter White, *A Man Called White* (Athens: University of Georgia Press, 1948, 1995), 169-70. I should note that antilynching legislation enjoyed widespread public support throughout the country. A 1937 Gallup Poll found 72 percent support nationally and 57 percent in the South. See Avis Thomas-Lester, "A Senate Apology for a History on Lynching," *Washington Post*, June 14, 2005. The Senate in 2005 voted to formally apologize for filibustering antilynching legislation.

97. On the black cabinet and its symbolic significance, see Stikoff, *A New Deal for Blacks*, pp. 77-83 and Nancy Weiss, *Farewell to the Party of Lincoln: Black Politics in the Age of FDR* (Princeton: Princeton University Press, 1982), ch. 7.

98. Louis Ruchames, *Race, Jobs and Politics: The Story of FEPC* (New York: Columbia University Press, 1953). Eventually FDR also advocated abolition of the poll tax and antilynching legislation, but he did not exert much effort to secure their passage.

99. Sitkoff, *A New Deal for Blacks*, p. 329.

100. Richard Morin, "The Ugly Way We Were," *Washington Post*, April 6, 1997.

101. Brinkley draws this distinction between economic and racial liberalism in *The End of Reform*.

102. Samuel Huntington, "Conservatism as an Ideology," *American Political Science Review*, p. 473.

103. Stephen Depoe, *Arthur Schlesinger Jr. and the Ideological History of American Liberalism* (Tuscaloosa: University of Alabama Press, 19944), ii. See also John Blum, "Arthur Schlesinger Jr.: Tory Democrat," in John Patrick Diggins, ed., *The Liberal Persuasion: Arthur Schlesinger Jr. and the American Left* (Princeton: Princeton University Press, 1997).

104. Arthur Schlesinger Jr., *The Cycles of American History* (Boston: Houghton Mifflin, 1986).

105. Schlesinger, *The Age of Jackson*, vol. 1 (Boston: Little, Brown, 1945), 391, as quoted in Defoe, *Arthur Schlesinger Jr. and the Ideological History of American Liberalism*, p. x.

106. Arthur Schlesinger Jr. *A Life in the Twentieth Century: Innocent Beginnings, 1917–1950* (Boston: Houghton Mifflin, 2000), 518. Of his father, also an eminent historian, Schlesinger wrote that he was the last white member of the board of the Association of African American History and on the editorial board of the *Journal of Negro History* as well as an "ardent supporter" of the work of Carter G. Woodson and a mentor to John Hope Franklin. "Still for all his support of black Americans in their struggle for equal rights, that struggle was never a major theme in my father's historical work (p. 32). Franklin discusses appreciatively Schlesinger's mentoring in his memoir *Mirror to America* (New York: Farrar, Straus, and Giroux, 2005), 74–76. As a political scientist I should note that racism and the struggle for civil rights were ignored by my profession until the 1960s. See Wilbur Rich, ed., *African American Perspectives on Political Science* (Philadelphia: Temple University Press, 2007), especially the essays by Jerry Watts and Hanes Walton Jr. and Robert C. Smith.

107. Schlesinger, *A Life in the Twentieth Century*, p. 274.

108. Ibid.

109. Schlesinger, *The Vital Center*, p. 274. A principal concern of *The Vital Center* was the danger Schlesinger saw to liberalism from left radicalism, especially the danger of the intertwining of domestic and international communism. Thus in a widely read *Life* magazine article he joined with southern conservatives in red baiting the civil rights movement, arguing in the article that the Communist Party was "sinking its tentacles into the NAACP." See "The Communist Party," *Life*, July 29, 1946, p. 90.

110. There are exceptions. For example, Hubert Humphrey made militant liberalism on race the centerpiece of his political career from its beginning to its end. See Timothy Thurber, *The Politics of Equality: Hubert Humphrey and the African American Freedom Struggle* (New York: Columbia University Press, 1999). But most liberals during the New Deal era simply ignored racism. John Kenneth Galbraith, another leading liberal-activist intellectual, in his memoir writes that looking back on the New Deal he was "astonished how little we were concerned" about racism. See *A Life in Our Times* (Boston: Houghton Mifflin, 1981), 41–42. On organized liberalism's ambivalent approach to racism and civil rights in the post–World War era see Steven Gillon, *Politics and Vision: The ADA and American Liberalism, 1947–1985* (New York: Oxford, 1987), chs. 4–5.

Chapter 5

1. Samuel Huntington, "Conservatism as an Ideology," *American Political Science Review*, pp. 457, 461.

2. Mack Jones, "Racism, Multiculturalism, the Black Conservative Movement and the Post Civil Rights Era," in Franklin Jones et. al, eds., *Readings in American Political Issues*, 2nd ed. (Dubuque, Iowa, 2004), 16–20.

3. Heather Richardson Cox, *The Death of Reconstruction: Race, Labor and Politics in the Post Civil War North* (Cambridge: Harvard University Press, 2001), 244–45. Richard Bensel similarly argues that conservative elites in the north feared that efforts to end planter dominance in the South and create a more racially equalitarian economy would lead white labor in the North to make similar demands for the redistribution of wealth. See *Yankee Leviathan: The Origins of Central State Authority in America, 1857–1877* (New York: Cambridge University Press, 1990).

4. Eric Foner, *Reconstruction: America's Unfinished Revolution, 1863–1877* (New York: Harper and Row, 1988), 305. See also pp. 309–10.

5. James Kluegel and Eliot Smith, *Beliefs about Inequality: American Views of What Is and What Ought to Be* (New York: Aldine De Gruyter, 1986), 289. Although African Americans may exhibit a kind of class consciousness, Klugel and Smith (pp. 129–30) show that they nevertheless share almost to the same degree as whites the chaste Lockean values of individualism, hard work and self-reliance.

6. Ralph Bunche, "A Critique of New Deal Planning as It Affects Negroes," in Charles Henry ed., *Ralph Bunche: Selected Speeches and Writings* (Ann Arbor: University of Michigan Press, 1995), 63–70. On Bunche's role along with sociologist E. Franklin Frazier and economist Abram Harris in advancing a tradition of left radicalism in social science research while on the faculty of Howard University in the 1930s, see Jonathan Scott Holloway, *Confronting the Veil: Abram Harris, E. Franklin Frazier, and Ralph Bunche* (Chapel Hill: University of North Carolina Press, 2002).

7. Quoted in Nikhil Pal Singh, *Black Is a Country: Race and the Unfinished Struggle for Democracy* (Cambridge: Harvard University Press, 2004), 89.

8. Elsewhere I have written of this ideological diversity as the "enduring dilemma" in African American politics because it inhibits the development of elite solidarity and mass mobilization; see "Ideology as the Enduring Dilemma," in Georgia Persons, ed., *Dilemmas of Black Politics: Issues of Leadership and Strategy* (New York: HarperCollins, 1993), 211–24. On how this diversity has historically undermined black leadership consensus, see Howard Bell, "National Negro Conventions of the Middle 1840s," *Journal of Negro History* 31 (1966): 435–43; Lawrence Wittner, "The National Negro Congress: A Reassessment," *American Quarterly* 22 (1968): 883–901; and Robert C. Smith, *We Have No Leaders: African Americans in the Post Civil Rights Era* (Albany: State University of New York Press, 1996), ch. 2.

9. Michael Dawson, *Black Visions: The Roots of Contemporary African-American Ideologies* (Chicago: University of Chicago Press, 2001).

10. Ibid.

11. James Forten, "A Philadelphia Negro Condemns Discriminatory Proposals, 1813," an excerpt from *A Series of Letters by a Man of Color* in Herbert Aptheker, ed., *A Documentary History of the Negro People in the United States*, vol. 1 (New

York: Citadel, 1967), 60. On Forten's remarkable career as businessman and citizen activist see, Julie Winch, *A Gentleman of Color: The Life of James Forten* (New York: Oxford, 2002).

12. "Slave Petitions for Freedom During the Revolution, 1773–1779," in Aptheker, *A Documentary History of the Negro People*, pp. 8–9.

13. Jeffrey Myers, *Frederick Douglass: Race and the Rebirth of American Liberalism* (Lawrence: University Press of Kansas, 2008), 7

14. Frederick Douglass, "Fourth of July Address, 1852," in Aptheker, *A Documentary History of the Negro People*, p. 333.

15. For a fine study of the speech see Drew Hansen, *The Dream: Martin Luther King Jr. and the Speech That Inspired a Nation* (New York: Ecco, 2003).

16. In a 2001 survey of African American political scientists DuBois was named the second (after King) most important or influential African American leader of all time, with one respondent writing that "he had a singularly crucial role" in defining the "conceptual parameters" of ideological discourse in America. See Robert C. Smith, "Rating Black Leaders," *National Political Science Review* 8 (2001): 124–38. DuBois' magnificent career is beautifully recounted in David Lewis' two volumes, *W. E. B. DuBois: Autobiography of Race, 1868–1919* (New York: Holt, 1973); and *W. E. B. DuBois: The Fight for Equality and the American Century, 1919–1963* (New York: Holt, 2000).

17. W. E. B. DuBois, *Dusk of Dawn: An Essay toward an Autobiography of a Race Concept* (New York: Schocken Books, 1940, 1968), 290.

18. W. E. B. DuBois, "The Conservation of Races," in Howard Brotz, ed., *Negro Social and Political Thought, 1850–1920: Representative Texts* (New York: Basic Books, 1966).

19. The 2000 survey of black political scientists overwhelmingly selected Dr. King as the greatest black leader of all time. All of the respondents listed King among their top five, and half listed him first. See Smith, "Rating Black Leaders," p. 129. Nor should King be understood only as the greatest African American leader; he should also be understood as one of the four great transformative leaders in American history: George Washington and the founding; Abraham Lincoln and the Union and emancipation; Franklin Roosevelt and the New Deal; and Martin Luther King Jr. and the civil rights revolution.

20. On Reagan's musings about the possibly of King being a Communist, see chapter 9.

21. See for example, his 1956 sermon, "Paul's Letter to the American Church," in Claybourne Carson, ed., *A Knock at Midnight* (New York: Warner Audio Books, 1998).

22. David Garrow, *Bearing the Cross: Martin Luther King Jr. and the Southern Christian Leadership Conference* (New York: Morrow, 1986), 367, 382, 434.

23. Harold Cruse, *The Crisis of the Negro Intellectual* (New York: Morrow, 1967), 4.

24. This was also the view of Jefferson, Lincoln, and Tocqueville. That is, each argued that it would be impossible for blacks and whites to live on Lockean terms of equality in the United States. Lincoln's view was discussed in chapter 4; Jefferson's view is in *Notes on Virginia,* ed. William Peden (Chapel Hill: University of North Carolina

Press, 1954), 162–63. Tocqueville discusses the problem in *Democracy in America*, vol. 1 ed. Phillip Bradley (New York: Vintage Books, 1945), ch. 18.

25. On the various nationalist ideologies and their historical roots, see Sterling Stuckey, *The Ideological Origins of Black Nationalism* (Boston: Beacon, 1972); and John Bracey, August Meier, and Elliott Rudwick, eds., *Black Nationalism in America* (New York: Bobbs Merrill, 1970).

26. Tommie Shelby, *We Who Are Dark: The Philosophical Foundations of Black Solidarity* (Cambridge: Harvard University Press, 2005), ch. 1.

27. Edwin Redkey, "The Flowering of Black Nationalism: Henry McNeal Turner and Marcus Garvey," in Nathan Huggins, Martin Kilson, and Daniel Fox, eds., *Key Issues in the Afro-American Experience* (New York: Harcourt Brace Jovanovich, 1971), 107–24.

28. Ibid.

29. Ibid.

30. See Dawson, *Black Visions*.

31. Washington is for sure the most controversial major black leader of all time. In the survey of black political scientists, he was tied with Garvey as the fifth most important black leaders; however, most respondents who selected him described his leadership as "negative" or "villainous"; see Smith, "Rating Black Leaders," p. 132. Louis Harlan presents a comprehensive and balanced assessment of Washington in his two volumes, *Booker T. Washington: The Making of a Black Leader* (New York: Oxford, 1972); and *Booker T. Washington: The Wizard of Tuskegee* (New York: Oxford, 1983).

32. W. E. B. DuBois, *The Souls of Black Folk* (New York: Fawcett, 1903, 1963), 48.

33. Gunnar Myrdal, *An American Dilemma: The Negro Problem and Modern Democracy* (New York: Harper and Row, 1944, 1962), ch. 34.

34. DuBois, *The Souls of Black Folk*, p. 49.

35. See August Meier, *Negro Thought in America, 1880–1915* (Ann Arbor: University of Michigan Press, 1968), 110–14.

36. Booker T. Washington, "Booker T. Washington's Plan to Achieve the Rights of Citizenship," in August Meier, Elliott Rudwick, and Francis Broderick, eds., *Black Protest Thought in the Twentieth Century* (New York: Bobbs-Merrill, 1971), 8–17.

37. Myrdal, *An American Dilemma*, p. 640–41.

38. George Schuyler, *Black and Conservative: The Autobiography of George Schuyler* (New York: Arlington House, 1966), 346.

39. The phrase is from Oscar Williams Jr., "The Lonely Iconoclast: George Schuyler and the Civil Rights Movement," in Gayle Tate and Lewis Randolph, eds., *Dimensions of Black Conservatism in the United States* (New York: Palgrave, 2002), 165.

40. Schuyler, *Black and Conservative*, pp. 121–22.

41. Ibid., p. 2.

42. Ibid., p. 345. Schuyler writes that his drift toward conservatism was "much influenced" by the writings of Alfred Jay Nock an obscure but cult like figure in the modern conservative movement. Nock's writings (especially his 1943 book *Memoirs of a Superfluous Man*) are said to have been influential on the thinking of Russell Kirk and William F. Buckley Jr. But Williams concludes that Schuyler "shrewdly . . . saw his chance to be part of the American mainstream and possibly be accepted by white

conservatives of the world," see "The Lonely Iconoclast," p. 165. For a diverse collection of Schuyler's writings see Timothy Leak, ed., *Race[]ing to the Right: Selected Essays of George S. Schuyler* (Knoxville: University of Tennessee Press, 2001).

43. Frederick Harris, *Something Within: Religion in African American Political Activism* (New York: Oxford, 1999), 8.

44. On the role of religion as an inspiration for slave rebellions, see Eugene Genovese, *From Rebellion to Revolution: Afro-American Slave Revolts in the Making of the New World* (New York: Vintage Books, 1984), and on it as force in encouraging political activism and participation, see Harris, *Something Within*.

45. Myrdal, *An American Dilemma*, ch. 40.

46. On Douglass, see Myers, *Frederick Douglass*, chs. 4–5; on Crummell, see William Moses, *Alexander Crummell: A Study of Civilization and Discontent* (New York: Oxford, 1989); and Alfred Moss, *The American Negro Academy: Voice of the Talented Tenth* (Baton Rouge: Louisiana State University Press, 1981). DuBois presents a moving tribute to Crummell in *The Souls of Black Folk*, essay 12.

47. Meier, *Negro Thought in America*, p. 42.

48. William Jeremiah Moses, *Creative Conflict in African American Thought: Frederick Douglass, Alexander Crummell, Booker T. Washington, W. E. B. DuBois, and Marcus Garvey* (New York: Cambridge University Press, 2004), 101.

49. Ibid.

50. W. E. B. DuBois, "The Talented Tenth Memorial Address," in Henry Louis Gates and Cornell West, *The Future of the Race* (New York: Vintage, 1997).

51. W. E. B. DuBois, "The Talented Tenth Memorial Address" *Boule Journal* 15 (1948), 3–13.

52. W. E. B. DuBois, *The Philadelphia Negro: A Social Study* (New York: Schocken Books, 1967).

53. On DuBois' aristocratic pretensions, see Adolph Reed, *W. E. B. DuBois and American Political Thought* (New York: Oxford, 1997), ch. 5; and Kevin Gaines *Uplifting the Race: Black Leadership, Politics and Culture in the Twentieth Century* (Chapel Hill: University of North Carolina Press, 1996), ch. 4.

54. Loury's ideas are discussed in chapter 6 on neoconservatism.

55. Bertrand Russell, *A History of Western Philosophy* (New York: Simon and Shuster, 1965), ix.

56. I emphasize "might" because like American Jews American blacks as a long-suffering, persecuted minority might have continued their adherence to liberalism.

57. Frederick Douglass, "What the Black Man Wants," in John Blassingame et al., eds., *The Frederick Douglass Papers*, vol. 4 (New Haven: Yale University Press, 1991), 59, 68.

58. Myers, *Frederick Douglass*, ch. 4–5.

Chapter 6

1. The origins and evolution of the civil rights movement are two of the most thoroughly researched and documented occurrences in the twentieth-century history of the United States. For a useful overview of this vast literature, see Stephen Lawson

"Freedom Then, Freedom Now: The Historiography of the Civil Rights Movement," *American Historical Review* 96 (1991): 466–71.

2. Quoted from Leronne Bennett, *Confrontation Black and White* (Baltimore: Penguin, 1965), 103.

3. Ibid.

4. See David Levering Lewis, *W. E. B. DuBois: Biography of a Race, 1868–1919* (New York: Holt, 1993), chs. 15, 17; and Daniel Walden, ed., *W. E. B. DuBois: The Crisis Writing* (Greenwich, CT: Fawcett Books, 1972).

5. Social movements are defined, following Charles Tilly, as "any organized, sustained self-conscious challenge to existing authorities." See his "Social Movements and National Politics," in C. Bright and S. Harding, eds., *State Making and Social Movements: Essays in History and Theory* (Ann Arbor: University of Michigan Press, 1984), 304.

6. "To Fulfill These Rights," *Public Papers of the President of the United States: Lyndon B. Johnson, 1965*, vol. 2 (Washington, DC, 1966), 635–40.

7. George Nash, *The Conservative Intellectual Movement in the United States Since 1945* (New York: Basic Books, 1976), xiii.

8. Sara Diamond, *Roads to Dominion: Right-Wing Movements and Political Power in the United States* (New York: Guilford, 1995), 2.

9. Peter Viereck, *Conservatism Revisited: The Revolt against the Revolt* (New York: Scribner's and Sons, 1949), x.

10. Ibid.

11. See Diamond, *The Roads to Dominion*, pp. 175, 179; *The Conservative Intellectual Movement in America*, p. 131; Godfrey Hodgson, *The World Turned Right Side Up: A History of Conservative Ascendancy in America* (Boston: Houghton Mifflin, 1996). Diamond refers to these three elements as the "three pillars of the right" (p. 7). She refers to the Lockean conservatives as "libertarian" capitalists and writes that the anti-Communist element was also interested generally in U.S. military hegemony. Nash refers to the Lockean conservatives as "classical liberals" or "libertarians" who resented the ever-expanding threat to liberty and individualism represented by the welfare state (p. xiii).

12. Frank Meyer, *In Defense of Freedom: A Conservative Credo* (Chicago: Regenery, 1962). On the significance of Meyer's contribution, see Kevin Smant, *Principles and Heresies: Frank S. Meyer and the Shaping of American Conservatism* (Wilmington, DE: ISI Books, 2002).

13. Diamond, however, contends that one of the values the traditionalists wished to maintain was "the supreme status of native born white male Americans." *Roads to Dominion*, p. 7.

14. The phrase "ill sorted" is from Hodgson, *The World Turned Right Side Up*, pp. 23–24; see also Charles Dunn and J. David Woodard, *The Conservative Tradition in America* (Boulder, CO: Rowman and Littlefield, 1996), 4–5.

15. Nash writes of the "centrality" of Hayek's work in the conservative movement, and Diamond refers to Kirk's book as a "landmark that became a classic on par with Hayek."

16. F. A. Hayek, *The Road to Serfdom* (Chicago: University of Chicago Press, 1944), 32, 36.

17. Ibid., p. 120.
18. Ibid., p. 121.
19. See Hayek, "Why I Am Not a Conservative," in *The Constitution of Liberty* (Chicago: University of Chicago Press, 1960). See chapter 4 for discussion of Schlesinger's work.
20. *Time Magazine* devoted its entire book section to Kirk's book; it was positively reviewed in the *New York Times* and serialized in *Reader's Digest*.
21. Russell Kirk, *The Conservative Mind: From Burke to Sartayana* (Chicago: Regenery, 1953, 1985), 152.
22. Ibid., p. 155.
23. Auerbach contrasts Kirk's racist views on *Brown* with Peter Vicreck's view, suggesting that while both men were interested in tradition, stability, and the prevention of racial conflict, Vicreck saw segregation as a moral evil and thus inconsistent with fundamental conservative values. See M. Morton Auerbach, *The Conservative Illusion* (New York: Columbia University Press, 1959), 185.
24. Milton Friedman, *Capitalism and Freedom* (Chicago: University of Chicago Press, 1962), 109.
25. Ibid., p. 111.
26. Ibid., p. 113.
27. Ibid., p. 115.
28. Nash, *The Conservative Intellectual Movement in the United States*, p. 250.
29. Ibid., p. 224.
30. Larry Kramer, *The People Themselves: Popular Constitutionalism and Judicial Review* (New York: Oxford, 2004), 222.
31. Alfred Regenery, *Upstream: The Ascendance of American Conservatism* (New York: Simon and Shuster 2008), 222.
32. *Patterson vs. Alabama*, 294, U.S., 660 (1934).
33. *Shelley vs. Kramer*, 334 U.S. 1(1948).
34. *Smith vs. Allwright*, 334, U.S. 649 (1944).
35. *Gaines vs. Canada*, 305, U.S. 337 (1938).
36. *Sweatt vs. Painter*, 339 U.S., 629 (1950). In 1949 the Justice Department submitted a brief in *Henderson vs. United States* (involving segregation in interstate transportation) in which it argued for the first time that "separate but equal [was] a constitutional anachronism no longer deserv[ing] a place in our law." See William Berman, *The Politics of Civil Rights in the Truman Administration* (Columbus: Ohio State University Press, 1970), 173.
37. The citation of Myrdal perhaps outraged southern racists and white supremacists even more so than the citing of the African American Clark, because Myrdal's *American Dilemma* had revealed in stark terms the brutal nature of the southern "caste" system. The Lockean conservatives were also upset that Myrdal was a socialist.
38. Warren here too was probably referring to Myrdal's work. In the introduction to *An American Dilemma*, Myrdal had written, "If the Negro was a 'failure' as he obviously was by every criterion that white society recognized as valid, then he was a failure because white America made him so." And he continued, "All recent attempts to reach scientific explanations of why the Negroes are what they are and why they live as they do have regularly led to determinants on the white side of the

race line." See vol. 1, p. ixxv. In their conference Warren had told his colleagues that in his view the only basis in which *Plessy* could be sustained was that of a belief in black inferiority, and if the Court choose to sustain it must do so honestly on that basis. See Richard Kluger, *Simple Justice: A History of Brown vs. Board of Education* (New York: Vintage Books, 1975), 679.

39. W. J. Cash, *The Mind of the* South; see p. 317. See also Richard Weaver, "Integration as Communization," *National Review*, July 13, 1957, pp. 67–68.

40. For the early makings of this bloc post-*Brown* see David Danzig "Rightist, Racists and Separatists: A White Bloc in the Making?" *Commentary*, August, 1964, pp. 28–32. I analyze the making of this bloc in detail in chapters 7 and 8.

41. Nash, *The Conservative Intellectual Movement in the United States*, p. 250. Of conservatism's embrace of majoritarianism Dunn and Woodward write, "The conservatism of the recent era is no longer suspicious of the masses," partly they conclude because it wants "limited action by government to redress racial and gender inequalities." *The Conservative Tradition in America*, p. 111. Thus, beginning with *Brown*, conservative intellectuals began to argue that conservatism should abandon its elitist, aristocratic pretensions and embrace the masses. Wilmore Kendall had long argued this position, and this tendency became especially pronounced with the emergence of the neoconservatives, who also viewed themselves as self-consciously Burkean. This ill-sorted arrangement of ideas is discussed in the next chapter.

42. L. Brent Bozell, *The Warren Revolution* (New York: Arlington, 1966) was an exception. Bozell while arguing that *Brown* was wrongly decided also argued against judicial supremacy contending that while the framers favored judicial review they also favored legislative supremacy in constitutional understandings. See also Nash, *The Conservative Intellectual Movement in the United States*, pp. 224–27.

43. See, for example, Frank Meyer, "In the Great Tradition," *National Review*, June 1, 1957. The response of this group was not to curb the imperial judiciary but to reconstitute the Supreme Court. Aside from embracing a quixotic campaign to impeach Chief Justice Warren, the conservative movement after *Brown* began a campaign to pack the Court with conservatives. This campaign began with Nixon in 1969 and continued in the Reagan and two Bush administrations. With the appointment of Clarence Thomas conservatives for the first time since Herbert Hoover achieved a narrow five-person conservative majority. This transformation of the Court, however, took a long time as the Senate rejected two Nixon nominees (forcing him to submit less conservative nominees) and Reagan's nomination of Robert Bork, the conservative movement's foremost legal scholar. Bork was rejected partly because of his opposition to the Civil Rights Act of 1964.

44. Barry Goldwater, *Conscience of a Conservative* (Shepherdsville, KY: Victor, 1960), 121.

45. Robert Bork, "Civil Rights: A Challenge," *New Republic*, August 31, 1963, p. 22.

46. Ronald Reagan adopted Bork's individual liberty principle as the basis of his opposition to the Civil Rights Act as well as his support for California's Proposition 14, the 1964 initiative that overturned the state's law banning racial discrimination in the sale of housing. See chapter 8.

47. Bork, "Civil Rights," p. 23.

48. See Richard Weaver, "The Regime of the South," *National Review*, March 14, 1959, pp. 587–89.

49. Nash, *The Conservative Intellectual Movement in America*, p. 202. David Chappel describes Kilpatrick as "the most credible and influential ideologue of the segregationist cause." See *A Stone of Hope: Prophetic, Religion and the Death of Jim Crow* (Chapel Hill: University of North Carolina Press, 2004), 160.

50. James J. Kilpatrick, *The Southern Case for School Segregation* (New York: Crowell-Collier, 1962), 93.

51. Ibid., pp. 192–93.

52. Ibid.

53. Ibid., p. 72.

54. Ibid., pp. 192–93.

55. Ibid.

56. Ibid.

57. Ibid., p. 50.

58. Ibid., pp. 23–24.

59. Ibid., p. 71.

60. Ibid., pp. 26–27.

61. Kilpatrick also offered intellectual respectability to the discredited Calhounian idea of interposition and nullification used by Alabama Governor George Wallace when he "stood in the schoolhouse door" to block the desegregation of the University of Alabama. See Kilpatrick, "The Right to Interpose," *Human Events*, December 24, 1955, pp. 9–15.

62. Hodgson, *The World Turned Right Side Up*, pp. 72, 74.

63. Nash, *The Conservative Intellectual Movement in America*, p. 153.

64. In contrast to his fusion of racism into the conservative movement, Buckley worked consistently and forthrightly to purge anti-Semitism from the movement. Indeed, "purging poisonous elements" such as anti-Semitism and anti-Catholicism is described as "something of a calling" for him. See Mark Gerson, *The Neo-Conservative Vision: From Cold War to the Culture of Wars* (New York: Madison Books, 1996), 43–44.

65. Buckley's militant anticommunism called for the rollback of communism by supporting—even at the cost of nuclear war—rebellions such as the Hungarian uprising in 1956. With the slogan "Better dead than red," *National Review* advocated preemptive attacks on China to prevent it from acquiring nuclear weapons.

66. "Why the South Must Prevail," *National Review*, August 24, 1957, pp. 4–7.

67. Buckley, *Up from Liberalism*, p. 146.

68. Ibid.

69. Ibid., p. 148.

70. Quoted in John Judis, *William F. Buckley, Jr.: Patron Saint of the Conservative Movement* (New York: Simon and Shuster, 1988), 168. Judis suggests that Buckley's racism and white supremacy may have had their origins in his childhood, writing that Buckley "had been raised to think that blacks were inferior to whites" (p. 138).

71. Ibid., p. 185.

72. See Frank Meyer, "Abdication of Responsibility," April 8, 1961; Jeffrey Hart, "African Gothic," July 6, 1966; James Burnham, "Tangle in Katanga," December 3, 1961; and James J. Kilpatrick et al., "Rhodesia: A Case History" May 16, 1967.

73. Frank Meyer, "The Negro Revolution," *National Review*, June 18, 1963, pp. 3–7.

74. See chapter 8 for discussion of YAF. In addition Buckley and the *National Review* crowd were instrumental in creating the American Conservative Union, the most successful conservative political action group.

75. Judis, *William F. Buckley*, p. 198.

76. Ibid., p. 381.

77. Although I shall follow the convention in referring to whites from southern and eastern Europe as white ethnics, I agree with Matthew Holden Jr. that "it is superficial and inaccurate to simultaneously define 'Italo-Americans' as ethnics but Anglo-Protestants as nonethnics. Each is as "ethnic" as the other. Moreover, I maintain that there is an implicit snobbery in the ordinary use of the term "ethnic," for it somehow implies that "ethnics" are merely those white people who somehow deviate from the "normal" cultural-political standards of the Anglo-Protestant population." See *The Politics of the Black "Nation"* (New York: Chandler, 1973), 209–10.

78. Judis, *William F. Buckley*, p. 252, citing a *New York Times* editorial of October 29, 1965. Buckley won 13 percent of the vote, John Lindsay 45 percent, and Abe Beame 41 percent. Buckley carried 1 percent of the black vote. On the significance of the Buckley campaign for the conservative movement, see Regenery, *Upstream*, pp. 108–09.

79. Ibid.

80. Clinton Rossiter, *Conservatism in America* (New York: Vintage Books, 1955), 177, 179.

81. Ibid.

Chapter 7

1. Claybourne Carson, *In Struggle: SNCC and the Black Awakening of the 1960s* (Cambridge: Harvard University Press, 1981); Robert C. Smith, *We Have No Leaders: African Americans in the Post Civil Rights Era* (Albany: State University of New York Press, 1996), ch. 2; William Van Deburg, *New Day in Babylon: The Black Power Movement and African American Culture, 1965–75* (Chicago: University of Chicago Press, 1992); Peniel Joseph, *Waiting Til the Midnight Hour: A Narrative History of Black Power* (New York: Holt, 2006); and Cedric Johnson, *Revolutionaries to Race Leaders: Black Power and the Making of African American Politics* (Minneapolis: University of Minnesota Press, 2007).

2. Joe Feagin and Harlan Hahn, *Ghetto Revolts* (New York: MacMillan, 1973); *Report of the National Advisory Commission on Civil Disorders* (New York: Bantam Books, 1968); Garry Wills, *The Second Civil War: Arming for Armageddon* (New York: New American Library, 1968); and T. M. Tomlinson, "The Development of a Riot Ideology among Urban Negroes," *American Behavioral Scientist* 2 (1968): 17–19.

3. King saw the war on Vietnam as a racist, imperialist adventure, growing he said out of a "morbid fear of communism." He also saw it as taking resources from the struggle against poverty at home. See Adam Fairclough, "Martin Luther King Jr.

and the War in Vietnam," in Michael Krenn, ed., *The African American Voice in U.S. Foreign Policy since World War II* (New York: Garland, 1999). By early 1967 King had also come to believe that in order to achieve a racially just society radical changes were required in the U.S. economic system, hence the poor people's campaign. Charles Fager, *Uncertain Resurrection: The Poor Peoples Campaign* (Grand Rapids, MI: Erdman, 1969). More generally see Thomas F. Jackson, *From Civil Rights to Human Rights: Martin Luther King Jr. and the Struggle for Economic Justice* (Philadelphia: University of Pennsylvania Press, 2007).

4. This was a phrase used in an early neoconservative text. See Richard Scammon and Ben Wattenberg, *The Real Majority* (New York: Coward-McCann, 1970).

5. *The Civil Rights Cases of 1883*, 3.S.Ct. 18(1883).

6. *Veto Message of President Andrew Johnson, The Freedmen's Bureau Act*, February 19, 1866, as reprinted in Amilear Shabazz, ed., *The Forty Acres Documents* (Baton Rouge: House of Songhay, 1994), 84.

7. Booker T. Washington, "The Future of the American Negro," as reprinted in August Meier, Elliott Rudwick, and Francis Broderick, eds., *Black Protest Thought in the Twentieth Century* (Indianapolis: Bobbs-Merrill, 1965), 17.

8. Jeffrey Hart, "The Negro in the City," *National Review*, June 18, 1968.

9. Frank Meyer, "Showdown with Insurrection," *National Review*, January 16, 1968.

10. William F. Buckley Jr., *The Jeweler's Eye* (New York: Putnam, 1968), as quoted in John Judis, *William F. Buckley Jr.: Patron Saint of the Conservative Movement in America* (New York: Simon and Shuster, 1988), 281.

11. Mark Gerson writes, "What was Good for Jews" was an important factor in the mobilization of neoconservatives. "The Jewish" factor he writes was "an important distinction between neo-conservatism and the rest of conservatism.... Neoconservatives tirelessly stressed that liberalism, 1970s style, was distinctively bad for the Jews." See *The Neoconservative Vision: From the Cold War to Cultural Wars* (New York: Madison Books, 1996), 192. If measured by effect on mass opinion and voting behavior, this is a neoconservative idea that has little consequence as Jews in America, after blacks, are the most distinctively liberal and Democratic group in the electorate. See Eard Raab and Seymour Martin Lipset, *The Political Future of American Jews* (New York: American Jewish Committee, n.d.), 4; and Lipset's "Jews Are Still Liberal and Proud of It," *Washington Post*, December 20, 1984. On the historical sources of Jewish Left/liberalism see Percy Cohen, *Jewish Radicals and Radical Jews* (London: Academic, 1980); and Arthur Liebman, *Jews and the Left* (New York: Wiley and Sons, 1979).

12. Irving Kristol, *Neo-conservatism: The Autobiography of an Idea* (New York: Free, 1995), ix. Kristol claims the label *neoconservative* for the "impulse" was invented "in a spirit of contempt for 'renegades' by the socialist Michael Harrington" (p. 33). For Harrington's early views, see "The New Class and the Left," in B. Bruce-Briggs, ed., *The New Class?* (New Brunswick, NJ: Transaction Books, 1979).

13. George Nash, *The Conservative Intellectual Movement in the United States Since 1945* (New York: Basic Books, 1976), 324.

14. See Sara Diamond, *Roads to Dominion: Right Wing Movements and Political Power in the United States* (New York: Guilford, 1995), 185; Peter Stienfels, *The*

Neoconservatives: The Men Who Are Changing America's Politics (New York: Simon and Shuster, 1979), 61; and Carol Horton, *Race and the Making of American Liberalism* (New York: Oxford University Press, 2005), 200.

15. Gerson lists the following as the four "fundamental principles" of the "neoconservative style of thought": life is infinitely complex; man can be good, but man also can be evil; man is a social animal; and ideas rule the world. See *The Neoconservative Vision*, pp. 16–19. On the Burkean influence on neoconservative thinking, see Isaac Kramnick, ed., *The Portable Burke* (New York: Penguin Books, 1999), xxxi–xxxv.

16. Quoted in Shadia Drury, *Leo Strauss and the American Right* (New York: St. Martin's, 1997), 155. Kristol writes that the new class "consists of scientists, lawyers, city planners, social workers, educators, criminologists, sociologists, public health doctors, etc.... [who] are acting on a hidden agenda: to propel the nation from the modified version of capitalism we call 'the welfare state' toward an economic system so stringently regulated in detail as to fulfill many of the traditional anti-capitalist aspirations of the left." See *Neo-Conservatism*, pp. 221–22.

17. George Wallace in his career also inveighed against a new class of "insulated, liberal, elitist cabal of lawyers, judges, editorial, writers, academics, government bureaucrats and planners" who wanted to impose their will on working-class whites. See Thomas Edsal, *Chain Reaction* (New York: Norton, 1992), 77–78.

18. For example, Kristol's major work *Neo-conservatism: The Autobiography of an Idea* is simply a collection of his previously published essays introduced by a long, meandering, partly autobiographical essay. There are several book-length studies of the movement, including Gerson's sympathetic, even celebratory account, *The Neoconservative Vision*; Stienfel, *The Neoconservatives*; Gary Dorrien, *The Neoconservative Mind: Politics, Culture and the War of Ideology* (Philadelphia: Temple University Press, 1993); and Sidney Blumenthal, *The Rise of the Counter-Establishment: From Conservatism to Political Power* (New York: Times Books, 1986), which discusses neoconservatives in the course of an overall assessment of the conservative movement, as does Nash in *The Conservative Intellectual Movement* and Diamond in *Roads to Dominion*. For an early critique of the neoconservatives from a leftist perspective, see Lewis Coser and Irving Howe, eds., *The New Conservatives: A Critique from the Left* (New York: Quadrangle/New York Times Books, 1973). This volume contains fifteen essays by, among others, Michael Harrington, Robert LeKachman, Hanna Pitkin, Michael Walzer, and Dennis Wrong, and it covers topics such as the welfare state, equality, the economy, and crime. There are, however, no contributions by African Americans or essays on the racial origins or consequences of the new movement. For an early and insightful analysis of the racist implications of neoconservatism by a black writer, see Orde Coombs, "The Retreat of the Liberal Sages," *New York Times*, May 17, 1976. For a more recent critique, see Houston Baker, *Betrayal: How Black Intellectuals Have Abandoned the Ideals of the Civil Rights Movement* (New York: Columbia University Press, 2008), 45–71.

19. See Nicholas Lemann, "Slumlord; Pat Moynihan Has Done Great Things—But Betraying the Poverty Warriors Isn't One of Them," *Washington Monthly*, May 1991; and see more generally Godfrey Hodgson, *The Gentleman from New York: Daniel Patrick Moynihan* (Boston: Houghton Mifflin, 2000). Of Moynihan Midge Decter writes, "He was one of us until he got elected, and then he broke our hearts." Quoted in Regenery, *Upstream*, p. 150.

20. John Saloma, *Ominous Politics: The New Conservative Labyrinth* (New York: Hill and Wang, 1984). See also Blumenthal, *The Rise of the Counter-Establishment*; and Alan Lichtman, *White Protestant Nation: The Rise of the American Conservative Movement* (New York: Atlantic Monthly Press, 2008), 302–10.

21. Blumenthal, *The Rise of the Counter-Establishment*, p. 21. For a thorough methodological critique of *Losing Ground,* see Christopher Jencks, *Rethinking Social Policy: Race, Poverty and the Underclass* (Cambridge: Harvard, 1992). Using as point of departure his 1965 report on the black family, Moynihan also presents a telling critique of Murray's book in *Family and Nation* (New York: Harcourt, 1986). Later the Manhattan Institute sponsored and promoted Murray's, *The Bell Curve*, which suggested that IQ was distributed to some degree genetically on the basis of race, and this genetic distribution of IQ explained to some extent racial inequality in the United States. See Richard Herrnstein and Charles Murray, *The Bell Curve: Intelligence and Class Structure in America* (New York: Free, 1995).

22. Kristol personally solicited major corporate leaders, telling them that capitalism and business were under attack from the "new class" and needed cheerleaders. With sufficient funding he indicated he was willing to become one and could recruit others. See *Neo-Conservatism*, pp. 230–34. Kristol subsequently became a regular contributor to the *Wall Street Journal* and wrote *Two Cheers for Capitalism* (New York: Basic Books, 1978), another rehash of essays previously published in *Commentary, The Public Interest,* and the *Wall Street Journal*. Michael Novak, a former leftist, liberal theologian, was among those recruited. See *The Catholic Ethic and the Spirit of Capitalism* (New York: Free, 1993).

23. During this period African American intellectuals who wished to write autonomously within the traditions of black thought were limited to two underfunded, limited circulation journals: *Black World* and *The Black Scholar*. *Black World* ceased publication in the mid-1970s because its parent company Johnson Publishing (publisher of *Ebony* and *Jet*) claimed that it could not financially sustain a serious journal of thought and opinion, with limited advertisements and circulation. Meanwhile, the NAACP's *Crisis* magazine was only a shadow of its magnificent DuBoisian years, when it did play an important role in shaping black thought and influencing public debate.

24. See Jerry Watts, "The Case of the Black Conservatives," *Dissent* (Summer, 1982); Martin Kilson, "Anatomy of Black Conservatism," *Transition* 59 (1990); Mack Jones, "The Political Thought of the New Black Conservatives," in Franklin Jones et al., ed., *Readings in American Political Issues* (Dubuque: Kendall/Hunt, 1987); Alex Willingham, "The Place of the New Black Conservatives in Black Social Thought: Groundwork for the Full Critique," paper presented at the annual meeting of the Association for the Study of Afro-American Life and History, Philadelphia, 1981; and more generally Houston Baker, *Betrayal*. See also Angela Dillard, *Guess Who Is Coming to Dinner Now: Multi-Cultural Conservatism in America* (New York: New York University Press, 2001), ch. 1.

25. As Mannheim would have it opposition to the youthful counterculture and later feminism and *Roe vs. Wade* allowed traditionalism to become an ideology, to become fused with concerns about the economy, race, and foreign policy.

26. This view is central to the analysis of both Hayek and Friedman.

27. Jennifer Nedlesky has it right when she writes that "the equalitarian conception of liberty and justice requires incursions on traditional property rights... [T]he equalitarian vision entails conceptions of liberty and justice fundamentally different from those on which our tradition was built.... Equalitarianism defines the inequality of property as the *source* of the problems to be remedied. Redistribution is not incidental, it is the objective." See *Private Property and the Limits of American Constitutionalism* (Chicago: University of Chicago Press, 1990), 262.

28. David Garrow presents a detailed account of the long-running debate between King and Rustin on the efficacy, strategic and tactical, of the poor people's campaign in *Bearing the Cross: Martin Luther King Jr. and the Southern Christian Leadership Conference* (New York: Morrow, 1968).

29. By politics Rustin meant a revitalized, more liberal New Deal coalition with the empowered southern black vote viewed as the key to breaking the power in the Democratic Party of the conservative coalition. See "From Protest to Politics: The Future of the Civil Rights Movement," *Commentary*, February, 1965 as reprinted in Rustin's *Down the Line: The Collected Writings of Bayard Rustin* (Chicago: Quadrangle Books, 1971).

30. Ibid., p. 117.

31. Ibid., p. 115.

32. Ibid., p. 118.

33. The adoption by the Democratic Party in 1972 of rules designed to assure the equitable representation of minorities in the party and in the nominating process was the most alarming evidence of this phenomenon for the neoconservatives. McGovern was the quintessential post–civil rights era liberal—the last nominated by the Democrats—in both domestic and foreign policy. See chapter 9.

34. Two useful assessments of this vast literature are David Lang, "Poverty Literature and the Underclass Concept" (Princeton University, School of Public Affairs, ND); and Richard Nathan and Kenneth Clark, "The Urban Underclass," in *National Urban Policy: A Reconnaissance and Agenda for Further Study* (Washington: National Academy of Science, 1987). See also ch. 6 of my *Racism in the Post Civil Rights Era* (Albany: State University of New York Press, 1995), where I present a thorough critique of the underclass literature and attempt to show that it has little scientific utility and is little more than a successful attempt to denigrate the black poor. Adolph Reed presents a similar critique in "The 'Underclass' as Myth and Symbol: The Poverty of Discourse on Poverty," in his *Stirrings in the Jug: Black Politics in the Post Segregation Era* (Minneapolis: University of Minnesota Press, 1999).

35. Specifically Lewis argued that a culture of poverty, passed down from generation to generation, emerges in highly stratified capitalist societies with few or none of the characteristics of a highly developed welfare state. See Oscar Lewis, *LaVida: A Puerto Rican Family in the Culture of Poverty in San Juan and New York* (New York: Random House, 1966).

36. Edward Banfield, *The Unheavenly City* (Boston: Little, Brown, 1968), 125.

37. Edward Rossin, "The Causes of Race Superiority," *Annals of the American Academy of Political and Social Science* 18 (1901): 72, 75.

38. Kristol, *Two Cheers for Capitalism*, p. 184.

39. Nathan Glazer, "Is Busing Necessary?" *Commentary*, March, 1972, pp. 39–52. In *Milliken vs. Bradley* (418 U.S., 717, 1995), the Supreme Court prohibited cross-districting busing between urban-suburban schools as a remedy to metropolitan school segregation. However, a more important decision relating to equality of educational opportunities was *San Antonio School District vs. Rodriquez* (411, U.S., 1278, 1973). In this 6–3 decision the Court held that education was not a "fundamental right," that "wealth discrimination" was an inherent feature of American capitalism, and therefore a state was not required to assure equality in funding between high- and low-income school districts. Of course Glazer likely would have objected to a decision to achieve wealth equality more so than to the Court's decisions to achieve racial equality in schooling. See for example, Aaron Wildavsky, "Robert Bork and the Crime of Inequality," *The Public Interest* 96 (1990): 98–117.

40. Mack Jones, "Affirmative Action—What Is the Question—Race or Oppression?" *National Political Science Review*, 7 (1999), 249–58. In light of what he describes as the "persistence of racial inequality" Glazer in the 1990s softened his opposition to affirmative action, see his "In Defense of Preferences," *New Republic*, April 6, 1998.

41. William Bowen and Derek Box, *The Shape of the River: Long-term Consequences of Race in College and University Admissions* (Princeton: Princeton University Press, 1998).

42. Daniel P. Moynihan, "The New Racism," *Atlantic Monthly*, August, 1968, p. 40, as quoted in Gerson, *The Neoconservative Vision*, p. 149.

43. Diamond, *Roads to Dominion*, p. 185.

44. John Donovan, *The Politics of Poverty* (New York: Pegasus, 1967), 107. Despite public protestations to the contrary, President Johnson clearly saw the War on Poverty as a war on black poverty, as a civil rights program necessary to his strategy of overcoming the bastardization of Locke and creating a racially equalitarian society. See Randall Woods, *LBJ: The Architect of American Ambition* (New York: Free, 2006), 452–66.

45. Frances Fox Piven and Richard Cloward, *Regulating the Poor: The Functions of Public Welfare* (New York: Vintage Books, 1993).

46. King made these remarks in his 1967 speech "Why I Am Opposed to War in Vietnam," where he specifically linked the war on Vietnam to the lack of resources for the War on Poverty.

47. Godfrey Hodgson, *America in Our Time: From World War II to Nixon* (New York: Vintage Books), 270–71.

48. Irving Kristol, "American Conservatism, 1965–95," *The Public Interest*, Fall 1995, p. 85.

49. Aaron Wildavsky, "Government and the People," *Commentary*, August, 1973, pp. 25–29; and Nathan Glazer, "The Limits of Social Policy," *Commentary*, September 1971, pp. 51–58. Glazer later developed his ideas in a book; see *The Limits of Social Policy* (Cambridge: Harvard University Press, 1988).

50. Glazer, "The Limits of Social Policy," p. 53.

51. Ibid., p. 53.

52. Ibid., p. 54.

53. Wildavsky, "Government and the People," p. 26.

54. Aaron Wildavsky, "The Empty-Headed Blues: Black Rebellion and White Reaction," *The Public Interest*, Spring 1968, pp. 3–11.

55. Wildavsky, "Government and the People," p. 26.

56. This view was articulated by Moynihan in his influential 1967 address at the American for Democratic Action. See "The Politics of Stability," *The New Leader*, October 9, 1967, pp. 6–10.

57. We do not know whether the War on Poverty was a failure because it was never really fought. After a few minor skirmishes President Johnson called a truce, and President Nixon surrendered, abolishing OEO in his first term. Nor was the War on Poverty or related welfare policies especially liberal or radical. Rather as Michael Harrington concludes in his critique of neoconservative critiques of welfare, "This critique of neo-conservatism can now be generalized: the failures of the welfare state in recent years are the result of its conservatism, not its excessive liberalism or, more preposterously, of its radicalism." "The Welfare State and Its Neoconservative Critics," in Coser and Howe, ed., *The New Conservatives*, p. 53. For an assessment see Robert Haveman, ed., *A Decade of Federal Antipoverty Programs* (New York: Academic, 1977).

58. Fred Barnes, "Invent a Negro, Inc." *The New Republic*, April 15, 1985, pp. 9–10. More generally see Mack Jones "Racism, Multiculturalism, the Black Conservative Movement and the Post Civil Rights Era," in Franklin Jones et al., eds., *Readings in American Political Issues*, 2nd ed. (Dubuque, Iowa, 2004), 20–23.

59. Saloma, *Ominous Politics*, ch. 12. See also Jones, "Racism, Multiculturalism, the Black Conservative Movement."

60. Adolph Reed Jr. posits that many black conservatives are not autonomous but mere opportunists, mainly interested not in ideas but in "getting paid." See "The Descent of Black Conservatism," *Progressive*, p. 19. See also Baker, *Betrayal*.

61. Samuel P. Huntington, "Conservatism as an Ideology," *American Political Science Review*, p. 455.

62. See, for examples, Rustin's "Black Power and Coalition Politics," in *Down the Line*; and "Black Power's Legacy," *Newsweek*, November 13, 1972. Rustin was also very sympathetic to Israel while after 1967 increasingly black intellectuals and political leaders embraced the cause of the Palestinians.

63. See Walter Williams, *The State against Blacks* (New York: Free, 1982); Thomas Sowell, *Race and Economics* (New York: McKay, 1975); and Sowell, *Markets and Minorities* (Oxford: Blackwell for the International Center for Economic Policy Studies, 1981).

64. See Sowell, *Race and Economics*; and Sowell, *The Economics and Politics of Race: An International Perspective* (New York: Morrow, 1983).

65. This cultural theory explains, for Sowell, why West Indian immigrants have done relatively better in the United States than native born blacks.

66. Glen Loury, "The Moral Quandary of the Black Community," *The Public Interest* 79 (1985): 9–12.

67. Shelby Steele, *The Content of Our Character* (New York: St. Martin's, 1990); and Steele, *A Dream Deferred: The Second Betrayal of Black Freedom in America* (New York: HarperCollins, 1998). Norman Podhoretz was perhaps the first conservative intellectual to elevate this notion of white guilt to analytic significance in understanding

black-white relations. In a crudely written, white supremacist essay, Podhoretz wrote of his liberal shame and guilt and of his fear, hatred, and envy of blacks. See "My Negro Problem—and Ours," *Commentary*, February 1963. Glazer also muses about guilt in his social policy essay.

68. Glen Loury, *The Anatomy of Racial Inequality* (Cambridge: Harvard University Press, 2002). In this book Loury appears to renounce or back away from many of the neoconservative tenets he advanced in his earlier essays.

69. Scott Gerber, *First Principles: The Jurisprudence of Clarence Thomas* (New York: New York University Press, 1999), 63, 193.

70. *Grutter et al. vs. Bollinger, et al.* (Slip Opinion), #0–241 (2003).

71. *U.S. Term Limits, Inc. et al. vs. Thornton et al.* (slip opinion) #93–1456 (1995).

72. Ibid. In *United States vs. Lopez* (slip opinion) #93–1260 (1995). Justice Thomas indeed indicated that he might be willing to revisit the Supreme Court's post–New Deal Commerce Clause jurisprudence.

73. The following are identified as "coherent themes" underlying black conservative thought: race is not an unavoidable determinant of individual thinking; taboos among blacks about discussion of deficiencies in ghetto-specific culture are conducive to ineffective social policies or even "social engineering fiascoes"; racism is not a sufficient cause for ghetto poverty and the belief that it is "demotivates the poor"; rejects on "moral and pragmatic" grounds "reliance on the "political capital of white guilt"; and challenges the relevance to the poor as well as the morality of affirmative action. See Joseph Conti and Brad Stetson, *Challenging the Civil Rights Establishment* (Westport, CT: Praeger, 1993), ch. 2.

74. Quoted in the preface to Bruce-Biggs, *The New Class*, p. xi.

75. In a 1971 editorial *National Review* recognized this fusion by celebrating *Commentary*'s embrace of the right. See "C'mon in, the Water's Fine," March 9, 1971.

76. On foreign policy, since the fall of the Soviet Union, traditional conservatives have been reluctant to use U.S. military power abroad, while neoconservatives have often exhibited a wish to remake the world—especially the Middle East—in accordance with American values and interests. For the traditional conservative view, see George Will, "The Slow Undoing: The Assault on and Underestimation of Nationality"; and for the neoconservative view, see William Kristol (Irving's son) and Robert Kagan, "National Interest and Global Responsibility," in Irwin Seltzer, ed., *The Neocon Reader* (New York: Grove, 2004). The "what's good for Jews" or, more precisely, Israel also plays a part in the conservative-neoconservative foreign policy dispute. For example, Russell Kirk, who might be described as the "godfather" of the conservative intellectual movement said of neoconservatism's godfather that "what really animates the neoconservatives, especially Irving Kristol, is the preservation of Israel. That lies in back of everything." Later in a speech at the Heritage Foundation, Kirk described the neoconservative foreign policy as a prescription for disaster and said they were "pursuing a fanciful democratic globalism rather than the national interests of the United States." He also said it seemed "as if some eminent neoconservatives mistook Tel Aviv for the capital of the United States." The first Kirk quote is from Gerson, *The Neoconservative Vision*, p. 315; the second is from Dorrien, *The Neoconservative Mind*, p. 324.

Chapter 8

1. Works that display a major role for racism in the ascendancy of conservatism include: William Berman, *America's Right Turn: From Nixon to Clinton* (Baltimore: Johns Hopkins University Press, 1994); Kevin Phillips, *Post Conservative America: People, Politics, and Ideology in a Time of Crisis* (New York: Random House, 1982); Earl and Merle Black, *The Rise of Southern Republicans* (Cambridge: Harvard, 2002); Amy Elizabeth Answell, *New Right, New Racism: Race and Reaction in the United States and Britain* (New York: New York University Press, 1997); Godfrey Hodgson, *The World Turned Right Side Up: A History of Conservative Ascendancy in America* (Boston: Houghton Mifflin, 1996); Sara Diamond, *Roads to Dominion: Right-Wing Movements and Political Power in the United States* (New York: Guilford, 1995); Edward Carmines and James Stimson, *Issue Evolution: Race and the Transformation of American Politics* (Princeton: Princeton University Press, 1989); Robert Huckfeldt and Carol Kohfeld, *Race and the Decline of Class in American Politics* (Urbana: University of Illinois Press, 1989); James Glaser, *Race, Campaign Politics and the Realignment of the South* (New Haven: Yale, 1996); Jeffrey Mayer, *Running on Race: Racial Politics in Presidential Campaigns, 1960–2000* (New York: Random House, 2002); Thomas Edsal, *Chain Reaction: The Impact of Race, Rights, and Taxes on American Politics* (New York: Norton, 1992); Kenneth O'Reilly, *Nixon's Piano: Presidents and Racial Politics from Washington to Clinton* (New York: Free, 1995); Tali Mendelberg, *The Race Card: Campaign Strategy, Implicit Messages and the Norm of Equality* (Princeton: Princeton University Press, 2001); Dan Carter, *From George Wallace to Newt Gingrich: Race in the Conservative Counterrevolution, 1963–1994* (Baton Rouge: Louisiana State University Press, 1996); Paul Krugman, *The Conscience of a Liberal* (New York: Norton, 2007); Alan Lichtman, *White Protestant Nation: The Rise of the American Conservative Movement* (New York: Atlantic Monthly, 2008); and Joseph Lowndes, *From the New Deal to the New Right: Race and the Southern Origins of Modern Conservatism* (New Haven: Yale, 2008).

2. This of course is a reformulation of Anthony Downs' famous axiom that "parties formulate policies in order to win elections, rather than win elections in order to formulate policies." See *An Economic Theory of Democracy* (New York: Harpers, 1957), 28, 34–35.

3. Mendelberg, *The Race Card*, ch. 3.

4. Paul Krugman, "Seeking Willie Horton," *New York Times*, August 24, 2007.

5. David Brooks, "History and Calumny," *New York Times*, November 9, 2007.

6. Ibid. Reagan's appearance was at the Neshoba County Fair, several miles from Philadelphia. In the speech Reagan attacked "big government," Washington bureaucrats, and welfare and declared, "I believe in states rights, I believe we've distorted the balance of power by giving powers that were never intended in the Constitution to the federal government."

7. Bob Herbert, "Righting Reagan's Wrongs," *New York Times*, November 13, 2007.

8. Lou Cannon, "Reagan's Southern Stumble," *New York Times*, November 18, 2007. See Cannon's balanced but sympathetic study of the Reagan presidency, *President Reagan: The Role of a Lifetime* (New York: Simon and Shuster, 1991).

9. Paul Krugman, "Republicans and Race," *New York Times*, November 19, 2007.

10. Ronald Reagan, *An American Life* (New York: Simon and Shuster, 1990), 401–02. During his campaign for governor Reagan angrily walked out of a debate when George Christopher, his primary opponent, suggested that Goldwater and Reagan's opposition to the Civil Rights Act of 1964 hinted of prejudice and bigotry. Storming off the stage muttering expletives, Reagan said, "I'll get that S.O.B." See Mathew Dallek, *The Right Moment: Ronald Reagan's First Victory and the Decisive Turning Point in American Politics* (New York: Oxford University Press, 2000), 200–01. In his memoir he writes of the incident "I'd grown up in a home where no sin was more grievous than racial bigotry, and I wasn't going to take it from Christopher" (p. 150).

11. Quoted in O' Reilly, *Nixon's Piano*, p. 357.

12. Douglas Brinkley, ed., *The Reagan Diaries* (New York: HarperCollins, 2007), 337–38.

13. Ibid., p. 549.

14. Carl Rowan, *Breaking Barriers: A Memoir* (New York: Harper Perennial, 1991), 326.

15. Ibid., p. 327. Laurence Barrett notes that Reagan often suffered "convenient memory [lapses] when his record on race was brought up." For example, when Barrett asked him in 1980 if he had explicitly opposed the major civil rights bills of the 1960s, Reagan responded, "I can't remember, I honestly can't." See *Gambling with History: Reagan in the White House* (New York: Penguin Books, 1984), 426. In the numerous and voluminous collections of Reagan's speeches and radio addresses published and on the Reagan library website, there is virtually nothing on his civil rights record. For example, I was not able to locate a single speech or address on his views on the civil rights bills of the 1960s.

16. For example, it is barely credible that Reagan did not know the white supremacist and racist implications of his repeated use of the "welfare queen" story or his reference to "young buck" to refer to male welfare recipients, given the salience of these as references to blacks in the popular culture. In addition, although he may have indeed opposed civil rights legislation on the basis of conservative principles, he never denounced or clearly disassociated himself from George Wallace's explicit racist opposition. And as Dallek writes, "Governors Orval Faubus of Alabama[sic.] and Ross Barnett of Mississippi, segregationist both, gave Reagan awards for his steadfast devotion to public service.... Reagan did not embrace the bigoted opinion and platforms of his southern friends, but the actor was more than willing to associate himself with racists and conspiracy theorists, demagogues and anticommunists." *The Right Moment*, p. 39.

17. See James Sundquist, "Whiter the American Party System," *Political Science Quarterly* 98 (1983–84): 586–87; Walter Dean Burnham, "The Reagan Heritage," in Gerald Pomper, ed., *The Election of 1988: Reports and Interpretations* (Chatham, NJ: Chatham House, 1989), 10; Rowland Evans and Robert Novak, *The Reagan Revolution*

(New York: Dutton, 1981), 8; Andrew Busch, *Ronald Reagan and the Politics of Freedom* (Lanham, MD: Rowman and Littlefield, 2001); Hugh Heclo, "Ronald Reagan and the American Public Philosophy," and Ted McAllister, "Reagan and the Transformation of American Conservatism," both in W. Elliot Brownlee and Hugh Davis Graham, eds., *The Reagan Presidency: Pragmatic Conservatism* (Lawrence: University Press of Kansas), 17-39, 40-60; and Berman, *America's Right Turn*, pp. 88-90.

18. Among his admirers who express this view, see David Stockman, *The Triumph of Politics* (New York: Harper and Row, 1986), 49. This is a recurring theme in his authorized biography by Edmund Morris, *Dutch: A Memoir of Ronald Reagan* (New York: Random House, 2000).

19. Heclo, "Ronald Reagan and the American Public Philosophy," p. 18.

20. Kiron Skinner and Annelise and Martin Anderson, eds., *Reagan's Path to Victory: The Shaping of Reagan's Visions, Selected Writings* (New York: Free, 2004); Skinner and Anderson and Anderson, eds., *Reagan: A Life in Letters* (New York: Free, 2003); and Skinner and Anderson, *Reagan, In His Own Hand* (New York: Free, 2001). Reagan's ideology was shaped by his reading of *National Review, Human Events,* and Hayek's *Road to Serfdom* and especially Chambers' *Witness*, with its apocalyptic portrayal of the cold war as a struggle between good and evil. Reagan paid tribute to the influence of *National Review* and leading conservative intellectuals (Frank Meyer, Von Mises, Russell Kirk, Milton Friedman) on the development of his thought and his election to the presidency. See "Remarks at Conservative Political Action Conference Dinner," in Reagan, *Speaking My Mind: Selected Speeches* (New York: Simon and Shuster, 1989), 96. The influence of Chambers and Hayek on Reagan's thinking is discussed throughout John Patrick Duggins, *Ronald Reagan: Fate, Freedom and the Making of History* (New York: Norton, 2007).

21. Locke's thought is implicit in the writings of most conservative intellectuals who like Reagan tend to cite the framers of the Constitution, especially Madison and Jefferson.

22. Heclo, "Ronald Reagan and the American Public Philosophy," p. 28.

23. Busch is useful because he consciously attempts to systematize Reagan's thought, but see also the essays by Heclo and McAllister.

24. Busch, *Ronald Regan and the Politics of Freedom*, p. xviii.

25. Ibid.

26. Ibid., p. 12. See also McAllister, "Reagan and the Transformation of American Conservatism."

27. Heclo, "Ronald Reagan and the American Public Philosophy," p. 19.

28. Reagan, *An American Life*, p. 380

29. Steven Hayward, *The Age of Reagan: The Fall of the Old Liberal Order, 1964-1980* (Roseville, CA: Prima, 2001), 452. Lee Lescaz, "Reagan Still Sure Some in New Deal Espoused Fascism," *Washington Post*, December 24, 1981.

30. Quoted in Black and Black, *The Rise of Southern Republicans*, p. 387

31. Dallek, *The Right Moment*, p. 188.

32. Reagan, *An American Life*, p. 401.

33. Dallek, *The Right Moment*, pp. 226-28.

34. Ronald Reagan, "Remarks at the 1981 Annual Convention of the NAACP," Denver, Colorado, http://www.reagan.utexas.edu/archives/speeches/1981/62981a.htm.

35. Ibid.

36. Gunner Myrdal, *An American Dilemma: The Negro Problem and Modern Democracy* (New York: Harper and Row, 1944, 1962), 1035–40.

37. Walter Dean Burnham, "The 1980 Election Earthquake: Realignment, Reaction or What," in Thomas Ferguson and Joel Rogers, eds., *The Hidden Election: Politics and Economics in the 1980 Presidential Campaign* (New York: Pantheon, 1981), 99.

38. Theodore White, *The Making of the President, 1960* (New York: Atheneum, 1980), appendix B, "Text of Statement Released by Governor Rockefeller," July 23, 1960.

39. Rick Perlstein, *Before the Storm: Barry Goldwater and the Unmaking of the American Consensus* (New York: Hill and Wang, 2001), 90.

40. *National Review*, "The 1960 Election," October 22, 1960 p. 234.

41. Brent Bozell, "The Challenge to Conservatism," *National Review*, October 22, 1961, p. 12.

42. Race was related to the anti-Communism element of the conservative movement since the view that the civil rights movement was Communist inspired, dominated, or, at a minimum, influenced was widespread in movement circles. Throughout the 1950s and 1960s books were published by obscure conservative outlets documenting the alleged relationship between Communism and civil rights. See Donald Critchlow, *The Conservative Ascendancy: How the GOP Right Made Political History* (Cambridge: Harvard, 2007), 304, note 67.

The relationship between southern traditionalism and racism was discussed in chapter 3, but the relationships among southern, conservative evangelical Christianity, racism, and the conservative ascendancy is less clear. This is an important area of inquiry because by the time of Reagan's election white southern evangelicals had become the core or base constituency of the Republican Party. Overwhelming support of the Republican Party by white evangelicals is usually attributed to opposition to liberal Democratic support for feminism, abortion, and gay rights. However, racism may also play a role (I am not aware of any empirical studies that correlate the relationship between racism and evangelicalism among southern whites). Southern evangelical leaders during the 1950s and 1960s were divided on the question of civil rights. While Jerry Falwell preached sermons justifying racism and segregation on biblical principles, Billy Graham preached against racism, desegregated his crusades, shared his pulpit with Martin Luther King Jr., and endorsed what he called the "social revolution King was leading in the South." In addition, shortly after *Brown*, the convention of southern Baptists passed a resolution supporting the decision and calling for peaceful compliance. On Falwell's racist and white supremacist preachings, see Walt Harrington, "Well Wrought," *Washington Post Magazine*, July 29, 1988, and on Graham's positions and on race generally among white evangelicals during the civil rights era, see David Chappel, *A Stone of Hope: Prophetic Religion and the Death of Jim Crow* (Chapel Hill: University of North Carolina Press), 107–14.

43. William Rusher, "Crossroads for the GOP," *National Review*, February 12, 1963, p. 111.

44. Republican leaders had flirted with the idea of a southern strategy, off and on, since the end of Reconstruction. In the 1928 election between Herbert Hoover and Al Smith, Hoover nearly equaled Goldwater's performance in 1964 by winning four

southern states (Texas, North Carolina, Virginia and Florida). Hoover became the first Republican nominee to receive substantial southern electoral support by adopting a "southern strategy of] ... shrewdly directing appeals to religious bigotry, prohibitionism and racism." Alan Lichtman, *Prejudice and Politics: The Presidential Election of 1928* (Chapel Hill: University of North Carolina Press, 1979), 151. Although many African American leaders and newspapers responded by endorsing Smith, most blacks voted for Hoover because the Democratic Party maintained its traditional racist, white supremacist posture and Smith did little to challenge it. (At the 1928 Democratic Convention black visitors were notoriously segregated behind a chicken wire barrier.)

45. Clifton White (with William Gill), *Suite 3505: The Story of the Draft Goldwater Movement* (New Rochelle: Arlington House, 1967), 174.

46. Ibid., p. 175.

47. Ibid., p. 97.

48. Quoted in Perlstein, *Before the Storm*, p. 190.

49. Ibid., p. 227. Rockefeller's view of the futility of the southern strategy was shared at the time by a leading student of the voting behavior of the electorate. In an article written two years before the 1964 election, Philip Converse dismissed the likelihood that the South would become "a reliably Republican region." Although he recognized that "the Negro problem" had the potential to bring about a realignment, he thought it unlikely because he did not believe the Republicans would "come forth to champion the Southern white." When Goldwater did come forth, Converse thought it was likely an aberration, because "[i]n the wake of the Republican catastrophe at the polls and the likely return to power of more familiar Republican Party leadership, it seems reasonable to expect that the Goldwater strategy will be reversed as hastily as possible." See "On the Possibility of Major Political Realignment in the South," in Angus Campbell et al., eds., *Elections and the Political Order* (New York: Wiley & Sons, 1966), 240–41.

50. Conservative control of the party was the real objective of the campaign. Even before he announced for the nomination, Goldwater reportedly told his senior campaign staff, "I want you to know from the start I believe it's a lost cause [but] there are a lot of people out there [who believe in our cause]. We can't let them down. Some day they are going to pick up where we left off.... First, let's take over the party, then go from there." Quoted in Mark Stern, *Calculating Visions: Kennedy, Johnson and Civil Rights* (New Brunswick: Rutgers University Press, 1992), 194.

51. White, *Suite 3505*, p. 171. See also Robert Novak, *The Agony of the GOP* (New York: MacMillan, 1965); and Nicol Rae, *The Decline and Fall of Liberal Republicans: From 1952 to the Present* (New York: Oxford University Press, 1989). Critchlow suggests that conservatives did not gain effective control of the party until 1980. However, without the support of Strom Thurmond and Goldwater, Reagan might have defeated Nixon in 1968, and Critchlow himself concludes that in 1976 Reagan lost to Ford by an "inch." See *The Conservative Ascendancy*. This suggests that White is correct when he concludes that conservatives have constituted a majority of Republican delegates since 1964.

52. William Rusher, *The Rise of the Right* (New York: Morrow 1984). Alfred Regenery, the son of the publisher of Regenery Books, in his somewhat personal

account of the movement also ignores the role of race and racism. See *Upstream: The Ascendency of American Conservatism* (New York: Simon and Shuster, 2008).

53. White, *Suite 3505*, p. 175. White goes on to write that the only time the Republicans had a place in southern politics was during "the vindictive period of Reconstruction when radical Republicans installed carpetbaggers and others in political office in the South with the aid of occupation troops" (p. 175).

54. Krugman, *The Conscience of a Liberal*.

55. In a review essay frequently cited by conservatives embarrassed by the movement's association with racism, Gerard Alexander rejects the idea that the South converted to the Republican Party on the basis of racism. Rather, he concludes that economic transformations in the region (creating an upwardly mobile, nonunion white middle class) and the party's commitment to traditionalism and religiosity were the principal agents in the partisan transformation of the region. See "The Myth of the Racist Republicans," *Claremont Review of Books*, Spring, 2004, pp. 11–13. Byron Shafer and Richard Johnston also argue that it was the economy rather than racism that was central in the transformation of southern politics. See *The End of Southern Exceptionalism: Class, Race, and Partisan Change in the Postwar South* (Cambridge: Harvard, 2006).

56. Hodgson, *The World Turned Right Side Up*, p. 67.

57. White, *Suite 3505*, p. 236.

58. Ibid., p. 237.

59. David Danzig, "Rightists, Racists, Separatists: A White Bloc in the Making," *Commentary*, August, 1964, p. 28.

60. Ibid., p. 30. Some evidence suggests that Republican voters tended strongly toward racial conservatism long before the events of the 1960s. See Anthony Chen, Robert Mickey, and Robert Van Houweling, "Explaining the Contemporary Alignment of Race and Party: Evidence from California's 1946 Ballot Initiative on Fair Employment," *Studies in American Political Development* 22 (2008): 204–28. More generally, see Gary Gerstle, "Race and the Myth of the Liberal Consensus," *Journal of American History* 82 (1995): 579–86.

61. Danzig, "Rightists, Racists, Separatists," p. 32.

62. White, *Suite 3505*, p. 237.

63. Clifton White (with William Gill), *Why Reagan Won: A Narrative History of the Conservative Movement, 1964–1981* (Chicago: Regnery, 1981), 75–81. A huge July 1963 rally in Washington, D.C., of more than nine thousand persons, organized by YAF, is credited by White with pushing Goldwater into seriously considering seeking the nomination.

64. Hayward, *The Age of Reagan*, p. 63.

65. John Andrew, *The Other Side of the Sixties: Young Americans for Freedom and the Rise of Conservative Politics* (New Brunswick, NJ: Rutgers University Press, 1997), 57.

66. Ibid., p. 59.

67. Gregory Schneider, *Cadres for Conservatism: Young Americans for Freedom and the Rise of the Contemporary Right* (New York: New York University Press, 1999), 58.

68. Ibid.

69. E. E. Schattsneider, *The Semi-Sovereign People: A Realist's View of Democracy in America* (New York: Holt, Rinehart, and Winston, 1960), 69.

70. Peter Bachrach and Morton Baratz, "The Two Faces of Power," *American Political Science Review* 56 (1962): 947–52.

71. Clinton's contribution to the two-party system's silence on race beginning in 1992 is discussed in the concluding chapter.

72. The classic study of these compromises and their ultimate failure is David Potter, *The Impending Crisis, 1848–1861* (New York: Harper and Row, 1976).

73. Mendelberg, *The Race Card*, p. 28.

74. Ibid., p. 29.

75. William Gillettee, *Retreat from Reconstruction, 1869–1879* (Baton Rouge: Louisiana State University Press, 1979).

76. The description of the brief Reconstruction period as a failed experiment resembles the characterization by neoconservatives of the War on Poverty during the 1960s and 1970s. For the Reconstruction era and how the understanding of it as failure became orthodoxy among American historians, see Eric Foner, *Reconstruction: America's Unfinished Revolution, 1863–1877* (New York: Harper and Row, 1988), chs. 10–13, epilogue.

77. Mendelberg, *The Race Card*, pp. 49–56.

78. Ibid.

79. On Wallace's racial liberalism during the campaign and especially his courageous campaigning in the South see Patricia Sullivan, *Days of Hope: Race and Democracy in the New Deal Era* (Chapel Hill: University of North Carolina Press, 1996), 244–47.

80. William C. Berman, *The Politics of Civil Rights in the Truman Administration* (Columbus: Ohio State University Press, 1970), 29.

81. Sullivan, *Days of Hope*, pp. 186–87.

82. Ibid., p. 15. See also Karl Schmidt, *Henry A. Wallace's Quixotic Crusade* (Tuscaloosa: University of Alabama Press, 1960).

83. Richard Russell of Georgia, the emerging leader of the Senate's southern bloc, accused Truman of "unconditional surrender to the Wallace campaign and to the treasonable civil disobedience ... of Randolph." Sullivan, *Days of Hope*, p. 117.

84. Henry Lee Moon, *Balance of Power: The Negro Vote* (Garden City, NY: Doubleday, 1948), 198.

85. Quoted in Paul Frymer, *Uneasy Alliances: Race and Party Competition in America* (Princeton: Princeton University Press, 1999), 96.

86. Mary Dudziak, *Cold War Civil Rights: Race and the Image of American Democracy* (Princeton: Princeton University Press, 2000), ch. 3.

87. Timothy Thurber, *The Politics of Equality: Hubert H. Humphrey and the African American Freedom Struggle* (New York: Columbia University Press, 1999), 62.

88. Berman, *The Politics of Civil Rights in the Truman Administration*, p. 95. Dewey received 23 percent of the black vote in 1948, compared to his 40 percent in 1944.

89. Richard Hofstader, "From Calhoun to the Dixiecrats," *Social Research* 16 (1949): 146–66.

90. Arthur Schlesinger Jr., *The Vital Center* (Cambridge, MA: Riverside, 1949, 1962), 190.

91. Chappel, *A Stone of Hope*, p. 34.

92. Jeff Broadwater, *Adlai Stevenson and American Politics* (New York: Twayne, 1994), 168.

93. John Bartlow Martin, *Adlai Stevenson of Illinois: The Life and Times* (New York: Doubleday, 1976), 554.

94. Broadwater, *Adlai Stevenson and American Politics*, p. 142.

95. Steven Gillon, *Politics and Vision: The ADA and American Liberalism, 1947–1985* (New York: Oxford University Press, 1987), ch. 4.

96. David Nichols, *A Matter of Justice: Eisenhower and the Beginning of the Civil Rights Revolution* (New York: Simon and Shuster, 2007).

97. Reluctantly and only under the glare of international publicity did Eisenhower intervene in Little Rock. For example, in 1956 the Mansfield, Texas, school district also defied a federal court order and denied admission to three black children. Yet Eisenhower flatly refused the NAACP's request for federal intervention. Indeed, in July 1957 Eisenhower told a press conference, "I can't imagine any set of circumstances that would ever induce me to send federal troops ... into any area to enforce the order of a federal court." This statement on the eve of the opening of the school year likely encouraged Oval Faubus' defiance and created the domestic and international uproar that Eisenhower could not imagine would require dispatch of the army. On the Mansfield incident and the Eisenhower quote, see Russell Riley, *The Presidency and the Politics of Civil Rights* (New York: Columbia University Press, 1993), 189–95.

98. Even the liberal stalwart Humphrey in the interest of sectional unity and his growing vice presidential and presidential ambitions begin to curry favor with southern racists and backtrack on civil rights. See Thurber, *The Politics of Equality: Hubert H. Humphrey and the African American Freedom Struggle*, pp. 98–101.

99. Joan Hoff, *Nixon Reconsidered* (New York: Basic Books, 1994), ch. 3; and Mayer, *Running on Race*, ch. 7.

100. Garry Wills, *Nixon Agonistes* (Boston: Houghton Mifflin, 1969), back flap.

101. Quoted in George Sinkler, *The Racial Attitudes of American Presidents* (Garden City, NY: Doubleday, 1971), 11.

102. See the interview with Schlesinger on C-Span's "In Depth," December 13, 2000. On the Dunning School's falsification of Reconstruction history, see the preface in Eric Foner, *Reconstruction: America's Unfinished Revolution* (New York: Harper and Row, 1988) and "The Propaganda of History," in DuBois, *Black Reconstruction* (New York: Athenaeum, 1935, 1969).

103. John F. Kennedy, *Profiles in Courage* (New York: Harper and Brothers, 1955), 126–27, 131. See also his profile of Reconstruction-era Mississippi senator Lucius Lamar for similar views. After his confrontations with Mississippi governor Ross Barnett and Alabama's Wallace over the desegregation of their states' universities Kennedy may have changed his views of Stevens and the South. Schlesinger recalls a conversation with him shortly after the murder of Mississippi NAACP director Medgar Evers, when he said, "I don't understand the South. I'm coming to believe that Thaddeus Stevens was right. I had always been taught to regard him as a man

of vicious bias. But, when I see this sort of thing, I begin to wonder how else you can treat them." Quoted in James David Barber, *The Presidential Character: Predicting Performance in the White House* (Englewood Cliffs, NJ: Prentice Hall, 1972), 341–42. In order to educate the president about the lies and distortions of the Dunning School, his brother, the attorney general, invited the historian David Donald to the White House to conduct a seminar that provided a more accurate account of Reconstruction. See James Giglio, *The Presidency of John F. Kennedy*, 2nd ed. (Lawrence: University Press of Kansas, 2006), 190.

104. Theodore White, *The Making of the President, 1960* (New York: Athenaeum, 1961, 1980), 385–87, and Arthur Schlesinger Jr., *Robert F. Kennedy and His Times* (Boston: Houghton Mifflin, 1978), 233–35.

105. Arthur Schlesinger Jr., *A Thousand Days: John F. Kennedy in the White House* (Boston: Houghton Mifflin, 1965), 929.

106. Ibid., p. 931.

107. Ibid.

108. Ibid.

109. Nick Kolz, *Judgment Days: Lyndon Baines Johnson, Martin Luther King Jr. and the Laws That Changed America* (Boston: Houghton Mifflin, 2005), 59.

110. In his memoir Stokely Carmichael recalls, "Given the administration's record, I was sure it would turn out to be just another cop-out. But I was surprised. It was accurate, clear and truthful. The clearest, they said, since Lincoln's second Inaugural Address (1864) a hundred years earlier.... I think this speech has to be what accounted for Kennedy's great popularity among ordinary black folk in the South." See *Ready for Revolution: The Life and Struggles of Stokely Carmichael* (New York: Scribner, 2003), 328.

111. John F. Kennedy, "Civil Rights Speech," in Richard Heffener, ed., *A Documentary History of the United States* (New York: Signet Books, 2003), 398, 400.

112. Schlesinger, *A Thousand Days*, p. 977.

113. This is a major theme in Randall Woods' biography, *LBJ: Architect of American Ambition* (New York: Free, 2006).

114. Kotz, *Judgment Days*, p. 23.

115. Robert Mann, *The Walls of Jericho: Lyndon Johnson, Hubert Humphrey, Richard Russell, and the Struggle for Civil Rights* (New York: Harcourt Brace, 1996).

116. Kotz, *Judgment Days*, p. 38.

117. Woods, *LBJ*, p. 480.

118. Barry Goldwater, *With No Apologies: The Personal and Political Memoirs* (New York: Morrow, 1979); and White, *Suite 3505*, pp. 252–53.

119. "Goldwater's Speech on Civil Rights, June 18, 1964," in White, *Suite 3505*, p. 430.

120. Goldwater also said the effective implementation of the law would require "the creation of a police state."

121. Johnson also addressed civil rights once in his famous "Nigger Speech" in New Orleans. Joining his wife at the end of her tour of the South (where in South Carolina she was booed and jeered by a hostile crowd of Goldwater supporters), Johnson told a largely white party fund-raiser, "[W]hatever your views are, we have a

Constitution ... and we have the law of the land [Civil Rights Act of 1964], I signed it and I intend to enforce it." He then said, "I would like to go back down there [to an unnamed southern state] and make them one more Democratic speech.... The poor old state, they haven't heard a Democratic speech in 30 years. All they ever hear at election time is 'nigger, nigger, nigger!'" Quoted in Wood, *LBJ*, p. 544.

122. Perlstein, *Before the Storm*, p. 460. Goldwater canceled a planned television ad called "The Choice" after allegations were made that it might be viewed as racist, telling White, "I'm not going to be made out a racist; you can't show it." *Suite 3505*, p. 415.

123. Perlstein, *Before the Storm*, p. 461-62.

124. Ibid.

125. Theodore White writes that of Goldwater's total vote one can "estimate that he received some 24 percent from the conservative, hereditary, white Republicans and 14 percent (the ultimate racist vote of George Wallace in 1968) from white racists who hate blacks." See *The Making of the President, 1968* (New York: Athenaeum, 1969), 363.

126. Quoted in Hayward, *The Age of Reagan*, p. 643.

127. Dan Carter, *The Politics of Rage*, p. 12.

128. Carmines and Stimson, *Issue Evolution*. See also Alan Abramowitz, "Issue Evolution Reconsidered: Racial Attitudes and Partisanship in the U.S. Electorate," *American Journal of Political Science* 38 (1994): 1–24. Although Abramowitz writes that "much of the evidence presented by Carmines and Stimson is incontrovertible" (p. 4), he nevertheless questions the strong relationship between race and partisan change suggested by Carmines and Stimson because "they do not control for other issues when examining the relationship between racial attitudes and partisanship." While an important methodological revision of Carmines and Stimson's work, their findings substantively remain incontrovertible.

129. It also produced a conservative grassroots base that would be instrumental in nominating and electing Reagan. Regenery estimates that as many as 3.5 million persons worked in the Goldwater campaign, and its list of more than a million small contributors became the genesis of the conservative movement's direct mail fundraising that was so effective in the 1970s and 1980s. See *Upstream*, pp. 97–99.

130. Dallek, *The Right Moment*, p. 67; and Clifton White, *Why Reagan Won*, pp. 120–23.

131. Ronald Reagan, "Televised Address on Behalf of Senator Barry Goldwater, October 27, 1964," in Ronald Reagan, *Speaking My Mind*.

132. These businessmen were militantly anticommunist, anti-New Deal and antilabor union, favoring an almost unregulated Lockean laissez faire capitalism. See Dallek, *The Right Moment*, pp. 73–77.

133. Ibid., chs. 9–10.

134. Ibid., p. 188.

135. White, *The Making of the President, 1968*, p. 35. Reagan delayed entering the 1968 race according to White because of the discovery of a "homosexual scandal" in his gubernatorial staff. By the time he announced, Nixon had already won the nomination by winning the support of Goldwater and Strom Thurmond. On the

significance of Thurmond's support in Reagan's defeat, see White, *Why Reagan Won*, pp. 92–104.

136. White, *The Making of the President, 1968*, p. 29.

137. Mendelberg, *The Race Card*, p. 95. See also Joel Olson, "Whiteness and the Polarization of American Politics," *Political Research Quarterly* 61 (2008): 704–18.

138. Dean Kotlowski, *Nixon's Civil Rights Record: Politics, Principles and Policy* (Cambridge: Harvard University Press, 2001).

139. O'Reilly, *Nixon's Piano*, p. 99.

140. John Ehrlichman, *Witness to Power* (New York: Auburn House, 1982), 222–23.

141. *Report of the National Advisory Commission on Civil Disorders* (New York: Bantam Books, 1968).

142. T. M. Tomlinson, "The Development of a Riot Ideology among Urban Negroes," *American Behavioral Scientist* 2 (1968): 17–29.

143. On Hoover's views see U.S. Senate, *Final Report of the Select Committee to Study Government Operations with Respect to Intelligence*, Washington, S.R. 94-755, 94th Congress, 2nd session, 1976. See also Garry Wills, *The Second Civil War: Arming for Armageddon* (New York: New American Library).

144. White, *The Making of the President, 1968*, p. 28.

145. Mendelberg, *The Race Card*, pp. 95–99. Ehrlichman writes that in Nixon's statements and speeches on schools and housing there was always a "subliminal appeal to the anti-black voter." *Witness to Power*, p. 223.

146. Ibid.

147. White, *The Making of the President, 1968*, p. 401.

148. Black and Black, *The Rise of Southern Republicans*, pp. 225–26.

149. When Theodore White started writing his making of the president series in the 1960s he averred that there were only three issues in American politics: "bread and butter, war and peace and black and white." By the 1970s as a result of the social and cultural changes of the 1960s one could add a fourth issue, which might be labeled "right and wrong." This issue deals with such matters as prayer in school, the rights of persons accused of crimes, the death penalty, abortion, and gay rights.

150. Bruce Miroff, *The Liberal's Moment: The McGovern Insurgency and the Identity Crisis of the Democratic Party* (Lawrence: University Press of Kansas, 2007), 123.

151. Ibid., p. 134.

152. "Democratic Party Platform, 1972," in Kirk Porter and Donald Johnson, eds., *National Party Platforms* (Urbana: University of Illinois Press, 1976). The platform adopted by the Democrats in 1972 resembles the agendas and budgets proposed by the Congressional Black Caucus during the 1970s and 1980s. See Robert C. Smith, *We Have No Leaders: African Americans in the Post Civil Rights Era* (Albany: State University of New York Press, 1996), ch. 8.

153. Hoff's *Nixon Reconsidered* makes this case. See also David Greenberg, *Nixon's Shadow: The History of an Image* (New York: Norton, 2003). Of course, Nixon being Nixon, calling him a liberal does not mean very much. Scholars of his presidency have argued about why Nixon embraced liberal policies during his first administration.

The explanations advanced include the following: he had to accommodate a liberal, Democratic Congress; he wanted to co-opt the opposition in preparation for the 1972 election; he was unduly influenced by his liberal advisors (especially Moynihan); he really did not care about domestic policy; and he wanted to do liberal things to leave a historical legacy as the American Disraeli.

154. White, *Why Reagan Won*, p. 132. On conservative disaffection from Nixon see also Rusher, *The Rise of the Right*, pp. 239–62; and White, *Why Reagan Won*, pp. 132–37. Hayward in *The Age of Reagan* titles part 2 of the book "The Failure of Richard Nixon," and Critchlow in *The Conservative Ascendancy* titles his chapter "Trust and Betrayal in the Nixon Years."

155. Hugh Davis Graham in the most detailed study of the origins and development of affirmative action is inconclusive as to why Nixon approved the policy, which was written by two African American deputy assistant secretaries of labor. See Graham, *The Civil Rights Era: Origins and Development of National Policy* (New York: Oxford University Press, 1990), chs. 12–13. However, Berman concludes flat out that Nixon embraced the policy "to increase strife between blacks and organized labor." See *America's Right Turn*, p. 11. This was certainty the view of labor and civil rights leaders at the time. AFL-CIO President George Meany said affirmative action was a "concoction and contrivance of some bureaucrat's imagination to offset criticism of the administration's civil rights record," and Clarence Mitchell, the NAACP's Washington lobbyist, described it as "calculated attempt coming right from the president's desk to break up the coalition between Negroes and labor unions. Most of the social progress in this country has come from this alliance." See *Civil Rights Progress Report* (Washington: CQ, 1971), 57–58.

156. Miroff, *The Liberal's Moment*, p. 50. Another factor cited by McGovern and Gary Hart, the campaign manager, was the controversy surrounding the replacement of the vice presidential nominee Thomas Eagelton because he had been treated for mental illness. The vociferous opposition to McGovern's candidacy by George Meany and the other leaders of organized labor was also a factor. Labor's opposition to McGovern in the general election led black trade unionists to form a separate group, the Coalition of Black Trade Unionists.

157. H. R. Halderman, *The Halderman Diaries: Inside the Nixon White House* (New York: Putnam, 1994), 473.

158. Ibid.

159. Critchlow, *The Conservative Ascendancy*, p. 170.

160. Miroff, *The Liberal's Moment*, pp. 261, 275. The most detailed study of the election labels it an ideological election with the Democratic Party viewed as far to the left and therefore out of touch with the Lockean electorate. Arthur Miller et al., "A Majority Party in Disarray: Policy Polarization in the 1972 Election," *American Political Science Review* 70 (1976): 753–78.

161. Miroff, *The Liberal's Moment*, p. 261.

162. Although Reagan lost the nomination, the platform adopted by the convention was a Reagan rather than a Ford document, "a full throated conservative manifesto" in Hayward's language. See *The Age of Reagan*, p. 478.

163. William Rusher, *The Making of the New Majority Party* (New York: Sheed and Ward, 1975).

164. White, *Why Reagan Won*, p. 168-69; Rusher, *The Rise of the Right*, pp. 263-90; and Hayward, *The Age of Reagan*, p. 449.

165. Jimmy Carter, *Turning Point: A Candidate, a State, and a Nation Come of Age* (New York: Times Books, 1992).

166. Hanes Walton Jr., *The Native Son Presidential Candidate: The Carter Vote in Georgia* (New York: Praeger, 1992).

167. Gerald Pomper, et al., *The Election of 1976: Reports and Interpretations* (New York: McKay, 1977), 79.

168. See Carmines and Stimson, *Issue Evolution*; and Jonathan Kinuckey, "Racial Resentment and the Changing Partisanship of Southern Whites," *Party Politics* 11 (2005): 15-32.

169. Wayne Greenshaw, *Elephant in the Cotton Field* (New York: MacMillan, 1982), 13.

170. Morris Fiorina, *Retrospective Voting in American National Elections* (New Haven: Yale, 1981).

171. All studies of the election demonstrate this. See, for examples, James Sundquist, "Whither the American Party System?—Revisited," *Political Science Quarterly* 98 (1983-84): 573-93; Everett Carl Ladd, "The Brittle Mondale: Electoral Realignment in 1980," *Political Science Quarterly* 96 (1981): 1-25; Paul Abramson, John Aldrich, and David Rhode, *Change and Continuity in the 1980 Election* (Washington: CQ, 1982); and Walter Dean Burnham, "The 1980 Election Earthquake: Realignment, Reaction, or What?" in Thomas Ferguson and Joel Rogers, eds., *The Hidden Election: Politics and Economics in the 1980 Presidential Campaign* (New York: Pantheon, 1980).

172. On Reagan advisers' efforts to keep "Reagan from being Reagan" and avoid campaign gaffes see Hayward, *The Age of Reagan*, pp. 674-94.

173. On the preparation of the statement see Jack Germond and Jules Witcover, *Blue Smoke and Mirrors: How Reagan Won and Why Carter Lost* (New York: Viking, 1981), 281.

174. Quoted in Hayward, *The Age of Reagan*, p. 698. Coretta Scott King and Andrew Young also made remarks suggesting Reagan was antiblack. Young described Reagan's remarks at the Philadelphia fair as "like a code word to me that it's going to be all right to kill niggers when he's President and Mrs. King said 'I am scared that if Ronald Reagan gets into office, we're going to see more Ku Klux Klan and a resurgence of the Nazi Party.'" These quotes are also from *The Age of Reagan*, p. 697.

175. Sundquist, "Whither the American Party System?" p. 583.

176. Ladd, "The Brittle Mandate," p. 121.

177. Ibid.

178. Burnham, "The 1980 Election Earthquake," p. 109.

179. Ladd, "The Brittle Mandate," p. 138.

180. Berman, *America's Right Turn*, p. 81.

181. Robert Dahl argues that whole idea of electoral mandates in presidential elections rests on shaky empirical foundations. See "The Myth of the Presidential Mandate," *Political Science Quarterly* 105 (1990): 355-72. On the absence of a conservative ideological mandate from the 1980 election specifically, see Ladd, "The Brittle Mandate."

182. Burnham, "The 1980 Election Earthquake," p. 97.

183. A week after the election the Heritage Foundation presented a three thousand-page set of policy recommendations to the Reagan transition team titled *Mandate for Change*, which called for reversing "48 years of liberal policies."

184. Carter did not carry a majority of the Jewish vote, the first Democratic nominee not to do so. This may have been partly because at the UN the United States apparently mistakenly cast a vote calling for the dismantlement of Jewish settlements in the occupied West Bank, including Jerusalem. This offended the Israeli lobby, and although Carter subsequently issued a statement saying the vote was a mistake, this may have eroded his support among Jews. See Germond and Witcover, *Blue Smoke and Mirrors*, pp. 152-53; and Burnham, "The 1980 Election Earthquake," p. 105.

185. Burnham, "The 1980 Election Earthquake," p. 105.

186. Matthew Holden Jr., "The President, Congress and Race Relations," Ernest Patterson Memorial Lecture, University of Colorado, Boulder, 1986, p. 69.

Chapter 9

1. Kenneth O'Reilly, *Nixon's Piano: Presidents and Racial Politics from Washington to Clinton* (New York: Free, 1995), 355.

2. Laughlin McDonald, "Voting Rights on the Chopping Block," *Southern Exposure*, Spring, 1981, as quoted in Abigail Thernstrom, *Whose Votes Count? Affirmative Action and Minority Voting Right* (Cambridge: Harvard University Press, 1987), 79-80.

3. Richard Newstadt, *Presidential Power and the Modern Presidents* (New York: Free, 1990).

4. Aaron Wildavsky, "The Two Presidencies," in Steven Shull, ed., *The Two Presidencies: A Quarter Century Assessment* (Chicago: Nelson-Hall, 1991). In a subsequent essay, Wildavsky concluded that the two presidencies no longer existed because foreign policy had become more complex, contentious, partisan, and ideological. See Duane Oldfield and Wildavsky "Reconsidering the Two Presidencies," in Shull, *The Two Presidencies*. I still think the formulation holds up pretty well. As the George W. Bush administration demonstrated, the president's command of the diplomatic and military corps allows him to generally have his way, even against the will of the Congress and the public.

5. Hugh Davis Graham, *The Civil Rights Era: Origins and Development of National Policy* (New York: Oxford, 1990). See also Hanes Walton Jr., *When the Marching Stopped: The Politics of Civil Rights Regulatory Agencies* (Albany: State University of New York Press, 1988).

6. Howard Schulman, Carlotta Steeth, and Lawrence Bobo, *Racial Attitudes in America: Trends and Interpretations* (Cambridge: Harvard, 1985).

7. Robert C. Smith, *Racism in the Post Civil Rights Era* (Albany: State University of New York Press, 1995), 37.

8. David Sears, "Symbolic Racism," in P. Katz and D. Taylor, eds., *Eliminating Racism* (New York: Plenum, 1988); Donald Kinder and Lynn Sanders, *Divided by*

Color: Racial Politics and American Democracy (Chicago: University of Chicago Press, 1996), 272–76; and Lawrence Bobo, J. Klugel, and R. Smith, "Laissez-Faire Racism: The Crystallization of 'A Kinder, Gentler' 'Anti-Black Ideology,' " in S. Tuch and J. Martin, eds., *Racial Attitudes in the 1990s* (Westport, CT: Praeger, 1997).

9. Paul Sniderman, "The New Look in Public Opinion Research," in A. Finifter, *The State of the Discipline, II* (Washington: American Political Science Association, 1993), 232.

10. Sears, "Symbolic Racism," p. 232. Jack Turner writes that it is not "a surprise that the language of individualism is the moral rhetoric of choice for prejudiced whites.... This preoccupation is rooted both in white Americans['] deep commitment to the idea of self-sufficiency and in the deep American assumption that self-sufficiency is white people's special province." See "American Individualism and Structural Injustice: Tocqueville, Gender and Race," *Polity* 4 (2008): 215. See also Donald Kinder and Tali Mendelberg, "Individualism Reconsidered: Principles and Prejudices in Contemporary American Opinion," in David Sears, Jim Sidanius, and Lawrence Bobo, eds., *Racialized Politics: Values, Ideology, and Prejudice in American Public Opinion* (Chicago: University of Chicago Press, 2000).

11. These are my calculations from Michael Barone and Grant Ujifusa, *The Almanac of American Politics, 1982* (Washington: Barone, 1982). Nicol Rae estimates fifteen liberal-moderate Republican senators and thirty in the House. See *The Decline and Fall of Liberal Republicans, 1952 to the Present* (New York: Oxford, 1989).

12. Harold Wolman and Norman Thomas, "Black Interests and Black Groups in the Federal Policy Process," *Journal of Politics* 32 (1970): 875–97.

13. Robert C. Smith, "Black Power and the Transformation from Protest to Politics," *Political Science Quarterly* 96 (1981): 431–44.

14. Dianne Pinderhughes, "Racial Interest Groups and Incremental Politics," unpublished manuscript, Notre Dame, 1980.

15. Dianne Pinderhughes, "Divisions in the Civil Rights Community," *PS: Political Science and Politics* 25 (1992): 485–87.

16. The National Welfare Rights Organization (NWRO), the first national organization devoted exclusively to the interests of poor black women and their children, was from 1967 to 1975 an effective grassroots lobbying presence in Washington, helping to, ironically, defeat Nixon's Family Assistance Plan. See Todd Shaw, "We Refused to Lay Down Our Spears: The Persistence of Welfare Rights Activism," in Ollie Johnson and Karin Stanford, eds., *Black Political Organizations in the Post Civil Rights Era* (New Brunswick, NJ: Rutgers University Press, 2002).

17. Douglass Imig, *Poverty and Power: The Political Representation of Poor Americans* (Lincoln: University of Nebraska Press, 1996), 10–13.

18. Ibid., p. 11.

19. Gwendolyn Mink, *Welfare's End* (Ithaca: Cornell University Press, 1998), 7. Mink's observation raises the question of intersectionality, the idea that the largely white, middle-class feminist movement cannot adequately represent the forms of subordination experienced by poor black women. See Patricia Hill Collins, "Gender, Black Feminism and the Black Political Economy," *Annals of the American Academy of Political and Social Science* 569 (2000): 41–53.

20. James David Barber, *The Presidential Character: Predicting Performance in the White House* (Englewood Cliffs, NJ: Prentice Hall, 1972). For an assessment of Barber's work, see Michael Nelson, "The Psychological Presidency," in Nelson, ed., *The Presidency and the Political System* (Washington: CQ, 1998).

21. Paul Quirk, "Presidential Competence," in Nelson, *The Presidency and the Political System*, p. 174.

22. Ibid., p. 175.

23. Bill Boyarsky, *Ronald Reagan: His Life and Rise to the Presidency* (New York: Random House, 1981), 11.

24. John Sloan, *FDR and Reagan: Transformative Presidents with Clashing Visions* (Lawrence: University Press of Kansas, 2008), 177, 290.

25. Ibid., p. 268.

26. See John Burke, "The Institutional Presidency," in Nelson, *The Presidency and the Political System*.

27. Hedrick Smith, *The Power Game: How Washington Works* (New York: Random House, 1988), 300.

28. Quirk, "Presidential Competence," p. 175.

29. Sara Diamond, *Roads to Dominion*, p. 206.

30. John Kessel, "The Structures of the Reagan White House," *Journal of Politics* 28 (1984): 231–58.

31. For an analysis similar to mine of the ideological identities of Reagan's staff and cabinet, see Sloan, *FDR and Reagan*, ch. 6.

32. Smith, *The Power Game*, pp. 302–30. On Reagan's appointments to the civil rights bureaucracies Detlefsen writes that they were "resolutely opposed" to affirmative action and race conscious jurisprudence. See *Civil Rights under Reagan* (San Francisco: Institute for Contemporary Studies, 1991), 47.

33. On the protests at Selma see David Garrow, *Protest at Selma: Martin Luther King Jr. and the Voting Rights Act of 1965* (New Haven: Yale, 1978). On King's conversation with Johnson see http://www.utex.edu/1bj/news/spring2008/mlk.php.

34. Hanes Walton Jr. and Robert C. Smith, *American Politics and the African American Quest for Universal Freedom*, 4th ed. (New York: Longman, 2008), 150.

35. *South Carolina vs. Katzenbach*, 383 US 301 (1966).

36. John Reid, "The Voting Behavior of Blacks," *Intercom* 9 (1981): 8–11.

37. Dean Kotlowski, *Nixon's Civil Rights: Politics, Principles and Policy* (Cambridge: Harvard University Press, 2001), ch. 3.

38. *Allen v. Board of Elections*, 393 U.S., 544(1969).

39. Thernstrom, *Whose Votes Count?* p. 242.

40. *City of Mobile vs. Bolden*, 466, US 55(1980).

41. See Frank Parker, *Black Votes Count: Political Empowerment in Mississippi After 1965* (Chapel Hill: University of North Carolina Press, 1990), 174–77.

42. For a comprehensive account of the act's renewal in 1982, see Thomas Boyd and Stephen Markham, "The 1982 Amendments to the Voting Rights Act: A Legislative History," *Washington and Lee Law Review* 40 (1983): 1174–1203. See also Thernstrom, *Whose Vote Counts?*

43. Memorandum from Michael Uhlmann to Craig Fuller, "DOJ's Report on Voting Rights Act," October 7, 1981, Edwin Meese Files, Ronald Reagan Library (RRL).

44. Uhlman to Meese, Baker, Anderson, and Fielding, "Voting Rights Extension," May 18, 1981, Edwin Meese Files, RRL.

45. Strom Thurmond to James Baker, October 7, 1981, Edwin Meese Files, RRL.

46. Uhlman to Meese, Baker, Anderson and Fielding, "Voting Rights Extension," May 18, 1991, Edwin Meese Files, RRL.

47. Memorandum from Melvin Bradley to Martin Anderson, Thru Ron Frankum, "The 1965 Voting Rights Act," September 24, 1981; Letter from Samuel Pierce to Craig Fuller, October 7, 1981, Edwin Meese Files, RRL.

48. Elizabeth Dole to Richard Darman, "Voting Rights Act," October 7, 1981, Edwin Meese Flies, RRL.

49. Martin Anderson to Edwin Meese, September 21, 1981, Edwin Meese Files, RRL.

50. Uhlman to Attorney General William French Smith, June 12, 1981, Edwin Meese Files, RRL.

51. William French Smith to Ronald Reagan, "Outlining Voting Rights Options: Re: Amending the Voting Rights Act," October 2, 1981, Edwin Meese Files, RRL.

52. Henry Hyde to Ronald Reagan, as quoted in Thernstrom, *Whose Vote Counts*, p. 115.

53. Memorandum from Richard Wirthlin to James Baker and Michael Deaver, "RE: Voting Rights Act," October 4, 1981, Edwin Meese Files, RRL.

54. Patrick Buchanan, "Toward Segregated Voting Districts," *Washington Times*, May 6, 1982; and Abigail Thernstrom, "Voting Rights: To What Are Minorities Entitled?" *Washington Post*, August 4, 1981.

55. Ed Thomas to Edwin Meese, "RE: Voting Rights Act," August 27, 1981, Edwin Meese Files, RRL. It is estimated that the creation of majority-minority districts contributed thirteen of the fifty-four-seat gain by the Republicans in 1994, exceeding their twelve-vote margin of control. See Morris Fiorina, *Divided Government*, 2nd ed. (New York: Longman, 2003), 137.

56. Kenneth Cribb Thru Craig Fuller to Edwin Meese, "RE: Voting Rights Act," Edwin Meese Files, RRL.

57. Ronald Reagan, "Remarks on Signing the Voting Rights Act Amendments of 1982," http://www.reagan.utexas.edu/archives/speeches/1982/62982b.htm.

58. In 2006 the Voting Rights Act was easily renewed for another twenty-five years. With the enthusiastic support of President Bush and the leaders of both parties in Congress, it passed the House 309 to 33 and the Senate 98 to 0. However, in early 2009 the Supreme Court agreed to hear a case—*Northwest Municipal District # 1.v vs. Mukasey*—to determine the constitutionality of section 5. In rejecting the claims of conservatives that Reagan sold out the movement on civil rights, Meese contends that he and Reagan always believed that the best way to bring about conservative reform on civil rights was through appointments to the courts. Both of President George W. Bush's appointments to the Supreme Court—the chief justice and Justice Samuel Alito—began their careers as low-level staff lawyers in the Reagan White House. In

these positions both wrote memos sharply critical of affirmative action and the Voting Rights Act. Perhaps, then, from the grave Reagan may yet have his way on these issues (see also note 83 in this chapter). In *Northwest Municipal District* in an 8-to-1 decision the Court in a narrow opinion avoided the constitutional question (by allowing the District to "bail out") with only Justice Thomas voting to declare section 5 unconstitutional. However, Chief Justice Roberts explicitly indicated that this may only be a temporary reprieve, writing, "Whether conditions continue to justify [section 5] is a difficult constitutional question we do not answer today."

59. *Grove City College vs. Bell*, 465 U.S. 555 (1984).

60. Memorandum for Faith Ryan Whittlesey," from J. Douglas Holladay, "Title IX," April 20, 1984, PQ White House Office Files (WHORM), Subject File, RRL.

61. Hugh Davis Graham, "The Storm over Grove City College: Civil Rights Regulation, Higher Education, and the Reagan Administration," *History of Education Quarterly* 38 (1998): 417.

62. Nicholas Laham, *The Reagan Presidency and the Politics of Race: In Pursuit of Colorblind Justice and Limited Government* (New York: Praeger, 1998), 159.

63. Ibid., pp. 156, 157.

64. Ronald Reagan, "Message to the Senate Returning without Approval the Civil Rights Restoration Act of 1987 and Transmitting Alternative Legislation," March 16, 1988, http://www.reagan.utexas.edu/archives/speeches/1988/031688e.htm. Grove City withdrew from the student loan program, electing to establish its own privately funded financial aid program.

65. Quoted in Hugh Davis Graham, "Civil Rights Policy," in W. Elliot Brownlee and Hugh Davis Graham, eds., *The Reagan Presidency: Pragmatic Conservatism and Its Legacies* (Lawrence: University Press of Kansas, 2003), 286.

66. Charlotte Steeth and M. Krysan, "Affirmative Action and the Public, 1970–1995," *Public Opinion Quarterly* 60(1996): 128–58; and Lee Sigelman and Susan Welch, *Black Americans Views of Inequality: The Dream Deferred* (New York: Cambridge University Press, 1991), 129.

67. "Colorblind coalition is used by Lahman," *The Reagan Presidency and the Politics of Race*, p. 94.

68. Ibid.

69. Mark Distler to Patrick Buchanan, March 10, 1986, quoted in ibid.

70. Minutes, Meeting of Domestic Policy Council, October 22, 1985, PQ WHORM, Subject File, RRL.

71. Ibid.

72. Ibid.

73. Several observers conclude Regan "kept the issue off the President's desk." See Rowland Evans and Robert Novak, "Stalemate on Quotas," *Washington Post*, December 30, 1985; Graham, "Civil Rights Policy," p. 285; and Smith, *The Power Game*, p. 304. Regan does not mention the issue in his memoirs. See Don Regan, *For the Record: From Wall Street to Washington* (San Diego: Harcourt, Brace, Jovanovich, 1988).

74. Hamilton Fish to Ronald Reagan, February 6, 1986, PQ WHORM, Subject File, RRL.

75. Mack Mattingly to Ronald Reagan, November 19, 1985, PQ, WHORM, Subject File.

76. Quoted in Lahmam, *The Reagan Presidency and the Politics of Race*, p. 79.

77. See, for example, the series of articles by Howard Kurz and Juan Williams in the *Washington Post*. Kurz, "Meese-Brock Set Hiring Plan Talk: White House Tries to Resolve Affirmative Action Stalemate," January 15, 1986; Kurz, "Minority Hiring Battle Illustrates Stalemate," January 18, 1986; Kurz, "Groups Challenge Draft Plan to Void Numerical Goals," August 16, 1985; Williams, "U.S. Softens Draft Plan on Affirmative Action," September 11, 1985; Williams, "Reagan Considers Stance on Affirmative Action," July 11, 1985; and Williams, "White House Split on Bias Underscored," July 24, 1985. See also Rowland Evans and Robert Novak, "Derailing Drive against Affirmative Action" *Washington Post*, August 26, 1985; and the *Post* editorial "A Giant Step Backward," August 16, 1985.

78. I spoke with Anderson in January 2006 for about a half hour at the Reagan library. Anderson's view of Reagan's presidency is a central theme in Richard Reeves' *President Reagan: The Triumph of Imagination* (New York: Simon and Shuster, 2005). And David Stockman writes that Meese was always "protecting the President from having to choose sides among his cabinet members.... [s]eeing to it Reagan never had to make a disagreeable choice in front of contending factions. That certainly kept him above the fray, but Presidents have to make unpleasant decisions.... Whenever there was disagreement, Meese would step in to suggest some kind of adhoc forum and Reagan would smile and say 'okay, you fellas work it out.'" See *The Triumph of Politics: Why the Reagan Revolution Failed* (New York: Harper and Row, 1986), 108.

79. Graham, "Civil Rights Policy," p. 290.

80. Edwin Meese, *With Reagan: The Inside Story* (Washington: Regenery Gateway, 1992), 315–16.

81. Ibid.

82. See *J. A. Croson vs. City of Richmond*, 488 U.S. 469(1989) and *Adrand Constructors vs. Pena* (slip opinion) 903–1841 (1995). Both these cases, involving set asides for minority contractors, reversed prior constitutional precedents of the Court. See *Fullilove vs. Klutznik* 448 U.S. 448(1980) and *Metro Broadcasters vs. Federal Communications Commission*, 110 s.ct. 2997(1990). In its 1988–89 term the Supreme Court, in what Justice Thurgood Marshall described as "a deliberate retrenching of the civil rights agenda," handed down six statutory decisions that significantly undermined the enforcement of antidiscrimination law in the area of employment. However, in a continuing demonstration of the leverage of the black lobby in the legislative process, Congress in 1991 passed the Civil Rights Restoration Act, which overturned the Court's decisions. Although President Bush vetoed the first version of the act, facing election-year pressures and the possibility of a veto override, he signed a second version of the bill. For analysis of the six cases and a legislative history of passage of the Civil Rights Restoration Act, see Robert C. Smith, *We Have No Leaders: African Americans in the Post Civil Rights Era* (Albany: State University of New York Press, 1996), 170–82.

83. Although the archival records indicate only a minor role in decision making by Roberts on affirmative action, it is interesting to note that in his first race-

related decision as chief justice he used the exact language written for Reagan in his undelivered speech on affirmative action. In Reagan's draft speech he was to declare, "The only way to end discrimination is to end discrimination." *Parents Involved in Community Schools, Inc. vs. Seattle School District and Meredith vs. Jefferson County Board of Education* (slip opinion, 05-915-2001), cases involving the use of race in pupil assignments, Roberts wrote, "The way to stop discrimination on the basis of race is to stop discriminating on the basis of race."

84. William Muir Jr., "Ronald Reagan: The Primacy of Rhetoric" in Fred Greenstein, ed., *Leadership in the Modern Presidency* (Cambridge: Harvard, 1988), 262.

85. Steven Shull and Robert Ringelstein, "Presidential Rhetoric in Civil Rights Policy Making, 1953-1992," in James Riddlesperger and Donald Jackson, eds., *Presidential Leadership and Civil Rights Policy* (Westport, CT: Greenwood, 1995). For an example of Reagan's antiaffirmative action rhetoric see his June 15, 1985, "Radio Address to the Nation on Civil Rights," http://www.reagan.utexas.edu/archives/speeches/1985/61585a.htm.

86. See Detlefsen, *Civil Rights under Reagan*, Raymond Wolters, *Right Turn: William Bradford Reynolds and Black Civil Rights Under Reagan* (Westport, CT: Praeger, 1998); and Terry Eastland, *Ending Affirmative Action: The Case for Colorblind Justice* (New York: Basic Books, 1996).

87. Lahman, *The Reagan Presidency and the Politics of Race*, pp. 92, 126.

88. Ibid. Lahman contends that not only did Reagan not reform affirmative action but that his initiatives to encourage minority businesses "represent[ed] perhaps the most sweeping expansion of minority set aside programs ever undertaken by any president" (p. 105). However, the administration through changes in budget and regulatory procedures effectively undermined the enforcement of affirmative action guidelines, exempting in effect 75 percent of federal contractors from compliance. See Harrell Rogers Jr., "Fair Employment Laws for Minorities: An Evaluation of Federal Implementation," in Charles Bullock and Charles Lamb, eds., *Implementation of Civil Rights Policy* (Monterey, CA: Brooks/Cole, 1984).

89. Steven Shull, *American Civil Rights Policy from Truman to Clinton* (Armonk, NY: Sharpe, 1999), 210.

90. Juliet Eilperin, "House Defeats Bill Targeting College Affirmative Action," *Washington Post*, May 7, 1997.

91. Pertaining to U.S. policy on South Africa the archives indicate, "Due to restrictions of PRA and FOIA all decision making correspondence and memos have been removed."

92. In 2007 the House passed 333 to 93 a bill overturning Bush's order. Kentucky Senator Jim Bunning put a hold on the bill in the Senate, and President Bush threatened a veto. See Charles Davis, "Who Gets to Write History?" *San Francisco Chronicle*, December 17, 2007; Mary Stuckey, "Presidential Secrecy: Keeping Archives Open," *Rhetoric and Public Affairs* 9 (2006): 138-44; and my "On Martin Luther King Jr. Day: Twenty-six Pages in the History of the Holiday," *San Francisco Chronicle*, January 21, 2008.

93. Richard Hull, *American Enterprises in South Africa: Historical Dimensions of Engagement and Disengagement* (New York: New York University, 1990).

94. George Frederickson, *White Supremacy: A Comparative Study in American and South African History* (New York: Oxford, 1981).

95. Elliot Skinner, *African Americans and U.S. Policy toward Africa, 1850–1924*, vol. 1 (Washington: Howard University Press, 1992).

96. Thomas Borstelmann, *Apartheid's Reluctant Uncle: The United States and Southern Africa in the Early Cold War* (New York: Oxford University Press, 1993). In addition to its cold war strategic concerns, Borstelmann suggest that most of Truman's advisors were also motivated by racist and white supremacist interests and attitudes.

97. Donald Culverson, *Contesting Apartheid: U.S. Activism, 1960–1987* (Boulder, CO: Westview, 1999), 45.

98. Anthony Lake, *The "Tar Baby" Option: American Policy toward Rhodesia* (New York: Carnegie Endowment for International Peace, 1976).

99. Walter Isaacson, *Kissinger: A Biography* (New York: Simon and Shuster, 2005), 686.

100. Eric Morgan, "Our Own Interests: Nixon, South Africa and Dissent at Home and Abroad," *Diplomacy and Statecraft* 17 (2006), 475–95.

101. Isaacson, *Kissinger*, p. 687.

102. Ibid.

103. Ibid., p. 688.

104. Glen Abernathy, et al., *The Carter Years* (London: Frances, 1980), 60–61. Cuban troops had been dispatched to Angola to help the government put down a South African–U.S.-backed insurgency.

105. Gaddis Smith, *Morality, Reason, and Power* (New York: Hill and Wang, 1986), 134.

106. Richard Deutsch, "Reagan's Africa Perspectives," *Africa Report*, July–August, 1980, pp. 4–7.

107. Culverson, *Contesting Apartheid*, pp. 28–30.

108. The African Liberation Support Committee, a leftist radical group organized in 1972, held mass demonstrations in Washington and elsewhere during the 1970s. These demonstrations raised awareness in the black community of conditions in southern Africa and the role of the United States in sustaining the colonial and racist regimes in the region. Although its direct impact on policy was marginal, the committee was part of the necessary groundwork for the successes of the more moderate TransAfrica. See Cedric Johnson, *Revolutionaries to Race Leaders: Black Power and the Making of African American Politics* (Minneapolis: University of Minnesota Press, 2007), 132–47.

109. Pauline Baker, *The United States and South Africa: The Reagan Years* (New York: Ford Foundation Foreign Policy Association, 1989), 8.

110. Chester Crocker, *High Noon in Southern Africa: Making Peace in a Rough Neighborhood* (New York: Norton, 1992).

111. Ibid., p. 253.

112. "Political theater" is used by Culverson, *Contesting Apartheid*, p. 146.

113. Baker, *The United States and South Africa*, pp. 6–7.

114. Culverson, *Contesting Apartheid*, p. 124.

115. Crocker, *High Noon*, p. 255.

116. Baker, *The United States and South Africa*, p. 35.
117. Notes from meeting Robert McFarlane, Subject: Meeting with PK Botha, August 8, 1985 WHORM, Subject File, RRL.
118. Ibid.
119. Ibid.
120. Crocker, *High Noon*, p. 259
121. The Sullivan Principles, after Rev. Leon Sullivan the first African American appointed to a major corporate board, required American businesses in South Africa to desegregate their facilities and employ persons on a nondiscriminatory basis.
122. Crocker, *High Noon*, p. 321.
123. Ibid.
124. Ibid., p. 319.
125. Ibid., p. 321.
126. Ibid.
127. Ibid., p. 322.
128. "Ronald Reagan, "Remarks to Members of the World Affairs Council and the Foreign Policy Association," July 22, 1986, http://www.reagan.utexas.edu/dtsearch/dtisapi6.dll?cmd=getdoc.DocId=5062.index=%.
129. Among other things, the legislation banned new investments and bank loans, ended South African air links to the United States, and prohibited a range of South African imports.
130. Baker, *The United States and South Africa*, p. 44.
131. For anti-King rhetoric of this sort see the *Congressional Record—House*, where Louisiana Congressman John Rarick refers to King as a "plain garden variety subversive tool" and a "communist puppet," April 2, 1970, p. 10036.
132. By 1981 twenty-one states and hundreds of cities had enacted the King holiday legislation, and more than 6 million signatures had been collected on petitions supporting the legislation. For a brief overview of the legislative history of the federal legislation, see Don Wolfensberger, "The Martin Luther King Jr. Holiday: The Long Struggle in Congress," prepared for the *Martin Luther King Jr. Holiday: How Did It Happen*, Woodrow Wilson International Center for Scholars, Seminar, January 14, 2008.
133. Memorandum for Melvin Bradley from Edwin Harper; Subj: MLK Holiday, requesting Bradley to investigate and consider alternatives to a legal holiday, January 18, 1983, WHORM Subject File, RRL.
134. On many of the routing sheets for staff attendance at meetings on civil rights, Bradley's name is often penciled in as an afterthought.
135. Memorandum for Edwin Harper from Melvin Bradley, "Option Paper for Martin Luther King Holiday, February 7, 1983, WHORM Subject File, RRL.
136. Ibid.
137. Ibid. The administration ultimately supported a day of "commemoration" rather than a paid national holiday.
138. Ibid.
139. Charles D. Brennan to Ronald Reagan, August 15, 1983, with "Martin Luther King Jr.: A Summary View," WHORM Subject File, RRL.
140. Ibid.

141. Ibid.

142. Memorandum for Fred Fielding from John G. Roberts, "Correspondence from C.D. Brennan," September 16, 1983, WHORM Subject File, RRL.

143. Memorandum for Jack Svahn from Mel Bradley, October 3, 1983. Senator Jesse Helms distributed material from the FBI files to his colleagues during the Senate debate, leading Senator Moynihan to throw the material on the Senate floor calling it a "packet of filth" unworthy of the consideration of his colleagues. See *Congressional Record, Senate*, October 3, 1983.

144. Daniel P. Moynihan, *In Secrecy: The American Experience* (New Haven: Yale University Press, 1998).

145. Memorandum for Ed Meese from Joe Wright, "Administration Options Regarding HR3345" August 31, 1983, WHORM Subject File, RRL. One reason Wright wrote there were no favorable indicators was at the same time the Senate was considering the King holiday, it was also considering legislation to restructure the U.S. Commission on Civil Rights in order to prevent Reagan from firing its two more liberal members. Wright wrote, "Strong Administration opposition to the paid holiday will be linked to this issue, and even the Administration's strongest supporters may find it difficult to vote with the Administration on both the paid holiday and the Commission." On the struggle over restructuring the Commission and Reagan's efforts to fire her, see Mary Frances Berry, *And Justice for All: The United States Commission on Civil Rights and the Continuing Struggle for Freedom in America* (New York: Knopf, 2009), 183–215. Interestingly, Clarence Pendelton, the conservative African American chair of the commission, wrote Reagan a letter as a "personal petition" urging him "to take a leadership role" in support of the King Holiday. See Clarence Pendelton to the president, August 3, 1983. WHORM Subject File, RRL.

146. Ibid.

147. Memorandum to Craig Fuller from Tom Gibson, N.D., "The Martin Luther King National Holiday, and the Celebration Thereof," WHORM Subject File, RRL.

148. Ibid. Making Columbus Day "the sacrificial lamb" Gibson wrote would not terribly upset Americans of either Italian or Spanish descent, concluding only the citizens of Columbus, Ohio "would mourn its passing."

149. Memorandum For Faith Ryan Whittlesey from Mel Bradley, "The Dr. King Holiday," September 8, 1983, WHORM Subject Files, RRL.

150. Ibid.

151. Ibid.

152. Lou Cannon writes, "The answer dismayed Reagan's advisors who had laughed earlier in the day when Reagan gave essentially the same reply at a rehearsal for the news conference. His advisors had thought the remark just another Reagan one-liner, not a serious reply. 'I just assumed he'll never say that in a press conference' said White House communications director David Gergen afterward. 'I almost lost my dinner over that.' " *President Reagan: The Role of a Lifetime* (New York: Simon and Shuster, 1991), 524.

153. Matthew Holden Jr., "The President, Congress and Race Relations," Ernest Patterson Memorial Lecture, University of Colorado, Boulder, 1986, p. 69.

154. Ibid., p. 10.

155. Reducing the role of the regulatory state generally was related specifically to the administration's efforts to cutback on the activities of the civil rights bureaucracies, and to its opposition to overturning the Supreme Court's decision in Grove City.

156. Milton Friedman, "The Limitations of Tax Limitations," *Policy Review*, Summer 1978, pp. 7–14.

157. Ronald Reagan, *An American Life* (New York: Simon and Shuster, 1990), 232. Bruce Bartlett traces the origins of the starve-the-beast "theory" among conservative intellectuals and policy makers in " 'Starve the Beast': Origins and Development of a Budget Metaphor," *The Independent Review* 12 (2007): 5–26.

158. Herbert McClosky and John Zaller, *The American Ethos: Public Attitudes toward Capitalism and Democracy* (Cambridge: Harvard, 1984), 1.

159. James Klugel and Eliot Smith, *Beliefs about Inequality: American Views of What Is and What Ought to Be* (New York: de Gruyter, 1986), 5.

160. Ibid.

161. Times Mirror Center for the People and the Press as cited in Walton and Smith, *American Politics and the African American Quest for Universal Freedom*, p. 262.

162. Michael B. Katz, *The Undeserving Poor: From the War on Poverty to the War on Welfare* (New York: Pantheon Books), 5.

163. Locke also drew this distinction. Huyler writes that Locke's charity was "always directed to encourage working, laborious, industrious people and not to relieve idle beggars.... people who had been industrious, but through age or infirmity passed labor, he was very bountiful to... believing they should be kept from starving or extreme misery." See Jerome Huyler, *Locke in America: The Moral Philosophy of the Founding Era* (Lawrence: University Press of Kansas), 145.

164. Martin Gilens, *Why Americans Hate Welfare: Race, Media and the Politics of Antipoverty Policy* (Chicago: University of Chicago Press, 1999). Alberto Alesina, Edward Glaeser, and Bruce Sacesdole wrote that "within the US, race is the single most important predictor of support for welfare. America's troubled race relations are clearly a major reason for the absence of an American welfare state." See "Why Doesn't the US Have a European Style Welfare State?" National Bureau of Economic Research, working paper # 0524, October, 2001, p. 79.

165. Walton and Smith, *American Politics and the African American Quest for Universal Freedom*, p. 262. See also Tali Mendelberg, *The Race Card* (Princeton: Princeton University Press, 2001), ch. 7.

166. On the political efficacy of the welfare queen metaphor in delegitimatizing welfare recipients see Angie Marie Hancock, *The Politics of Disgust: The Public Identity of the Welfare Queen* (New York: New York University Press, 2004).

167. Katz, *The Undeserving Poor*, p. 5.

168. Stockman, *The Triumph of Politics*, pp. 8–9.

169. Klugel and Smith, *Beliefs about Equality*, p. 201.

170. Martin Anderson, *Welfare: The Political Economy of Welfare Reform in the United States* (Stanford, CA: Hoover Institution, 1978).

171. Minutes of meeting, A Welfare Program for the Reagan Administration, Blair House, January 6, 1981, Martin Anderson Files, RRL.

172. Ibid.

173. Ibid.

174. Anderson, *Welfare*, pp. 42–43. James Q. Wilson argues that single mothers claiming welfare benefits are not "decent citizens" and should be compelled to work in order to induce changes in their behavior concerning sex, childbearing, and marriage. See "Paternalism, Democracy, and Bureaucracy," in Lawrence Mead, ed., *The New Paternalism: Supervisory Approaches to Poverty* (Washington: Brookings Institution, 1997), 340–41.

175. Anderson, Personal Interview, January 11, 2006, at the Ronald Reagan Library. In 1982 Reagan did propose abolishing AFDC by returning the program to the states. The proposal was ignored by the Congress; however Moynihan notes that "had it been proposed in the swirl of the first 100 days, as it were, it might well have succeeded." See Daniel Patrick Moynihan, *Came the Revolution: Argument in the Reagan Era* (New York: Harcourt Brace Jovanovich, 1988), 94. Moynihan described the Reagan proposal "as close to cruel as any that had come from downtown" (p. 94).

176. Ronald Reagan, "Radio Address to the Nation on Welfare Reform," http://www.reagan.utexas.edu/archives/speeches/1986/2158a.htm.

177. Ibid.

178. *Up from Dependency: A New National Public Assistance Strategy*, December 1986.

179. Memorandum from Ed Feulner to Stuart Butler, "Republicans and Welfare Reform," July 1, 1987, Juanita Duggins File, RRL.

180. Ibid.

181. Memorandum for the President from Ken Cribb, Joe Wright, Chuck Hobbs, July 15, 1988, Daniel Crippen File, RRL.

182. Mark Rom, "The Family Support Act of 1988: Federalism, Developmental Policy, and Welfare Reform," *Publius* 19 (1989): 57–73.

183. In much of Western Europe welfare policies are specifically designed to ensure that all children receive the same benefits and are treated equally before the law. And there is little stigma attached to couples living together or to single parents or their children. In contrast, in the United States welfare, under both liberal and conservative administrations, is designed to encourage marriage. Meanwhile, in the United States and elsewhere out-of-wedlock births are relatively high: 38 percent in Great Britain, 41 in France, 31 in Ireland, and 62 in Iceland. Tamar Levin, "The Decay of Families Is Global," *New York Times*, May 30, 1995; and Sarah Lyall, "With the Blessing of Society, Europeans Opt Out of Marriage," *New York Times*, May 24, 2002. European democracies of course are much more Roussean than Lockean in their approach to welfare and families. For a Lockean, neoconservative critique of the American welfare system and the valorization of marriage, see James Q. Wilson, *The Marriage Problem: How Our Culture Weakened Families* (New York: HarperCollins, 2002). For a Roussean critique, see Mink's *Welfare Ends*, where she proposes that reform be reconceived to view "welfare as income *owed* to persons who work inside the home caring for, nurturing and protecting children" (p. 19).

184. Andrew Busch, *Ronald Reagan and the Politics of Freedom* (Lanham, MD: Rowman & Littlefield, 2001), 37.

185. Milton Kotler and Nelson Rosenbaum, "Strengthening the Democratic Party through Strategic Marketing: Voters and Donors," a confidential report prepared for the Democratic National Committee by CRG Research Institute, Washington, 1985. This report urged the party and its candidates to "de-market" the party to the social and economic underclass and focus on the concerns of the white middle class. This nexus between racism, taxes, and welfare is a principal thesis of Thomas Edsal, *Chain Reaction* (New York: Norton, 1992). Clinton read the book, and it reportedly shaped his approach to the 1992 campaign strategy. (See the concluding chapter.)

186. David Ellwood, *Poor Support: Poverty in the American Family* (New York: Basic Books, 1988).

187. In his memoir Clinton writes that welfare reform was "one of the most important decisions of [my] presidency." Noting that "most advocates of the poor wanted me to veto.... I decided to sign the legislation because I thought it was the best chance America would have for a long time to change the incentives in the welfare system from dependence to empowerment through work." See *My Life* (New York: Knoff, 2004), 720. The president does not mention political considerations in the decision, but his wife in her memoir writes that while troubled by parts of the bill "pragmatic politics had to be considered." "If he had vetoed welfare reform a third time, Bill would be handing the Republicans a potential political windfall." See Hillary Rodham Clinton, *Living History* (New York: Simon and Shuster, 2003), 369.

188. Quoted in Barbara Vobejda, "Moynihan Observing from the Wings," *Washington Post*, June 4, 1995. Subsequently in *Miles to Go: A Personal History of Social Policy* (Cambridge: Harvard, 1996) Moynihan described the legislation "as truly awful.... Those involved will take this disgrace to their grave" (pp. 39, 41).

189. One of those aides, Peter Edelman, wrote a harsh critique of Clinton's decision. See "Clinton's Worst Mistake," *Atlantic Monthly*, May, 1997. On the tenth anniversary of the act's passage, Bill Clinton celebrated the legislation as a "great success" and excellent example of bipartisanship. See "How We Ended Welfare, Together," *New York Times*, August 22, 2006. Donald Mauhewson and Shelly Arsneault present a penetrating analysis of how the welfare reform legislation served simultaneously the conservative values of (1) defending inequality and (2) federalism or states rights. See "Conservatives, Federalism, and the Defense of Inequality," *National Political Science Review* 11 (2007): 335–54.

190. Morris subsequently was forced to resign from the campaign after it was learned that he had fathered a child out of wedlock and was exposed (on the last night of the 1996 Democratic Convention) as having a long-time relationship with a prostitute. Nevertheless, Morris writes that he urged Clinton to sign the bill because doing so would symbolize his support for "family values" and opposition to promiscuous sex and out-of-wedlock births. Morris also said he told the president that a third veto of the bill would cost him the election, transforming a 15 percent win into a 3 percent loss. See *Behind the Oval Office: Winning the Presidency in the Nineties* (New York: Random House, 1997), 300.

191. Robert Pear, "Many Subtleties Shaped Welfare Vote," *New York Times*, August 4, 1996.

192. Rebecca Blank, "Was Welfare Reform Successful?" *Economist's Voice*, March 2006, pp. 4–5. For detailed studies of how women struggled to survive under welfare reform, see Lynneil Hancock, *Hands to Work: The Stories of Three Families Facing the Welfare Clock* (New York: Morrow, 2002); and Dana-ain Davis, *Battered Women and Welfare Reform: Between a Rock and a Hard Place* (Albany: State University of New York Press, 2006).

193. Sheldon Danziger, "Budget Cuts as Welfare Reform," *American Economic Review* 73 (1983): 65. Danziger concludes that these cuts "clearly reduced welfare dependency in the short run" and that it was "generally accepted" that they would also "increase poverty and inequality" (p. 65).

194. Imig, *Poverty and Power*, p. 17. See also Glazer, *The Limits of Social Policy* (Cambridge: Harvard, 1988), 55.

195. Imig, *Poverty and Power*, pp. 16–17.

196. Demetrios Caraley, "Washington Abandons the Cities," *Political Science Quarterly* 107 (1992): 1–37.

197. Quoted in Imig, *Poverty and Power*, p. 21.

198. The concept of institutional racism deals with the effects or consequences of public policies rather than their intent. See Jenny Williams, "Redefining Institutional Racism," *Ethnic and Racial Studies* 8 (1985): 323–37; Joe Feagin and N. Bencksrits, "Institutional Racism: In Search of a Perspective," in Charles Willie, ed., *Institutional Racism: In Search of a Perspective* (New Brunswick, NJ: Transaction, 1974); and Robert C. Smith, *Racism in the Post Civil Rights Era: Now You See It, Now You Don't* (Albany: State University of New York Press, 1995), ch. 4. The concept of institutional racism is akin to the legal doctrine of disparate impact used by the Supreme Court in employment discrimination cases. See *Griggs vs. Duke Power Company* 401 U.S. 424 (1971).

199. Img, *Poverty and Power*, p. 21.

200. Martin Anderson, *Revolution: The Reagan Legacy* (Stanford, CA: Hoover Institution, 1990), 177.

201. Glazer, *Limits of Social Policy*, p. 42.

202. Sloan, *FDR and Reagan*, p. 318.

203. Mark Smith, *The Right Talk: How Conservatives Transformed the Great Society into the Economic Society* (Princeton: Princeton University Press, 2008).

204. Diamond, *Roads to Dominion*, p. 310.

205. Before his death, Myrdal was near completion of a reevaluation of the conclusions of *An American Dilemma* "in the light of how race relations in America had evolved in the ensuing decades, and to express my worried thoughts about future developments." See Sissela Bok, "Introduction to the Transaction Fiftieth Anniversary Edition," *An American Dilemma*, vol. 1 (New Brunswick, NJ: Transaction, 1999).

Chapter 10

1. Hamilton Jordan, "Can the Whole Be More Than the Sum of Its Parts," *New Republic*, June 6, 1983, pp. 15–19.

2. Harry McPhearson, "How Race Destroyed the Democrat's Coalition," *New York Times*, November 20, 1988.

3. "Does Race Doom Democrats?" *New York Times*, November 20, 1988.

4. Thomas Edsal and Mary Edsal, "Race," *Atlantic Monthly*, May 1991, pp. 53–86.

5. Thomas Edsal, *Chain Reaction* (New York: Norton, 1992).

6. Stanley Greenberg, *Middle Class Dreams: The Politics and Power of the New American Majority* (New York: Times Books, 1995), 39.

7. Milton Kotler and Nelson Rosenbaum, "Strengthening the Democratic Party through Strategic Marketing: Voters and Donors," a confidential report prepared for the Democratic National Committee, 1985. See also Peter Brown, "85 Dem Report Urges De-marketing Party," *Houston Chronicle*, April 17, 1989.

8. Elaine Kamarck and William Galston, *The Politics of Evasion* (Washington: Progressive Policy Institute, 1989). This pattern of blaming race for the Democratic Party's electoral defeats continued after the Republicans won control of both houses of Congress in 1994. See Cokie and Steven Roberts, "Democrats Must Face Race Issue," *West County Times*, December 16, 1994.

9. Stephen Skowronek, *The Politics Presidents Make: Leadership from John Adams to George Bush* (Cambridge: Harvard, 1993), 428. On the reconstructive character of the Reagan presidency, see also Sean Wilentz, *The Age of Reagan: A History 1974–2008* (New York: HarperCollins, 2008). Wilentz is sharply critical of the Reagan presidency, concluding that it "brought about inequalities of living standards reminiscent of the nineteenth century robber barons' gilded age" (p. 275).

10. William Berman, *America's Right Turn: From Nixon to Clinton* (Baltimore: Johns Hopkins University Press, 1994), 97.

11. Andrew Busch, *Ronald Reagan and the Politics of Freedom* (Lanham, MD: Rowman, Littlefield, 2001), 253.

12. Berman, *America's Right Turn*, p. 114.

13. On the use of the "L" word during the 1988 campaign, see Charles O. Jones, "Meeting Low Expectations: Strategy and Prospects of the Bush Presidency," in Colin Campbell and Bert Rockman, eds., *The Bush Presidency: First Appraisals* (Chatham, NJ: Chatham House, 1991).

14. Kenneth Baer, *Reinventing the Democrats: The Politics of Liberalism from Reagan to Clinton* (Lawrence: University Press of Kansas, 2000), 9.

15. Ibid., p. 163.

16. Busch, *Ronald Reagan and the Politics of Freedom*, p. 264. See also Matt Bai, "The Clinton Referendum," *New York Times Magazine*, December 23, 2007, and Robert C. Smith, "In the Shadows of Ronald Reagan: Civil Rights Policymaking in the Clinton Administration." Paper prepared for the annual Alan B. Larkin Symposium on the American Presidency, Civil Rights and the Presidency: From Nixon to Obama, Florida Atlantic University, Boca Raton, February 12–13, 2009.

17. Baer, *Reinventing the Democrats*, pp. 168–70, 79.

18. Ibid.

19. Ibid.

20. Ibid.

21. Jon F. Hale, "The Making of the New Democrats," *Political Science Quarterly* 110 (1995): 224.

22. Arthur Schlesinger Jr., "For Democrats, Me-Too Reaganism Will Spell Disaster," *New York Times*, July 6, 1986. The DLC early on had a close relationship with the conservative Heritage Foundation. Baer writes of a "cross-pollination of ideas between the two." *Reinventing the Democrats*, p. 136.

23. Randall Rotherberg, *The Neoliberals: Creating the New American Politics* (New York: Simon and Shuster, 1984).

24. Baer, *Reinventing the Democrats*, pp. 184–85.

25. Ibid., p. 181.

26. Ibid., p. 187.

27. Jesse Jackson, "For Democrats: A Strategy of Inclusion," *Washington Post*, May 22, 1991 as cited in ibid.

28. When Clinton left office 87 percent of blacks approved of his performance as president, compared to 45 percent of whites. Toni Morrison, the Nobel laureate, famously described him as the first black president. See her essay "Clinton as First Black President," *New Yorker*, August 22, 2006. More seriously the African American columnist Dewayne Wickham wrote, "Bill Clinton was not the first black president, but in the long line of white men who ascended to this nation's presidency he was the next best thing." See *Bill Clinton and Black America* (New York: Ballentine Books, 2002), 239.

29. On the captive status of blacks in the Democratic Party, see Paul Frymer, *Uneasy Alliances: Race and Party Competition in America* (Princeton: Princeton University Press, 1999), chs. 2, 4. See also Robert C. Smith, *We Have No Leaders: African Americans in the Post Civil Rights Era* (Albany: State University of New York Press, 1996), ch. 10.

30. C. Wright Mills, *The Power Elite* (New York: Oxford University Press, 1956), 333, 335.

31. Ibid., p. 334.

32. Ibid., p. 244.

33. Randall Wood, *LBJ: Architect of American Ambition* (New York: Free, 2006), ch. 27.

34. Mills, *The Power Elite*, pp. 337–38.

35. Rex Texeira and John Judis, *The Emerging Democratic Majority* (New York: A Lisa Drew Book, 2002).

36. Paul Krugman, *The Conscience of a Liberal* (New York: Norton, 2007).

37. Paul Starr, *Freedom's Power: The True Force of Liberalism* (New York: Basic Books, 2007).

38. Berman, *America's Right Turn*, p. 109.

39. Even William Julius Wilson, who did so much to popularize the term in the 1980s, now wants to abandon it. In his 1990 presidential address at the American Sociological Association, Wilson said the "underclass" ought to be rejected because it had become a "code word" for inner-city blacks enabling journalists to focus on unflattering behavior in the ghetto. He also said he now believed the term had little scientific utility. See Thomas Edsal, "Underclass Term Falls from Favor," *Washington*

Post, August 13, 1990. Wilson popularized the term and gave it scientific respectability in his influential work, *The Truly Disadvantaged: The Inner-City, the Underclass and Public Policy* (Chicago: University of Chicago Press, 1987).

40. Sharon Wright Austin, *The Transformation of Plantation Politics: Black Politics, Concentrated Poverty, and Social Capital in the Mississippi Delta* (Albany: State University of New York Press, 2006).

41. It is often forgotten that Moynihan identified black male joblessness as the central reason for the rise of single-parent families and the incidence of racialized poverty.

42. Harvey Brenner, "Estimating the Effects of Economic Change on National Health and Well Being," paper prepared for the Subcommittee on Economic Goals and Intergovernmental Policy, Joint Economic Committee, July 15, 1984. See also William Julius Wilson, *When Work Disappears: The World of the New Urban Poor* (New York: Knopf, 1996).

43. Quoted in Smith, *We Have No Leaders*, p. 202.

44. Janny Scott, "Nearly Half of Black Men Found Jobless," *New York Times*, February 28, 2004.

45. Thomas Hobbes, *Leviathan*, intro by John Plamenalz (Cleveland: Meridian Books, 1963), 143.

46. Herbert McClosky and John Zaller, *The American Ethos: Public Attitudes toward Capitalism and Democracy* (Cambridge: Harvard, 1984), 300.

47. These data are from the University of Michigan's National Election Studies as reported in Samuel Eldersveld and Hanes Walton Jr., *Political Parties in American Society*, 2nd ed. (Boston: Bedford/St. Martin's, 2000), 381.

48. Stanley Feldman and John Zaller, "The Political Culture of Ambivalence: Ideological Responses to the Welfare State," *American Journal of Political Science* 36 (1992).

About the Author

Robert C. Smith, professor of political science, San Francisco State University, is the author of the *Encyclopedia of African American Politics*, as well as many books including *Race, Class, and Culture: A Study in Afro-American Mass Opinion; Racism in the Post Civil Rights Era: Now You See It, Now You Don't, We Have No Leaders: African Americans in the Post Civil Rights Era;* and *African American Leadership*, all published by the State University of New York Press. He is currently completing a book comparing the Irish Catholic and African American experiences in the United States and the election of the first Irish Catholic and first African American presidents.

Index

Abernathy, Glen, 166
accommodationism, 70–71, 78
Ackerman, Bruce, 57
Ackerman, Gary, 181
Adrand Constructors v. Pena, 248n82
affirmative action
   Burkean principles and, 99
   Democratic Leadership Council and, 189–90
   Fourteenth Amendment and, 104
   John Roberts and, 248n83
   Lockean principles and, 99
   McGovern and, 134
   Nathan Glazer and, 99
   neoconservatism and, 99, 104
   Nixon and, 133, 135, 241n155
   Orrin Hatch and, 154
   racial equality and, 98–99
   Reagan presidency and, 112, 143, 147, 157–63, 174, 188, 189, 248n83, 249n88
   Supreme Court and, 151
Affirmative Discrimination (Glazer), 99
African Americans. *See* blacks
African Liberation Support Committee, 250n108
Aid to Families with Dependent Children (AFDC), 56, 178
Aid to Families with Dependent Children—Unemployed Parent (AFDC-UP), 179
Alexander, Gerard, 235n55
Allen v. Board of Education, 151
Anderson, Martin, 153, 153, 162, 178, 182

Andrew, John A., III, 118
anticommunism, 80, 116, 233n42
aristocratic theory, 9
Aristotle, 25–26
Aronson, Arnold, 146
autonomous theory, 9

Bachrach, Peter, 119
Baker, Howard, 149
Baker, James, 149, 153, 160
Banfield, Edward, 94, 98, 133
Baraka, Amiri, 64
Baratz, Morton, 119
Barber, James David, 147
Barnett, Randy, 58
Barnett, Ross, 90
"Bastille Day Declaration," 115–16
Beard, Charles, 29
Becker, Carl, 28
Bell, Daniel, 94
Bennett, William, 160
Berman, William C., 124, 187, 192
Bethune, Mary Macleod, 60
Black, Hugo, 151
black radicalism during Reconstruction, 63–64
black thought, 63–64, 66
   black nationalism as residual stratum in, 69–70
   classical, 66–67
   Du Bois and, 67–69
   modern, 67–68
blacks and conservatism, 1, 2. *See also specific topics*
Blank, Rebecca, 181–82

Blumenthal, Sidney, 95
Blyden, Edward Wilmot, 69
Bolden, City of Mobile v., 152
Booth, John Wilkes, 44
Bork, Robert, 85, 174
Botha, P. W., 166, 169
Bowles, Chester, 165
Boyarsky, Bill, 148
Bozell, Brent, 114
Bradley, Joseph, 92
Bradley, Melvin, 153, 171–73
Bradley, Tom, 189
Brennan, Charles, 172
Brinkley, Alan, 7–8
Brinkley, Douglas, 15
Brock, William, 160
Broder, David, 111
Brooks, David, 108
Brown, Edmund G. "Pat," 132
Brown v. Board of Education, 78, 79, 83–86
Bryan, William Jennings, 134
Bryce, Lord, 127
Brzezinski, Zbigniew, 166
Buchanan, James, 42
Buchanan, Patrick, 154, 160, 166, 170
Buckley, William F., Jr.
  Brown v. Board of Education and, 85
  civil rights revolution and, 145
  and fusion of racism in conservative intellectual movement, 87–90
  on repression, 93
  Russell Kirk and, 82
  Willmore Kendall and, 18
  Young Americans for Freedom and, 118
Bunche, Ralph, 64, 167
Burke, Edmund, 3, 8, 33–35
  Locke and, 3, 32
  Reflections on the Revolution in France, 7
  Samuel Huntington on, 9–10
Burnham, Walter Dean, 141, 143
Burns, James Macgregor, 58–59
Busch, Andrew, 110, 111

Bush, George W., 164
Butler, Stuart, 179

Calhoun, John C., 3, 18, 34–38
Cannon, Lou, 108, 252n152
Capitalism and Freedom (Friedman), 81, 82
Carlson, Robert, 177
Carmichael, Stokely, 11, 238n110
Carmines, Edward G., 132
Carter, Jimmy
  election of 1976 and, 137–38
  election of 1980 and, 139–41
  Full Employment and Balanced Growth Act of 1978 and, 192
  Grove City case and, 155
  Jews and, 243n184
  South Africa and, 166
Casey, William, 170
Cash, W. J., 34, 84
Chappell, David L., 125
Christianity, evangelical, 233n42
citizenship, residency vs. national, 47
civil rights. *See specific topics*
Civil Rights, Committee on, 124, 125
Civil Rights Act of 1875, 48
Civil Rights Act of 1964, 85, 129, 130, 156, 174
Civil Rights Cases of 1883, 69, 92
civil rights era presidential elections, racism and conservatism in. *See under* presidential elections
civil rights legislation, 83
civil rights movement, 78
  Buckley on, 88, 89
  conservative movement and, 79
  starting point of, 77
  turn toward radicalism, 91–93, 97
Civil Rights Restoration Act of 1988, 156–57
Civil Rights Restoration Act of 1991, 248n82
Civil War, 38, 120
Civil War amendments, 48. *See also specific amendments*

Clark, Kenneth, 84
Clark, William, 149
classified documents, 163–64
Clifford, Clark, 123, 124
Clinton, Bill, 136–37, 187
   blacks and, 6, 190, 258n28
   Democratic Leadership Council and, 188–91
   welfare and, 180–81, 255n187
Cold War, 123
Colfax massacre, 47
collectivism, 81
communism, 80, 116
   civil rights and, 233n42
Congressional Black Caucus, 147
conservatism
   in America, 7–8
   defined, 8, 63
   manifestations in the Western world, 204n4
   philosophical, 16–17
   racism and, 1–4, 108–10. *See also specific topics*
   understanding, 8–10
Conservatism in America (Kirk), 81
conservative institutional arrangements, Lockean, 28–32
Conservative Mind (Kirk), 10, 82
conservative (intellectual) movement, 77–79
   Buckley and the fusion of racism in the, 87–90
   origins, 80–87
Conservative Opportunity Society, 169
conservative remnant, 73–75
Constitution, 28–32, 85. *See also* Fourteenth Amendment
   adoption of, 57
   Clarence Thomas on, 104
   principles in framing, 29
   racism and, 30
   undemocratic elements, 29–30
Converse, Philip, 234n49
Conyers, John, 64, 171
Cox, Heather, 63

"Creative Society," 112
Crocker, Chester, 168–70
Cruikshank v. the United States, 47
Crummell, Alexander, 73–74
Cruse, Harold, 69
cultural lag and racial inequality, 103
Cummings v. Board of Education, 48

Dahl, Robert, 29–30
Danzig, David, 117
Danziger, Sheldon, 182
Davidson, Donald, 39
Dawson, Michael, 66
Deaver, Michael, 149
Declaration of Independence, 28
Decter, Midge, 94
Delany, Martin, 66, 69, 74
Dellums, Ronald, 64, 169
democracy, 46
   Alexander Crummell and, 73–74
   Andrew Jackson and, 50–51
   Constitution and, 29–30
   James Madison and, 29–31
   Locke and, 25
   Robert Dahl on, 29–30
   Rousseau on, 21–22, 200n33
Democratic Leadership Council (DLC)
   Bill Clinton and, 188–91
   race and, 189–90
Democratic National Committee (DNC), 186
Democratic Party, 185–86
Depoe, Stephen, 61
desegregation, 85–87. See also *Brown v. Board of Education*
Dewey, Thomas, 124
Diamond, Sara, 80, 99, 183
Diggs, Charles, 167
Discourse on Inequality (Rousseau), 19, 20
Dole, Bob, 154, 169–70, 170, 179
Dole, Elizabeth, 153, 160
Douglass, Frederick, 30, 43, 66, 67, 73, 75–76
Douglass, William O., 151

Draft Goldwater Committee, 115
Drake, St. Clair, 64–66
Du Bois, W. E. B., 64
　on aristocracy of talent, 73
　black thought and, 67–68, 69
　Booker T. Washington and, 70–71
　bourgeois values, 74–75
　early civil rights movement and, 78
　Niagara Conference and, 77
　Pan African Conferences and, 167
　Progressive Party and, 122
　on Reconstruction, 46

Edsal, Thomas, 185–86
Edwards, Don, 152, 161
Eisenhower, Dwight D.
　conservative movement and, 113–14
　presidency, 125–26
　South Africa and, 165
Elliot, Martha, 45–46
Ellwood, David, 180
Emancipation Proclamation, 42
Enforcement Act of 1870, 47
Engels, Friedrich, 19
equalitarianism, 96, 97, 134, 226n27
equality, 96–100
Ervin, Sam, 153
evangelical Christianity, 233n42
Executive Order 8802, 60
Executive Order 11246, 158
Executive Order 13233, 164

Fair Employment Practices, Committee on, 60
Fair Labor Standards Act, 56
Falwell, Jerry, 167, 233n42
Family Support Act of 1988, 180
Farr, James, 26–27
Farrakhan, Louis, 69
Faubus, Orval, 126
Feagin, Joe, 12
Federal Bureau of Investigation (FBI) and Martin Luther King, 172

federalism, 31, 48, 111
　southern conservatism and, 34
Fehrenbacher, Don, 34
feudalism, 17, 34, 35
Feulner, Ed, 179
Fielding, Fred, 153
Fish, Hamilton, 161
Fitzhugh, George, 34–36
Foner, Eric, 63–64
Ford, Gerald R., 137–38
Forten, James, 66
Fourteenth Amendment, 45–49, 84, 85, 104
Free South Africa movement, 168
Freedman's Bureau Act, 92
freedom, Frank Meyer on, 80–81
Freedom of Information Act, 164
Freehling, William, 27–28
Friedman, Milton, 53, 81–83, 85, 175
Friendly, Fred, 45–46
From, Al, 188, 190
Frymer, Paul, 31
Fuller, Craig, 173

Garnett, Henry Highland, 64
Garvey, Marcus, 69, 167
Genovese, Eugene, 3
Gephardt, Dick, 189
Gerber, Scott, 104
Gerstle, Gary, 15–16
Gibson, Tom, 173
Gilens, Martin, 176
Gingrich, Newt, 163, 169
Girvetz, Clifford, 16
Glazer, Nathan, 94, 99, 101
Goldwater, Barry, 234nn49–50
　Brown v. Board of Education and, 84–85
　Buckley and, 90
　Civil Rights Act of 1964 and, 138
　election of 1964 and, 116, 117, 130–31, 136
　on Nelson Rockefeller, 114
government, limiting the power of (national), 29–32, 58

Index   267

government ownership of various enterprises, race and attitudes toward, 64, 65t
government spending on various programs, race and attitudes toward, 64, 65t
gradualism, doctrine of, 86
Graham, Hugh Davis, 145, 162
Gray, Bill, 189, 190
Great Society, 112
  as a neoconservative bogeyman, 100–102
Greeley, Horace, 121
Greenberg, Stanley, 186, 187

Hamilton, Charles, 11
Hammett, William, 95
Harlan, John Marshall, 48
Harper, Edwin, 171
Hart, Jeffrey, 93
Hartz, Louis, 33
  on American tradition, 17
  on Franklin Roosevelt, 53
  The Liberal Tradition in America, 2, 8, 18, 35
  on liberalism, 2, 8, 15, 17, 41, 53
  on southern thought, 35
Haste, William, 60
Hatch, Orrin, 154, 156
Hawkins, Augustus, 161
Hayek, Frederick, 81–82
Hayes, Rutherford B., 121, 143
Hegel, Georg Wilhelm Friedrich, 12
Helco, Hugh, 110, 111
Helms, Jesse, 153, 166–68, 173
Herbert, Bob, 108
Himmelfarb, Gertrude, 94
Hobbes, Thomas, 20, 193
  Locke, Rousseau, and, 21, 23–24
  as natural rights theorist, 16, 17
  on slavery, 26, 201n60
Hobbs, Charles, 179–80
Hodgson, Geoffrey, 116
Hofstadter, Richard, 51–53, 58
Holden, Matthew, Jr., 174

Holladay, J. Douglas, 156
Hooks, Benjamin, 109
Hoover, Herbert C., 52, 233n44
Hoover, J. Edgar, 133
Humphrey, Hubert, 123–24, 133
Huntington, Samuel P., 9, 33–34
  on the American liberal in Europe, 61
  on autonomous conservatism, 102–3
  on conservatism, 8–10
  Edmund Burke and, 9–10
  on Kirk's *Conservative Mind*, 10
  on liberalism, 9–10
  on manifestations of conservatism in Western world, 204n4
Hyde, Henry, 152

Ickes, Harold, 61
individualism, 17

J.A. Croson Co., City of Richmond v., 248n82
Jackson, Andrew, 50–51
Jackson, Jesse, 64, 189–90
"Jacksonian Revolution," 50
Jaffa, Henry, 36, 131
Jefferson, Thomas, 28, 43, 50
"Jeffersonian Revolution," 50
Jeffries, James, 161
Jews, 99, 159, 243n184
Johnson, Andrew, 31, 45, 127
Johnson, Lyndon B., 62, 79, 92
  "brief liberal hour" and, 191
  defeat of Barry Goldwater, 117
  election of 1964 and, 130–31, 134
  Great Society reforms, 100
  as Kennedy's running mate, 127
  as militant liberal on civil rights, 129–30, 238n121
  on racial equality, 93–94
  South Africa and, 165
  Voting Rights Act of 1965 and, 150
  War on Poverty, 91
Jordan, Hamilton, 185
Judis, John B., 90

just-war theory of slavery, 26, 27

Kant, Immanuel, 12
Kassellbaum, Nancy, 170
Kendall, Willmore, 18, 43
Kennedy, Edward M., 156–57
Kennedy, John F., 62
   Africa and, 165
   civil rights speech, 129
   Martin Luther King and, 128–29
   on race, 127, 129
Kennedy, Robert F., 128
Kessel, John, 148–49
Key, V. O., 39
Kilpatrick, James J., 85–87
King, Martin Luther, Jr., 64, 146, 193, 215n19. *See also* Martin Luther King Jr. holiday
   black thought and, 66
   Carter and, 137, 140
   "I Have A Dream" oration, 67
   increasing radicalism of, 91
   joblessness as principal focus of, 192
   John F. Kennedy and, 128–29
   poor people's campaign and, 96
   Reagan's slander of, 173
   as transformative leader, 68
   Voting Rights Act of 1965 and, 150
King, Martin Luther, Sr., 137
Kirk, Paul, 186–87
Kirk, Russell, 10, 30, 32, 80–82, 103
Kirkpatrick, Jeanne, 149, 170
Kissinger, Henry, 137, 165–66
Kluegel, James, 64, 175
Kotler, Milton, 186–87
Kramnick, Isaac, 32
Kristol, Irving, 93, 94, 95, 98, 225n22
Krugman, Paul, 108–9, 116, 192

Ladd, Everett Carll, 141
Laham, Nicholas, 163
Leadership Conference on Civil Rights (LCCR), 146, 156
Lee, Richard, 28

Leuchtenberg, William, 53, 57, 58
Lewis, Drew, 149
Lewis, John, 189
Lewis, Oscar, 98
liberal ascendancy, periods of, 41–42
liberal remnant, 41
   Lincoln and, 42–44
   three periods in the emergence of, 41–42
Liberal Tradition in America, The (Hartz), 2, 8, 18, 35
liberalism, 50, 52–53, 188. *See also specific topics*
   Arthur Schlesinger on, 59
   classical/constitutional *vs.* modern (democratic), 15–16
   Franklin Roosevelt and, 188
   as a philosophy (*vs.* an ideology), 15–18
   and racial liberalism, future of, 190–94
liberty *vs.* equality, 96
Lincoln, Abraham, 127
   conservative ambivalence toward, 43–44
   liberal remnant and, 42–44
   as racist, 120
   use of presidential power, 43
Lochner v. New York, 49
Locke, John, 3, 33, 35. *See also specific topics*
   African slaves and, 26–27
   American tradition and, 8
   bastardization of, 27–28, 54, 75, 79, 105, 112, 202n72
   C. B. Macpherson on, 15, 25
   Edmund Burke and, 3, 32
   ideological conservatism, 18, 22–25
   Lochner decision and, 49
   as natural rights theorist, 16, 17, 21, 23, 27, 28, 33, 42
   property and, 17, 22–25, 30, 32, 33, 37
   The Second Treatise of Government, 28, 32

Lockean conservative institutional
    arrangements, 28–32
Lockean conservativism. *See also specific
    topics*
  Reagan and, 110–13
Lockean legacy, challenges to, 50
Lockean principles. *See also specific
    topics*
  and the South, 33
"Lockean settlement," 175
Logan, Rayford, 122
Lopez, United States v., 211n82
Lott, Trent, 153
Loury, Glenn, 75, 103–4
Lugar, Richard, 169–70
Lusaka Declaration, 165

MacDonald, Laughlin, 143
MacPherson, C. B., 23–24
  on Locke, 15, 25
Madison, James, 29–31
Malcolm X, 64, 69
Mandela, Nelson, 170
Mannheim, Karl, 8–9, 17–18
Marshall, Thurgood, 109
Martin Luther King Jr. holiday, 163–64,
    170–73
"master bias," 113
Mathias, Charles, 152
Mattingly, Mack, 161
McClosky, Herbert, 175, 193
McFarlane, Robert, 169
McGovern, George, 134–36, 189–90,
    241n156
McPhearson, Harry, 185
McPhearson, James
  on Fourteenth Amendment, 49
  on Lincoln as conservative
    revolutionary, 44
Medicare, 176–77
Meese, Edwin, 149, 153, 154, 160, 162,
    172–73, 178
Meier, August, 73
Mendelberg, Tali, 120–21, 133
Meyer, Frank, 80–81, 93

Meyers, Jeffrey, 67
militant liberalism, 63–64
Miller, Kelly, 3
Miller, Samuel, 47–48
Mills, Wright, 190–91
Mink, Gwendolyn, 147
Miroff, Bruce, 134
Mitchell, Clarence, 146
mobilization of bias, 6, 118–20, 185
  and demobilization of bias, 120–25
  Democratic Leadership Council, Bill
    Clinton, and, 188–90
  in presidential elections 1948–1960,
    121–25
Mondale, Walter, 166
Moon, Henry Lee, 123
Morris, Dick, 181, 255n190
Moses, William Jeremiah, 73–74
movement conservatives, 149
Moynihan, Daniel Patrick, 94, 99, 172,
    179, 181, 192
Muhammad, Elijah, 69
Muir, William, 162–63
Murray, Charles, 95, 176
Myrdal, Gunnar, 2–3, 87, 219nn37–38
  on accommodationism, 70
  on Booker T. Washington, 71
  Brown v. Board of Education and, 84
  on ideology as "master bias," 113

Nash, George, 3, 50, 80, 83, 84, 87
National Association for the
    Advancement of Colored People
    (NAACP), 55, 56, 78, 123, 146, 147
National Labor Relations Act, 55
National Review, 88–90, 92–93, 115,
    145, 166
National Welfare Rights Organization
    (NWRO), 244n16
natural rights. *See also* civil rights
  Frederick Douglass and, 66–67
  George Fitzhugh and, 35
  John Calhoun and, 36
  John Randolph and, 206n25
  liberalism and, 16

natural rights *(continued)*
  Lincoln and, 42, 43
  Locke and, 16, 17, 21, 23, 27, 28, 33, 42
  philosophical conservatism and, 18
  philosophical liberalism and, 26
  slavery and, 26, 27, 33, 42
natural rights theorists, 16
nature, state of, 16–23, 200n47
  functions found wanting in, 23
Neas, Ralph, 146
Nedelsky, Jennifer, 49, 58, 226n27
neoconservatism, 79, 91–93, 102, 105, 224n15
  equality, affirmative action, and, 95–100
  foreign policy and, 229n76
  Great Society and, 100–102
  origins, 91–96
  writings on, 224n18
neoconservatives, black, 102–5
New Deal, 9, 49, 53–59
  racism and, 59–62
New Deal liberalism, 10, 50–53
Niagara Manifesto, 77–78
Nixon, Richard M., 92, 105
  affirmative action and, 158, 241n155
  Africa and, 165
  coalition between racists and rightists and, 117
  conservative movement and, 113–15
  election of 1960 and, 126–28
  election of 1968 and, 133–34
  election of 1972 and, 135–36, 138
  as "last liberal president," 135, 240n153
  racism, 133
  Voting Rights Act of 1965 and, 151
Nixon Nationality Security Study Memorandum, 165
Norquist, Grover, 175
North, blacks in the, 11

Obama, Barack, 164, 194

party system, race and the, 118–20
Pendleton, Clarence, 149, 160
Phillips, Kevin, 2
Pierce, Franklin, 42
Pierce, Samuel, 149, 153, 160
Pinderhughes, Dianne, 146
Plato, 25
Plessy v. Ferguson, 48, 83
Podhoretz, Norman, 94, 95
populist movement of 1890s, 51
Populist Party, 51
positive (resistance) state, 41. *See also* liberal remnant
Powell, Adam Clayton, Jr., 64, 126
Power Elite, The (Mills), 190–91
presidential elections
  1948–1960, mobilization of bias in, 121–25
  1952 and 1956, 125–30
  1960, 126–30
  1964, 130–32
  1968, 132–34
  1972, 134–37
  1976, 137–38
  1980, 138–41
Presidential Records Act, 164
progressive movement, 51–52
property (rights)
  Alexander Crummell and, 73–74
  Charles Beard and, 29
  Constitution and, 27–29, 47
  Edmund Burke and, 30, 32
  equality *vs.* inequality of, 226n27
  Fourteenth Amendment and, 47, 49
  James Madison and, 29
  Lincoln and, 42, 44
  Locke and, 17, 22–25, 30, 32, 33, 37
  meanings, 23
  in one's person, 23, 24, 26, 37
  in other persons, 29–31, 44
  private, 19–21, 23
  origin of, 23
  Reagan and, 111, 112
  Rousseau and, 17–21

slavery and, 28, 30, 42, 44
suffrage and, 25
Proposition 14, 112

quadrilateralism, 145
Quirk, Paul, 147–48

Race Card, The (Mendelberg), 120
racial equality. *See* equality
racial resentment, 145
racism
  definitions, 11, 12
  periods of liberal ascendancy and struggles against, 41–42
  post-civil rights era, 145–46
  prevalence, 145
  "symbolic"/"modern"/"laissez-faire," 145, 150
  systemic, 12
  understanding, 10–13
Randolph, A. Phillip, 60, 62, 64, 122, 146, 193
Ransom, John Crowe, 38
Rauh, Joseph, 128
Reagan, Ronald, 6, 7, 49, 92, 95, 185
  affirmative action and, 158–63
  budget and antipoverty programs, 182–83
  civil rights and, 109–12, 168–69, 173–74, 231n15
  as conservative icon, 1–2
  conservative movement and, 113–18
  controversy over racism of, 108–10
  election of 1964 and, 132
  election of 1976 and, 137
  election of 1980 and, 138–41
  Grove City case and, 155–58
  Lockean conservatism and, 110–13
  Martin Luther King holiday and, 163–64, 170–73
  as movement conservative, 110, 113
  as "passive"/"minimalist" president, 147–50
  on policies of 1960s, 101
  racism and, 108–9, 112, 140, 231nn15–16, 242n174
  as "reconstructive" president, 187–88
  seeds of election of, 107
  South African sanctions and, 163–70
  staff/administration, 147–49
  Voting Rights Act and, 152–55
  welfare and antipoverty policies, 175–82
Reagan Democrats, 186
Reagan presidency
  blacks and, 143
  and the constraints of power, 144–47
  presidential character in, 147–50
"Reagan Revolution," 187
Reardon, Thomas, 22
Reconstruction, 57
  and the conservative counterrevolution, 46–50
  as liberalism's finest hour, 45–46
  radicalism of blacks during, 63–64
Reconstruction presidential elections, racism and conservatism in, 120–21
Regan, Don, 149, 160, 161
Regenery, Alfred, 83
Rehnquist, William, 57, 131, 162
Republican Party, 121
Reynolds, William Bradford, 149, 160
Riker, William, 31
"riot ideology," 133
Road to Serfdom (Hayek), 81, 82
Roberts, John, 162, 172, 248n83
Robertson, Pat, 137
Robeson, Paul, 64, 122, 167
Robinson, Donald, 11, 31
Robinson, Randall, 168
Rockefeller, Nelson, 114–15
  "Bastille Day Declaration" by, 115–16
Rodino, Peter, 152
Roosevelt, Franklin Delano, 83
  election of 1932 and, 134
  fate of liberalism and, 191
  leadership style, 58
  New Deal and, 53–59

Roosevelt, Franklin Delano *(continued)*
  New Deal liberalism and, 50–53
  and the term "liberal," 188
Roosevelt, Theodore, 52
"Roosevelt Revolution," 50, 53
Rosenbaum, Nelson, 186–87
Ross, Edmund, 127
Rossin, Edward, 98
Rossiter, Clinton, 7, 30, 39, 49, 50, 90
Rousseau, Jean-Jacques
  ideological liberalism, 18–22
  as natural rights theorist, 16–17
  on slavery, 26
"Rousseaun settlement," 176
Rowan, Carl, 109–10
Rusher, William, 115, 116, 137
Russell, Bertrand, 75
Russell, Richard, 129
Rustin, Bayard, 64, 96–97, 103

Saloma, John, 95
Schattsneider, E. E., 119
Schlesinger, Arthur, Jr., 59, 61–62, 84, 124, 128, 189
school segregation, 85–87. See also *Brown v. Board of Education*
Schuyler, George, 92
  "conservatism," 71–73
Schweiker, Richard, 149
Scott, Hugh, 151
Sears, David, 146
segregation, 85–87. See also *Brown v. Board of Education*
Sensenbrenner, James, 157
separate but equal, doctrine of, 48
Sharon Statement, 118
Sharpeville massacre, 167
Shulz, George, 160
Sigler, Jay, 3
Sitkoff, Harvard, 60
Skowronek, Stephen, 187
Slaughterhouse Cases, 46–48
slavery, 11, 31. See also property, in other persons; Reconstruction
  and the Burkean variant of southern aristocratic conservatism, 34–38

  Lincoln and, 42–44
  natural rights and, 26, 27, 33, 42
  in the philosophy of liberalism, 25–28
Sloan, John, 148
Smith, Eliot, 64, 175
Smith, Gaddis, 166
Smith, Rogers, 17
social contract, 16, 18, 19, 199n9
  broken, 66–67
  racial, 69
Social Contract, The (Rousseau), 19–21, 26
social contract theorists, 16
Social Security, 176–77
Social Security Act of 1935, 54, 55
  Title IV, 181
social welfare responsibilities of government, race and attitudes toward, 64, 65t
South, 3
  racism in, 11
South African sanctions, 163–70
southern agrarianism, 38–39
southern aristocratic conservatism, slavery and the Burkean variant of, 33–38
Southern Case for Segregation, The (Kilpatrick), 85–87
southern conservatism, 82, 233n42
Soviet Union, 113
Sowell, Thomas, 103
Sparkman, John, 126
Starr, Paul, 16, 192
Steele, Shelby, 103–4
Stevens, John Paul, 104
Stevens, Thaddeus, 43–45, 127
Stevenson, Adlai, 125–26
Stimson, James A., 132
Stockman, David, 177
Sumner, Charles, 43, 45
  congressional reconstruction and, 45
Supreme Court, 46–49, 57, 83, 162. See also *specific cases*
Sweatt v. Painter, 83

Taft, Robert, 125
Tar Baby Option, 165
Thernstrom, Abigail, 154
Thomas, Clarence, 103-4, 149, 160
Thurmond, Strom, 124, 146, 153
Title IX of the Education Amendments Act of 1972, 155-56
TransAfrica, 167-68
Trefousse, Hans L., 44, 45
Trotter, William Monroe, 77
Truman, Harry S., 122
   civil rights and, 122, 124
   liberal retreat and, 125
   South Africa and, 165
Turner, Henry M., 69

Uhlman, Michael, 153
ultraconservativism of Buckley, 90. *See also* Buckley, William F.
"underclass," 192, 226n34, 258n39
Urban League, 55, 146, 147

Van den Berghe, Pierre, 11-12
Vance, Cyrus, 166
Viereck, Peter, 30, 80
Virginia plan, 31
Vital Center (Schlesinger), 61, 62
Voting Rights Act of 1965, 150-55, 174, 246n58

Waite, Morrison, 47
Wallace, George, 90, 92, 105, 146
   attempted murder of, 135
   1964 election campaign, 131-32
   1968 election campaign, 133-34, 137
   opposition to school integration, 129
   "white backlash" and, 117
Wallace, Henry, 61, 122
war, periods of liberal ascendancy and, 41
War on Poverty, 100-101
Warren, Earl, 84, 126
Washington, Booker T., 92, 216n31
   "conservatism," 70-71
   death, 77
Watson, Tom, 51

Watt, James, 149
Watts Riots of 1965, 100, 133
Weaver, Richard, 38
Weaver, Robert, 60
welfare and antipoverty policies, 254n183. *See also* New Deal; welfare reform
   1981-1987, 147, 175-77
   and the budget, 182-83
   public attitudes toward, 176
   race and, 64, 65t
welfare reform, 147, 177-82, 255n187
White, Clifton, 115-18, 122, 135
White, Theodore, 132-34
White, Walter, 59
white supremacy, 145. *See also* South African sanctions
   Brown v. Board of Education and, 84, 85
   Buckley and, 85, 87-88
   James Kilpatrick and, 85-87
   National Review and, 88, 90
   presidential elections and, 119-21
   roots of the ideology of, 12
Whittlesey, Faith Ryan, 156
Wildavsky, Aaron, 94, 101-2, 144
Wilkins, Roy, 146
Will, George, 131
Williams, G. Mennen, 165
Williams, Walter, 103
Wills, Gary, 43, 126-27
Wilson, James Q., 94
Wilson, William Julius, 258n39
Wilson, Woodrow, 52
Wirthlin, Richard, 154
Wish, Harvey, 36
workfare, 178
Wright, Joe, 172-73
Wright, Richard, 64

Young, Andrew, 166, 167
Young Americans for Freedom (YAF), 90, 118

Zaller, John, 175, 193

Made in the USA
Coppell, TX
30 November 2020